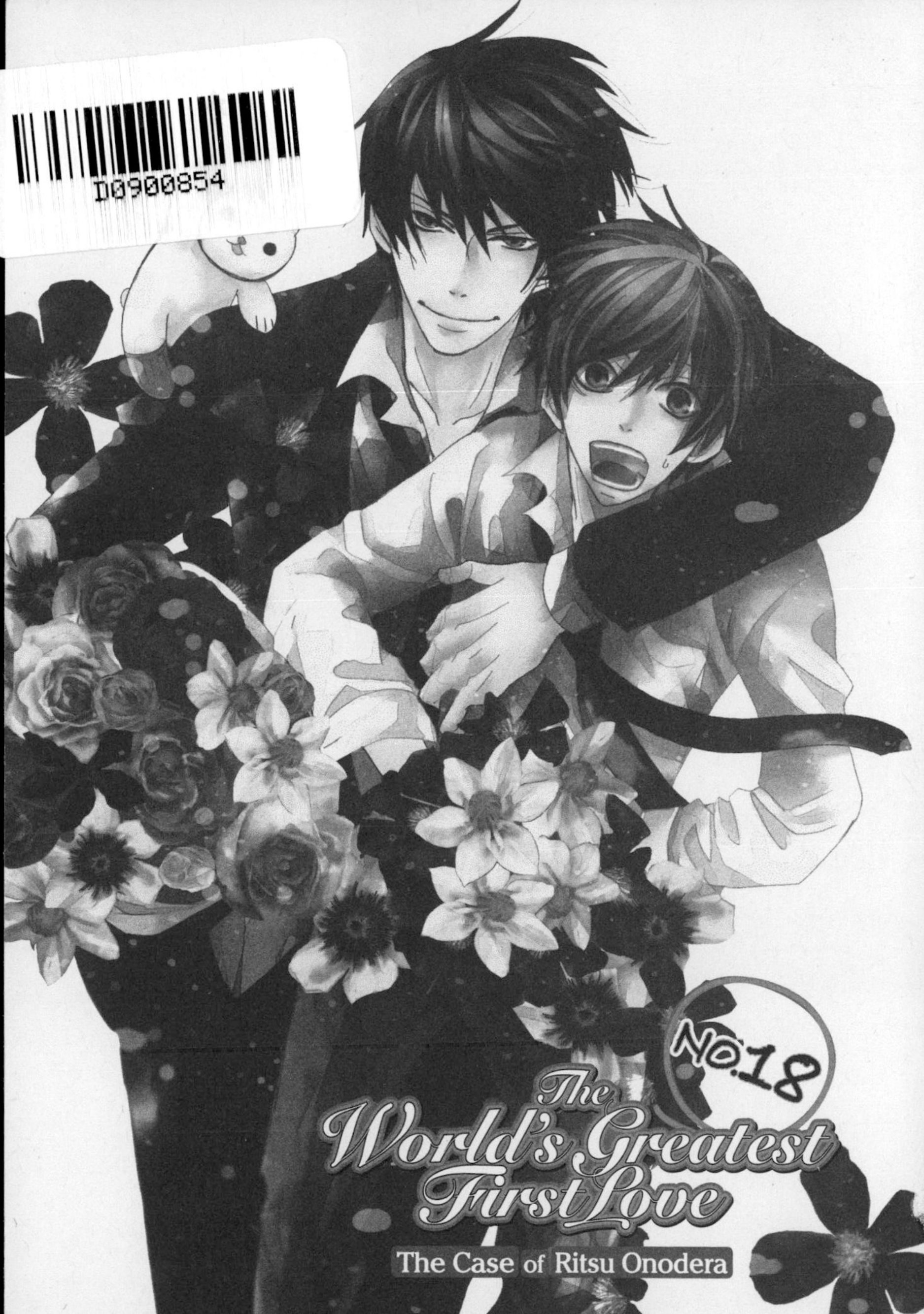
NO.18
The World's Greatest First Love
The Case of Ritsu Onodera

*I WONDER...
WHAT
COMES
AFTER THE
HAPPY
ENDING?*

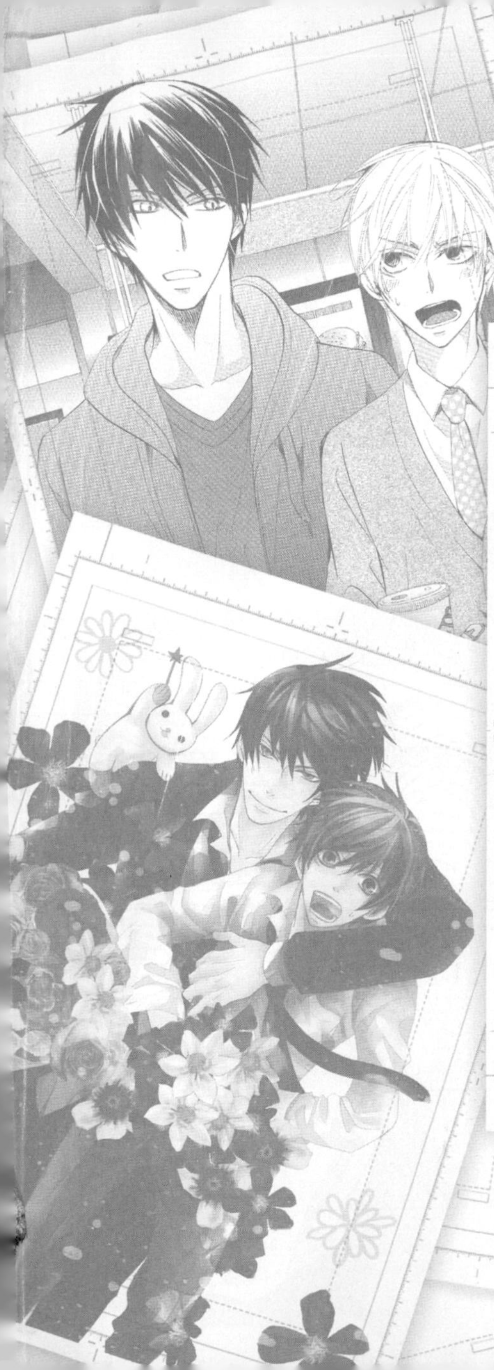
¥450

The World's Greatest First Love

The Case of Ritsu Onodera 10

Contents

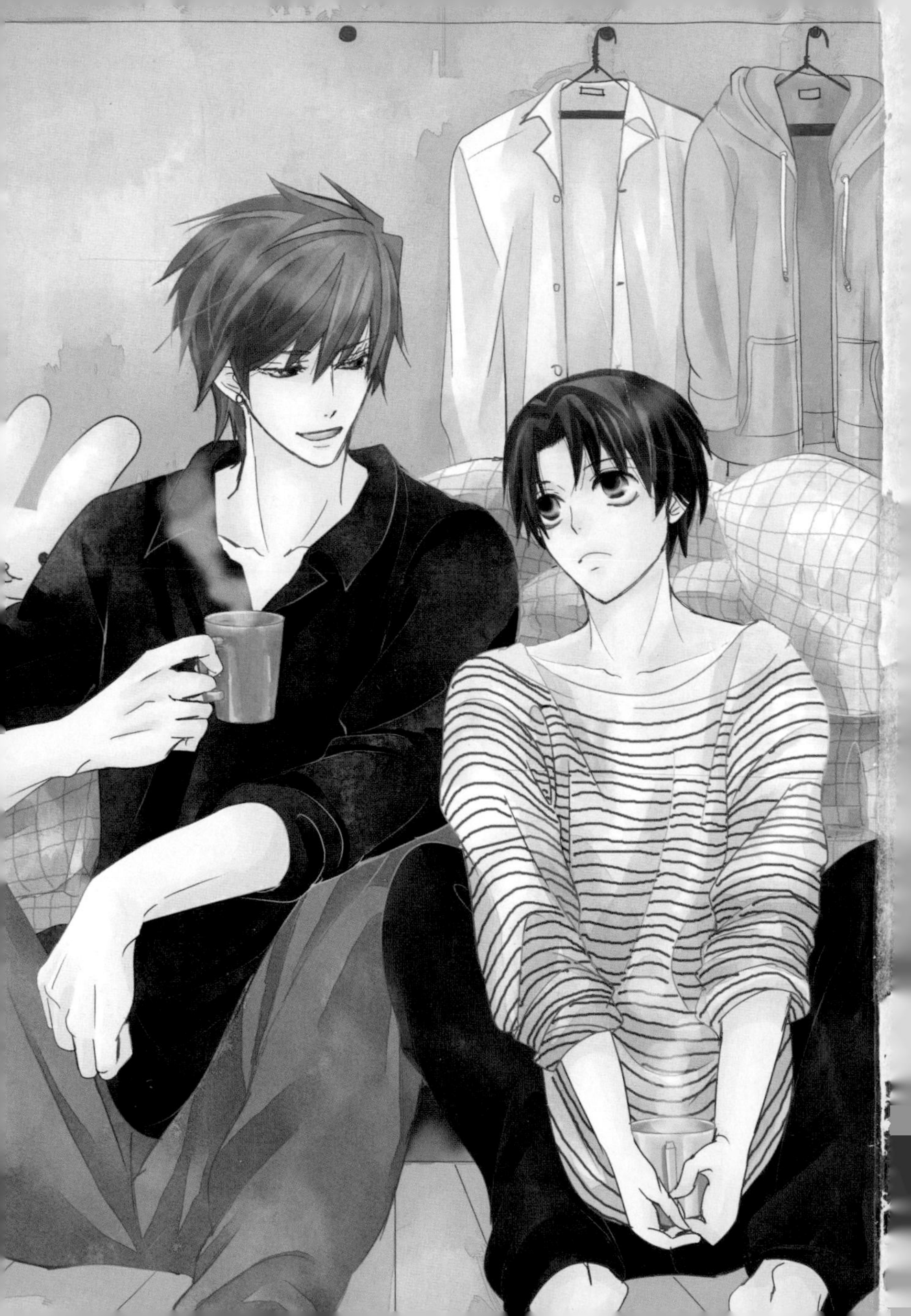

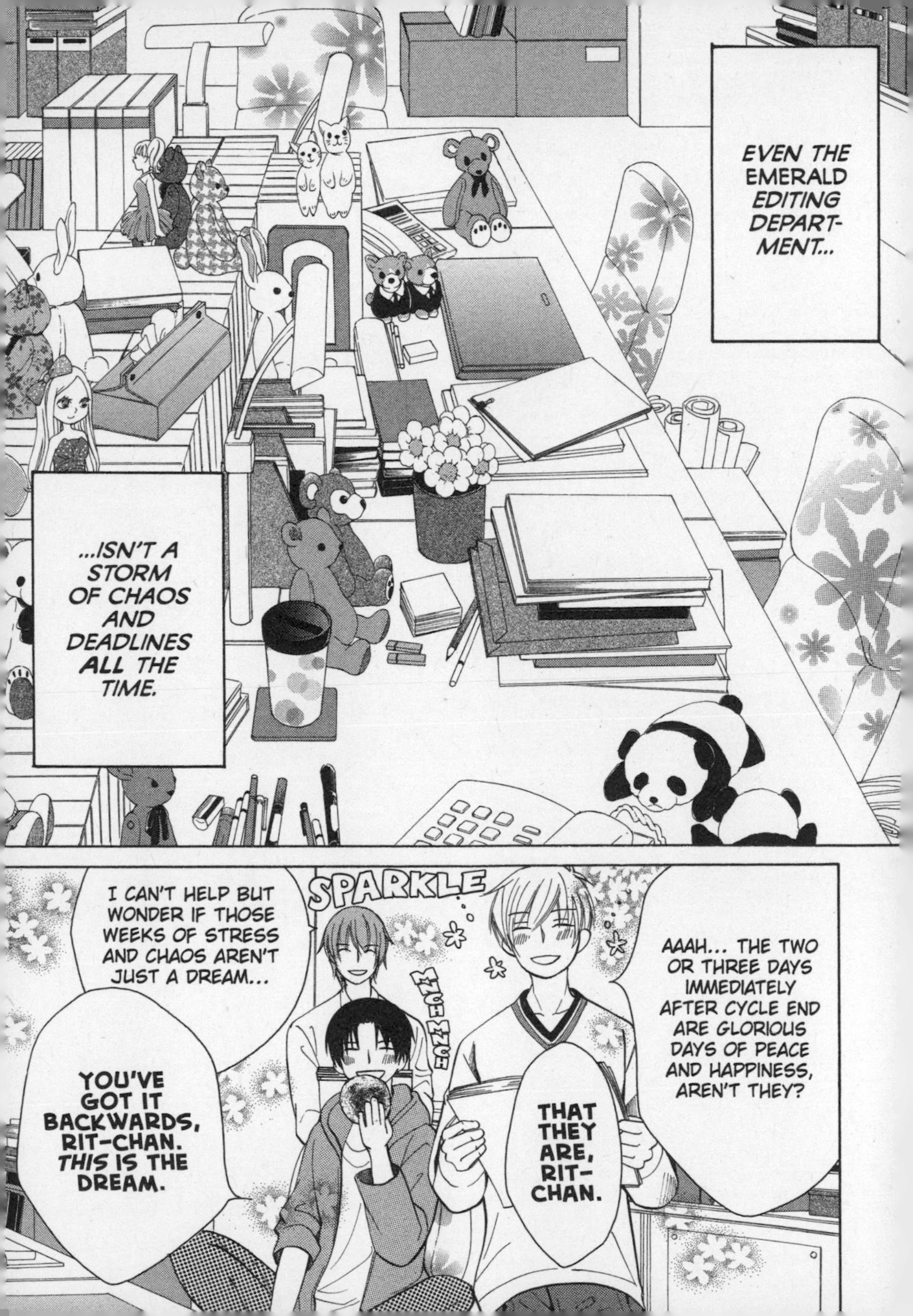
EVEN THE EMERALD EDITING DEPARTMENT...
...ISN'T A STORM OF CHAOS AND DEADLINES ALL THE TIME.
AAAH... THE TWO OR THREE DAYS IMMEDIATELY AFTER CYCLE END ARE GLORIOUS DAYS OF PEACE AND HAPPINESS, AREN'T THEY?
THAT THEY ARE, RIT-CHAN.
SPARKLE
I CAN'T HELP BUT WONDER IF THOSE WEEKS OF STRESS AND CHAOS AREN'T JUST A DREAM...
MUNCH MUNCH
YOU'VE GOT IT BACKWARDS, RIT-CHAN. THIS IS THE DREAM.

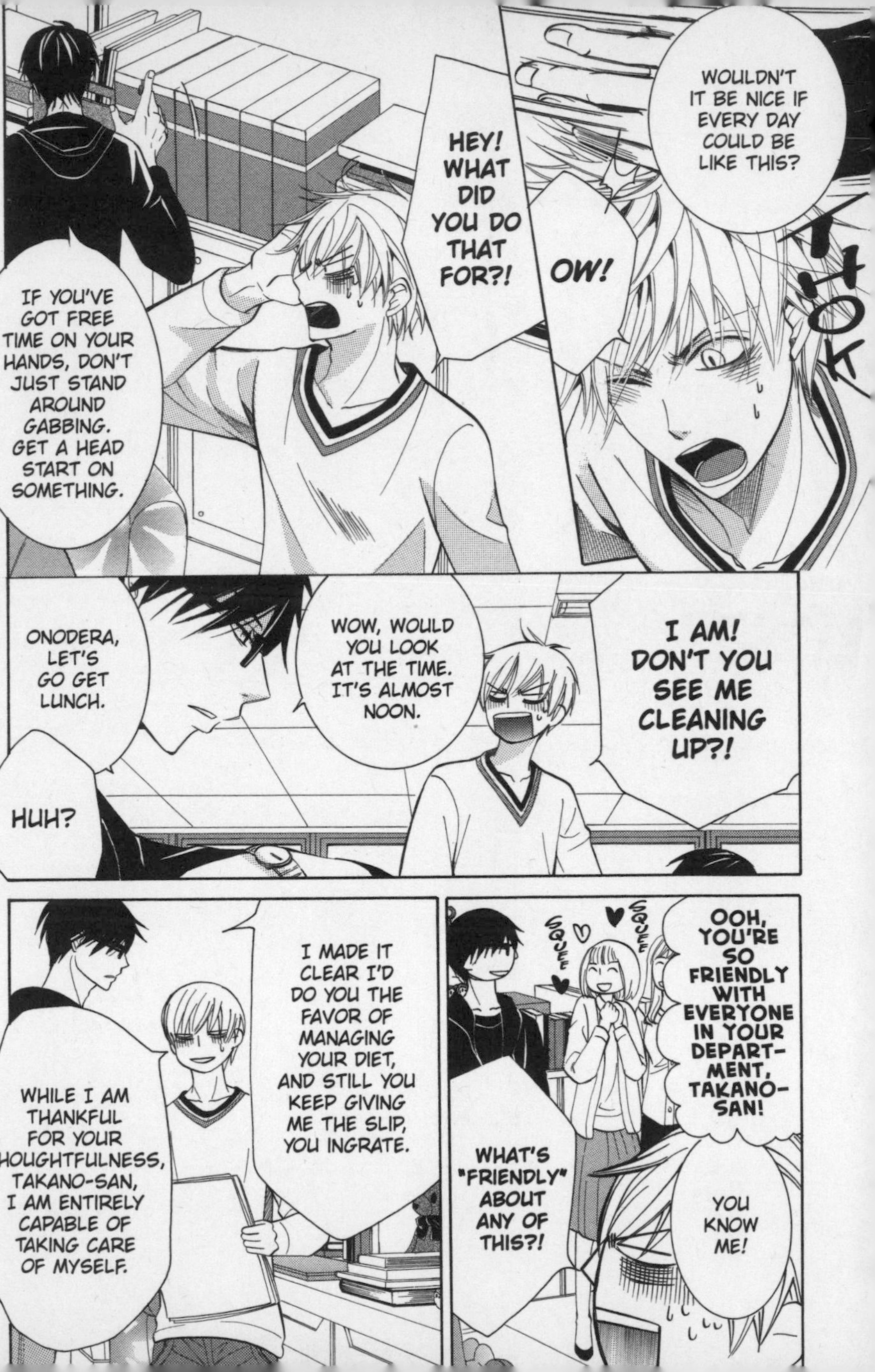
WOULDN'T IT BE NICE IF EVERY DAY COULD BE LIKE THIS?
THOK
OW!
HEY! WHAT DID YOU DO THAT FOR?!
IF YOU'VE GOT FREE TIME ON YOUR HANDS, DON'T JUST STAND AROUND GABBING. GET A HEAD START ON SOMETHING.
I AM! DON'T YOU SEE ME CLEANING UP?!
WOW, WOULD YOU LOOK AT THE TIME. IT'S ALMOST NOON.
ONODERA, LET'S GO GET LUNCH.
HUH?
OOH, YOU'RE SO FRIENDLY WITH EVERYONE IN YOUR DEPARTMENT, TAKANO-SAN!
SQUEE
SQUEE
YOU KNOW ME!
WHAT'S "FRIENDLY" ABOUT ANY OF THIS?!
I MADE IT CLEAR I'D DO YOU THE FAVOR OF MANAGING YOUR DIET, AND STILL YOU KEEP GIVING ME THE SLIP, YOU INGRATE.
WHILE I AM THANKFUL FOR YOUR THOUGHTFULNESS, TAKANO-SAN, I AM ENTIRELY CAPABLE OF TAKING CARE OF MYSELF.

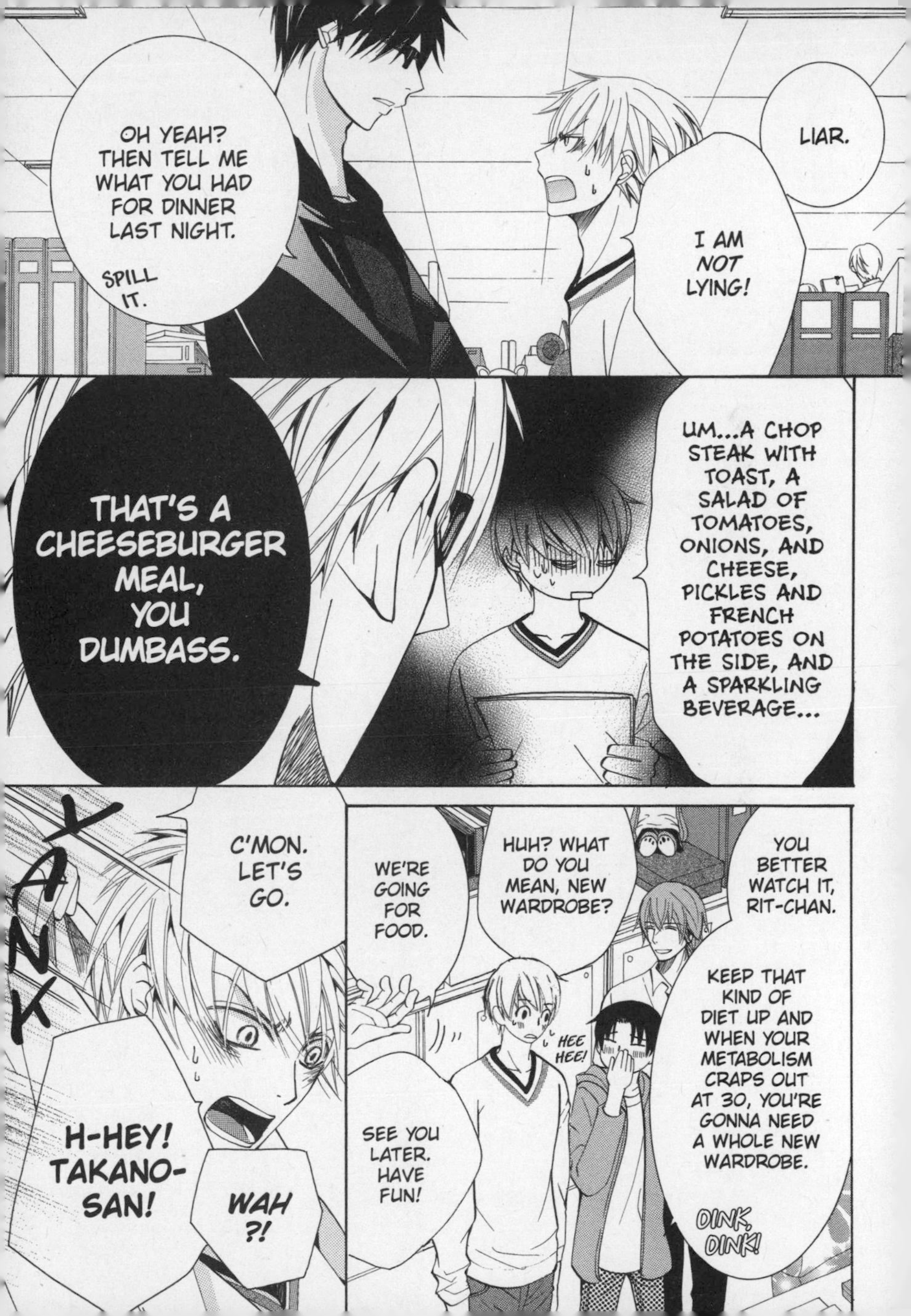
LIAR.
I AM NOT LYING!
OH YEAH? THEN TELL ME WHAT YOU HAD FOR DINNER LAST NIGHT.
SPILL IT.
UM...A CHOP STEAK WITH TOAST, A SALAD OF TOMATOES, ONIONS, AND CHEESE, PICKLES AND FRENCH POTATOES ON THE SIDE, AND A SPARKLING BEVERAGE...
THAT'S A CHEESEBURGER MEAL, YOU DUMBASS.
YOU BETTER WATCH IT, RIT-CHAN.
KEEP THAT KIND OF DIET UP AND WHEN YOUR METABOLISM CRAPS OUT AT 30, YOU'RE GONNA NEED A WHOLE NEW WARDROBE.
DINK, DINK!
HUH? WHAT DO YOU MEAN, NEW WARDROBE?
HEE HEE!
WE'RE GOING FOR FOOD.
SEE YOU LATER. HAVE FUN!
C'MON. LET'S GO.
YANK
H-HEY! TAKANO-SAN!
WAH ?!

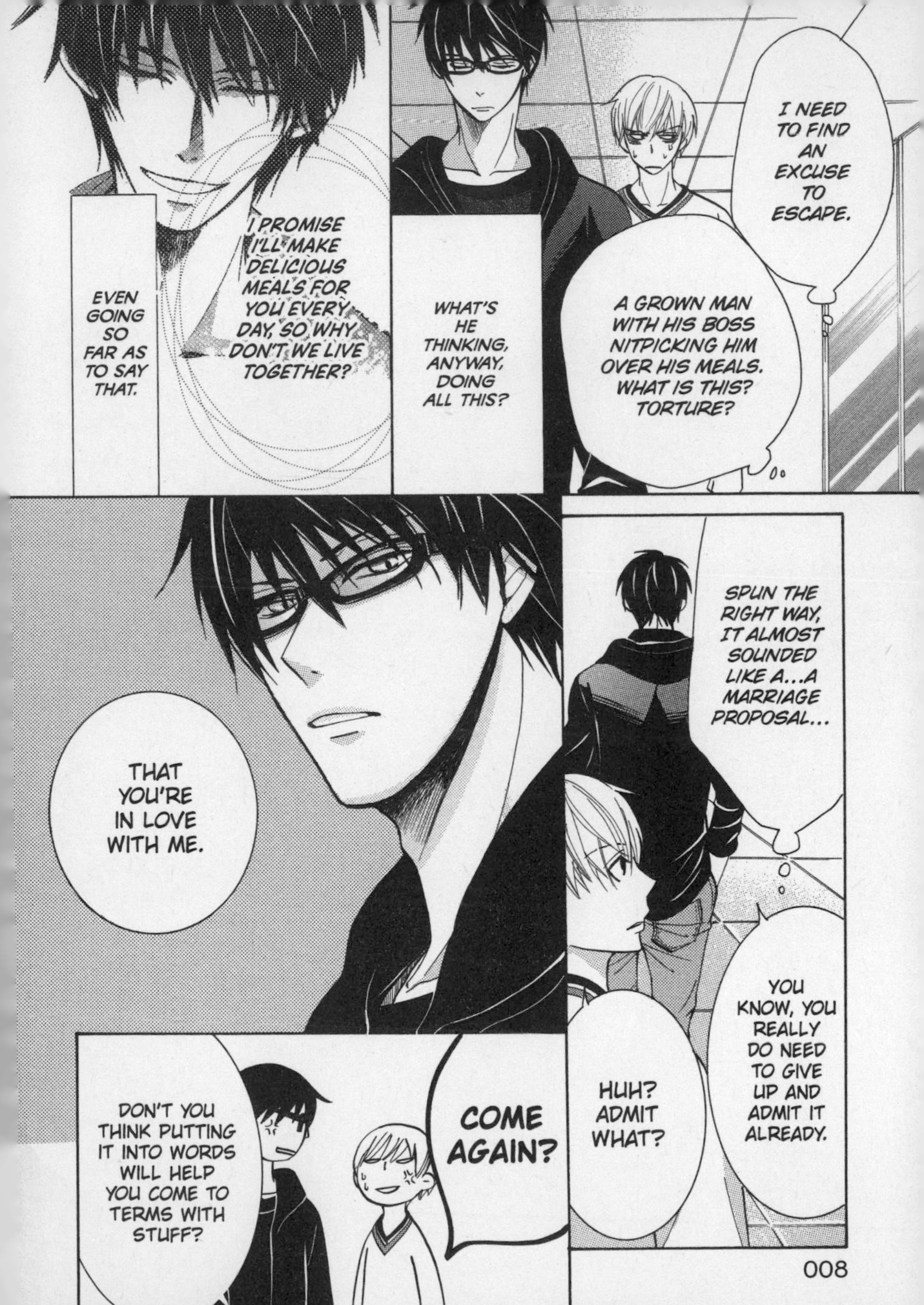
I NEED TO FIND AN EXCUSE TO ESCAPE.
A GROWN MAN WITH HIS BOSS NITPICKING HIM OVER HIS MEALS. WHAT IS THIS? TORTURE?
WHAT'S HE THINKING, ANYWAY, DOING ALL THIS?
I PROMISE I'LL MAKE DELICIOUS MEALS FOR YOU EVERY DAY, SO WHY DON'T WE LIVE TOGETHER?
EVEN GOING SO FAR AS TO SAY THAT.
SPUN THE RIGHT WAY, IT ALMOST SOUNDED LIKE A...A MARRIAGE PROPOSAL...
YOU KNOW, YOU REALLY DO NEED TO GIVE UP AND ADMIT IT ALREADY.
HUH? ADMIT WHAT?
THAT YOU'RE IN LOVE WITH ME.
COME AGAIN?
DON'T YOU THINK PUTTING IT INTO WORDS WILL HELP YOU COME TO TERMS WITH STUFF?

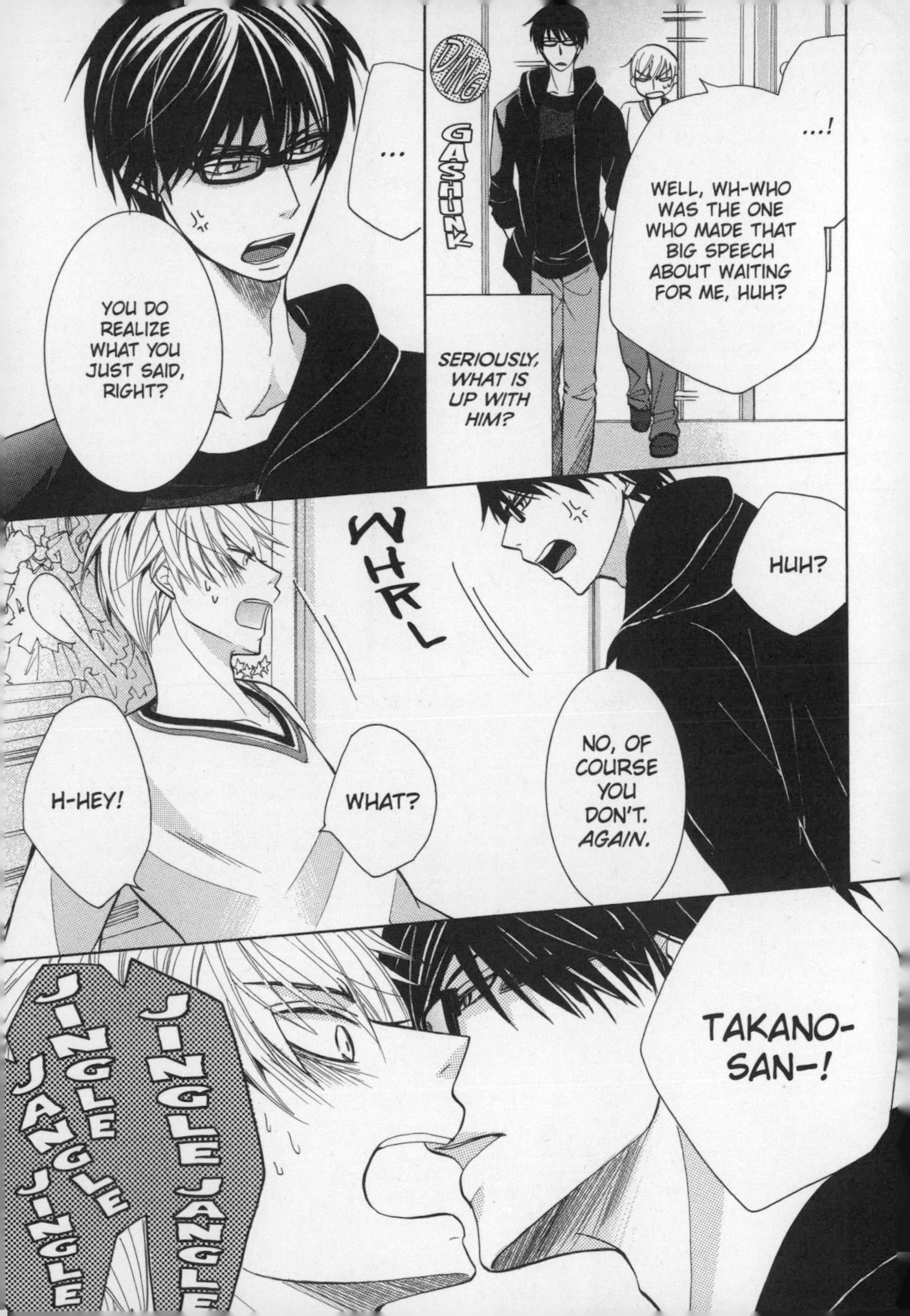
...!
WELL, WH-WHO WAS THE ONE WHO MADE THAT BIG SPEECH ABOUT WAITING FOR ME, HUH?
DING
GASHUNK
SERIOUSLY, WHAT IS UP WITH HIM?
...
YOU DO REALIZE WHAT YOU JUST SAID, RIGHT?
HUH?
WHRL
NO, OF COURSE YOU DON'T. AGAIN.
WHAT?
H-HEY!
TAKANO-SAN-!
JINGLE JANGLE
JINGLE JANGLE

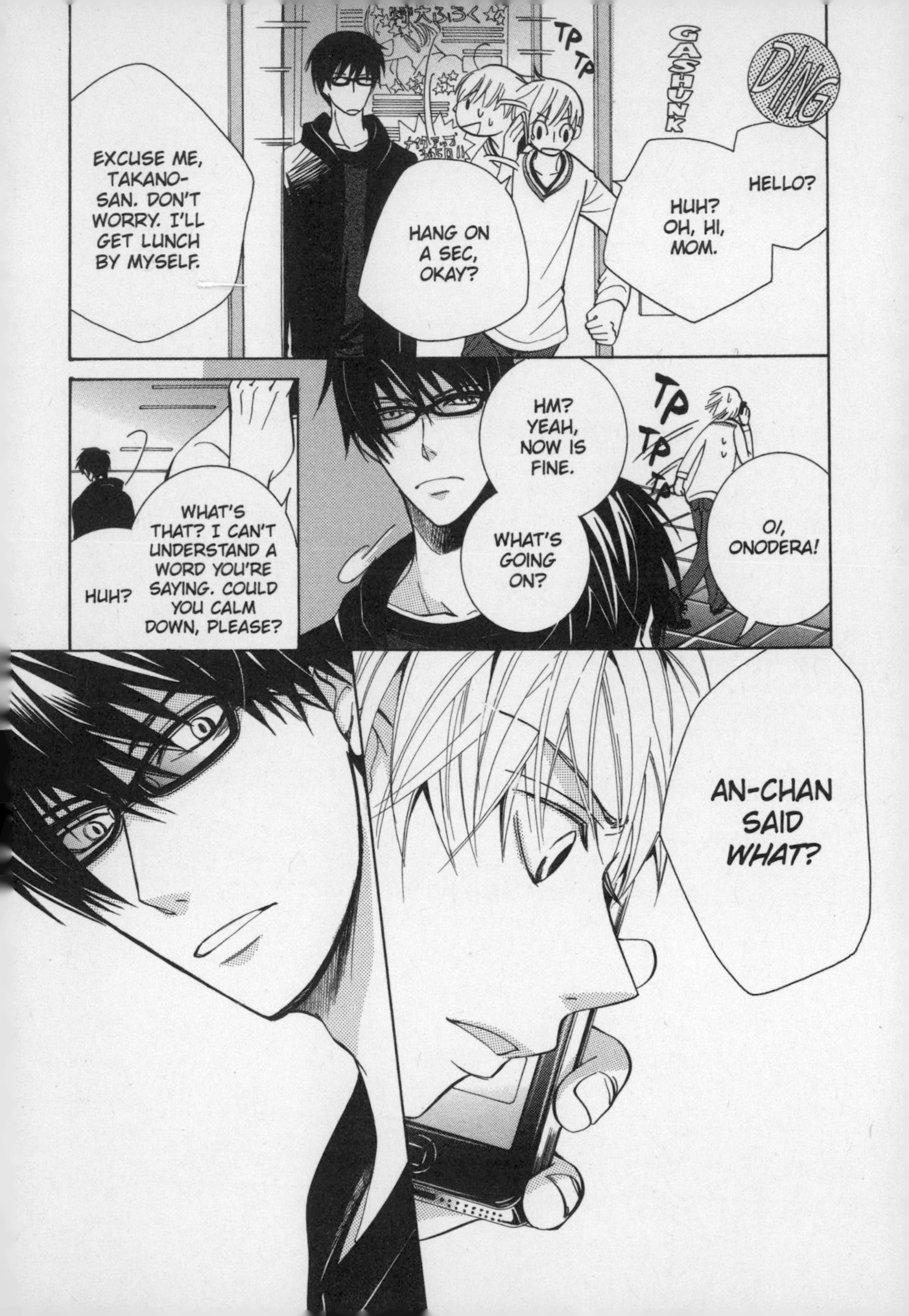
DING
GASHUNK
TP TP
HELLO?
HUH? OH, HI, MOM.
HANG ON A SEC, OKAY?
EXCUSE ME, TAKANO-SAN. DON'T WORRY. I'LL GET LUNCH BY MYSELF.
TP TP TP
OI, ONODERA!
HM? YEAH, NOW IS FINE.
WHAT'S GOING ON?
WHAT'S THAT? I CAN'T UNDERSTAND A WORD YOU'RE SAYING. COULD YOU CALM DOWN, PLEASE?
HUH?
AN-CHAN SAID *WHAT?*

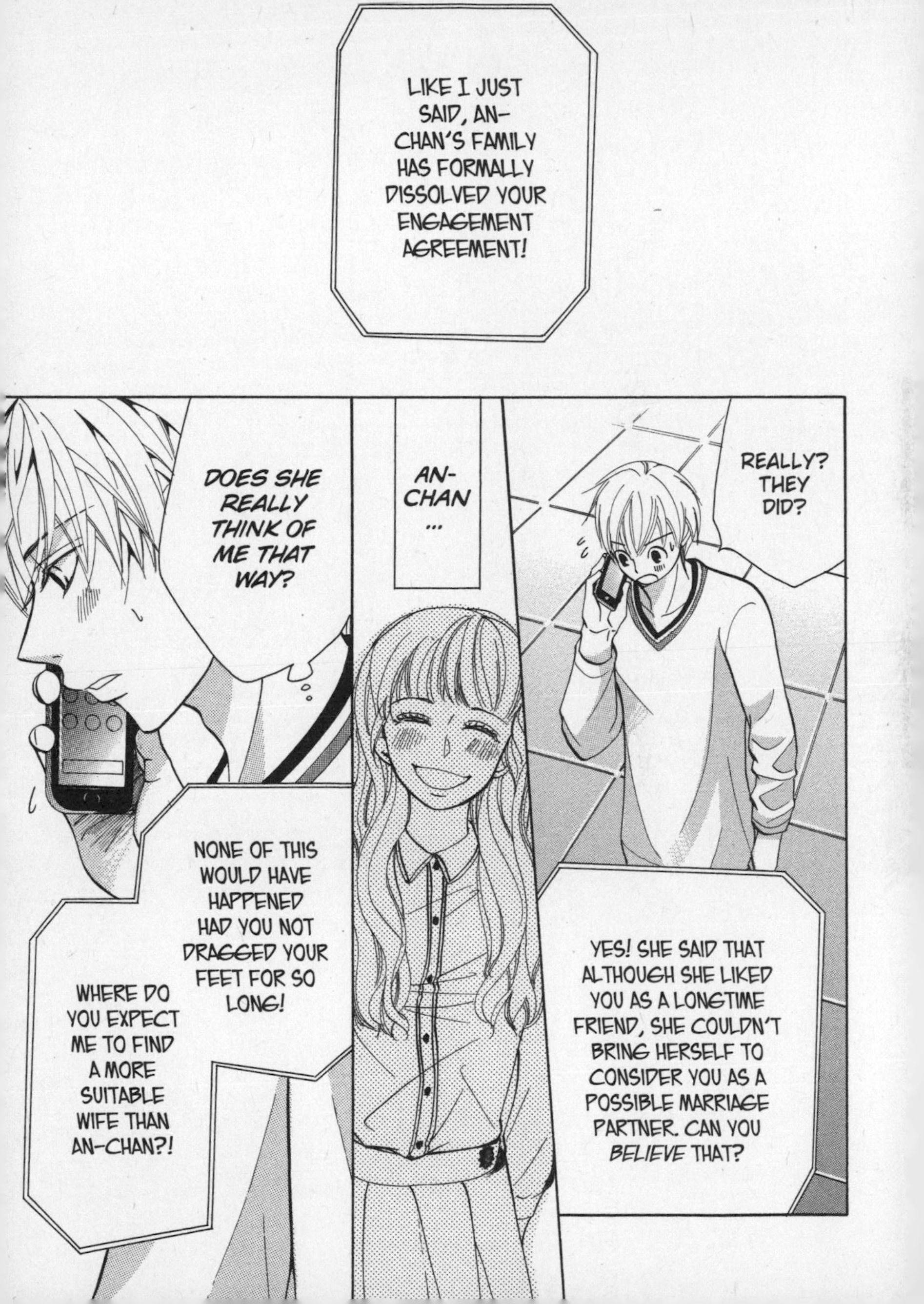
LIKE I JUST SAID, AN-CHAN'S FAMILY HAS FORMALLY DISSOLVED YOUR ENGAGEMENT AGREEMENT!
REALLY? THEY DID?
YES! SHE SAID THAT ALTHOUGH SHE LIKED YOU AS A LONGTIME FRIEND, SHE COULDN'T BRING HERSELF TO CONSIDER YOU AS A POSSIBLE MARRIAGE PARTNER. CAN YOU *BELIEVE* THAT?
AN-CHAN...
DOES SHE REALLY THINK OF ME THAT WAY?
NONE OF THIS WOULD HAVE HAPPENED HAD YOU NOT DRAGGED YOUR FEET FOR SO LONG!
WHERE DO YOU EXPECT ME TO FIND A MORE SUITABLE WIFE THAN AN-CHAN?!

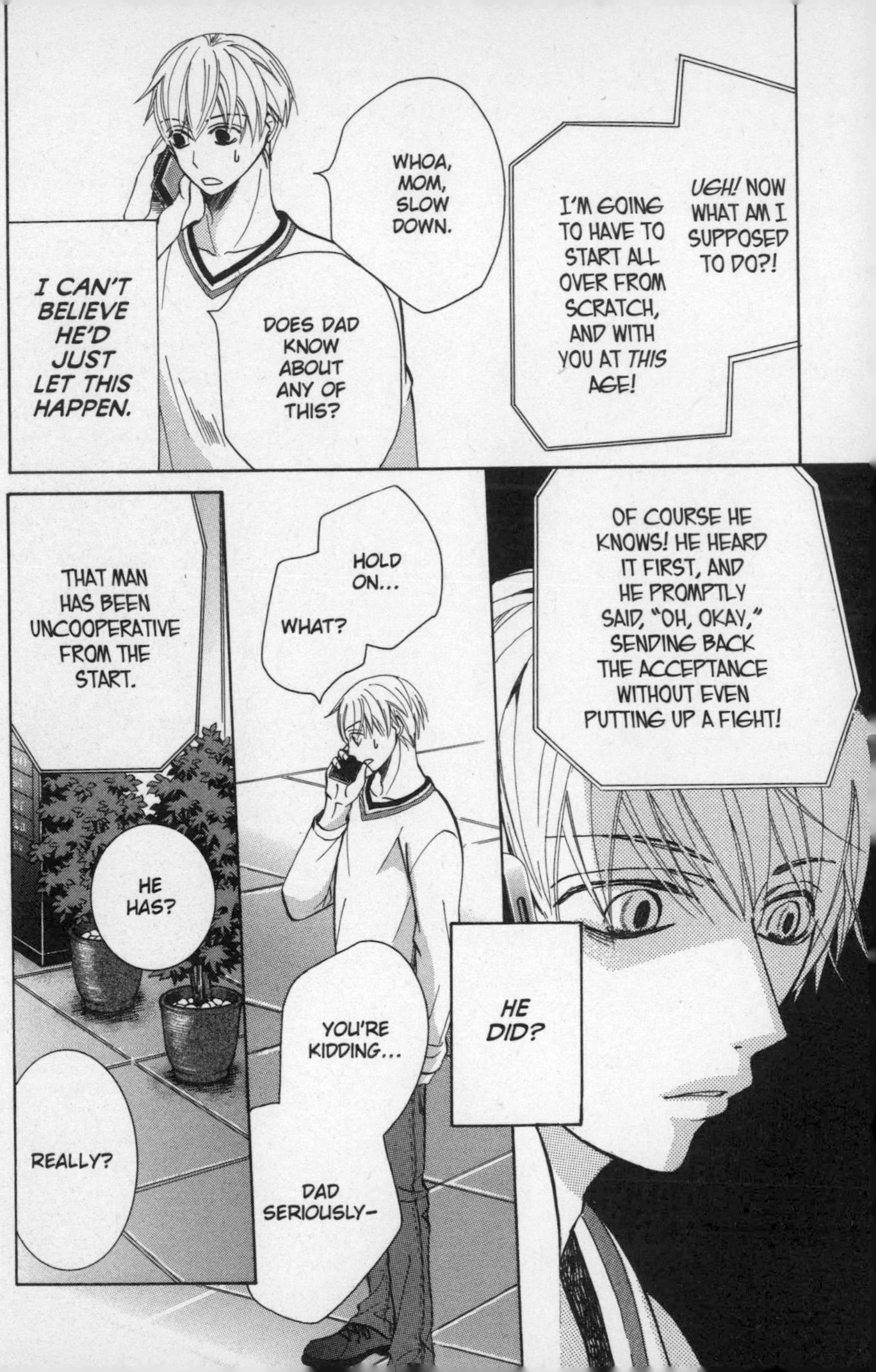
UGH! NOW WHAT AM I SUPPOSED TO DO?! I'M GOING TO HAVE TO START ALL OVER FROM SCRATCH, AND WITH YOU AT THIS AGE!
WHOA, MOM, SLOW DOWN.
DOES DAD KNOW ABOUT ANY OF THIS?
I CAN'T BELIEVE HE'D JUST LET THIS HAPPEN.
OF COURSE HE KNOWS! HE HEARD IT FIRST, AND HE PROMPTLY SAID, "OH, OKAY," SENDING BACK THE ACCEPTANCE WITHOUT EVEN PUTTING UP A FIGHT!
HE DID?
HOLD ON...
WHAT?
YOU'RE KIDDING...
DAD SERIOUSLY-
THAT MAN HAS BEEN UNCOOPERATIVE FROM THE START.
HE HAS?
REALLY?

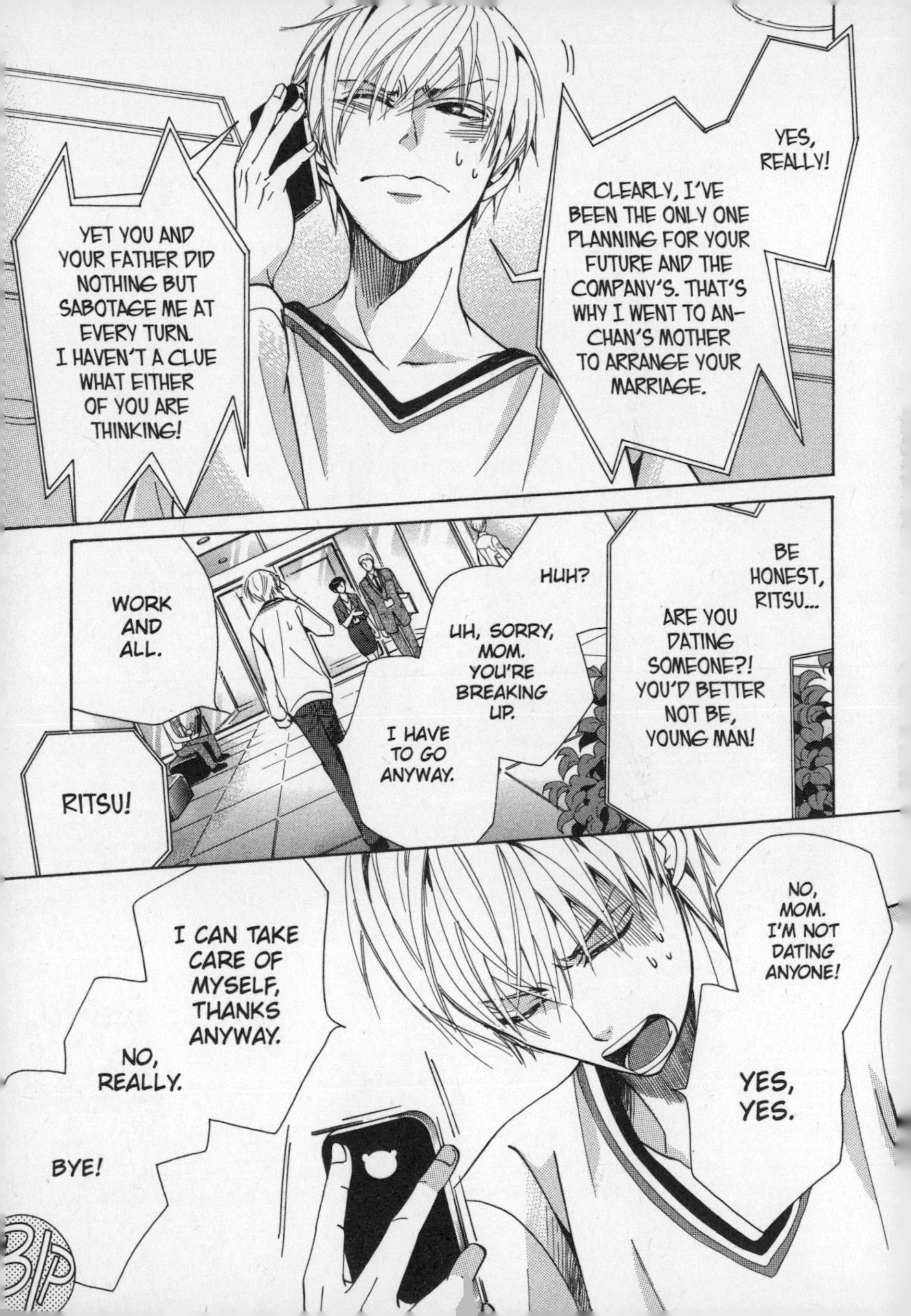
YES, REALLY!
CLEARLY, I'VE BEEN THE ONLY ONE PLANNING FOR YOUR FUTURE AND THE COMPANY'S. THAT'S WHY I WENT TO AN-CHAN'S MOTHER TO ARRANGE YOUR MARRIAGE.
YET YOU AND YOUR FATHER DID NOTHING BUT SABOTAGE ME AT EVERY TURN. I HAVEN'T A CLUE WHAT EITHER OF YOU ARE THINKING!
BE HONEST, RITSU...
ARE YOU DATING SOMEONE?! YOU'D BETTER NOT BE, YOUNG MAN!
HUH?
UH, SORRY, MOM. YOU'RE BREAKING UP.
I HAVE TO GO ANYWAY.
WORK AND ALL.
RITSU!
NO, MOM. I'M NOT DATING ANYONE!
YES, YES.
I CAN TAKE CARE OF MYSELF, THANKS ANYWAY.
NO, REALLY.
BYE!

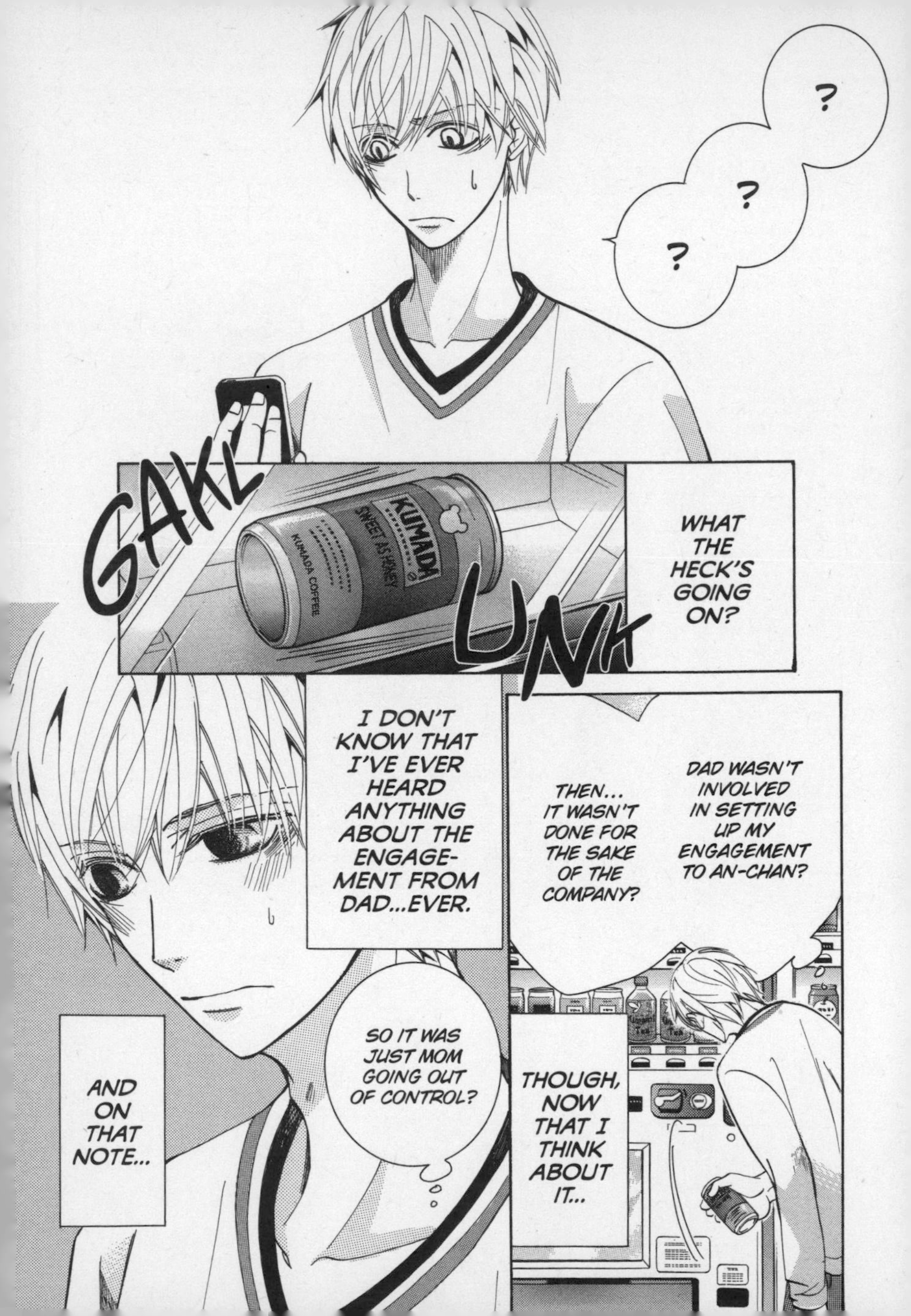

? ? ?
WHAT THE HECK'S GOING ON?
GAKLUNK
KUMADA
SWEET AS HONEY
KUMADA COFFEE
DAD WASN'T INVOLVED IN SETTING UP MY ENGAGEMENT TO AN-CHAN?
THEN... IT WASN'T DONE FOR THE SAKE OF THE COMPANY?
THOUGH, NOW THAT I THINK ABOUT IT...
I DON'T KNOW THAT I'VE EVER HEARD ANYTHING ABOUT THE ENGAGE-MENT FROM DAD...EVER.
SO IT WAS JUST MOM GOING OUT OF CONTROL?
AND ON THAT NOTE...

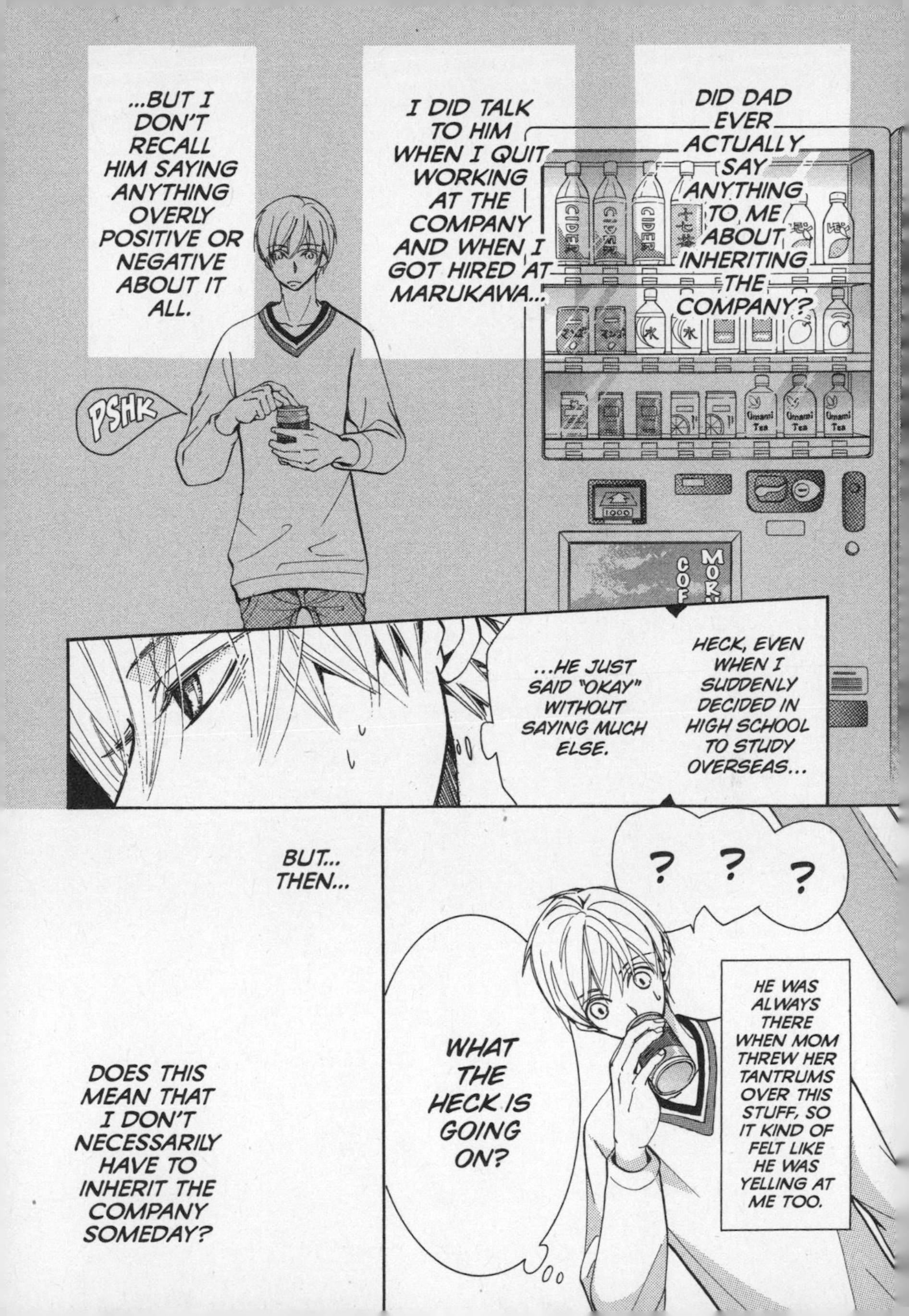
DID DAD EVER ACTUALLY SAY ANYTHING TO ME ABOUT INHERITING THE COMPANY?
I DID TALK TO HIM WHEN I QUIT WORKING AT THE COMPANY AND WHEN I GOT HIRED AT MARUKAWA...
...BUT I DON'T RECALL HIM SAYING ANYTHING OVERLY POSITIVE OR NEGATIVE ABOUT IT ALL.
PSHK
HECK, EVEN WHEN I SUDDENLY DECIDED IN HIGH SCHOOL TO STUDY OVERSEAS...
...HE JUST SAID "OKAY" WITHOUT SAYING MUCH ELSE.
? ? ?
HE WAS ALWAYS THERE WHEN MOM THREW HER TANTRUMS OVER THIS STUFF, SO IT KIND OF FELT LIKE HE WAS YELLING AT ME TOO.
WHAT THE HECK IS GOING ON?
BUT... THEN...
DOES THIS MEAN THAT I DON'T NECESSARILY HAVE TO INHERIT THE COMPANY SOMEDAY?

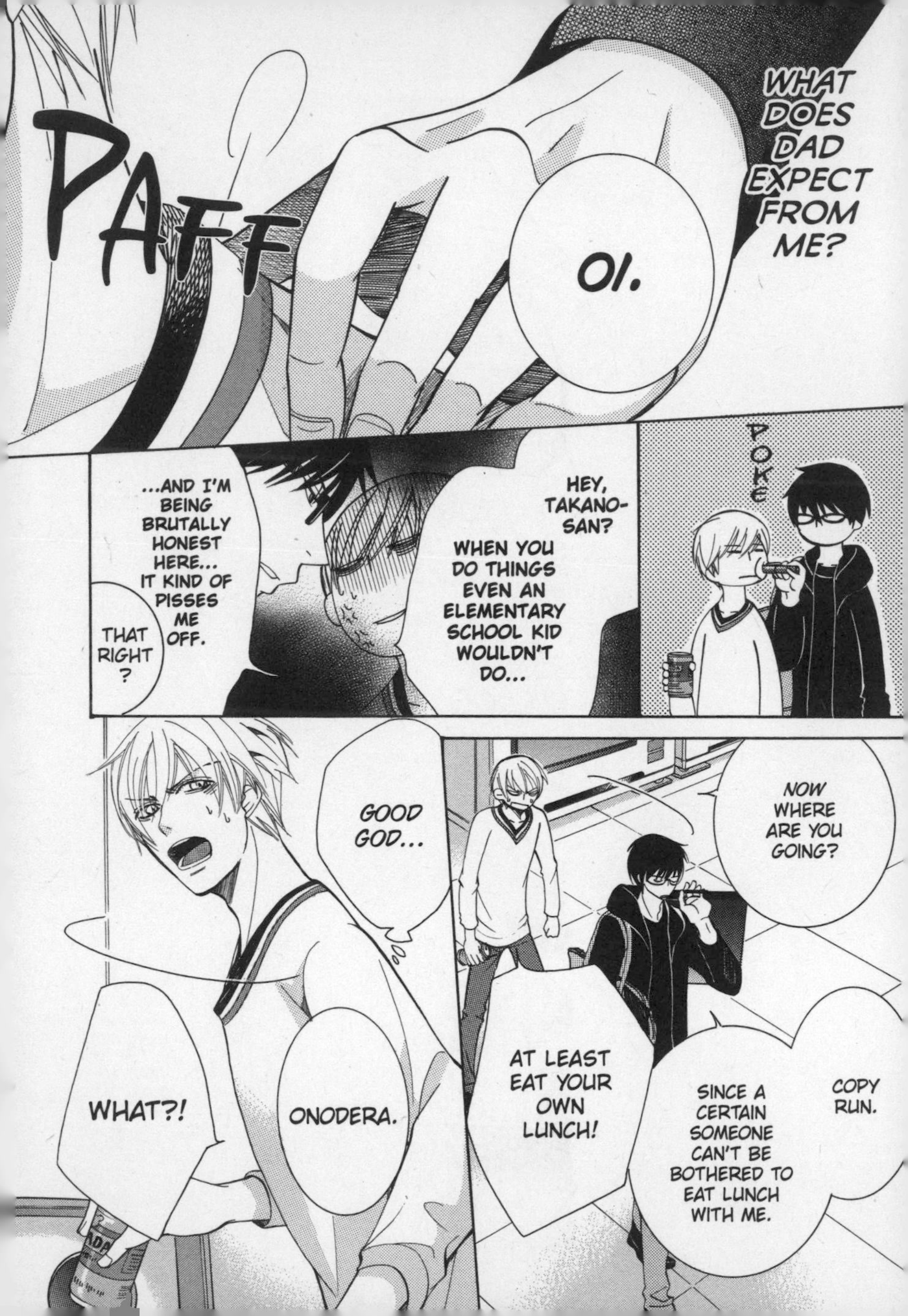
WHAT DOES DAD EXPECT FROM ME?
OI.
PAFF
POKE
HEY, TAKANO-SAN?
WHEN YOU DO THINGS EVEN AN ELEMENTARY SCHOOL KID WOULDN'T DO...
...AND I'M BEING BRUTALLY HONEST HERE... IT KIND OF PISSES ME OFF.
THAT RIGHT?
NOW WHERE ARE YOU GOING?
COPY RUN.
SINCE A CERTAIN SOMEONE CAN'T BE BOTHERED TO EAT LUNCH WITH ME.
AT LEAST EAT YOUR OWN LUNCH!
GOOD GOD...
ONODERA.
WHAT?!

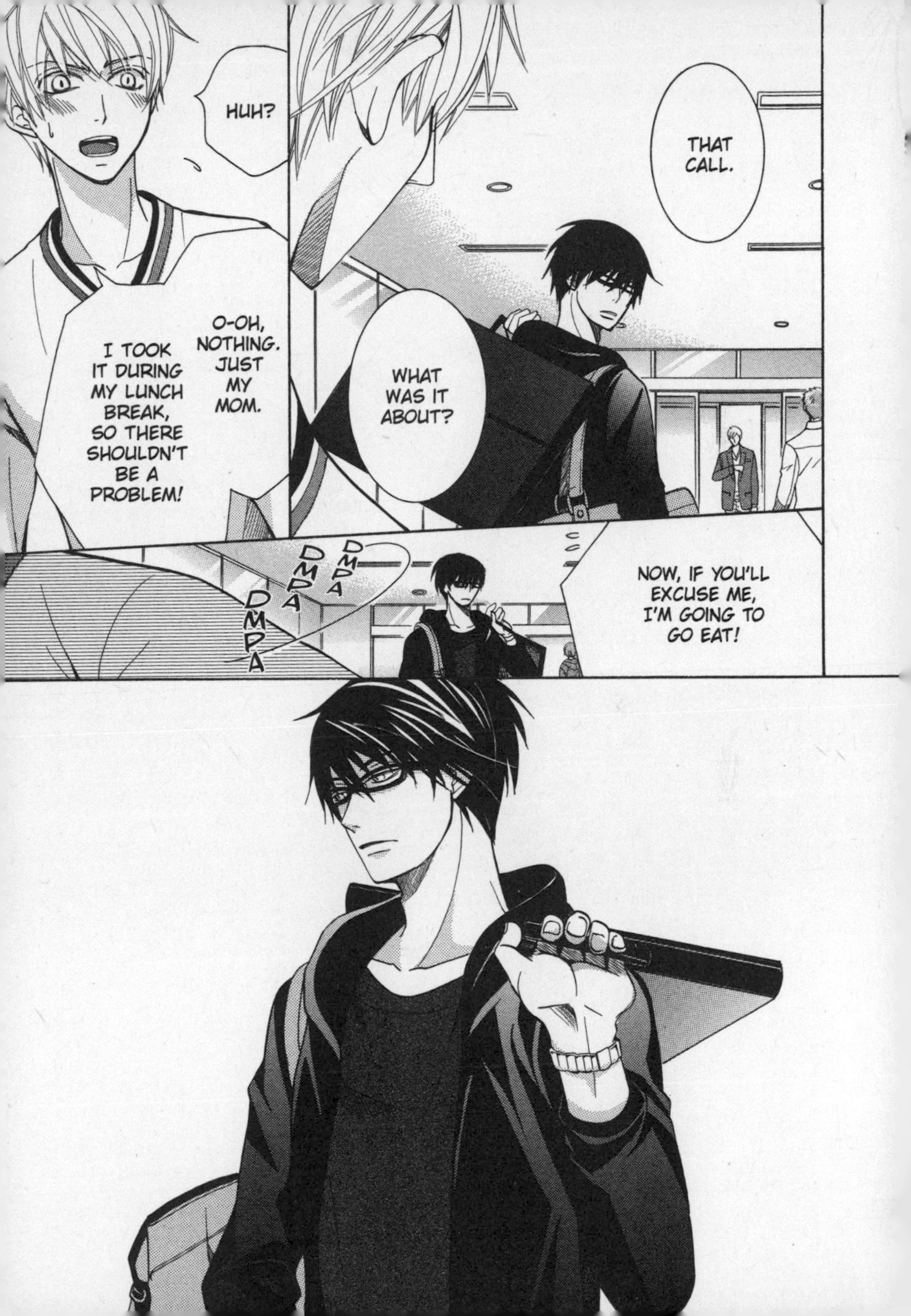
THAT CALL.
WHAT WAS IT ABOUT?
HUH?
O-OH, NOTHING. JUST MY MOM.
I TOOK IT DURING MY LUNCH BREAK, SO THERE SHOULDN'T BE A PROBLEM!
NOW, IF YOU'LL EXCUSE ME, I'M GOING TO GO EAT!
DMPA DMPA DMPA

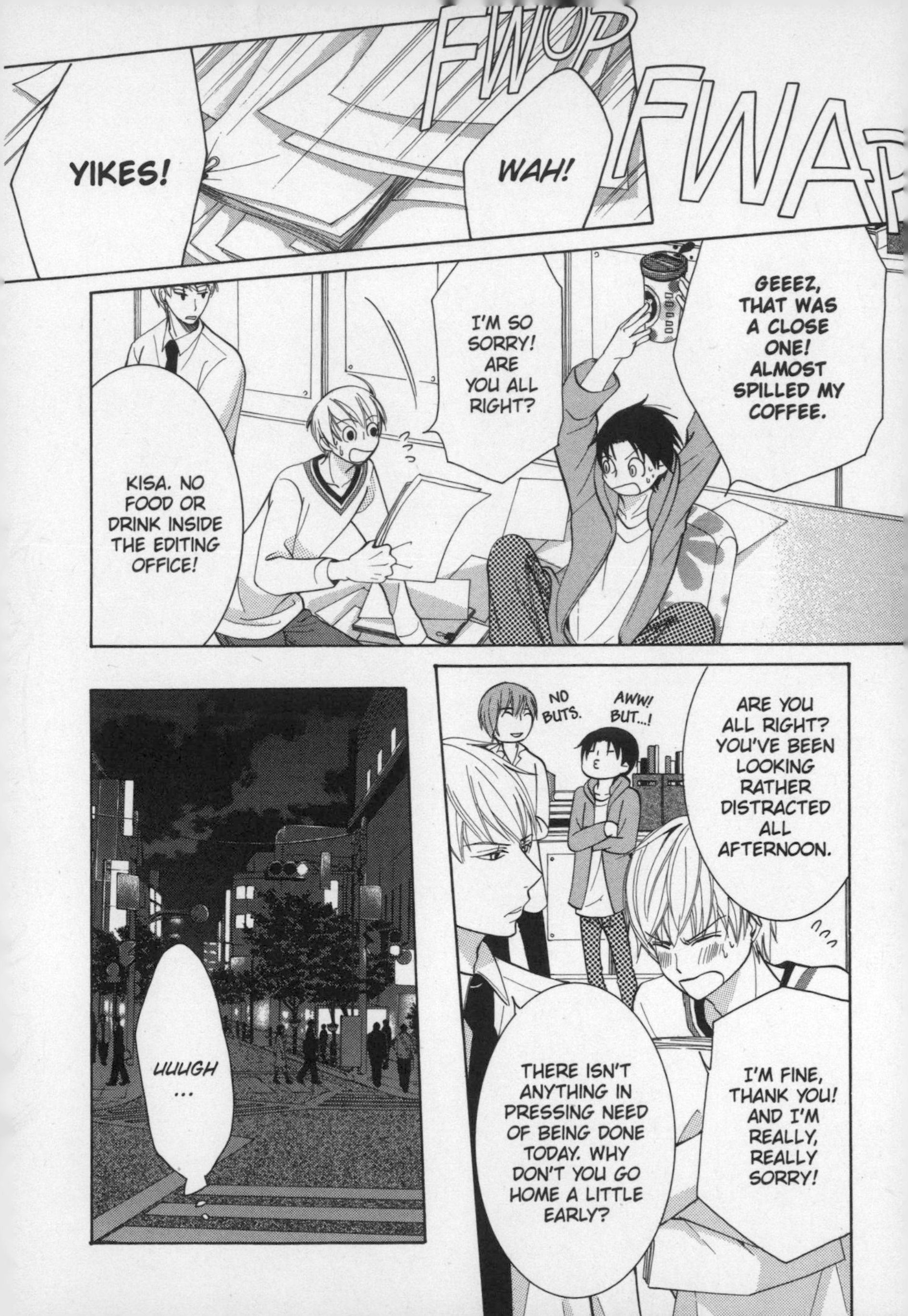
FWOP
FWAP
WAH!
YIKES!
GEEEZ, THAT WAS A CLOSE ONE! ALMOST SPILLED MY COFFEE.
I'M SO SORRY! ARE YOU ALL RIGHT?
KISA. NO FOOD OR DRINK INSIDE THE EDITING OFFICE!
ARE YOU ALL RIGHT? YOU'VE BEEN LOOKING RATHER DISTRACTED ALL AFTERNOON.
AWW! BUT...!
NO BUTS.
I'M FINE, THANK YOU! AND I'M REALLY, REALLY SORRY!
THERE ISN'T ANYTHING IN PRESSING NEED OF BEING DONE TODAY. WHY DON'T YOU GO HOME A LITTLE EARLY?
UUUGH ...

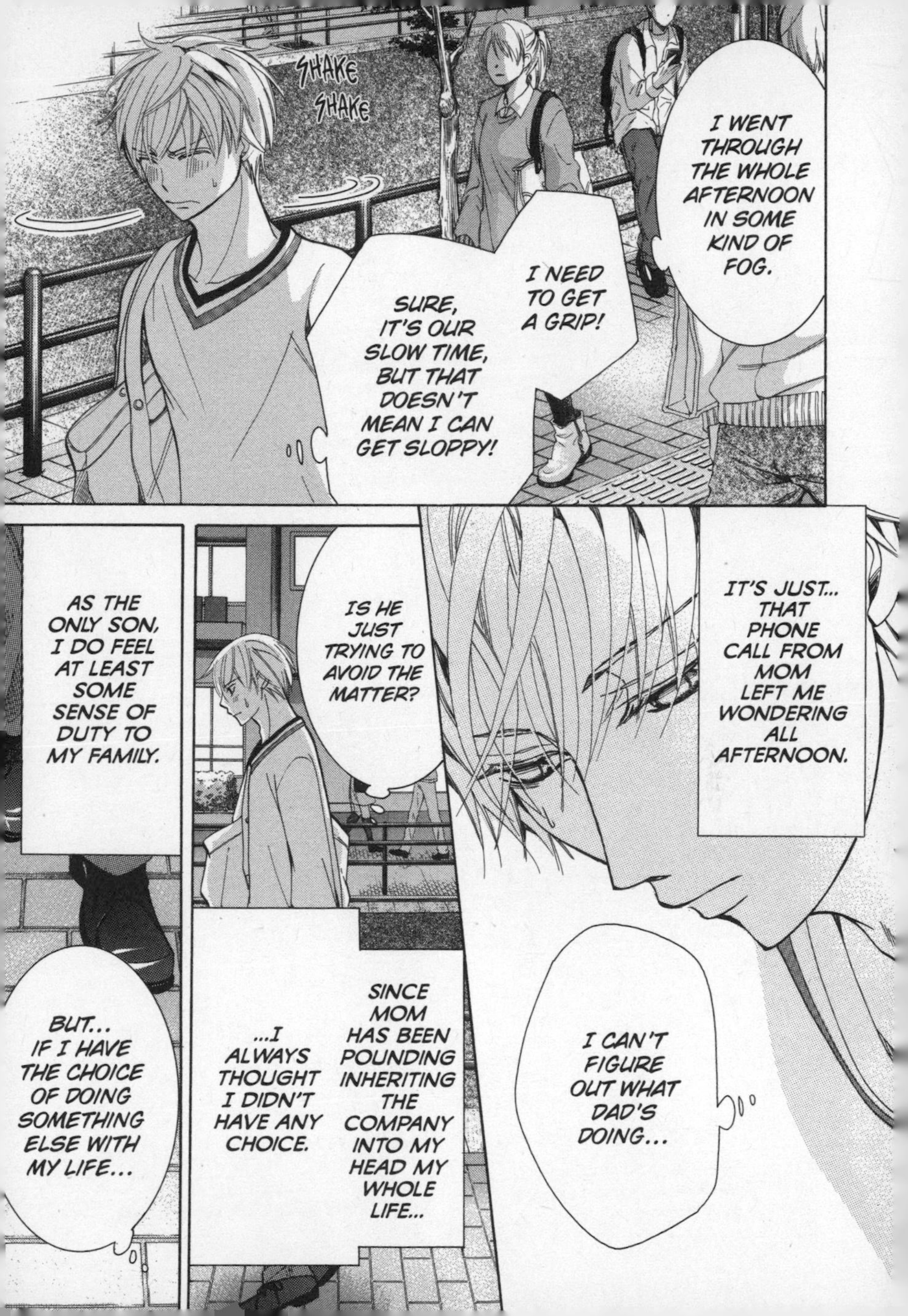
I WENT THROUGH THE WHOLE AFTERNOON IN SOME KIND OF FOG.
I NEED TO GET A GRIP!
SURE, IT'S OUR SLOW TIME, BUT THAT DOESN'T MEAN I CAN GET SLOPPY!
SHAKE
SHAKE
IT'S JUST... THAT PHONE CALL FROM MOM LEFT ME WONDERING ALL AFTERNOON.
I CAN'T FIGURE OUT WHAT DAD'S DOING...
IS HE JUST TRYING TO AVOID THE MATTER?
AS THE ONLY SON, I DO FEEL AT LEAST SOME SENSE OF DUTY TO MY FAMILY.
SINCE MOM HAS BEEN POUNDING INHERITING THE COMPANY INTO MY HEAD MY WHOLE LIFE...
...I ALWAYS THOUGHT I DIDN'T HAVE ANY CHOICE.
BUT... IF I HAVE THE CHOICE OF DOING SOMETHING ELSE WITH MY LIFE...

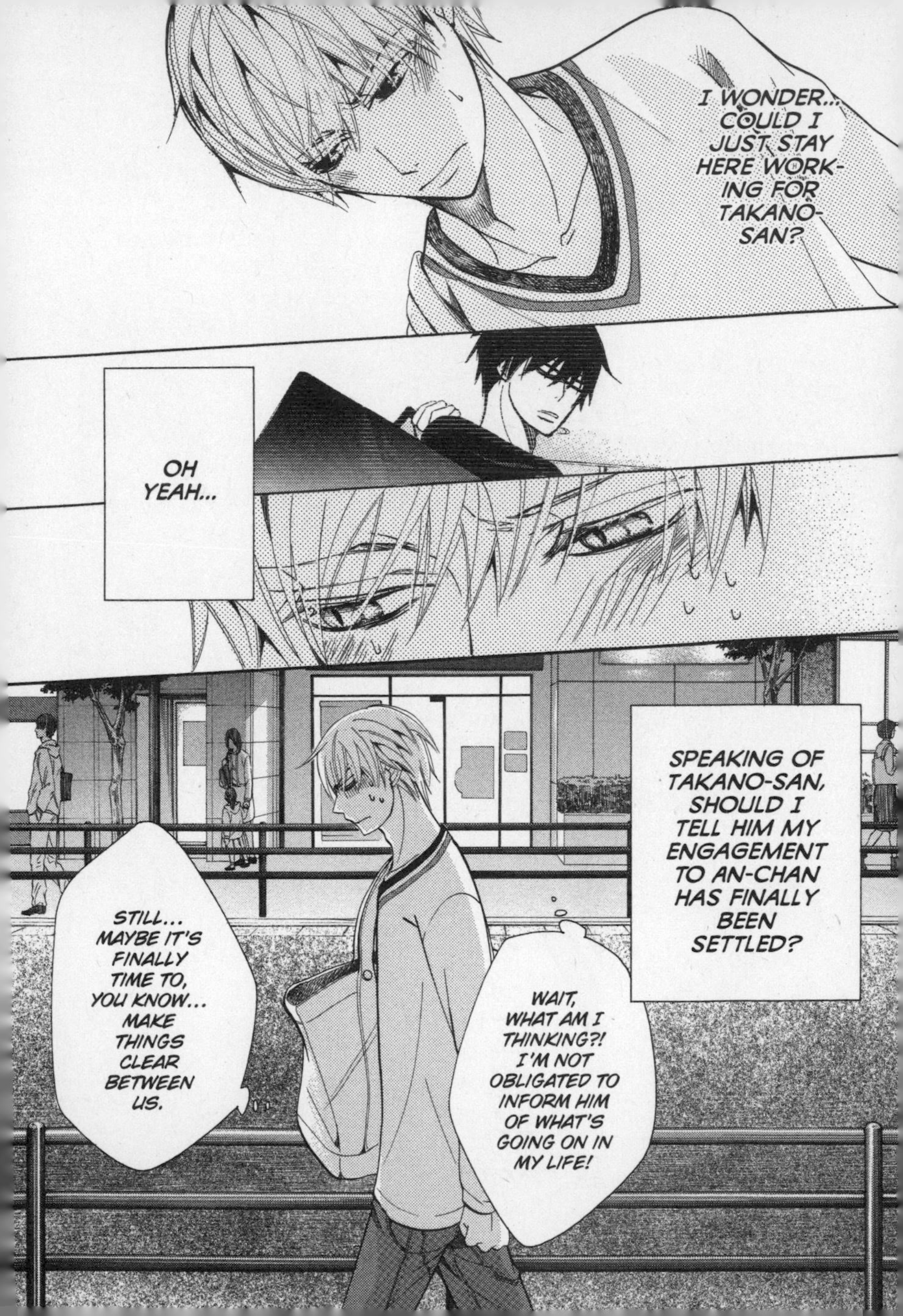
I WONDER... COULD I JUST STAY HERE WORKING FOR TAKANO-SAN?
OH YEAH...
SPEAKING OF TAKANO-SAN, SHOULD I TELL HIM MY ENGAGEMENT TO AN-CHAN HAS FINALLY BEEN SETTLED?
WAIT, WHAT AM I THINKING?! I'M NOT OBLIGATED TO INFORM HIM OF WHAT'S GOING ON IN MY LIFE!
STILL... MAYBE IT'S FINALLY TIME TO, YOU KNOW... MAKE THINGS CLEAR BETWEEN US.

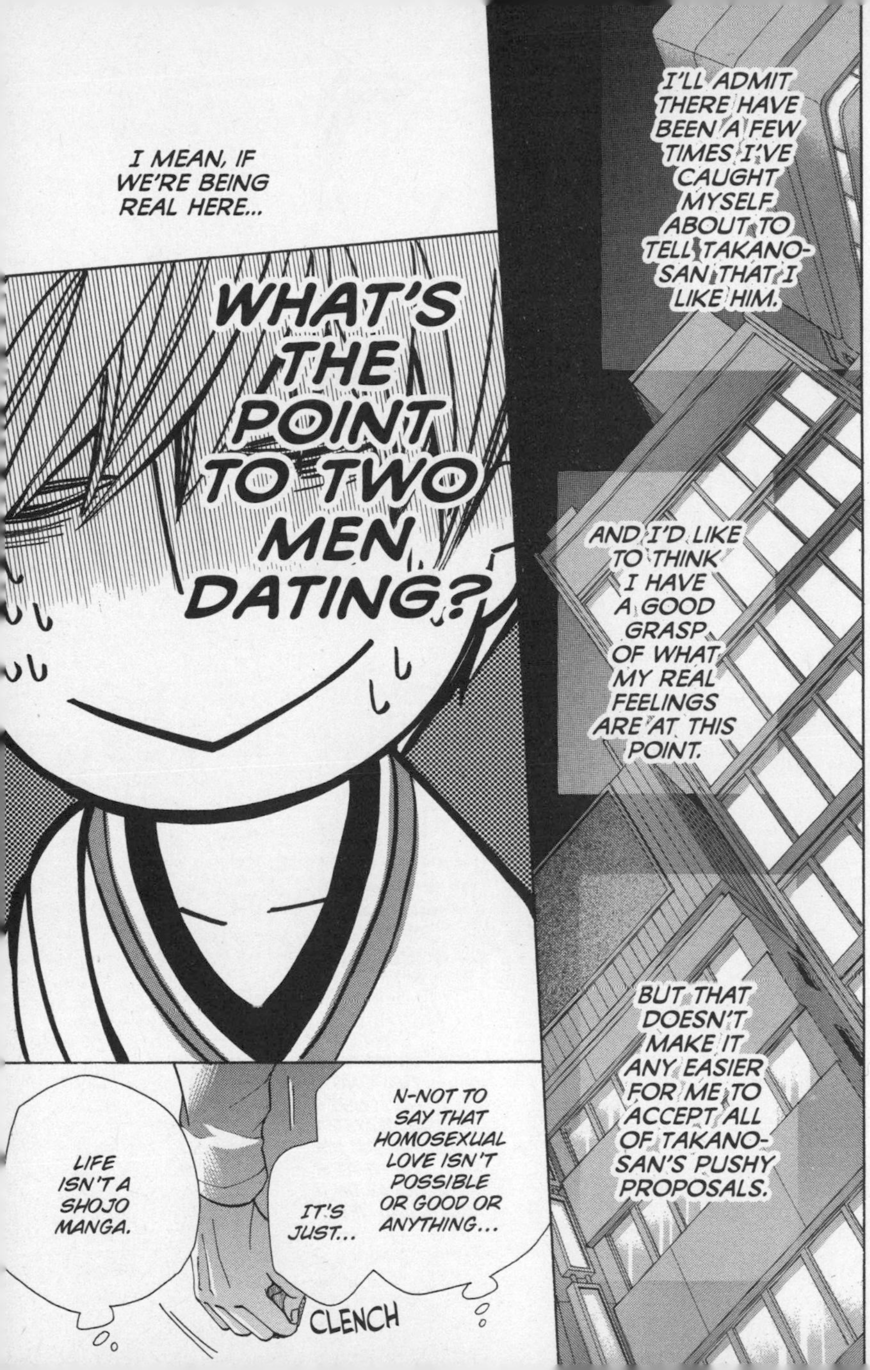
I'LL ADMIT THERE HAVE BEEN A FEW TIMES I'VE CAUGHT MYSELF ABOUT TO TELL TAKANO-SAN THAT I LIKE HIM.
AND I'D LIKE TO THINK I HAVE A GOOD GRASP OF WHAT MY REAL FEELINGS ARE AT THIS POINT.
BUT THAT DOESN'T MAKE IT ANY EASIER FOR ME TO ACCEPT ALL OF TAKANO-SAN'S PUSHY PROPOSALS.
I MEAN, IF WE'RE BEING REAL HERE...
WHAT'S THE POINT TO TWO MEN DATING?
N-NOT TO SAY THAT HOMOSEXUAL LOVE ISN'T POSSIBLE OR GOOD OR ANYTHING...
IT'S JUST...
LIFE ISN'T A SHOJO MANGA.
CLENCH

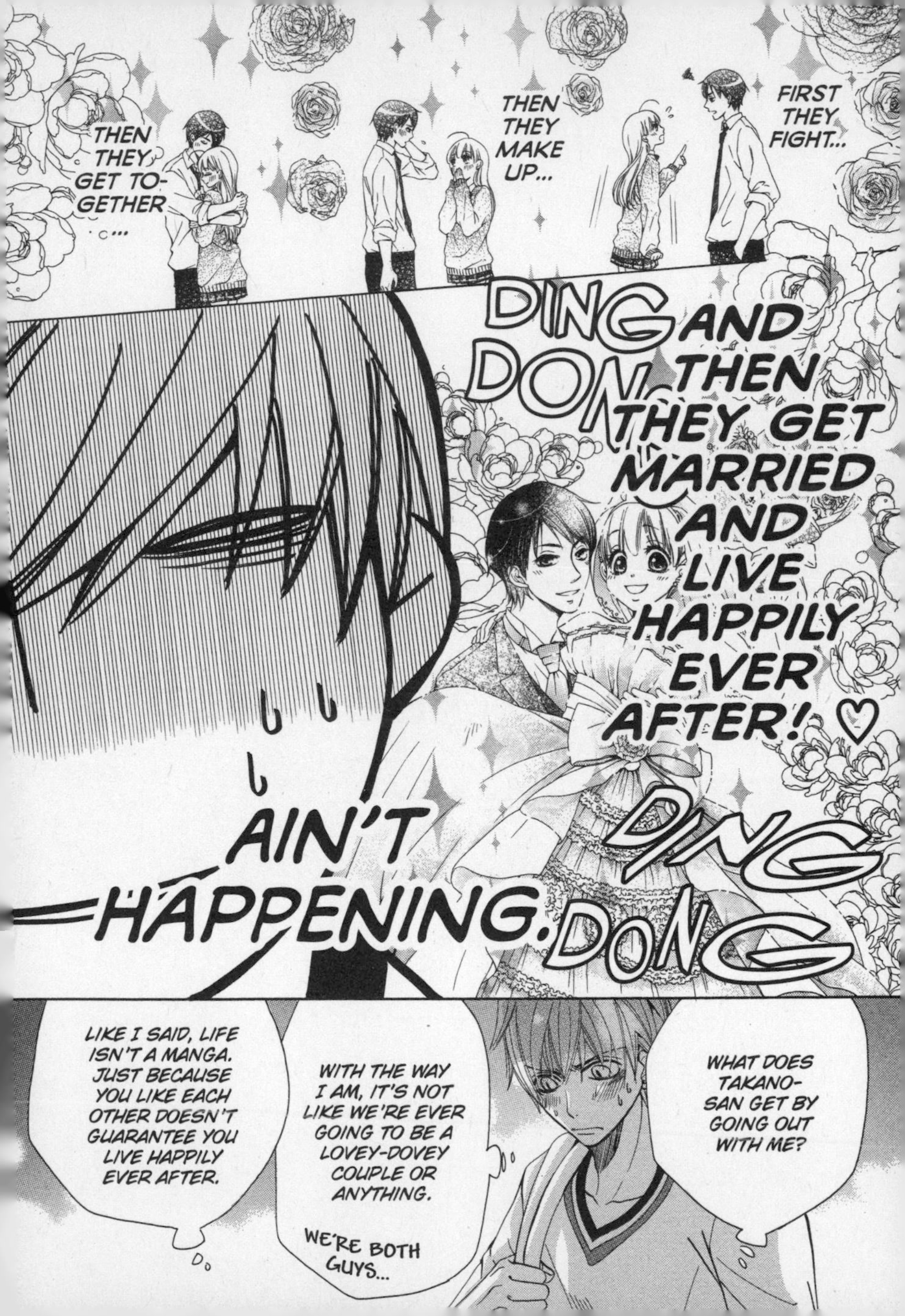
FIRST THEY FIGHT...
THEN THEY MAKE UP...
THEN THEY GET TO-GETHER...
DING DONG
AND THEN THEY GET MARRIED AND LIVE HAPPILY EVER AFTER! ♡
DING DONG
AIN'T HAPPENING.
WHAT DOES TAKANO-SAN GET BY GOING OUT WITH ME?
WITH THE WAY I AM, IT'S NOT LIKE WE'RE EVER GOING TO BE A LOVEY-DOVEY COUPLE OR ANYTHING.
WE'RE BOTH GUYS...
LIKE I SAID, LIFE ISN'T A MANGA. JUST BECAUSE YOU LIKE EACH OTHER DOESN'T GUARANTEE YOU LIVE HAPPILY EVER AFTER.

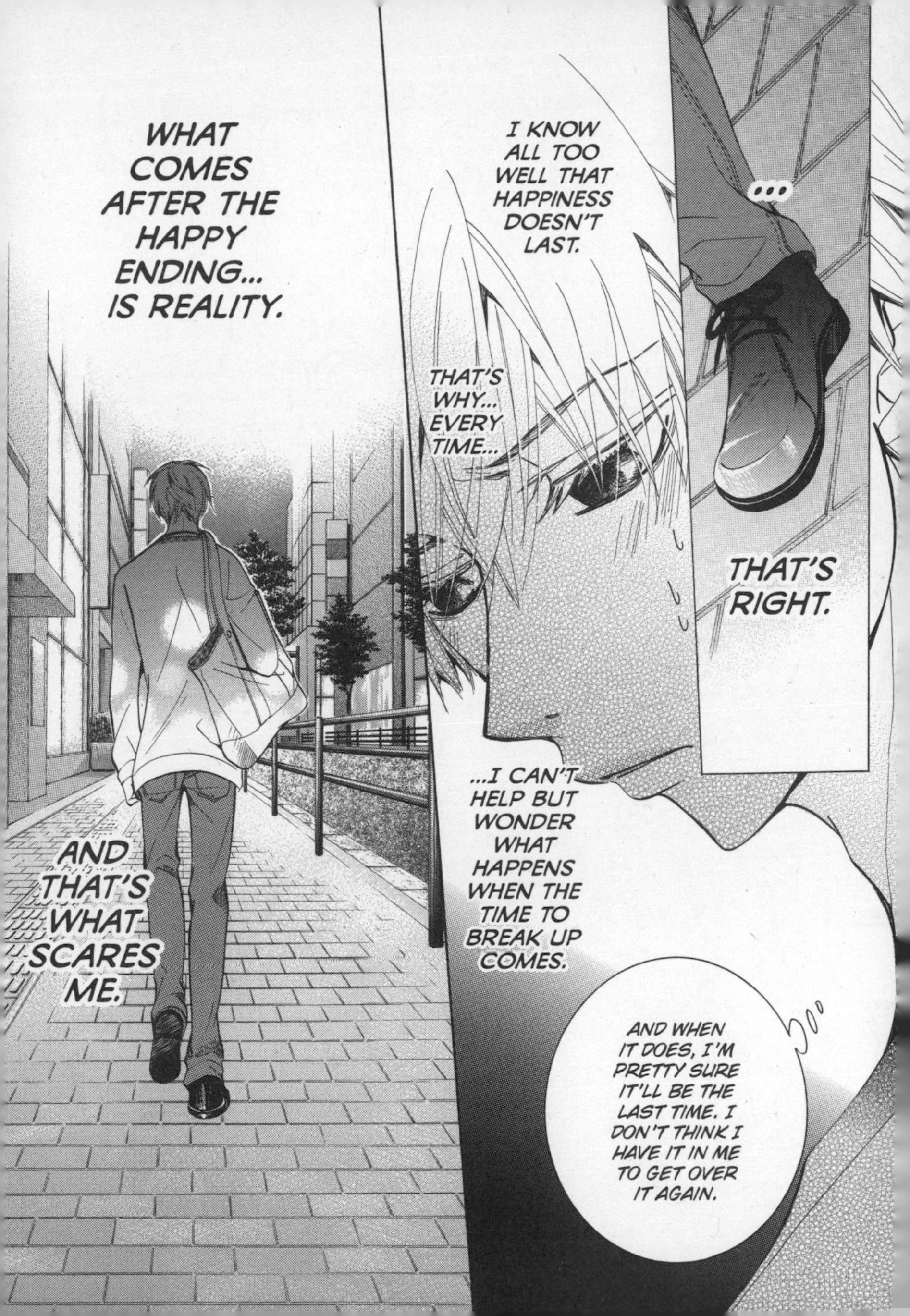
...
THAT'S RIGHT.
I KNOW ALL TOO WELL THAT HAPPINESS DOESN'T LAST.
THAT'S WHY... EVERY TIME...
...I CAN'T HELP BUT WONDER WHAT HAPPENS WHEN THE TIME TO BREAK UP COMES.
AND WHEN IT DOES, I'M PRETTY SURE IT'LL BE THE LAST TIME. I DON'T THINK I HAVE IT IN ME TO GET OVER IT AGAIN.
WHAT COMES AFTER THE HAPPY ENDING... IS REALITY.
AND THAT'S WHAT SCARES ME.

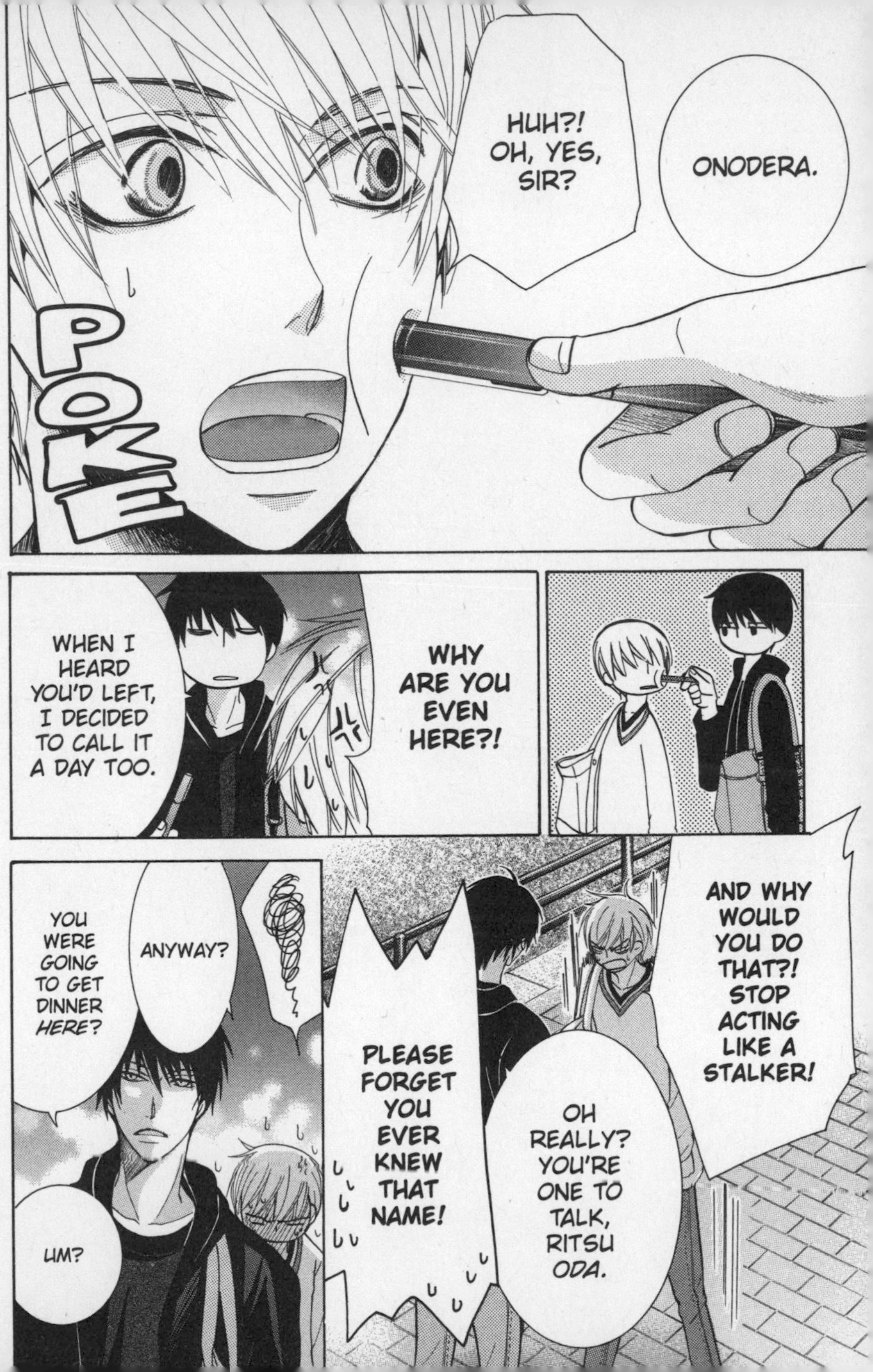
ONODERA.
HUH?! OH, YES, SIR?
POKE
WHY ARE YOU EVEN HERE?!
WHEN I HEARD YOU'D LEFT, I DECIDED TO CALL IT A DAY TOO.
AND WHY WOULD YOU DO THAT?! STOP ACTING LIKE A STALKER!
OH REALLY? YOU'RE ONE TO TALK, RITSU ODA.
PLEASE FORGET YOU EVER KNEW THAT NAME!
ANYWAY?
YOU WERE GOING TO GET DINNER *HERE*?
UM?

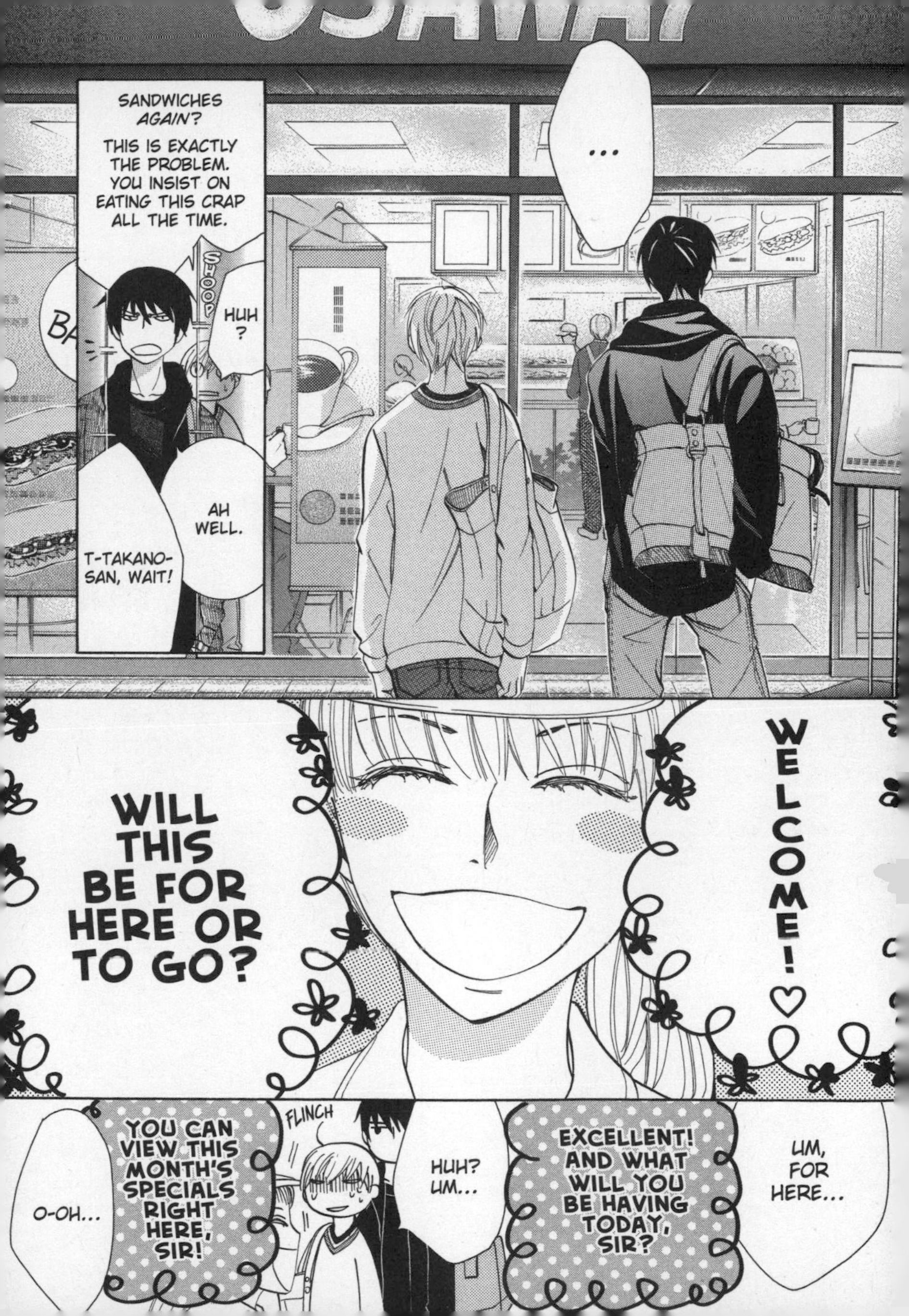
...
SANDWICHES AGAIN? THIS IS EXACTLY THE PROBLEM. YOU INSIST ON EATING THIS CRAP ALL THE TIME.
SHOOP
HUH?
BA
AH WELL.
T-TAKANO-SAN, WAIT!
WELCOME! ♡
WILL THIS BE FOR HERE OR TO GO?
UM, FOR HERE...
EXCELLENT! AND WHAT WILL YOU BE HAVING TODAY, SIR?
HUH? UM...
FLINCH
YOU CAN VIEW THIS MONTH'S SPECIALS RIGHT HERE, SIR!
O-OH...

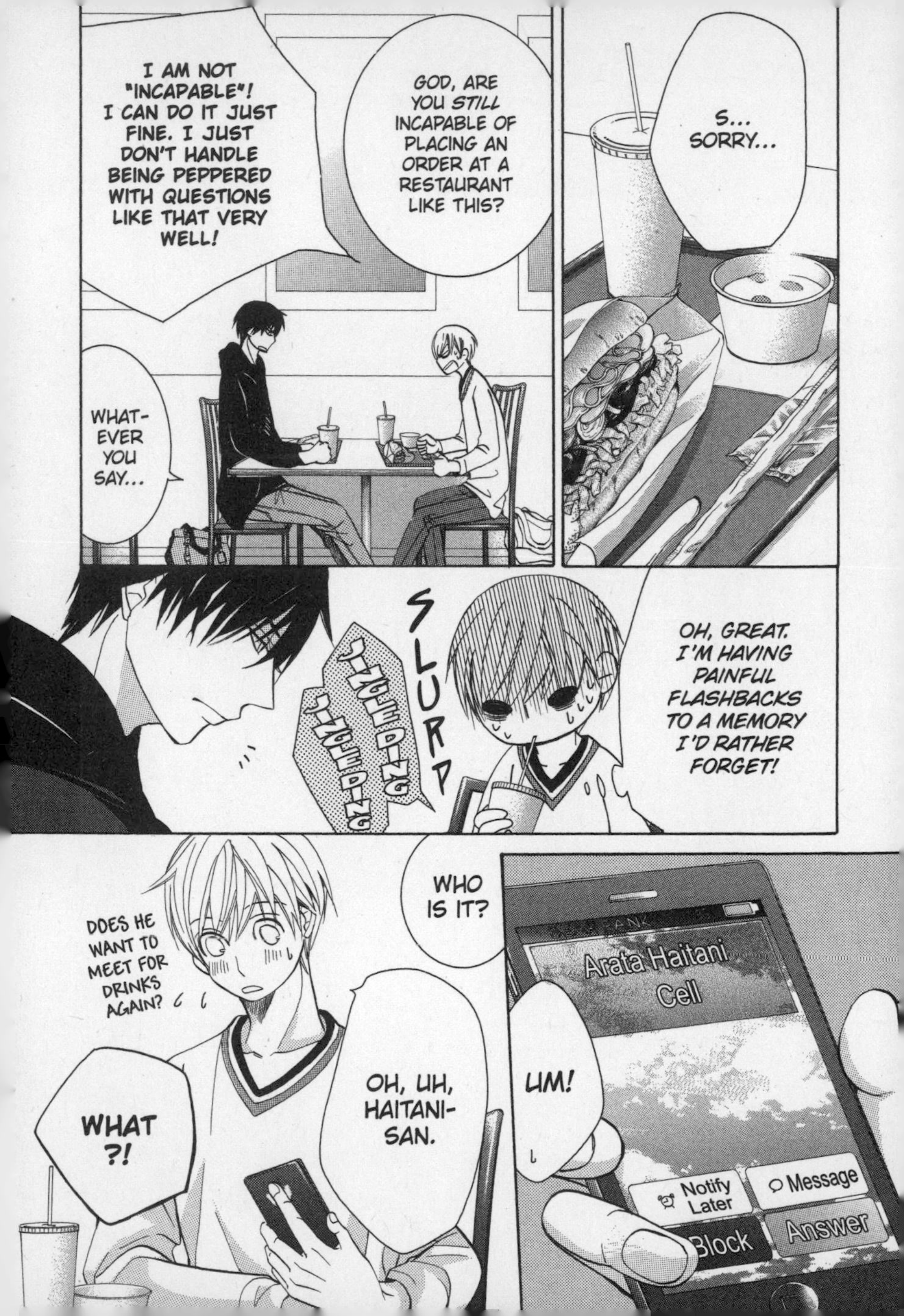
S... SORRY...
GOD, ARE YOU *STILL* INCAPABLE OF PLACING AN ORDER AT A RESTAURANT LIKE THIS?
I AM NOT "INCAPABLE"! I CAN DO IT JUST FINE. I JUST DON'T HANDLE BEING PEPPERED WITH QUESTIONS LIKE THAT VERY WELL!
WHAT-EVER YOU SAY...
OH, GREAT. I'M HAVING PAINFUL FLASHBACKS TO A MEMORY I'D RATHER FORGET!
SLURP
JINGLEDING JINGLEDING
Arata Haitani Cell
Notify Later
Message
Block
Answer
UM!
WHO IS IT?
DOES HE WANT TO MEET FOR DRINKS AGAIN?
OH, UH, HAITANI-SAN.
WHAT?!

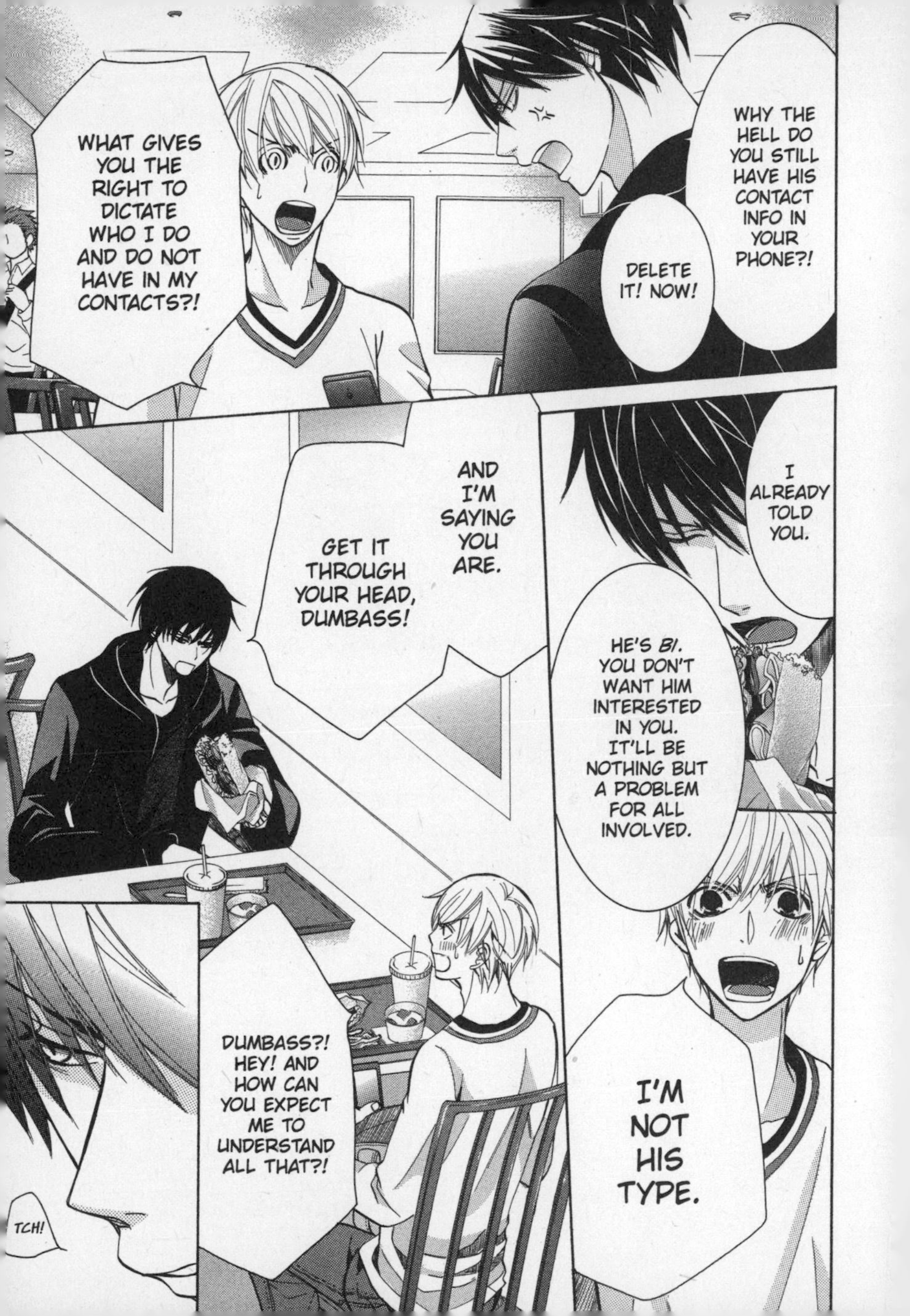
WHY THE HELL DO YOU STILL HAVE HIS CONTACT INFO IN YOUR PHONE?!
DELETE IT! NOW!
WHAT GIVES YOU THE RIGHT TO DICTATE WHO I DO AND DO NOT HAVE IN MY CONTACTS?!
I ALREADY TOLD YOU.
HE'S *BI*. YOU DON'T WANT HIM INTERESTED IN YOU. IT'LL BE NOTHING BUT A PROBLEM FOR ALL INVOLVED.
I'M NOT HIS TYPE.
AND I'M SAYING YOU ARE.
GET IT THROUGH YOUR HEAD, DUMBASS!
DUMBASS?! HEY! AND HOW CAN YOU EXPECT ME TO UNDERSTAND ALL THAT?!
TCH!

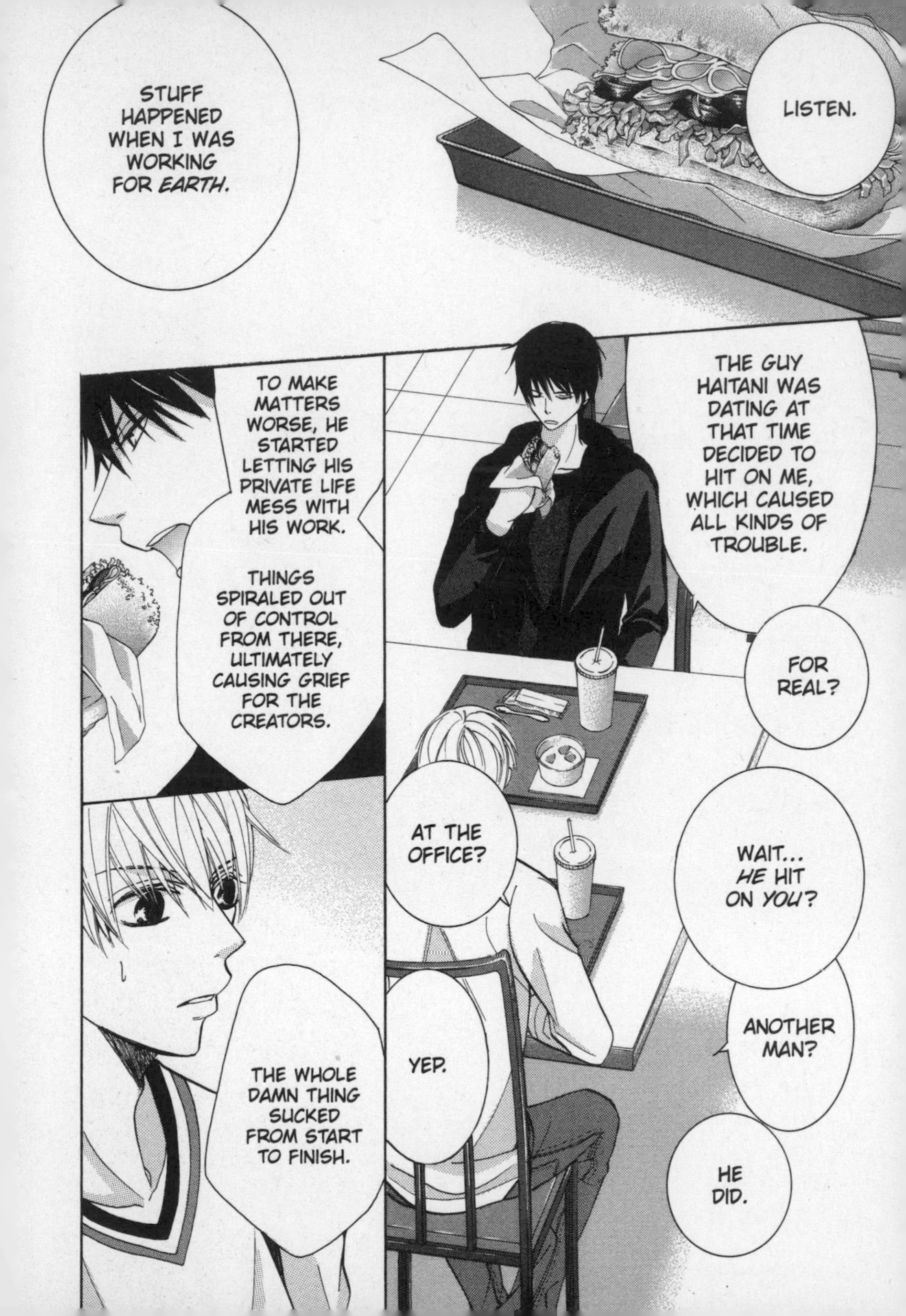
LISTEN.
STUFF HAPPENED WHEN I WAS WORKING FOR *EARTH*.
THE GUY HAITANI WAS DATING AT THAT TIME DECIDED TO HIT ON ME, WHICH CAUSED ALL KINDS OF TROUBLE.
FOR REAL?
WAIT... *HE* HIT ON *YOU*?
ANOTHER MAN?
HE DID.
AT THE OFFICE?
YEP.
TO MAKE MATTERS WORSE, HE STARTED LETTING HIS PRIVATE LIFE MESS WITH HIS WORK.
THINGS SPIRALED OUT OF CONTROL FROM THERE, ULTIMATELY CAUSING GRIEF FOR THE CREATORS.
THE WHOLE DAMN THING SUCKED FROM START TO FINISH.

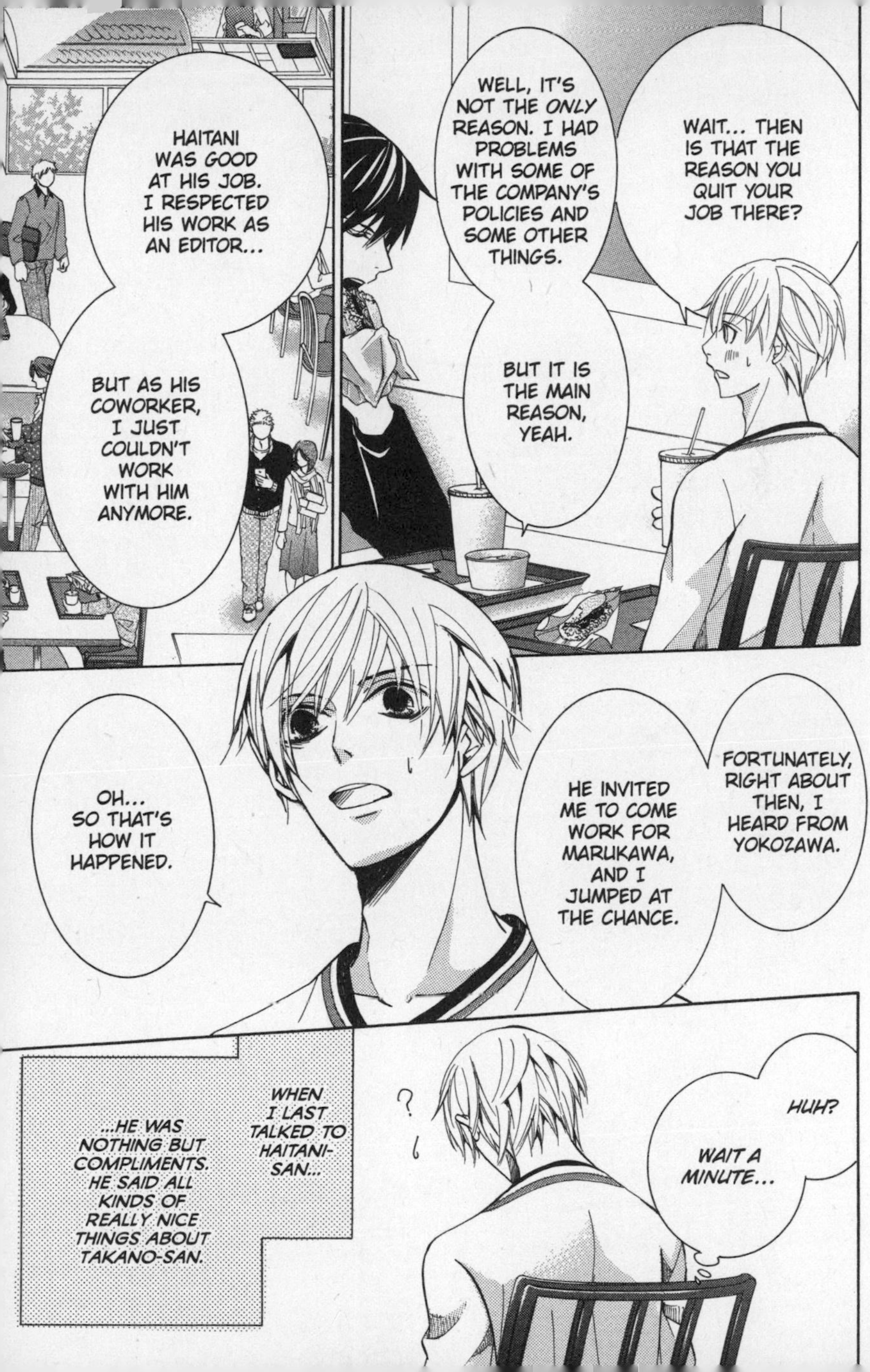
WAIT... THEN IS THAT THE REASON YOU QUIT YOUR JOB THERE?
WELL, IT'S NOT THE *ONLY* REASON. I HAD PROBLEMS WITH SOME OF THE COMPANY'S POLICIES AND SOME OTHER THINGS.
BUT IT IS THE MAIN REASON, YEAH.
HAITANI WAS GOOD AT HIS JOB. I RESPECTED HIS WORK AS AN EDITOR...
BUT AS HIS COWORKER, I JUST COULDN'T WORK WITH HIM ANYMORE.
FORTUNATELY, RIGHT ABOUT THEN, I HEARD FROM YOKOZAWA.
HE INVITED ME TO COME WORK FOR MARUKAWA, AND I JUMPED AT THE CHANCE.
OH... SO THAT'S HOW IT HAPPENED.
HUH?
WAIT A MINUTE...
?
WHEN I LAST TALKED TO HAITANI-SAN...
...HE WAS NOTHING BUT COMPLIMENTS. HE SAID ALL KINDS OF REALLY NICE THINGS ABOUT TAKANO-SAN.

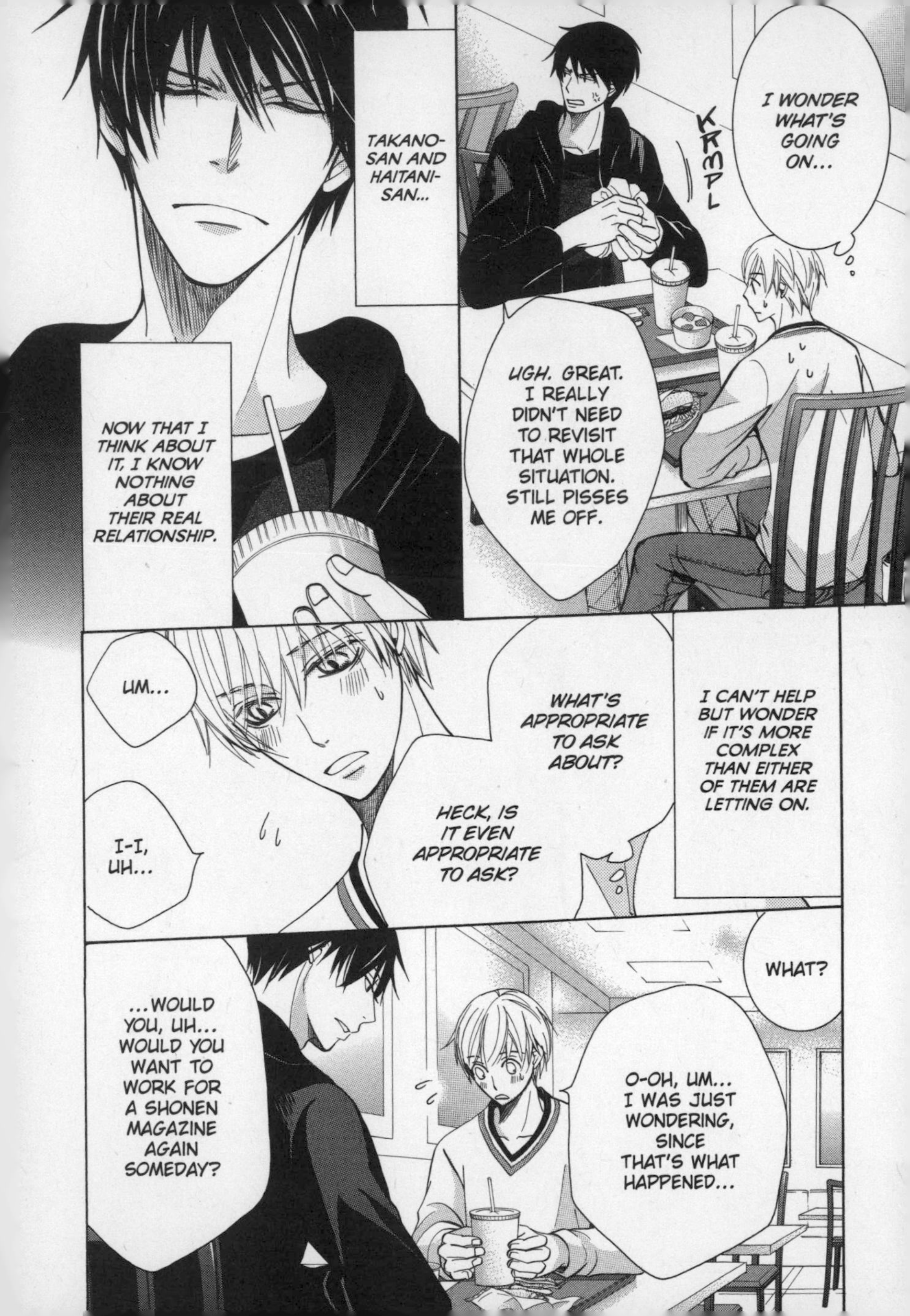
I WONDER WHAT'S GOING ON...
KRMPL
UGH. GREAT. I REALLY DIDN'T NEED TO REVISIT THAT WHOLE SITUATION. STILL PISSES ME OFF.
TAKANO-SAN AND HAITANI-SAN...
NOW THAT I THINK ABOUT IT, I KNOW NOTHING ABOUT THEIR REAL RELATIONSHIP.
I CAN'T HELP BUT WONDER IF IT'S MORE COMPLEX THAN EITHER OF THEM ARE LETTING ON.
WHAT'S APPROPRIATE TO ASK ABOUT?
HECK, IS IT EVEN APPROPRIATE TO ASK?
UM...
I-I, UH...
WHAT?
O-OH, UM... I WAS JUST WONDERING, SINCE THAT'S WHAT HAPPENED...
...WOULD YOU, UH... WOULD YOU WANT TO WORK FOR A SHONEN MAGAZINE AGAIN SOMEDAY?

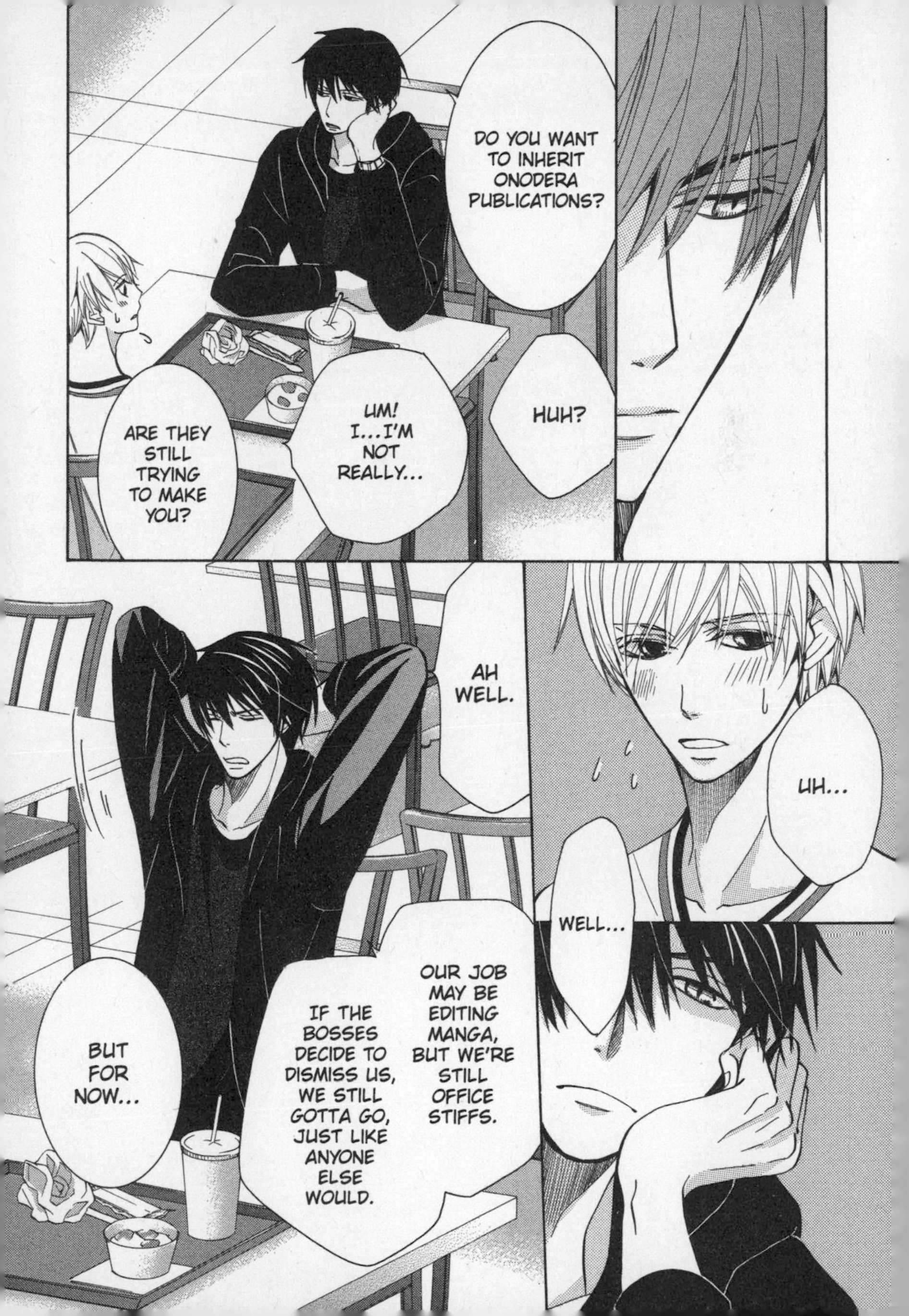
DO YOU WANT TO INHERIT ONODERA PUBLICATIONS?
HUH?
UM! I...I'M NOT REALLY...
ARE THEY STILL TRYING TO MAKE YOU?
UH...
WELL...
AH WELL.
OUR JOB MAY BE EDITING MANGA, BUT WE'RE STILL OFFICE STIFFS.
IF THE BOSSES DECIDE TO DISMISS US, WE STILL GOTTA GO, JUST LIKE ANYONE ELSE WOULD.
BUT FOR NOW...

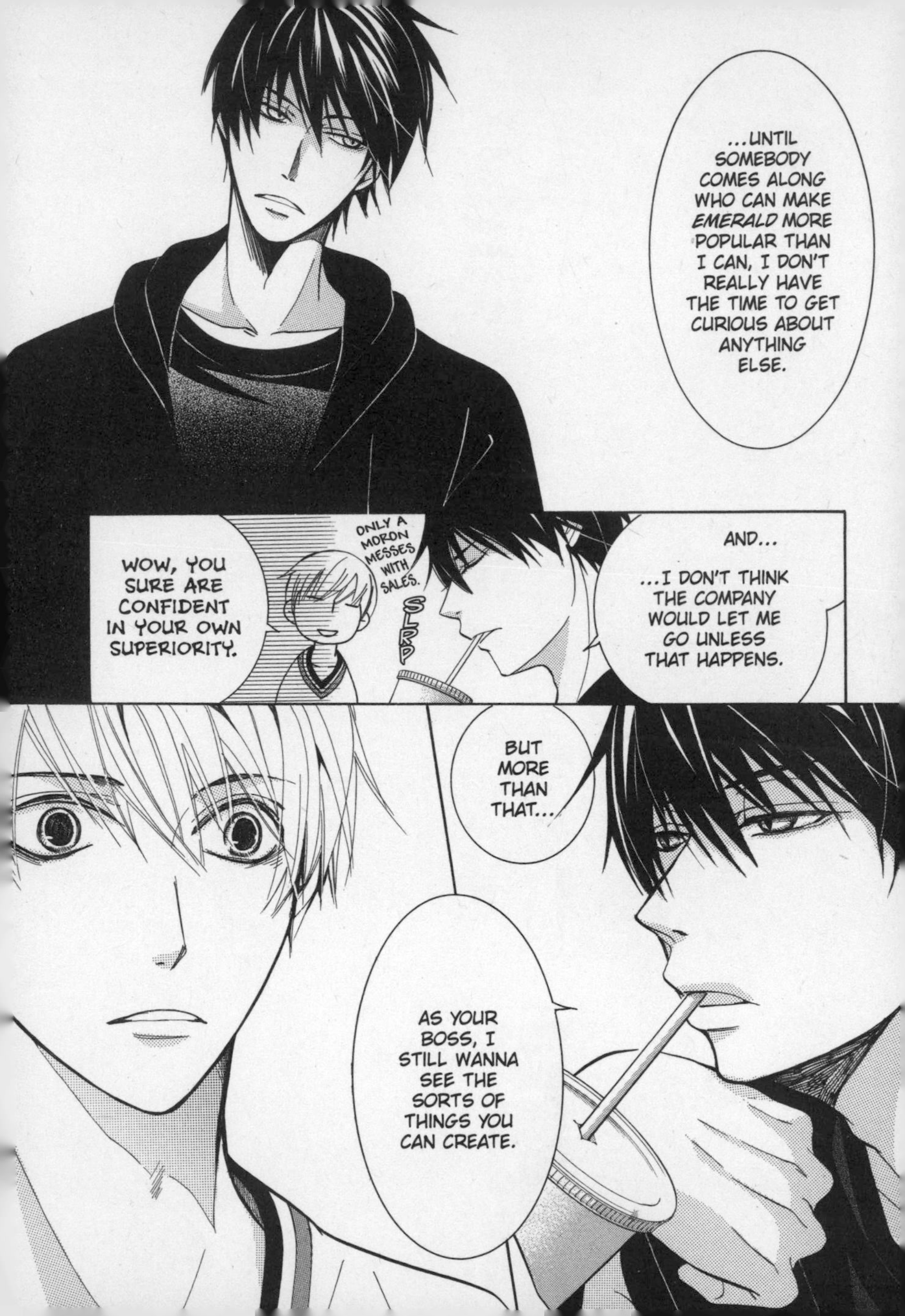
...UNTIL SOMEBODY COMES ALONG WHO CAN MAKE *EMERALD* MORE POPULAR THAN I CAN, I DON'T REALLY HAVE THE TIME TO GET CURIOUS ABOUT ANYTHING ELSE.
AND...
...I DON'T THINK THE COMPANY WOULD LET ME GO UNLESS THAT HAPPENS.
ONLY A MORON MESSES WITH SALES.
SLRP
WOW, YOU SURE ARE CONFIDENT IN YOUR OWN SUPERIORITY.
BUT MORE THAN THAT...
AS YOUR BOSS, I STILL WANNA SEE THE SORTS OF THINGS YOU CAN CREATE.

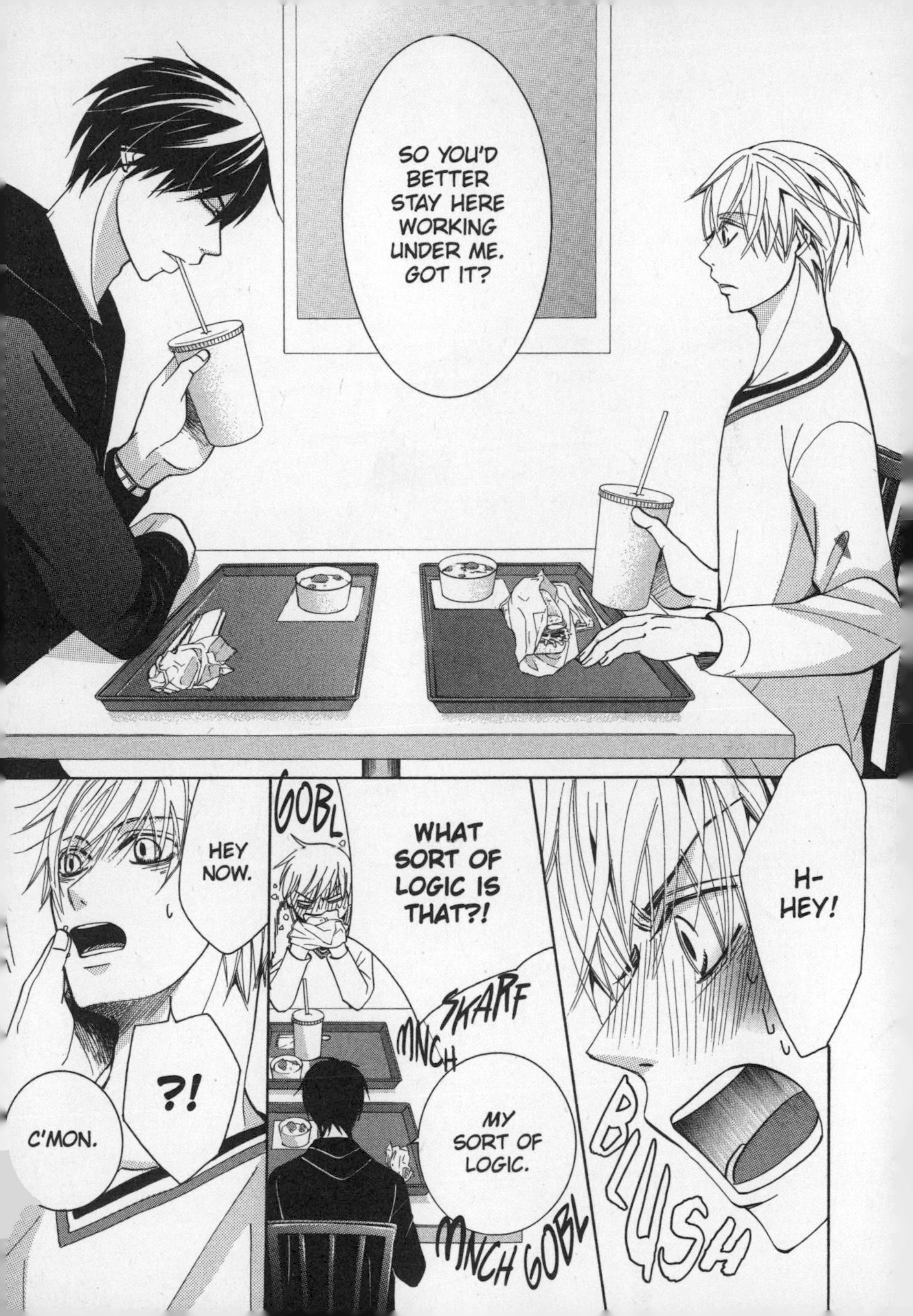
SO YOU'D BETTER STAY HERE WORKING UNDER ME. GOT IT?
H- HEY!
BLUSH
GOBL
WHAT SORT OF LOGIC IS THAT?!
SKARF
MNCH
MY SORT OF LOGIC.
MNCH GOBL
HEY NOW.
?!
C'MON.

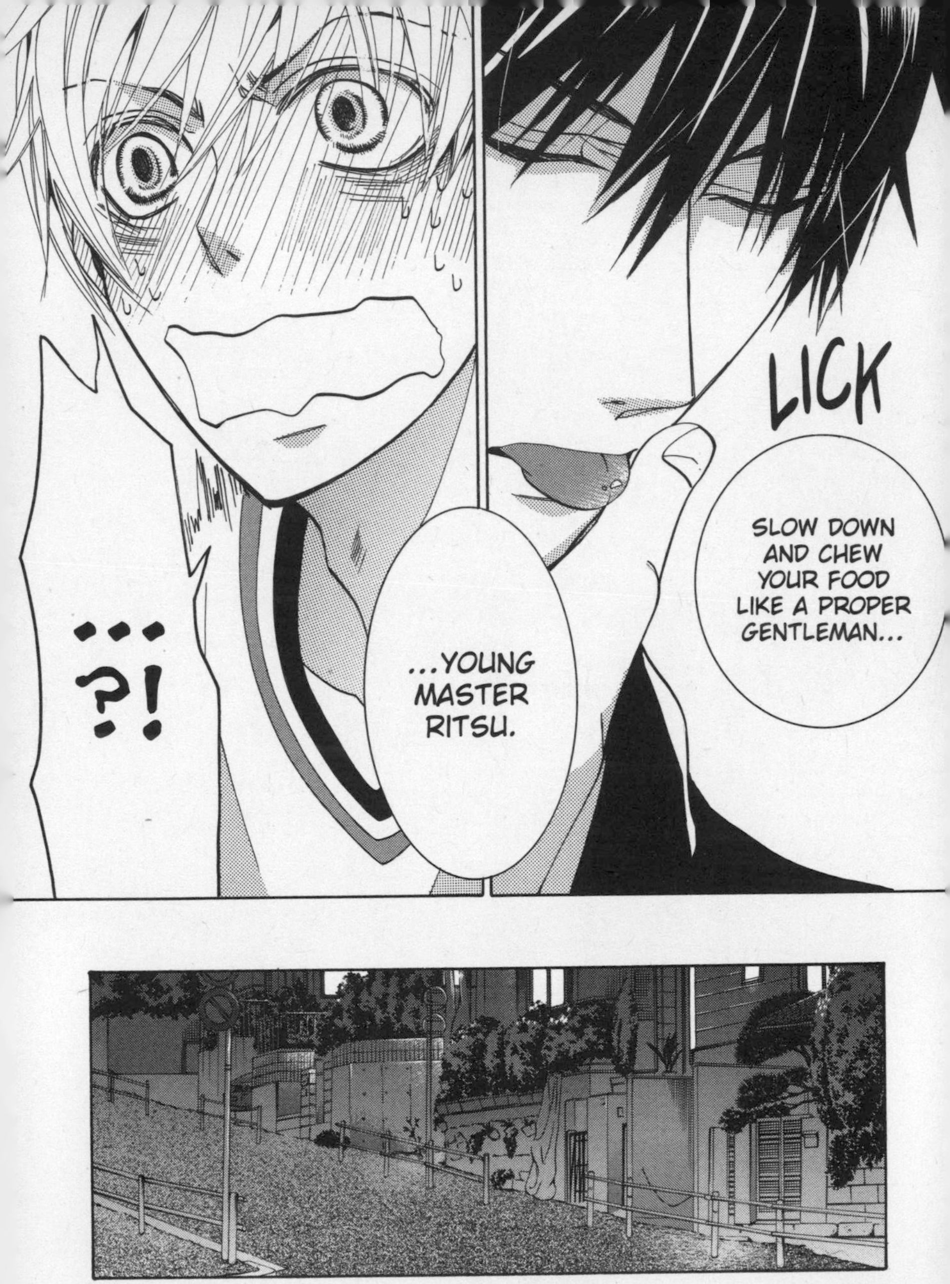
LICK
SLOW DOWN AND CHEW YOUR FOOD LIKE A PROPER GENTLEMAN...
...YOUNG MASTER RITSU.
...?!

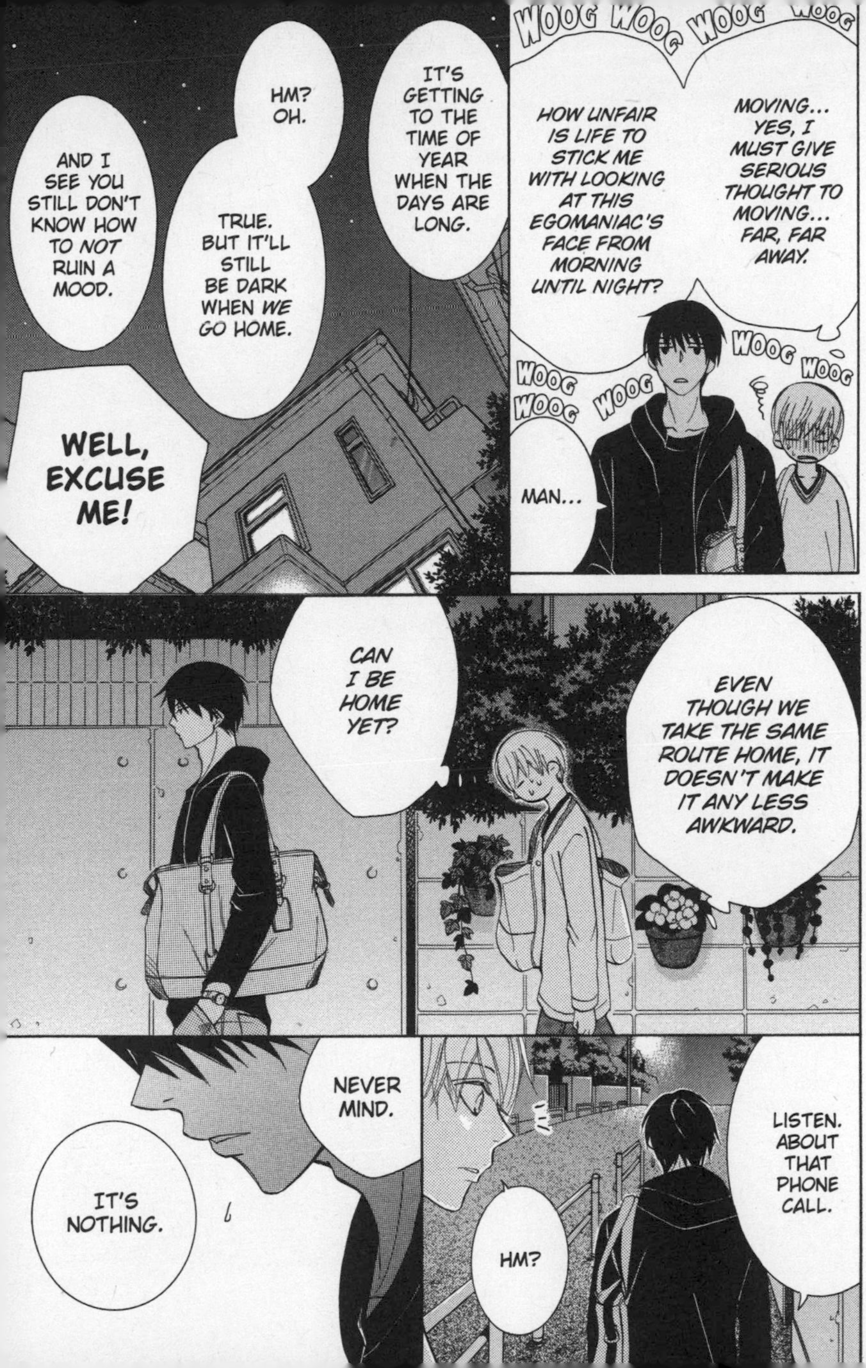
WOOG WOOG WOOG WOOG
MOVING... YES, I MUST GIVE SERIOUS THOUGHT TO MOVING... FAR, FAR AWAY.
HOW UNFAIR IS LIFE TO STICK ME WITH LOOKING AT THIS EGOMANIAC'S FACE FROM MORNING UNTIL NIGHT?
WOOG WOOG
WOOG WOOG WOOG
MAN...
IT'S GETTING TO THE TIME OF YEAR WHEN THE DAYS ARE LONG.
HM? OH.
TRUE. BUT IT'LL STILL BE DARK WHEN WE GO HOME.
AND I SEE YOU STILL DON'T KNOW HOW TO NOT RUIN A MOOD.
WELL, EXCUSE ME!
EVEN THOUGH WE TAKE THE SAME ROUTE HOME, IT DOESN'T MAKE IT ANY LESS AWKWARD.
CAN I BE HOME YET?
LISTEN. ABOUT THAT PHONE CALL.
HM?
NEVER MIND.
IT'S NOTHING.

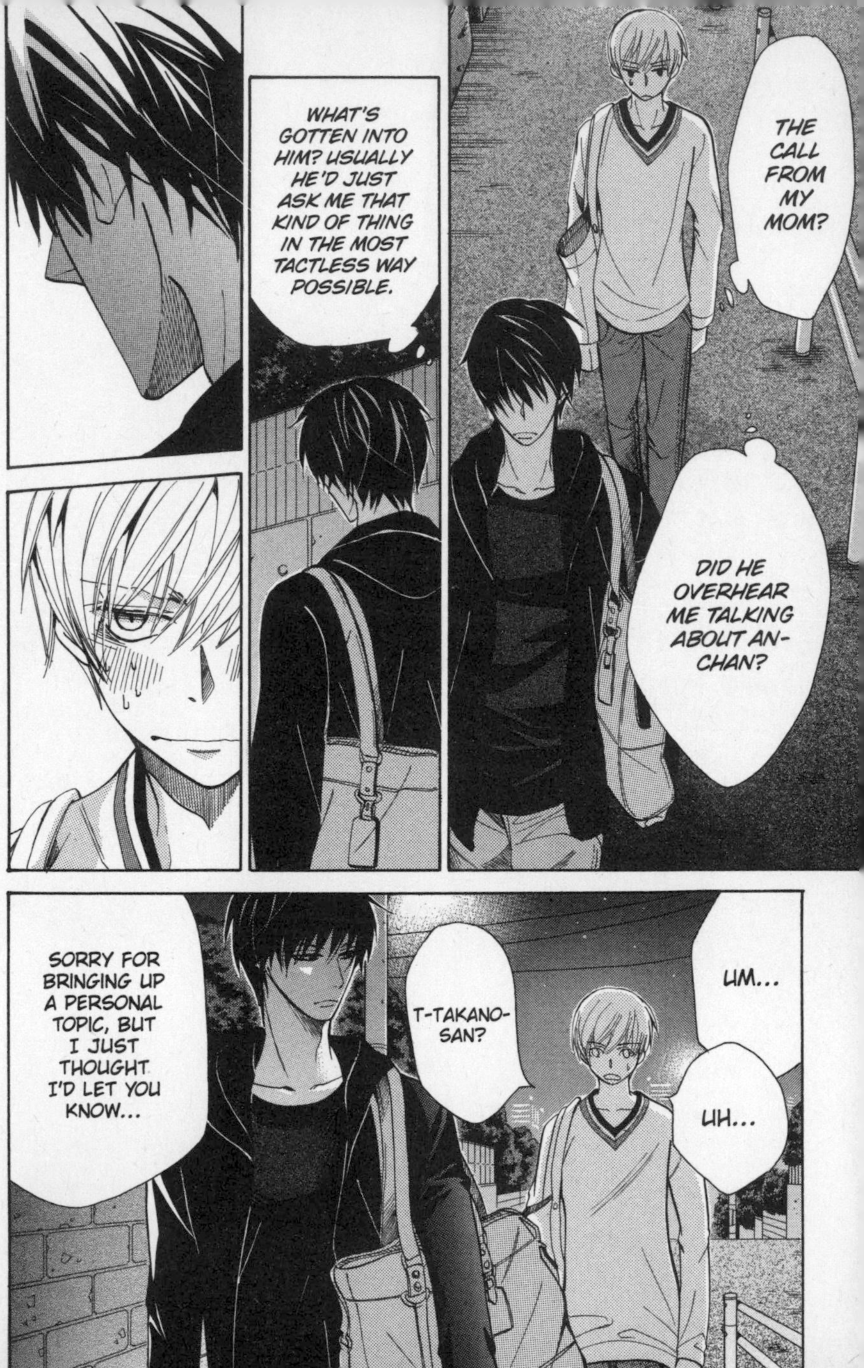
THE CALL FROM MY MOM?
DID HE OVERHEAR ME TALKING ABOUT AN-CHAN?
WHAT'S GOTTEN INTO HIM? USUALLY HE'D JUST ASK ME THAT KIND OF THING IN THE MOST TACTLESS WAY POSSIBLE.
UM...
UH...
T-TAKANO-SAN?
SORRY FOR BRINGING UP A PERSONAL TOPIC, BUT I JUST THOUGHT I'D LET YOU KNOW...

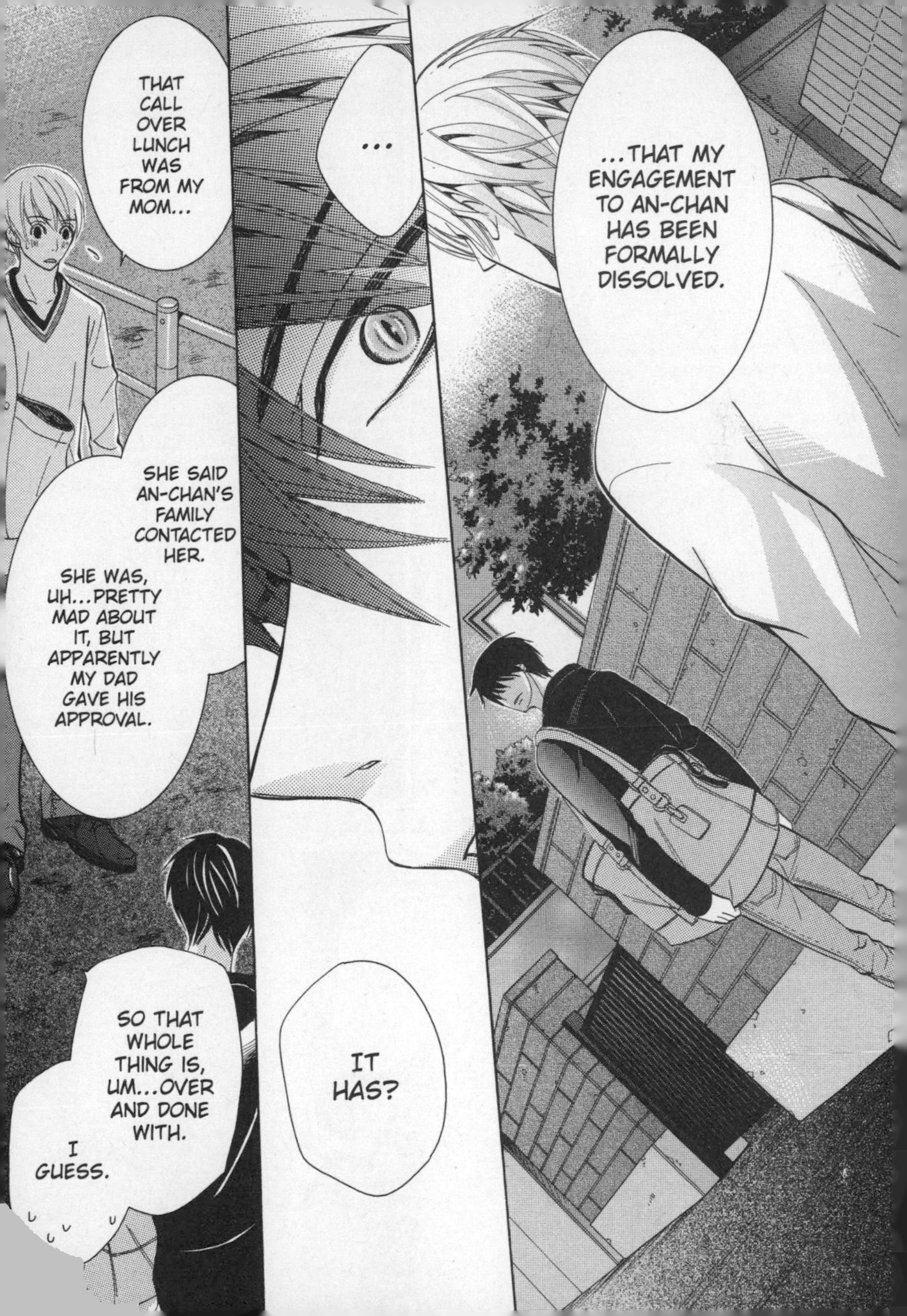
...THAT MY ENGAGEMENT TO AN-CHAN HAS BEEN FORMALLY DISSOLVED.
...
IT HAS?
THAT CALL OVER LUNCH WAS FROM MY MOM...
SHE SAID AN-CHAN'S FAMILY CONTACTED HER.
SHE WAS, UH...PRETTY MAD ABOUT IT, BUT APPARENTLY MY DAD GAVE HIS APPROVAL.
SO THAT WHOLE THING IS, UM...OVER AND DONE WITH.
I GUESS.

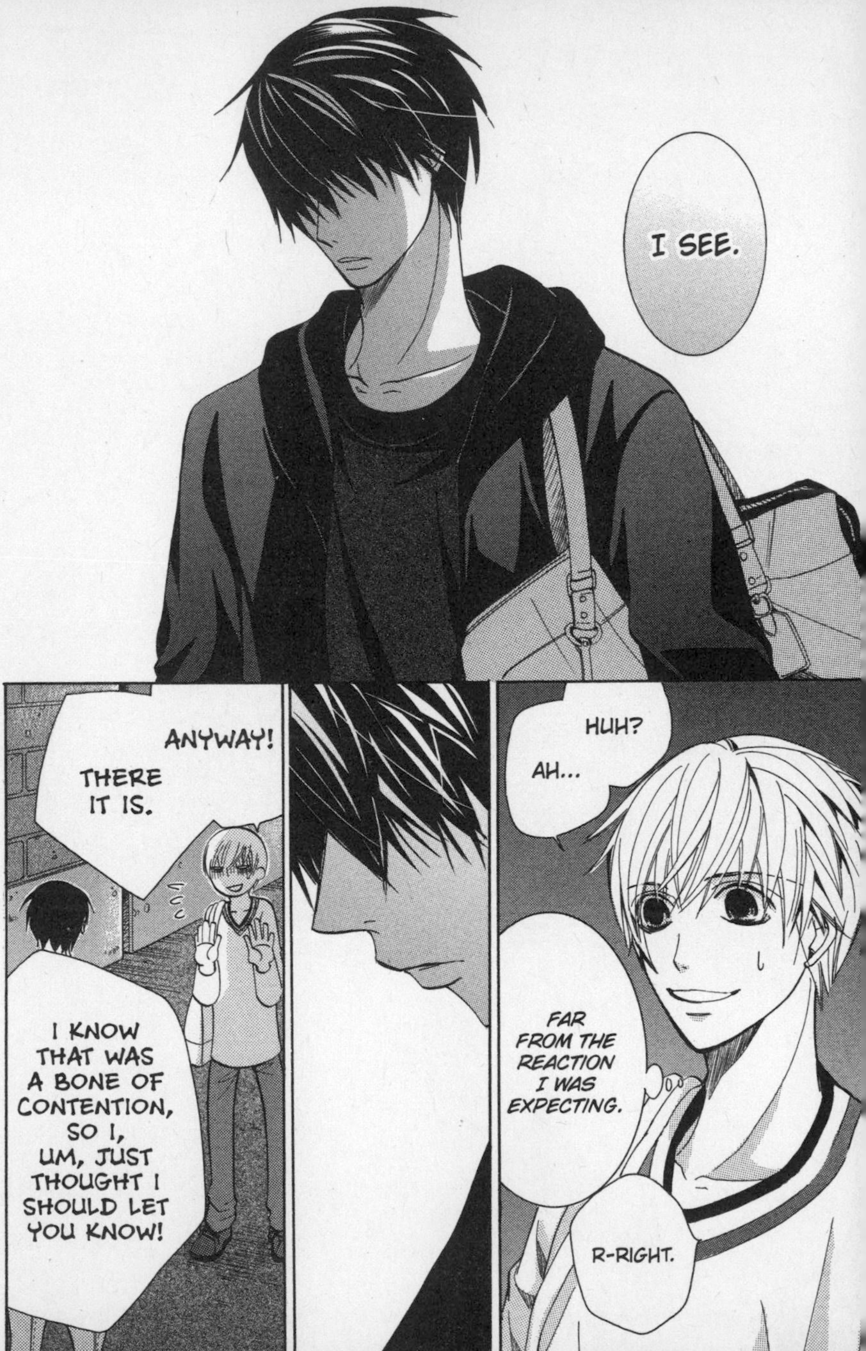
I SEE.
HUH? AH...
FAR FROM THE REACTION I WAS EXPECTING.
R-RIGHT.
ANYWAY! THERE IT IS.
I KNOW THAT WAS A BONE OF CONTENTION, SO I, UM, JUST THOUGHT I SHOULD LET YOU KNOW!

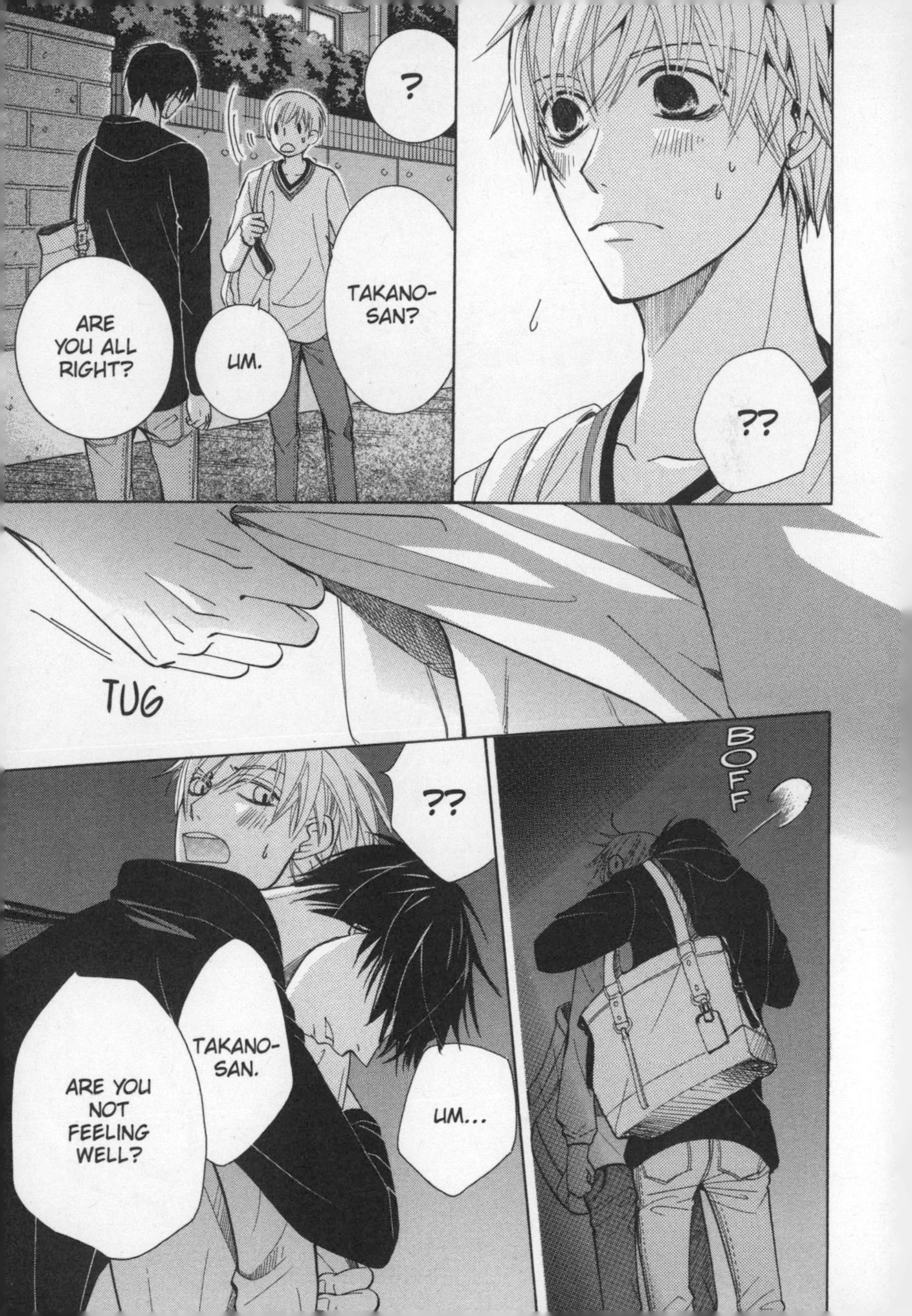
??
?
TAKANO-SAN?
UM.
ARE YOU ALL RIGHT?
TUG
BOFF
??
UM...
TAKANO-SAN.
ARE YOU NOT FEELING WELL?

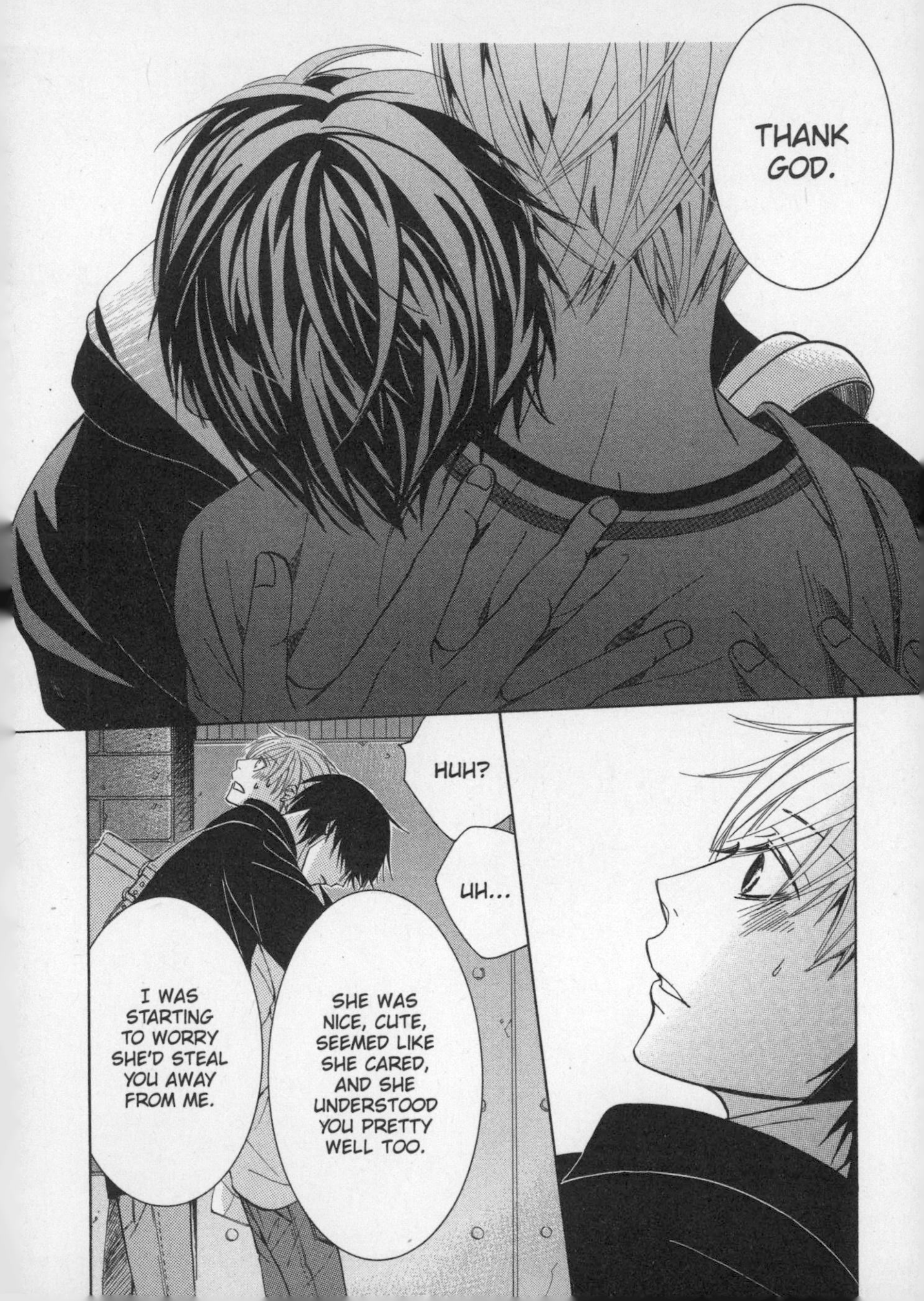
THANK GOD.
HUH?
UH...
SHE WAS NICE, CUTE, SEEMED LIKE SHE CARED, AND SHE UNDERSTOOD YOU PRETTY WELL TOO.
I WAS STARTING TO WORRY SHE'D STEAL YOU AWAY FROM ME.

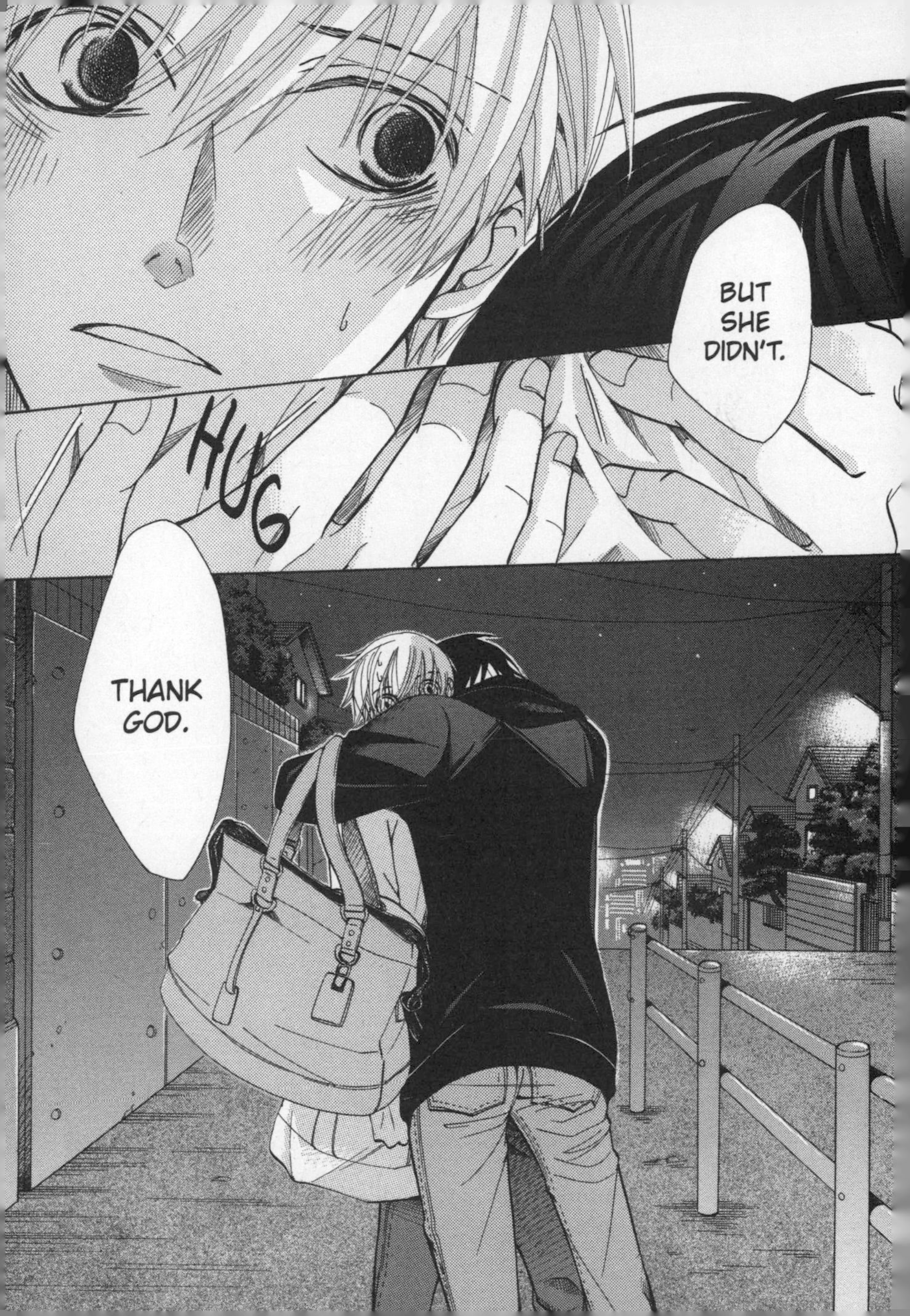
BUT SHE DIDN'T.
HUG
THANK GOD.

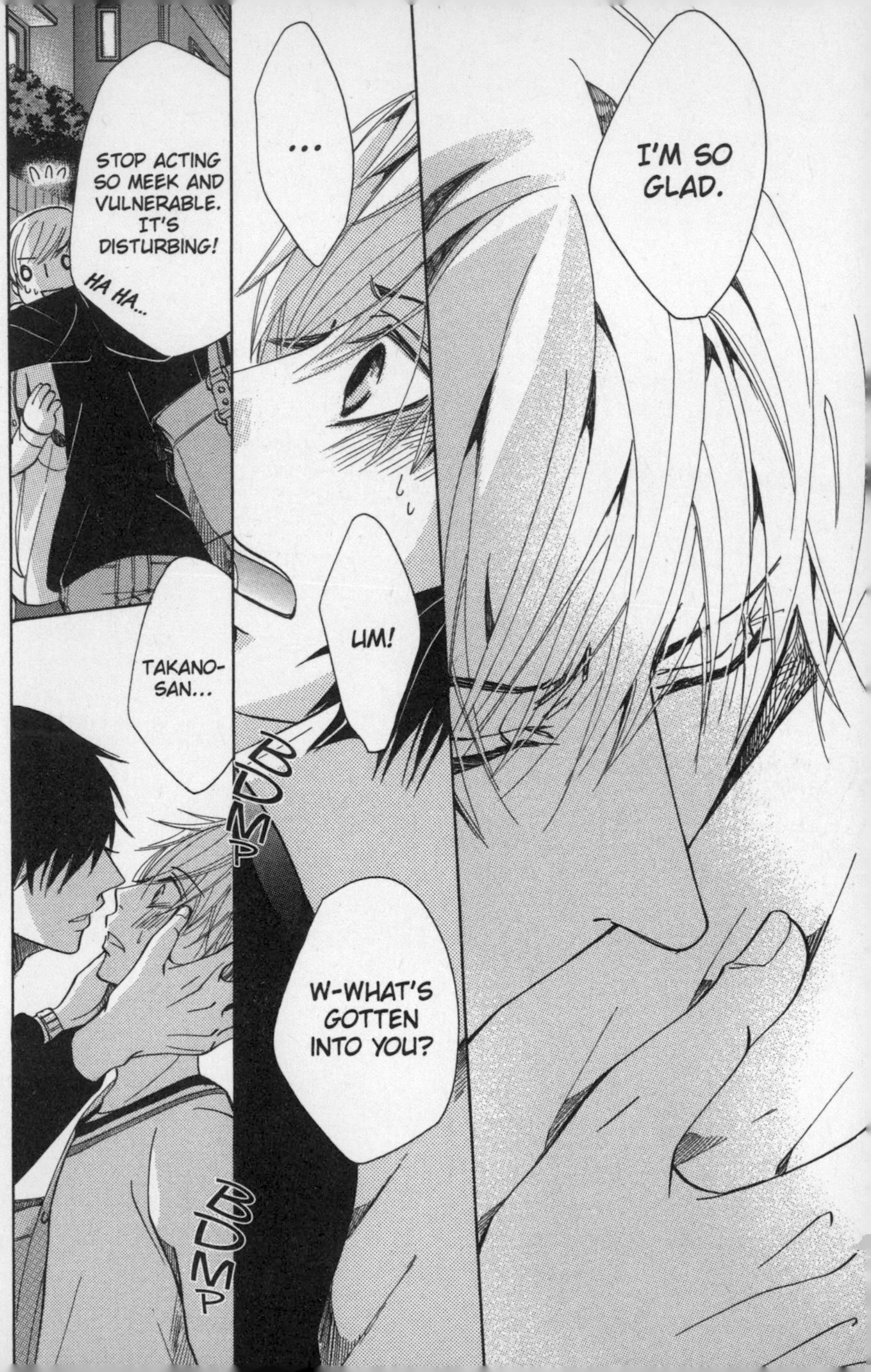
I'M SO GLAD.
...
UM!
W-WHAT'S GOTTEN INTO YOU?
STOP ACTING SO MEEK AND VULNERABLE. IT'S DISTURBING!
HA HA...
TAKANO-SAN...
BUMP
BUMP

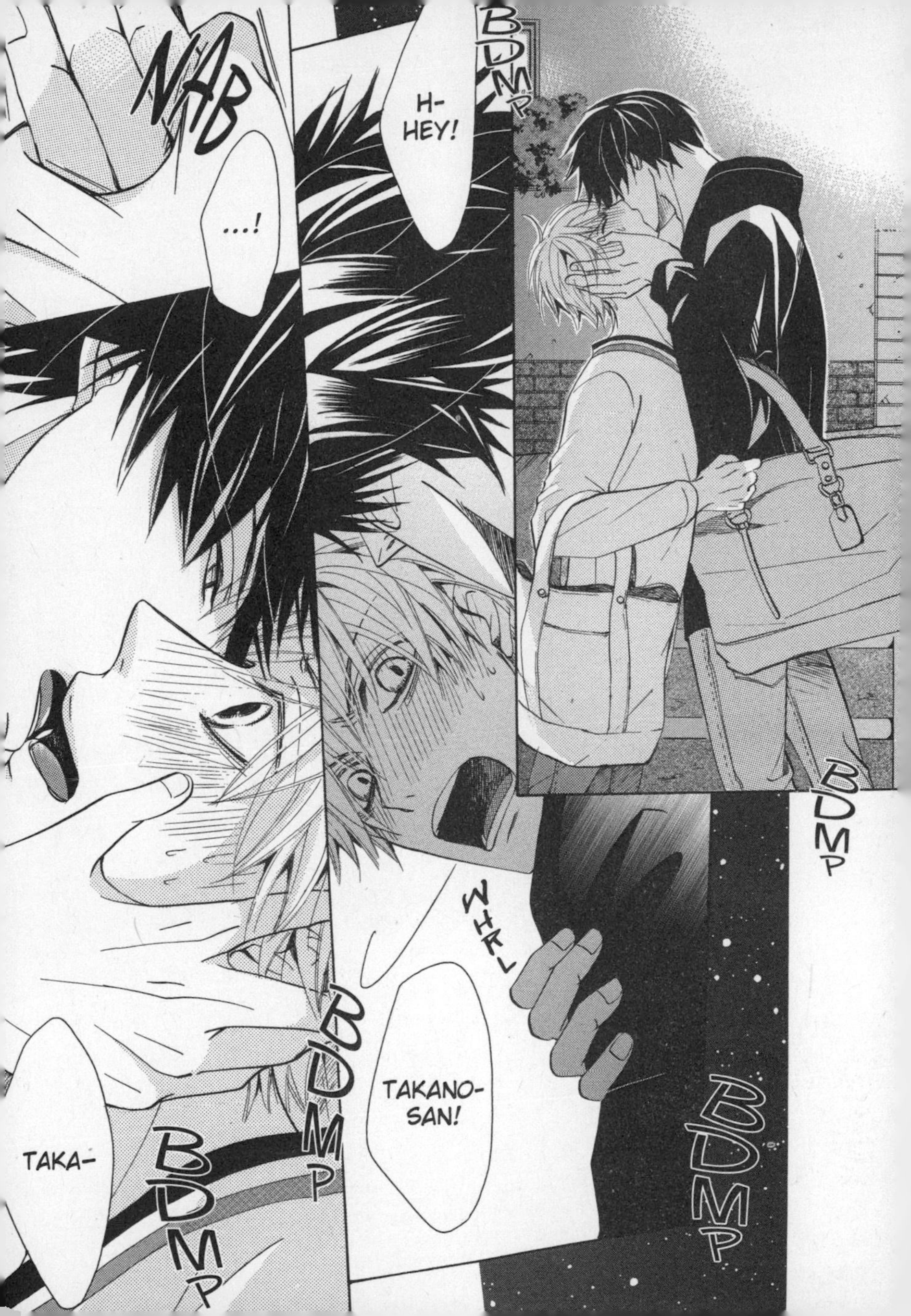
BDMP
BDMP
H-HEY!
NAB
...!
BDMP
WHRL
TAKANO-SAN!
BDMP
TAKA-
BDMP

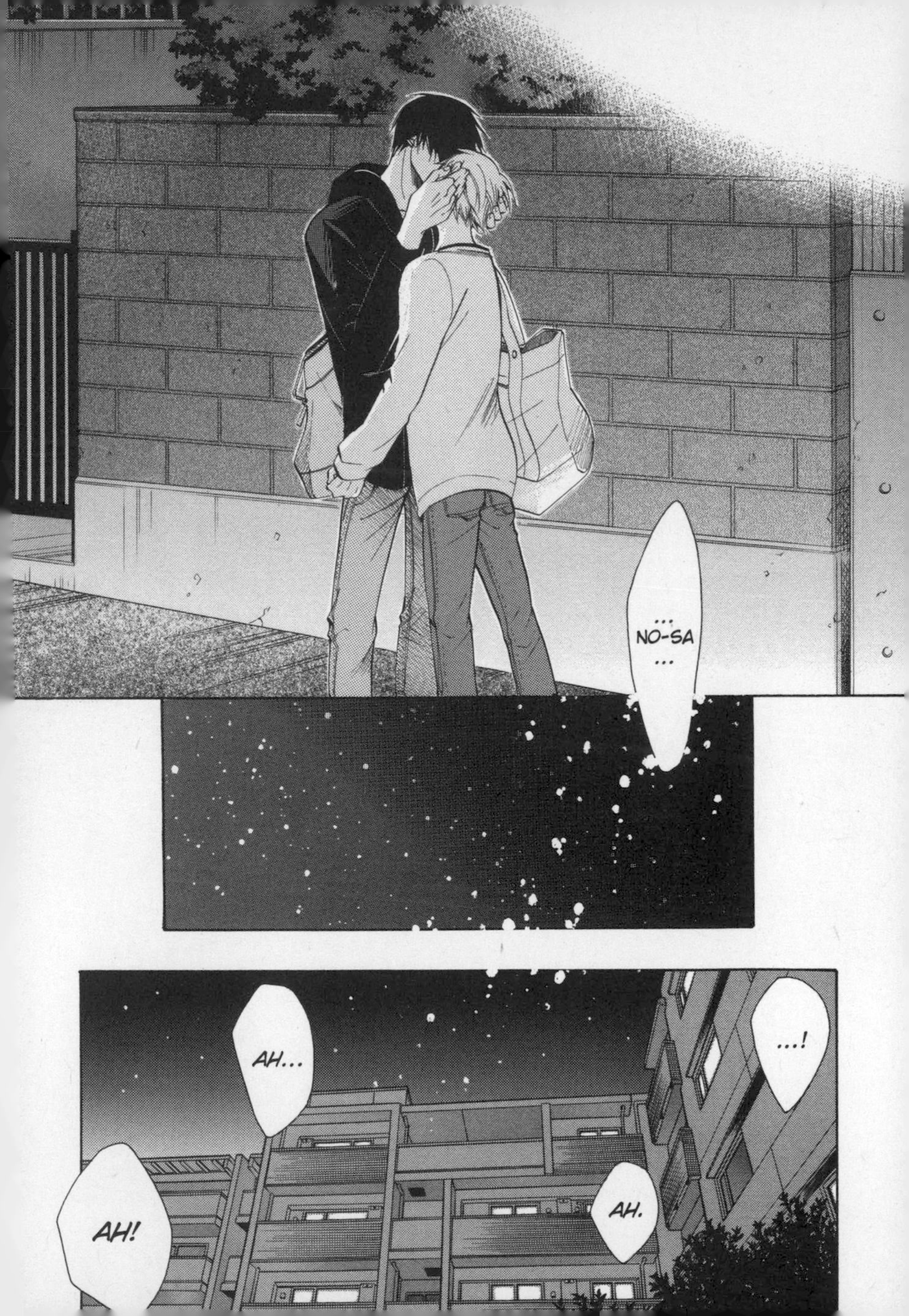
...NO-SA...
...!
AH...
AH.
AH!

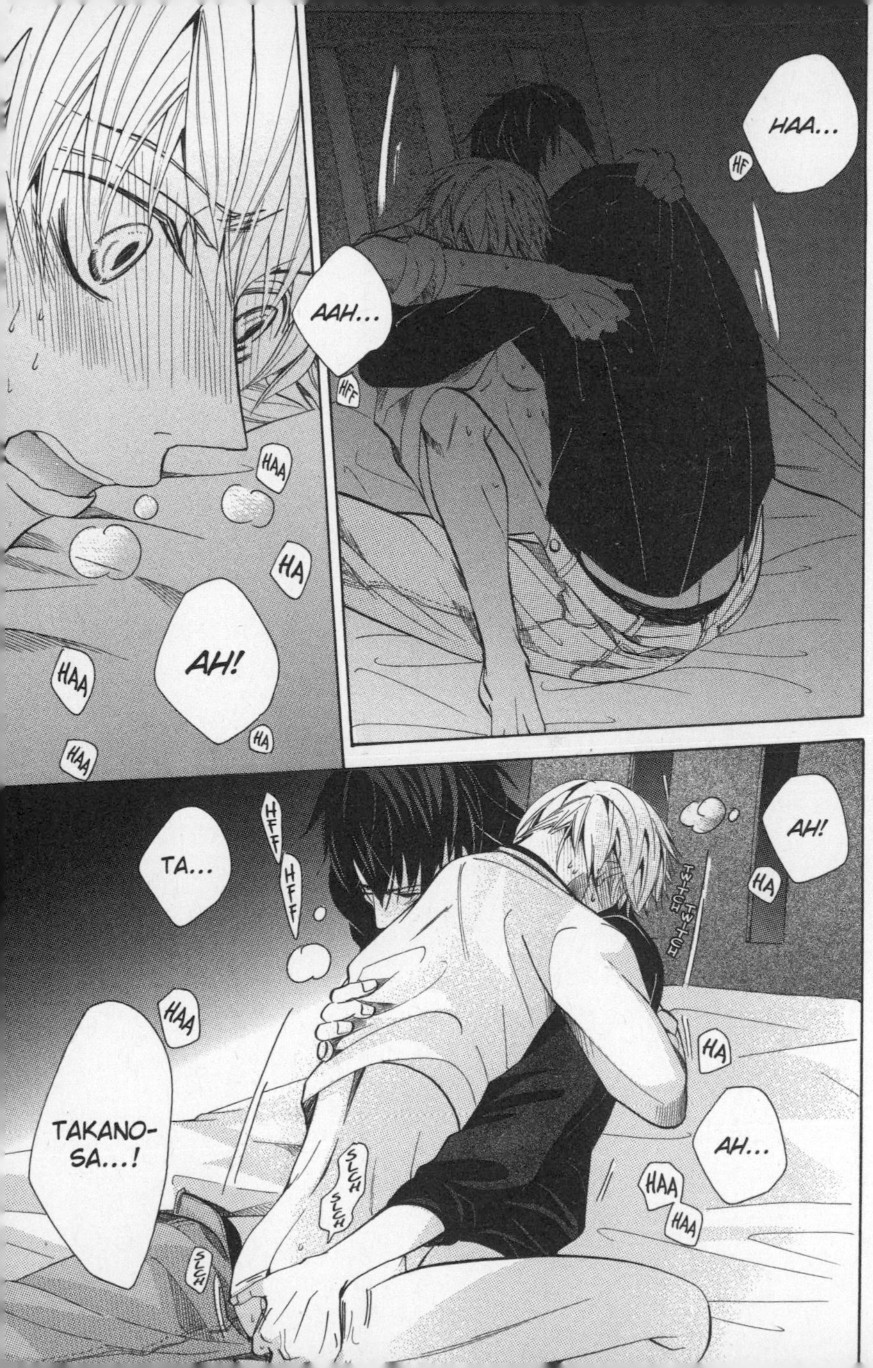
HAA...
HF
AAH...
HFF
HAA
HA
AH!
HAA
HA
HAA
AH!
HA
TWITCH TWITCH
HFF
HFF
TA...
HAA
HA
AH...
HAA
HAA
TAKANO-SA...!
SLCH SLCH
SLCH

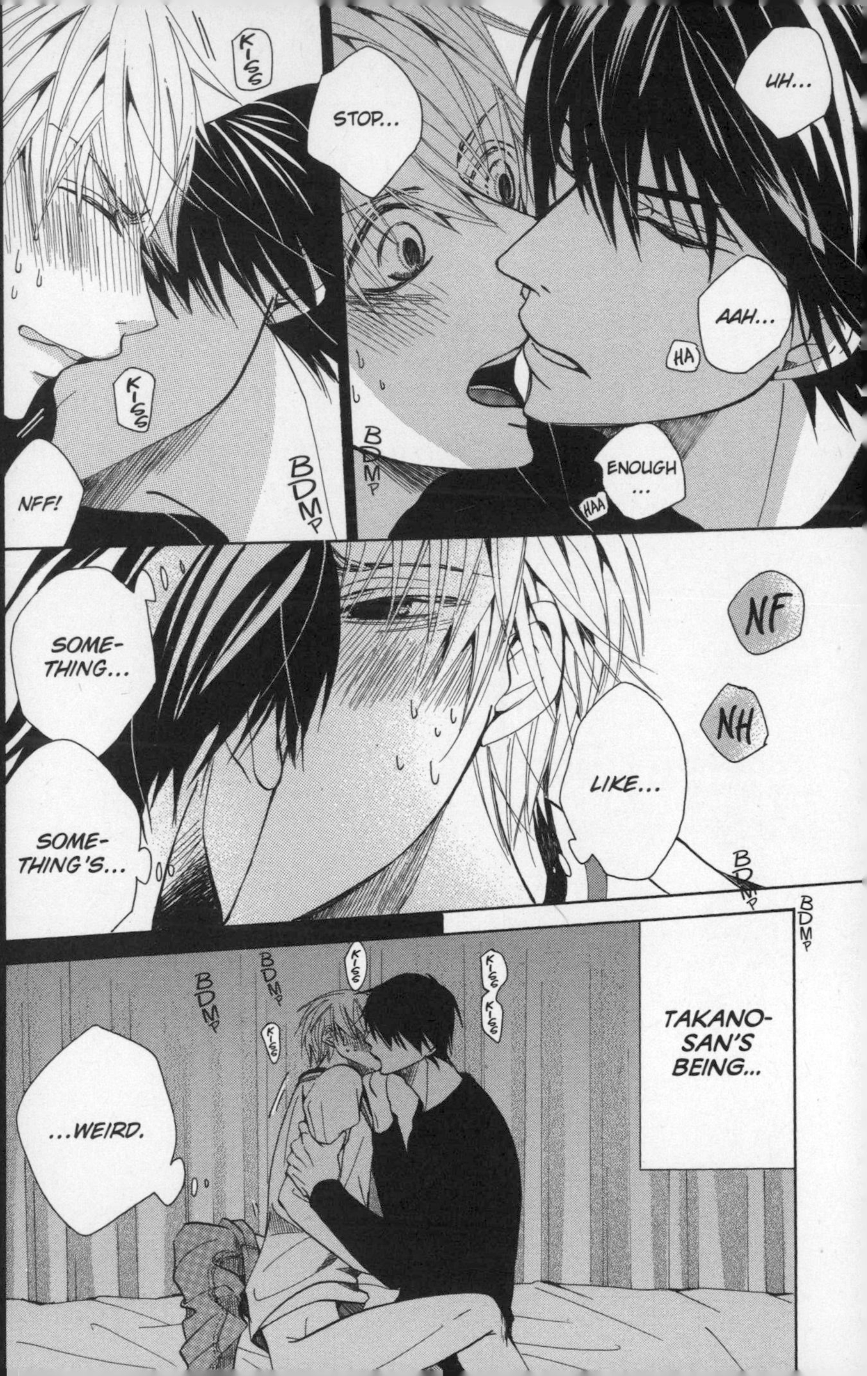
UH...
STOP...
AAH...
HA
ENOUGH...
HAA
BDMP
KISS
KISS
NFF!
BDMP
NF
NH
LIKE...
SOME-THING...
SOME-THING'S...
BDMP
BDMP
TAKANO-SAN'S BEING...
KISS KISS
KISS
BDMP
BDMP
KISS
...WEIRD.

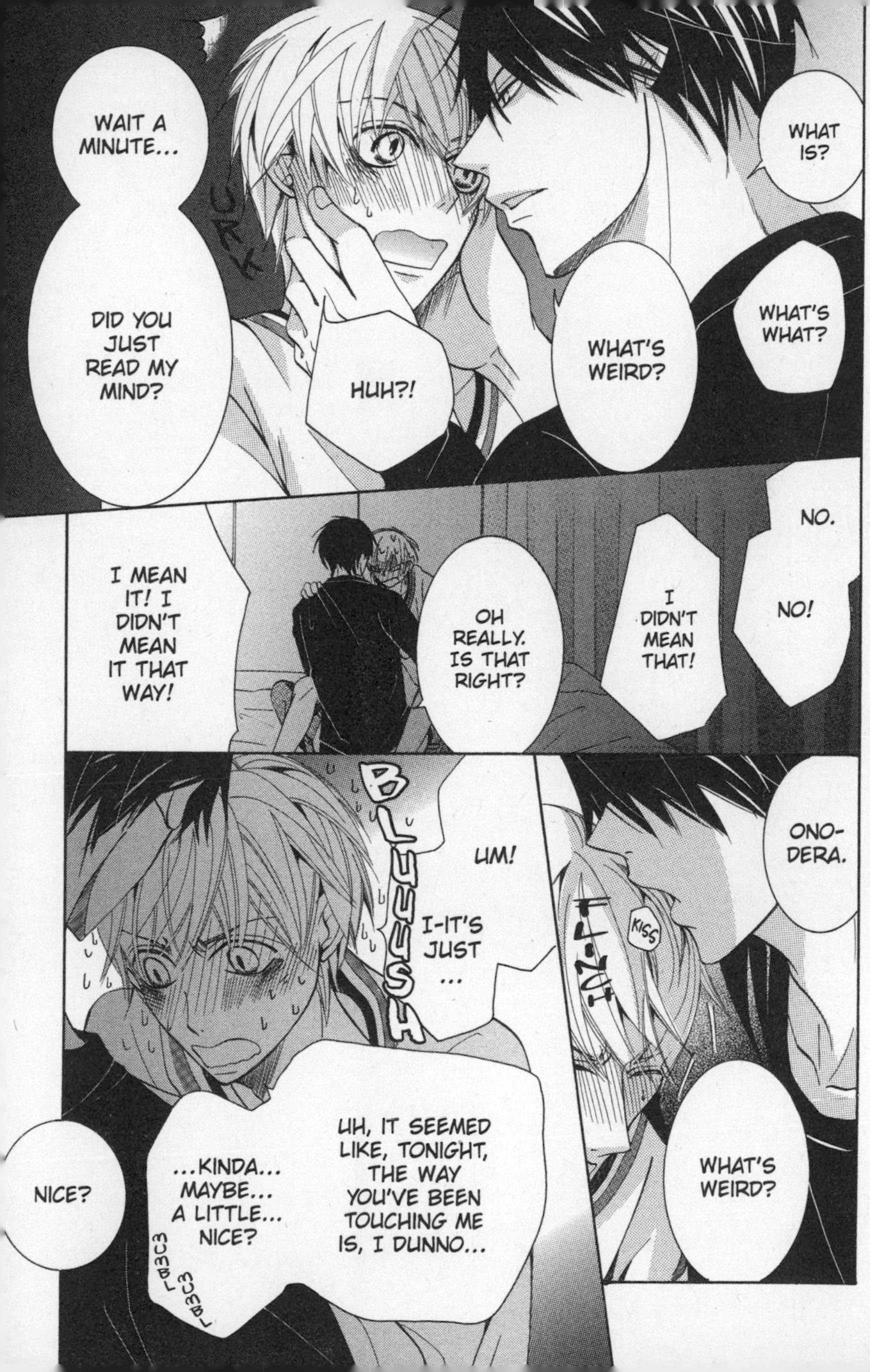
WHAT IS?
WHAT'S WHAT?
WHAT'S WEIRD?
HUH?!
WAIT A MINUTE...
URK
DID YOU JUST READ MY MIND?
NO. NO!
I DIDN'T MEAN THAT!
OH REALLY. IS THAT RIGHT?
I MEAN IT! I DIDN'T MEAN IT THAT WAY!
ONO-DERA.
KISS
WHAT'S WEIRD?
UM!
BLUUUSH
I-IT'S JUST ...
UH, IT SEEMED LIKE, TONIGHT, THE WAY YOU'VE BEEN TOUCHING ME IS, I DUNNO...
...KINDA... MAYBE... A LITTLE... NICE?
NICE?

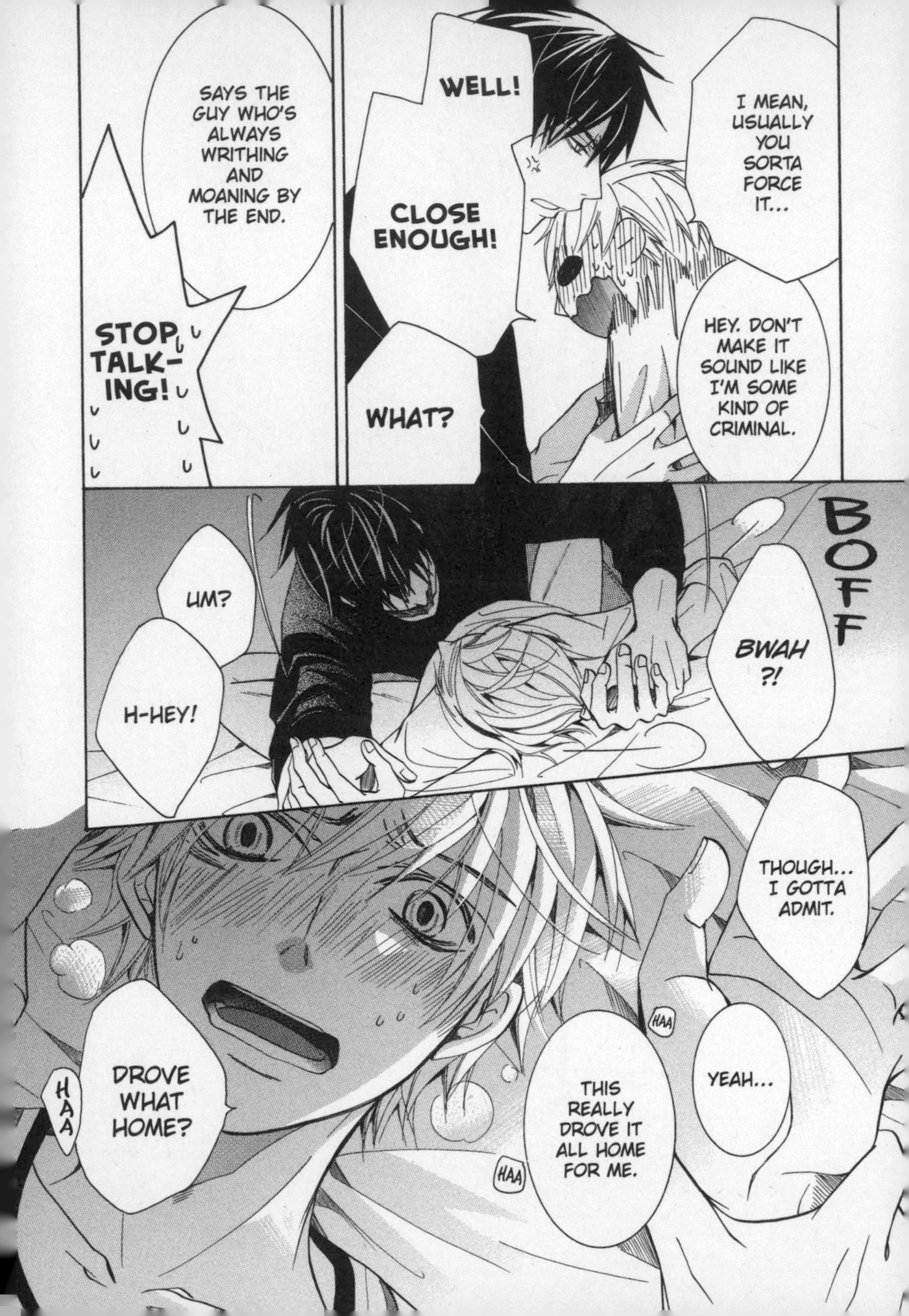
I MEAN, USUALLY YOU SORTA FORCE IT...
HEY. DON'T MAKE IT SOUND LIKE I'M SOME KIND OF CRIMINAL.
WELL!
CLOSE ENOUGH!
WHAT?
SAYS THE GUY WHO'S ALWAYS WRITHING AND MOANING BY THE END.
STOP TALKING!
BOFF
BWAH ?!
UM?
H-HEY!
THOUGH... I GOTTA ADMIT.
YEAH...
HAA
THIS REALLY DROVE IT ALL HOME FOR ME.
HAA
DROVE WHAT HOME?
HAA

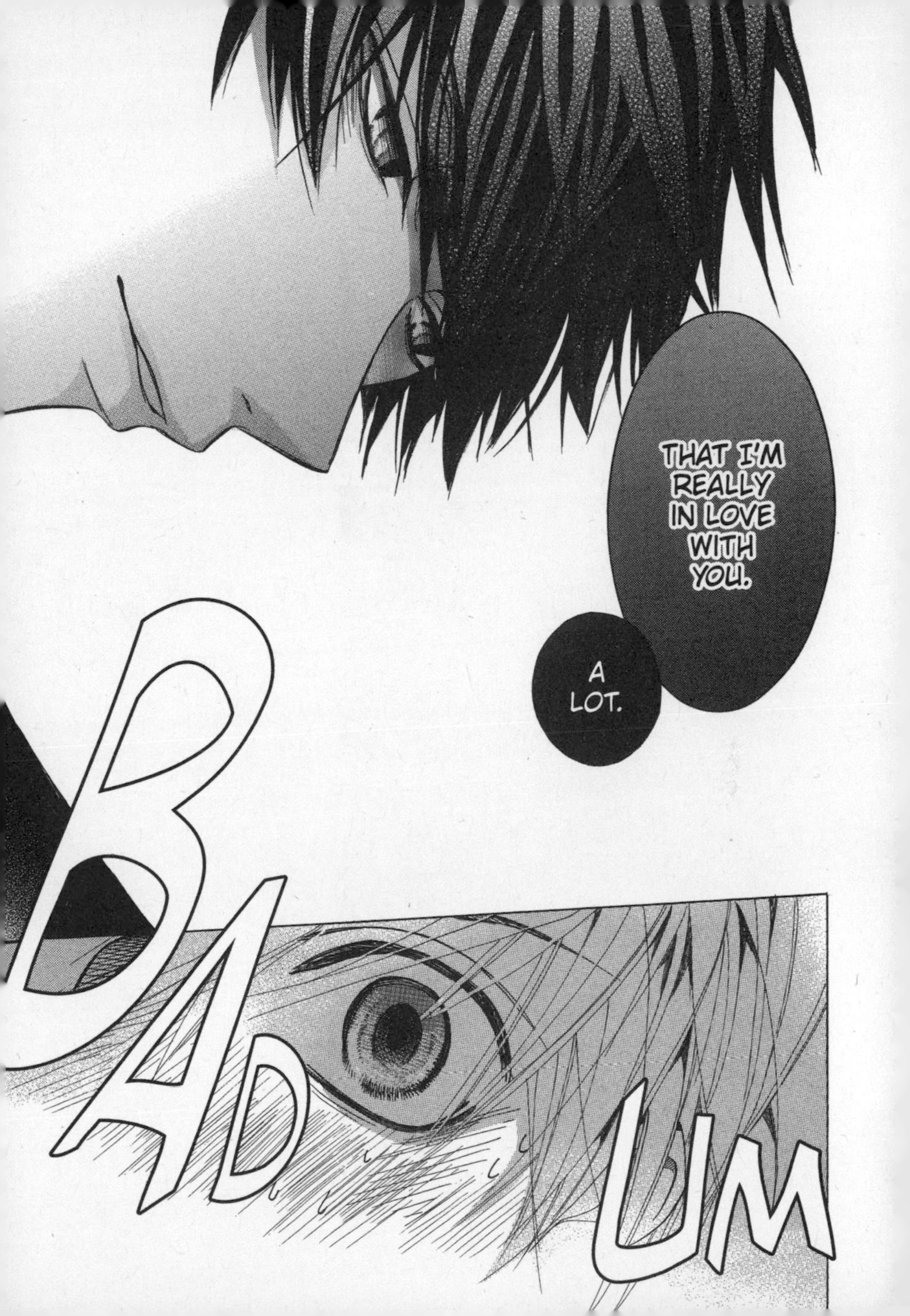
THAT I'M REALLY IN LOVE WITH YOU.
A LOT.
BADUM

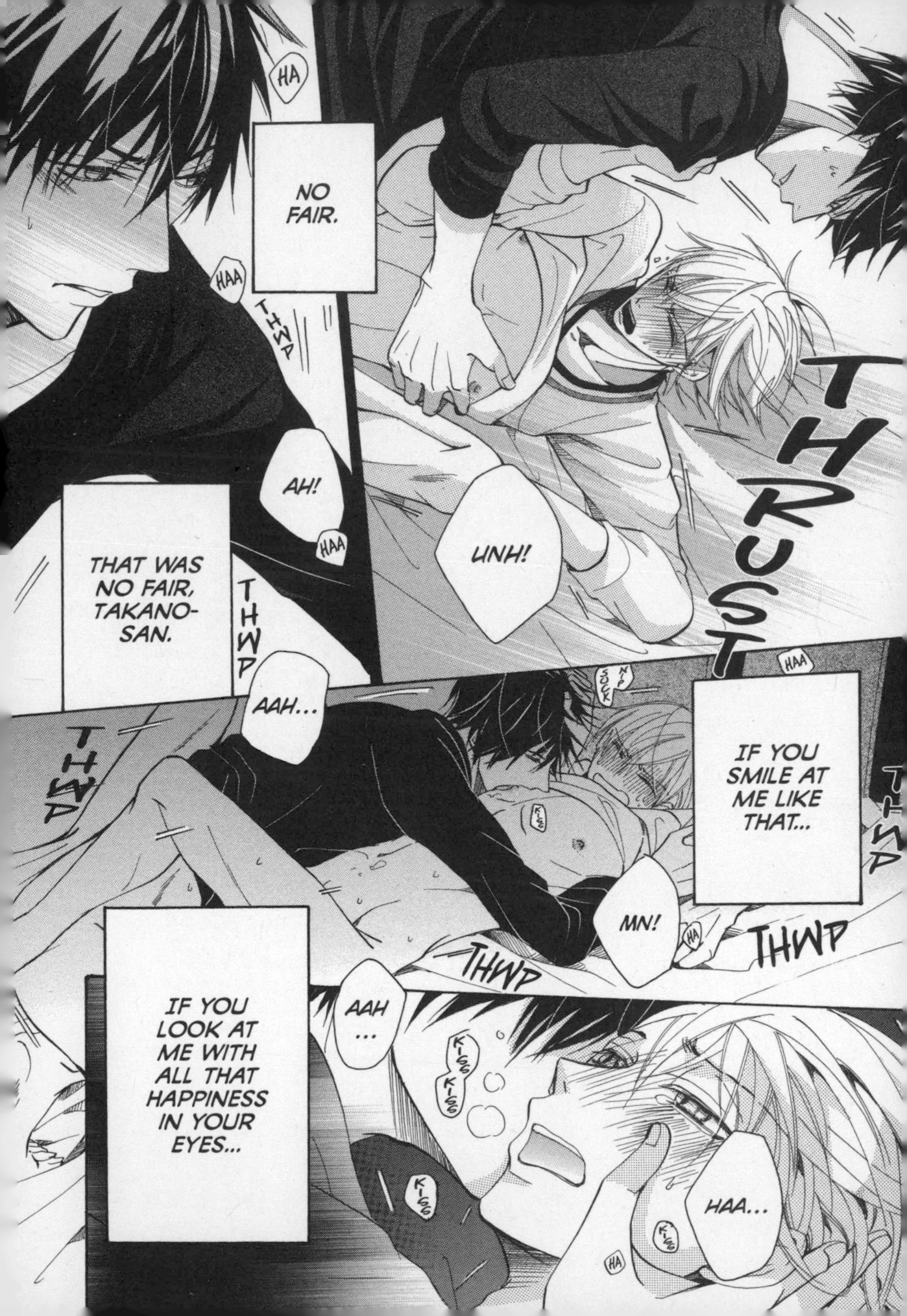
THRUST
UNH!
HA
NO FAIR.
HAA
THWP
AH!
HAA
THAT WAS NO FAIR, TAKANO-SAN.
THWP
HAA
SUCK
NIP
IF YOU SMILE AT ME LIKE THAT...
THWP
AAH...
KISS
THWP
MN!
HA
THWP
THWP
AAH ...
KISS KISS
IF YOU LOOK AT ME WITH ALL THAT HAPPINESS IN YOUR EYES...
HAA...
KISS
KISS
HA

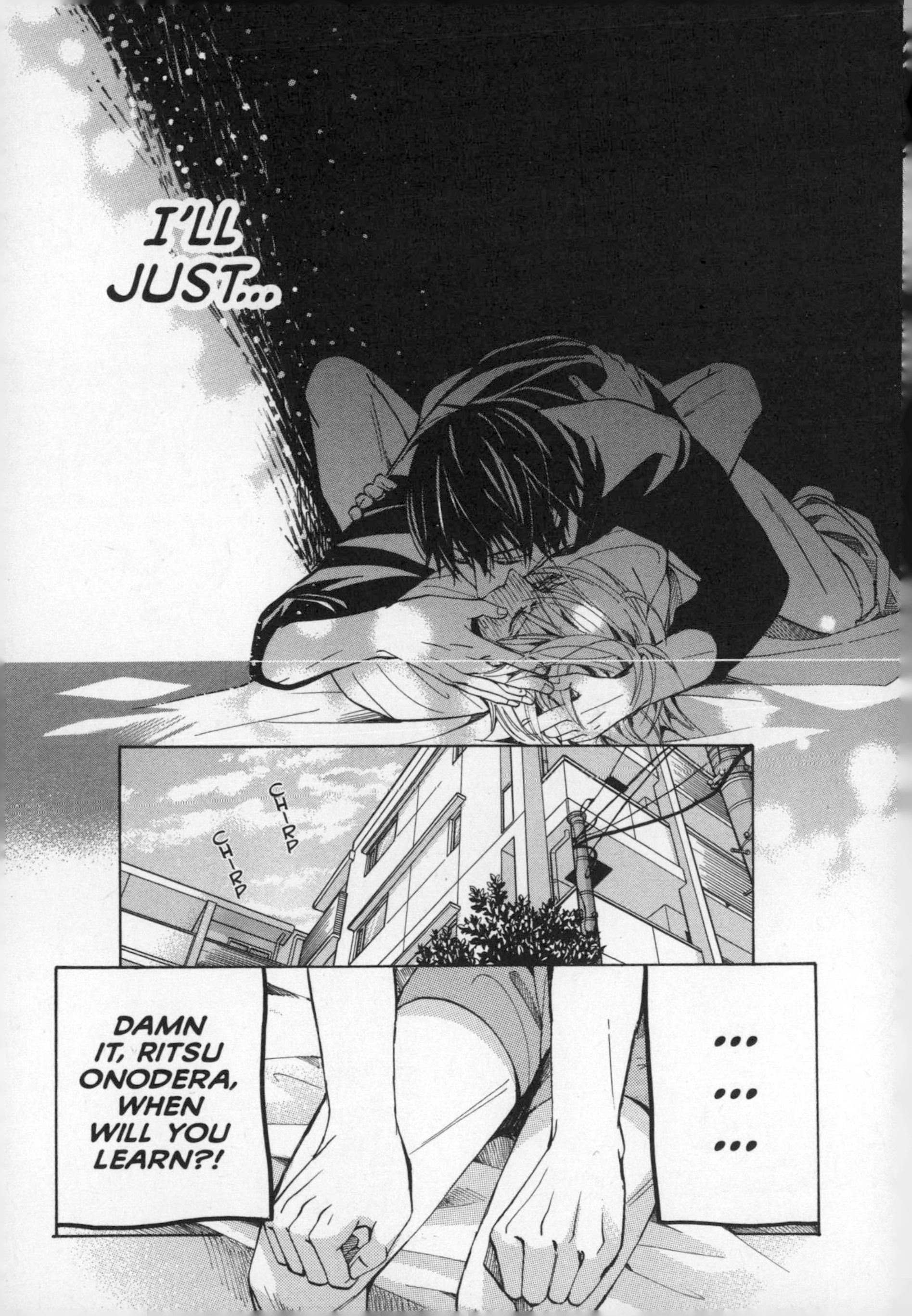
I'LL JUST...
CHIRP
CHIRP
...
...
...
DAMN IT, RITSU ONODERA, WHEN WILL YOU LEARN?!

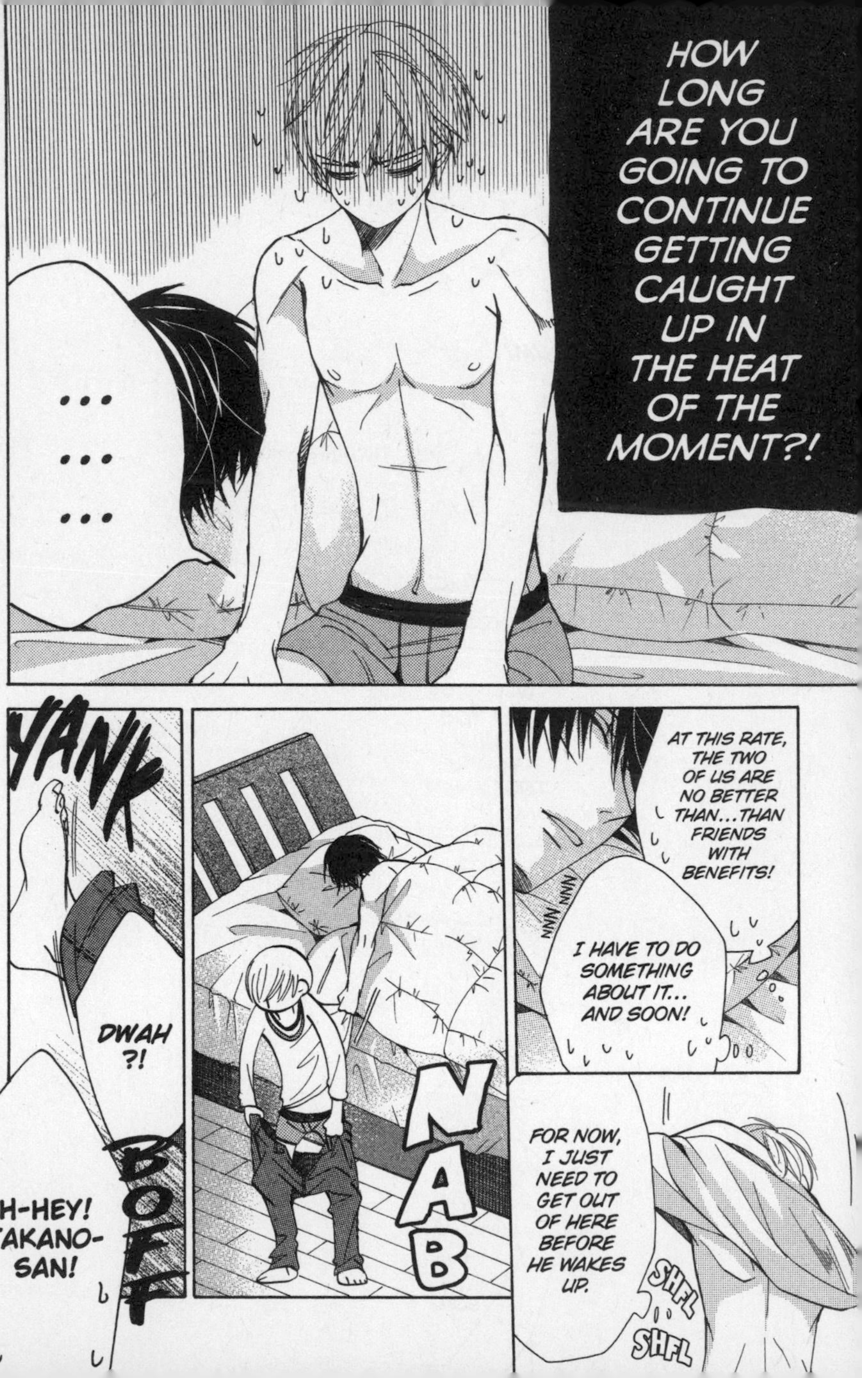
HOW LONG ARE YOU GOING TO CONTINUE GETTING CAUGHT UP IN THE HEAT OF THE MOMENT?!
...
...
...
AT THIS RATE, THE TWO OF US ARE NO BETTER THAN...THAN FRIENDS WITH BENEFITS!
NNN NNN
I HAVE TO DO SOMETHING ABOUT IT... AND SOON!
FOR NOW, I JUST NEED TO GET OUT OF HERE BEFORE HE WAKES UP.
SHFL
SHFL
NAB
YANK
DWAH ?!
BOFF
H-HEY! TAKANO-SAN!

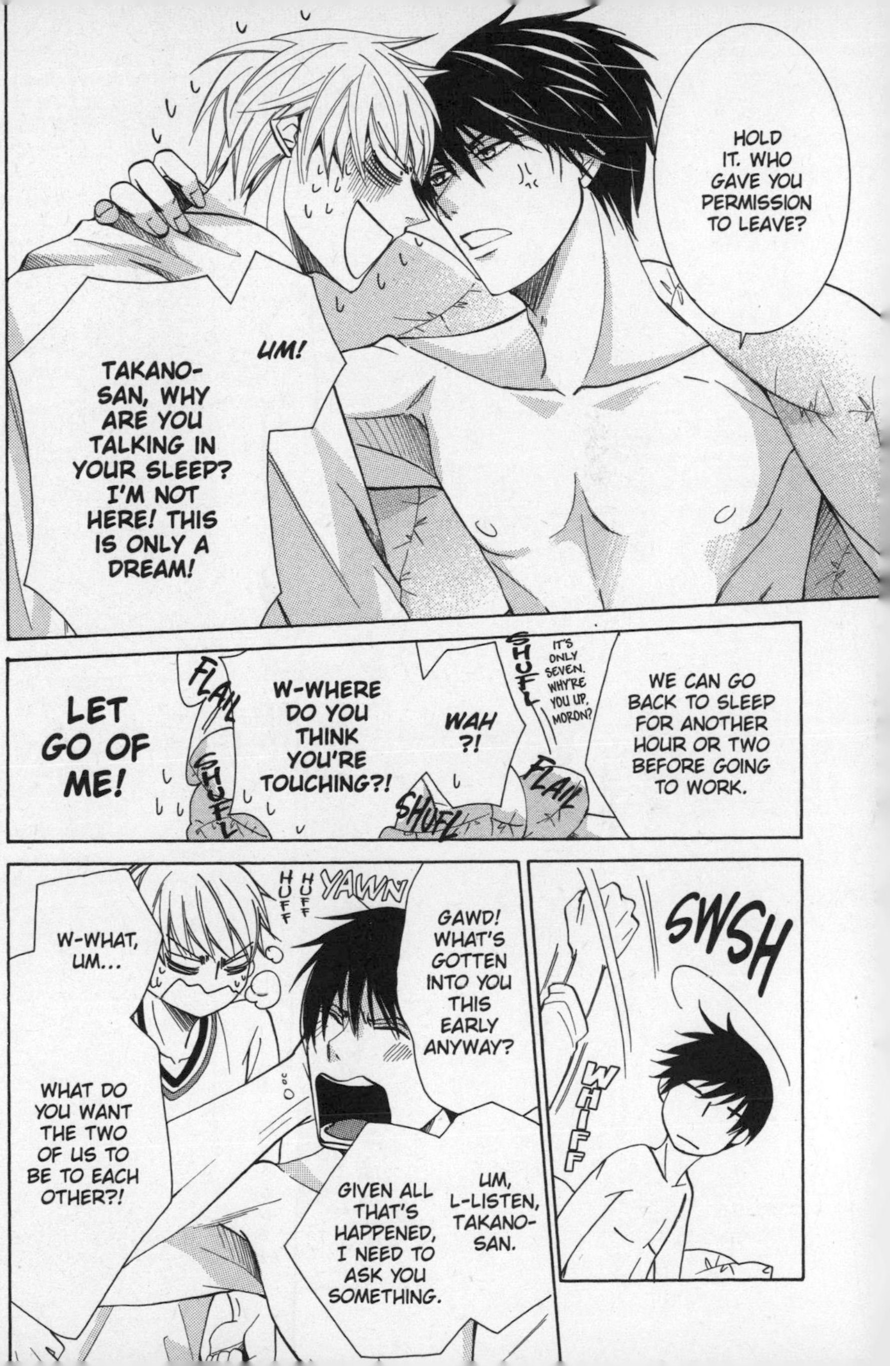
HOLD IT. WHO GAVE YOU PERMISSION TO LEAVE?
UM!
TAKANO-SAN, WHY ARE YOU TALKING IN YOUR SLEEP? I'M NOT HERE! THIS IS ONLY A DREAM!
WE CAN GO BACK TO SLEEP FOR ANOTHER HOUR OR TWO BEFORE GOING TO WORK.
IT'S ONLY SEVEN. WHY'RE YOU UP, MORON?
SHUFL
FLAIL
WAH?!
SHUFL
W-WHERE DO YOU THINK YOU'RE TOUCHING?!
FLAIL
SHUFL
LET GO OF ME!
SWSH
WHIFF
YAWN
GAWD! WHAT'S GOTTEN INTO YOU THIS EARLY ANYWAY?
UM, L-LISTEN, TAKANO-SAN.
GIVEN ALL THAT'S HAPPENED, I NEED TO ASK YOU SOMETHING.
HUFF HUFF
W-WHAT, UM...
WHAT DO YOU WANT THE TWO OF US TO BE TO EACH OTHER?!

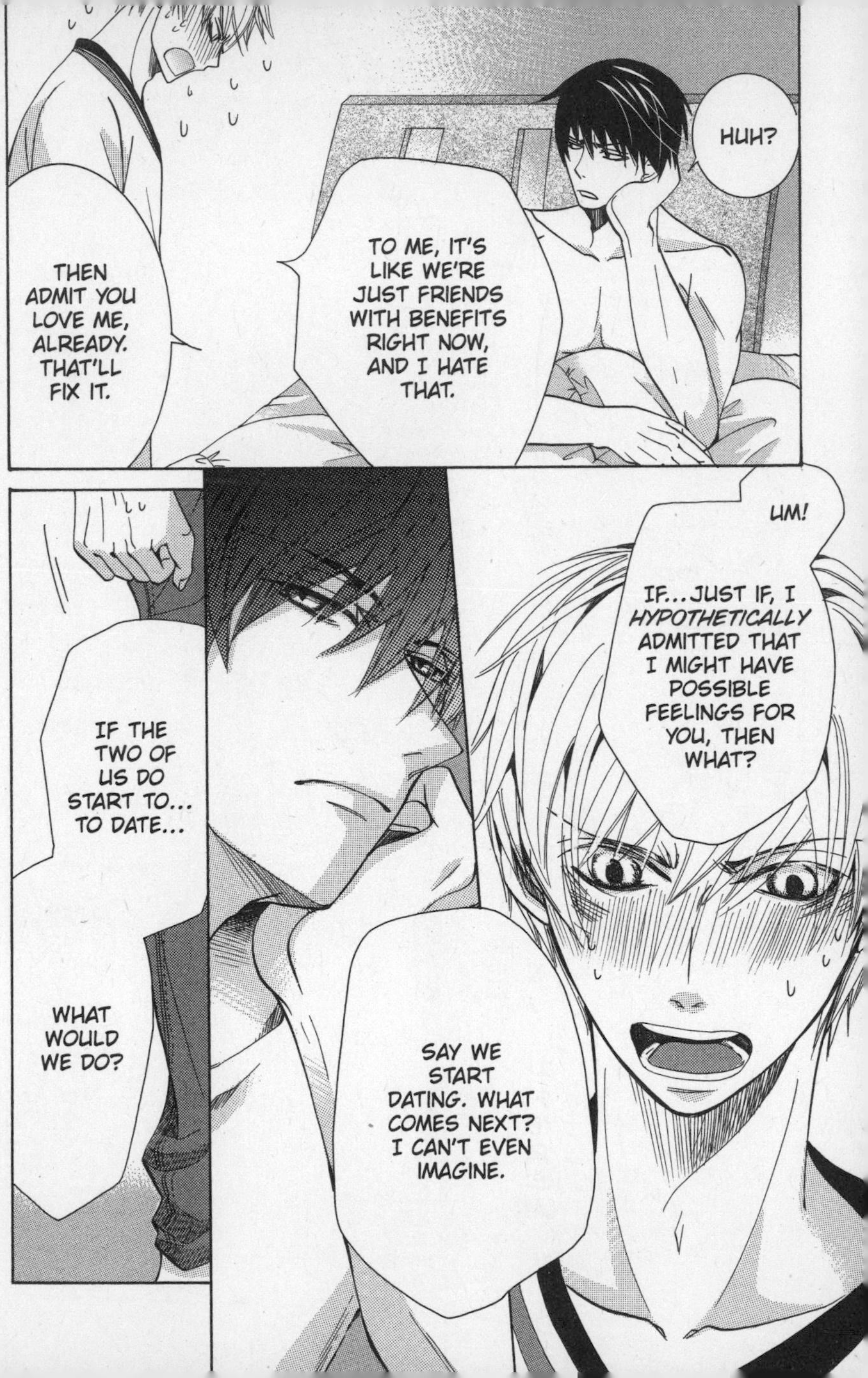
HUH?
TO ME, IT'S LIKE WE'RE JUST FRIENDS WITH BENEFITS RIGHT NOW, AND I HATE THAT.
THEN ADMIT YOU LOVE ME, ALREADY. THAT'LL FIX IT.
UM!
IF...JUST IF, I *HYPOTHETICALLY* ADMITTED THAT I MIGHT HAVE POSSIBLE FEELINGS FOR YOU, THEN WHAT?
SAY WE START DATING. WHAT COMES NEXT? I CAN'T EVEN IMAGINE.
IF THE TWO OF US DO START TO... TO DATE...
WHAT WOULD WE DO?

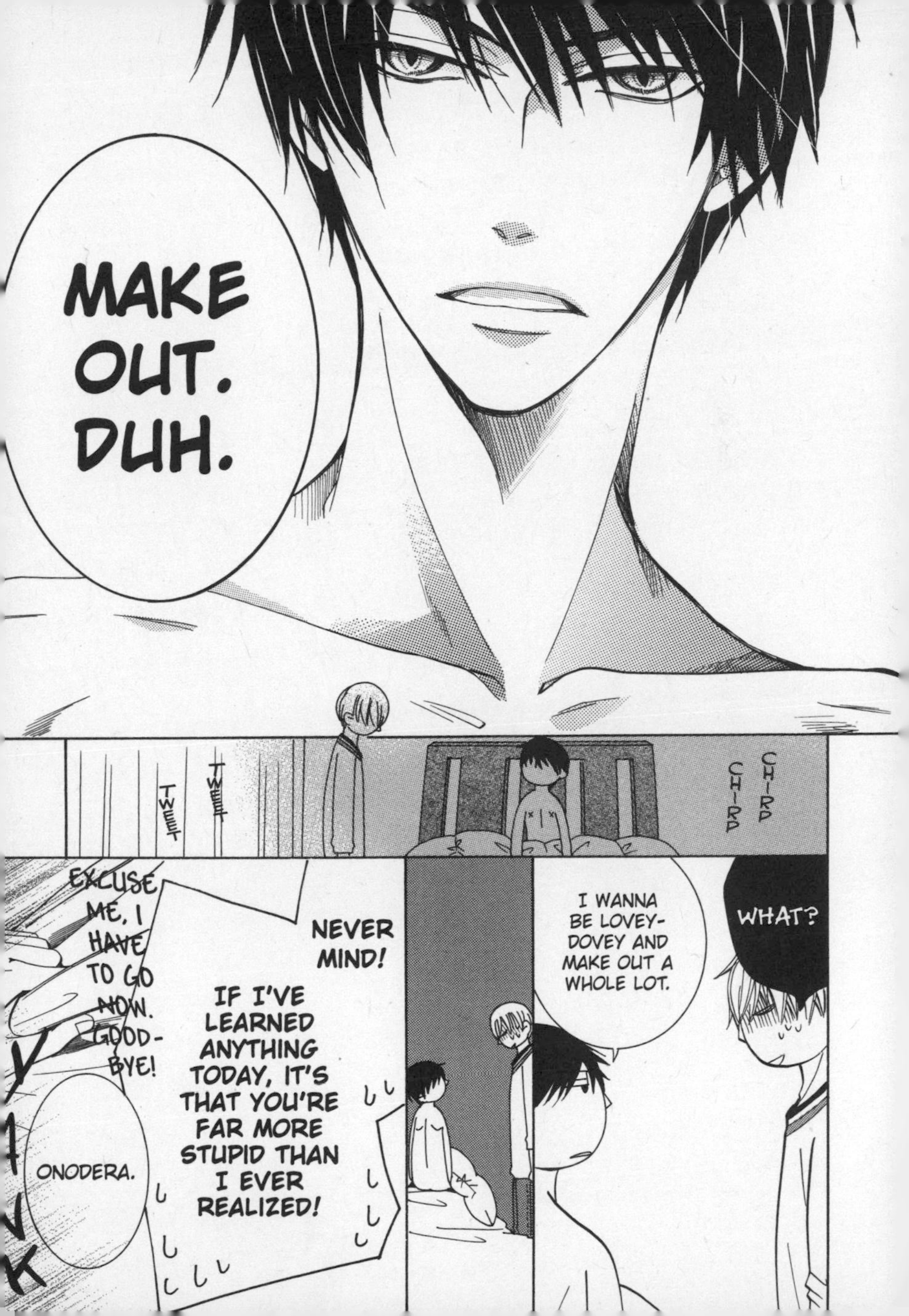
MAKE OUT. DUH.
CHIRP CHIRP
TWEET TWEET
WHAT?
I WANNA BE LOVEY-DOVEY AND MAKE OUT A WHOLE LOT.
NEVER MIND!
IF I'VE LEARNED ANYTHING TODAY, IT'S THAT YOU'RE FAR MORE STUPID THAN I EVER REALIZED!
EXCUSE ME, I HAVE TO GO NOW. GOOD-BYE!
ONODERA.
YANK

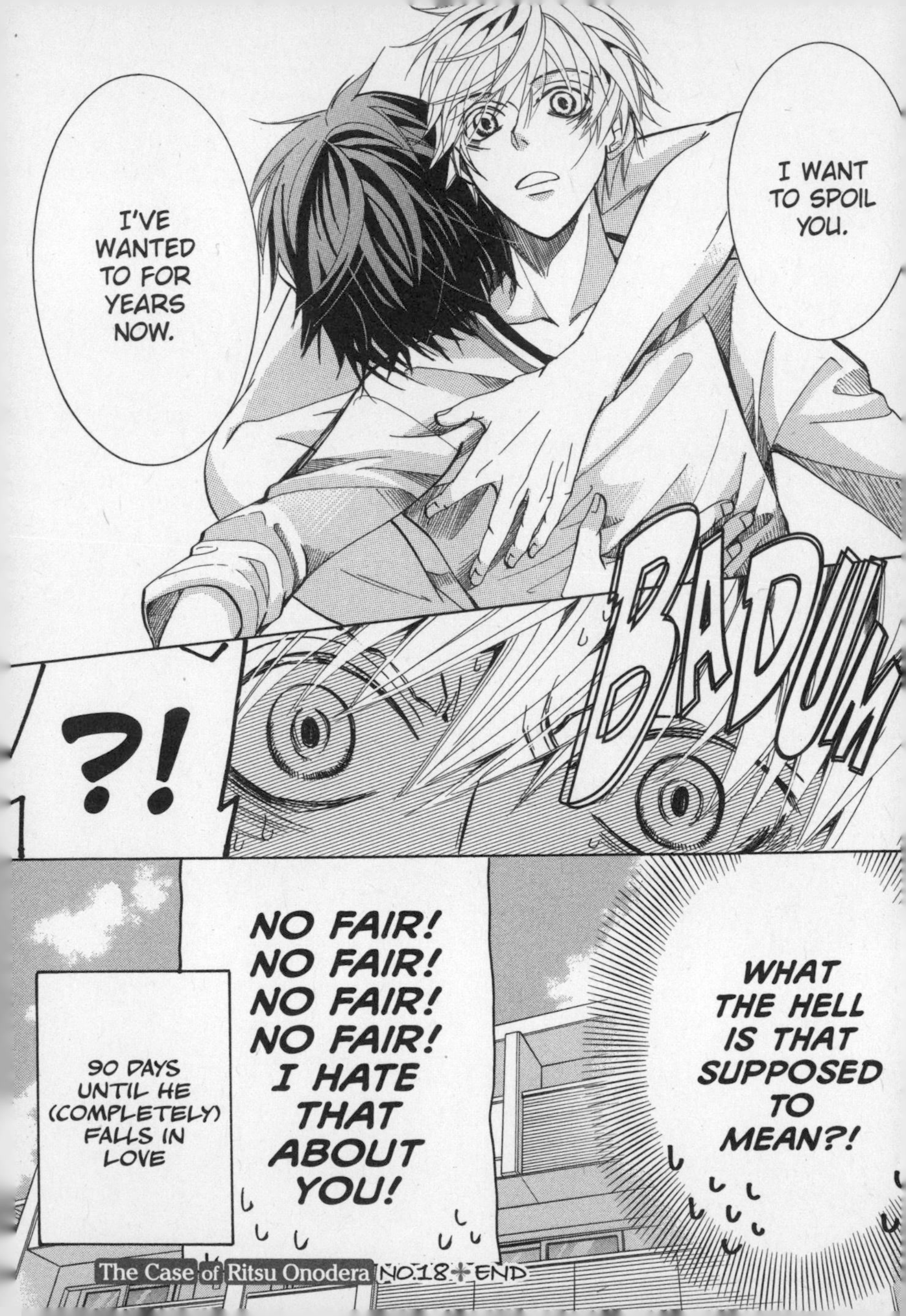
I WANT TO SPOIL YOU.
I'VE WANTED TO FOR YEARS NOW.
BADUM
?!
WHAT THE HELL IS THAT SUPPOSED TO MEAN?!
NO FAIR! NO FAIR! NO FAIR! NO FAIR! I HATE THAT ABOUT YOU!
90 DAYS UNTIL HE (COMPLETELY) FALLS IN LOVE
The Case of Ritsu Onodera NO.18 END

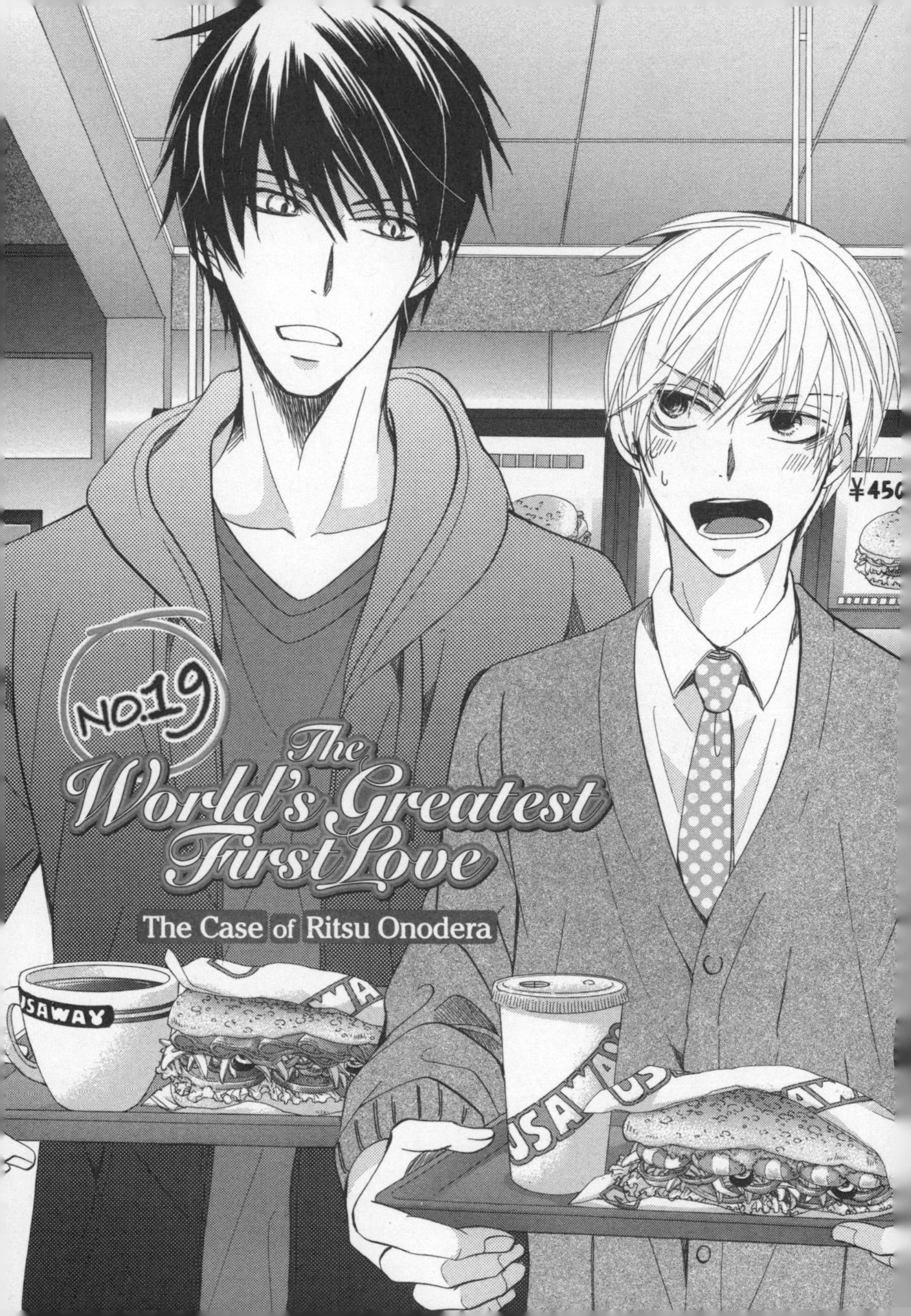

No.19
The World's Greatest First Love
The Case of Ritsu Onodera
¥450
USAWAY

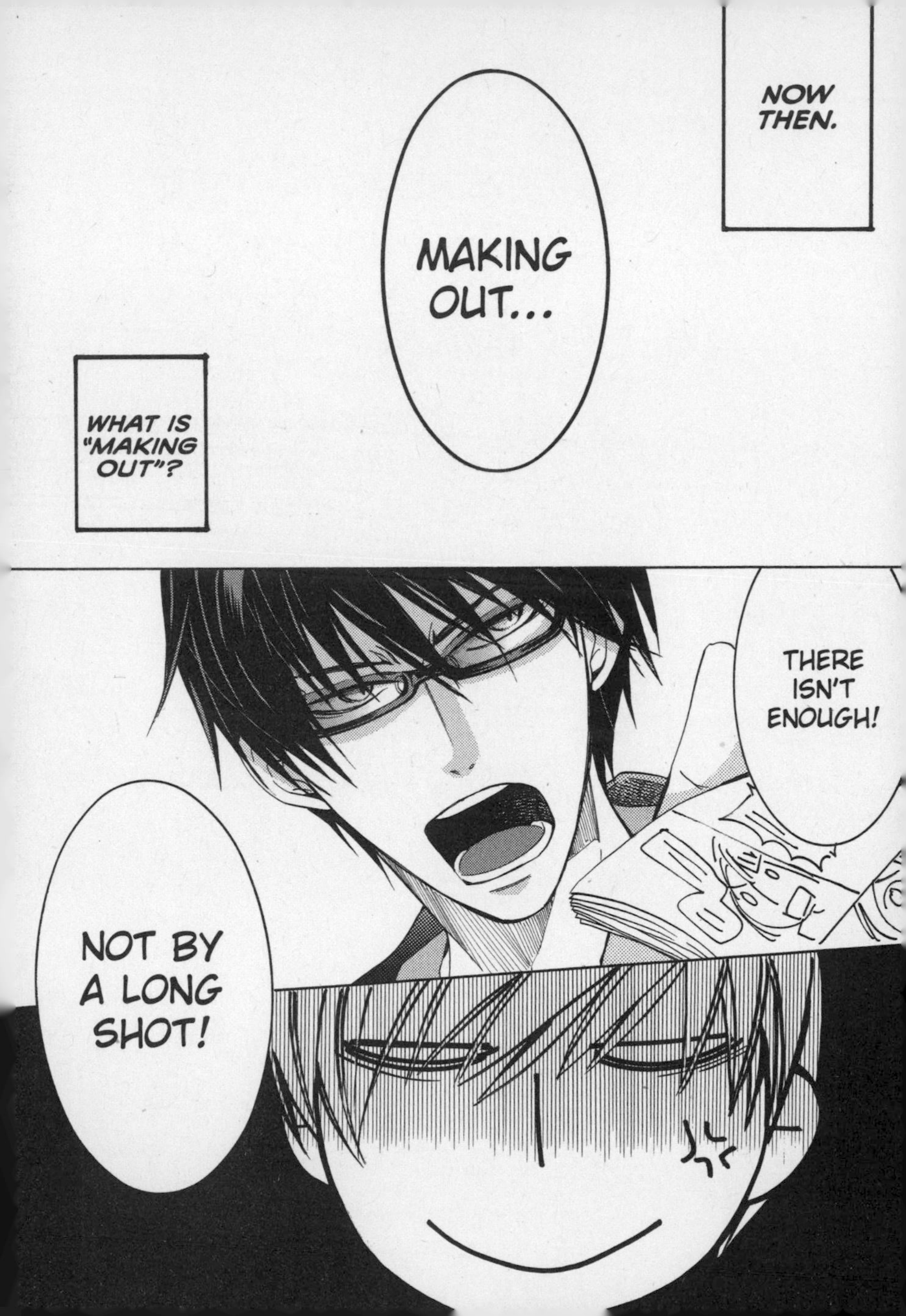
NOW THEN.
MAKING OUT...
WHAT IS "MAKING OUT"?
THERE ISN'T ENOUGH!
NOT BY A LONG SHOT!

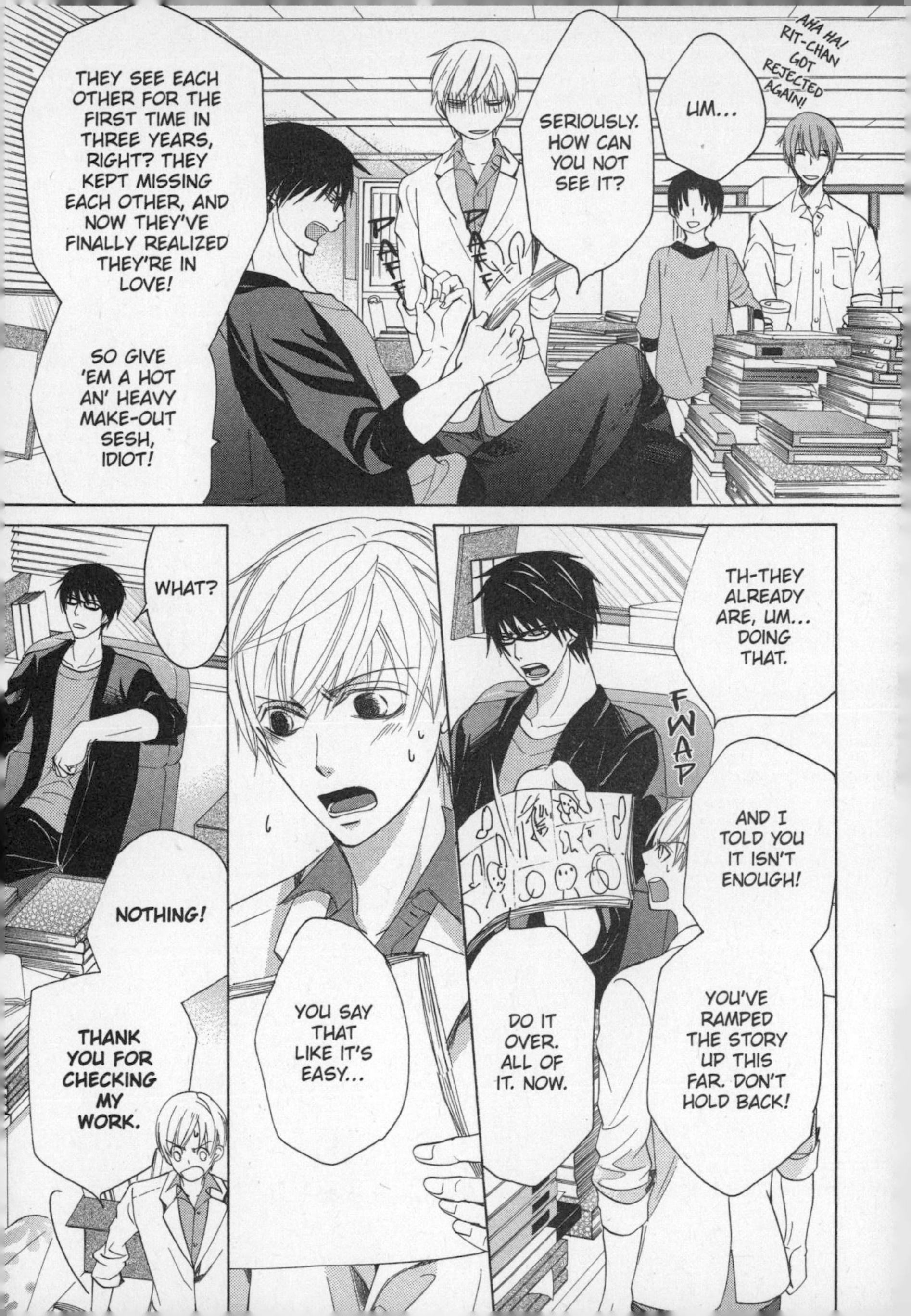
AHA HA! RIT-CHAN GOT REJECTED AGAIN!
UM...
SERIOUSLY. HOW CAN YOU NOT SEE IT?
PAFF
PAFF
THEY SEE EACH OTHER FOR THE FIRST TIME IN THREE YEARS, RIGHT? THEY KEPT MISSING EACH OTHER, AND NOW THEY'VE FINALLY REALIZED THEY'RE IN LOVE!
SO GIVE 'EM A HOT AN' HEAVY MAKE-OUT SESH, IDIOT!
TH-THEY ALREADY ARE, UM... DOING THAT.
FWAP
AND I TOLD YOU IT ISN'T ENOUGH!
YOU'VE RAMPED THE STORY UP THIS FAR. DON'T HOLD BACK!
DO IT OVER. ALL OF IT. NOW.
YOU SAY THAT LIKE IT'S EASY...
WHAT?
NOTHING!
THANK YOU FOR CHECKING MY WORK.

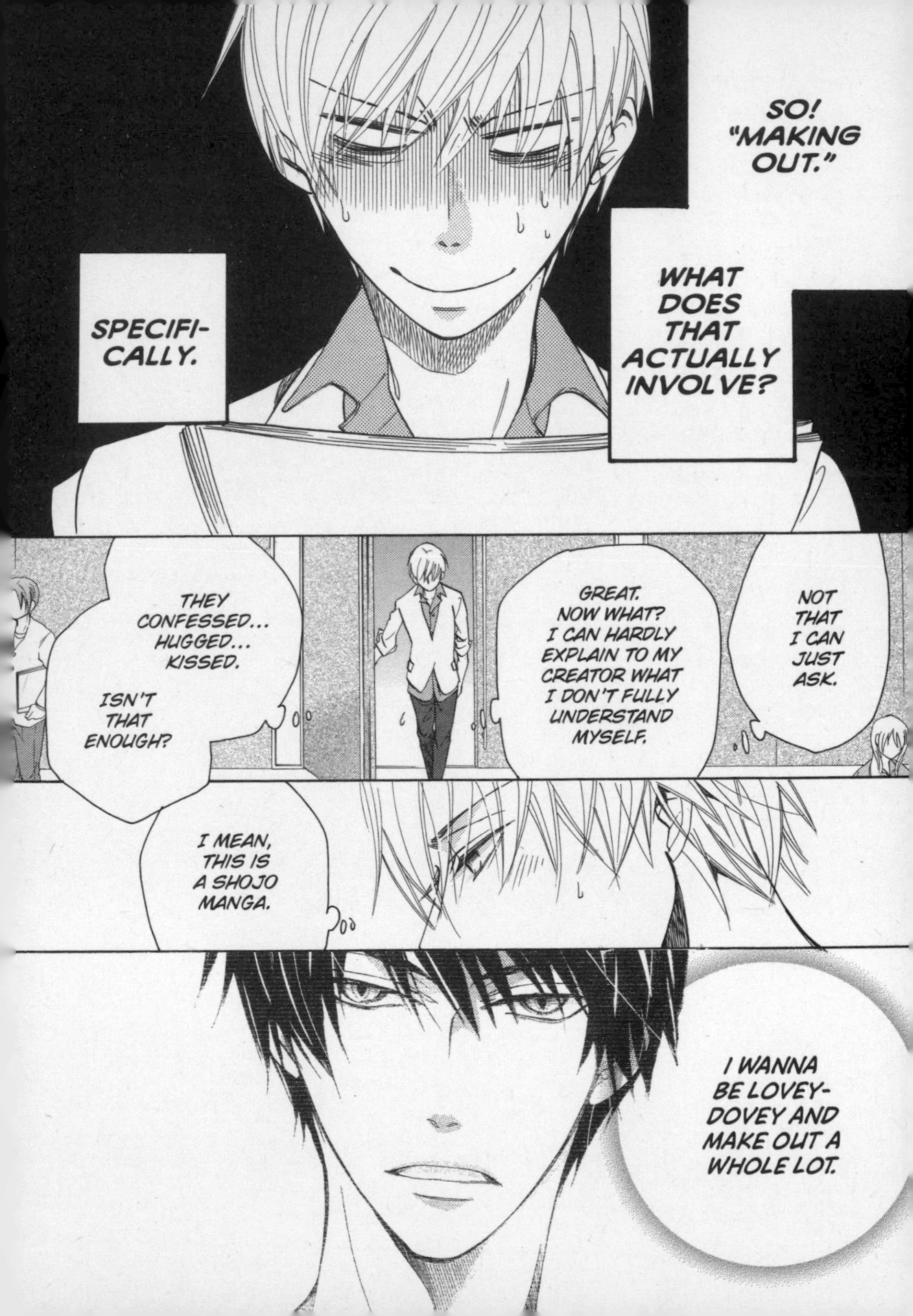
SO! "MAKING OUT."
WHAT DOES THAT ACTUALLY INVOLVE?
SPECIFI-CALLY.
NOT THAT I CAN JUST ASK.
GREAT. NOW WHAT? I CAN HARDLY EXPLAIN TO MY CREATOR WHAT I DON'T FULLY UNDERSTAND MYSELF.
THEY CONFESSED... HUGGED... KISSED.
ISN'T THAT ENOUGH?
I MEAN, THIS IS A SHOJO MANGA.
I WANNA BE LOVEY-DOVEY AND MAKE OUT A WHOLE LOT.

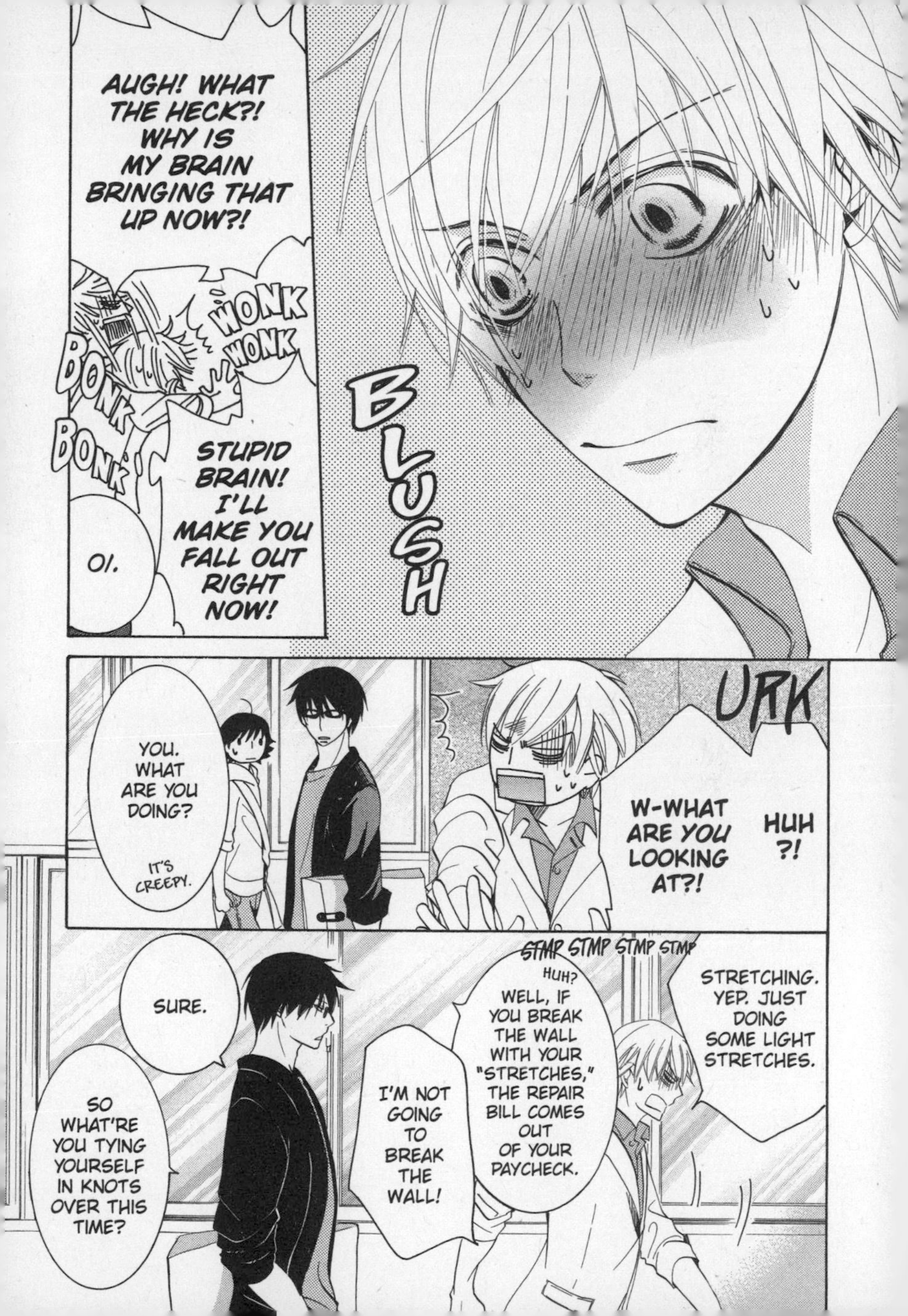
BLUSH
AUGH! WHAT THE HECK?! WHY IS MY BRAIN BRINGING THAT UP NOW?!
WONK WONK
BONK BONK
STUPID BRAIN! I'LL MAKE YOU FALL OUT RIGHT NOW!
OI.
URK
HUH ?!
W-WHAT ARE YOU LOOKING AT?!
YOU. WHAT ARE YOU DOING?
IT'S CREEPY.
STRETCHING. YEP. JUST DOING SOME LIGHT STRETCHES.
STMP STMP STMP STMP
HUH?
WELL, IF YOU BREAK THE WALL WITH YOUR "STRETCHES," THE REPAIR BILL COMES OUT OF YOUR PAYCHECK.
I'M NOT GOING TO BREAK THE WALL!
SURE.
SO WHAT'RE YOU TYING YOURSELF IN KNOTS OVER THIS TIME?

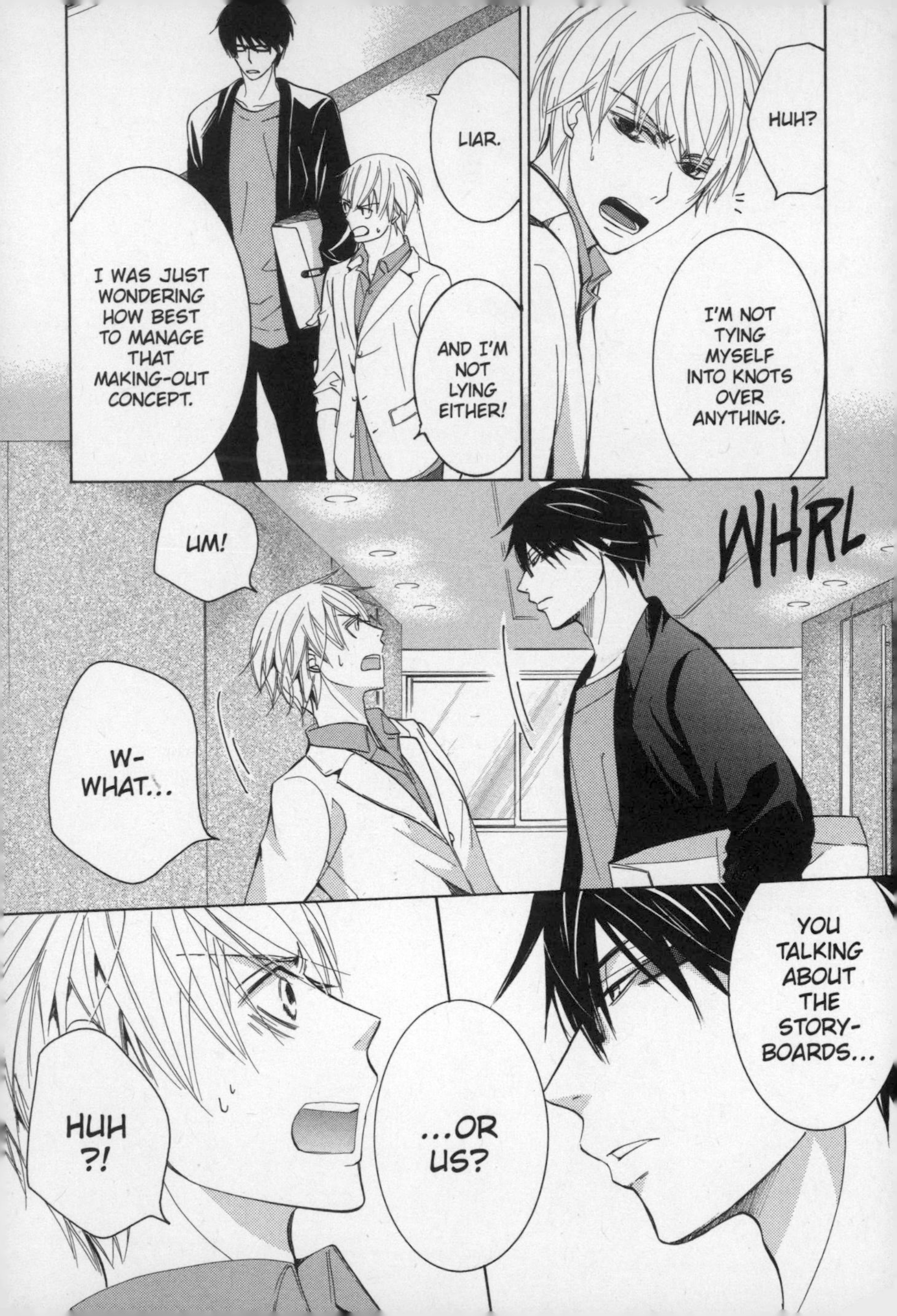
HUH?
I'M NOT TYING MYSELF INTO KNOTS OVER ANYTHING.
LIAR.
AND I'M NOT LYING EITHER!
I WAS JUST WONDERING HOW BEST TO MANAGE THAT MAKING-OUT CONCEPT.
WHRL
UM!
W-WHAT...
YOU TALKING ABOUT THE STORY-BOARDS...
...OR US?
HUH?!

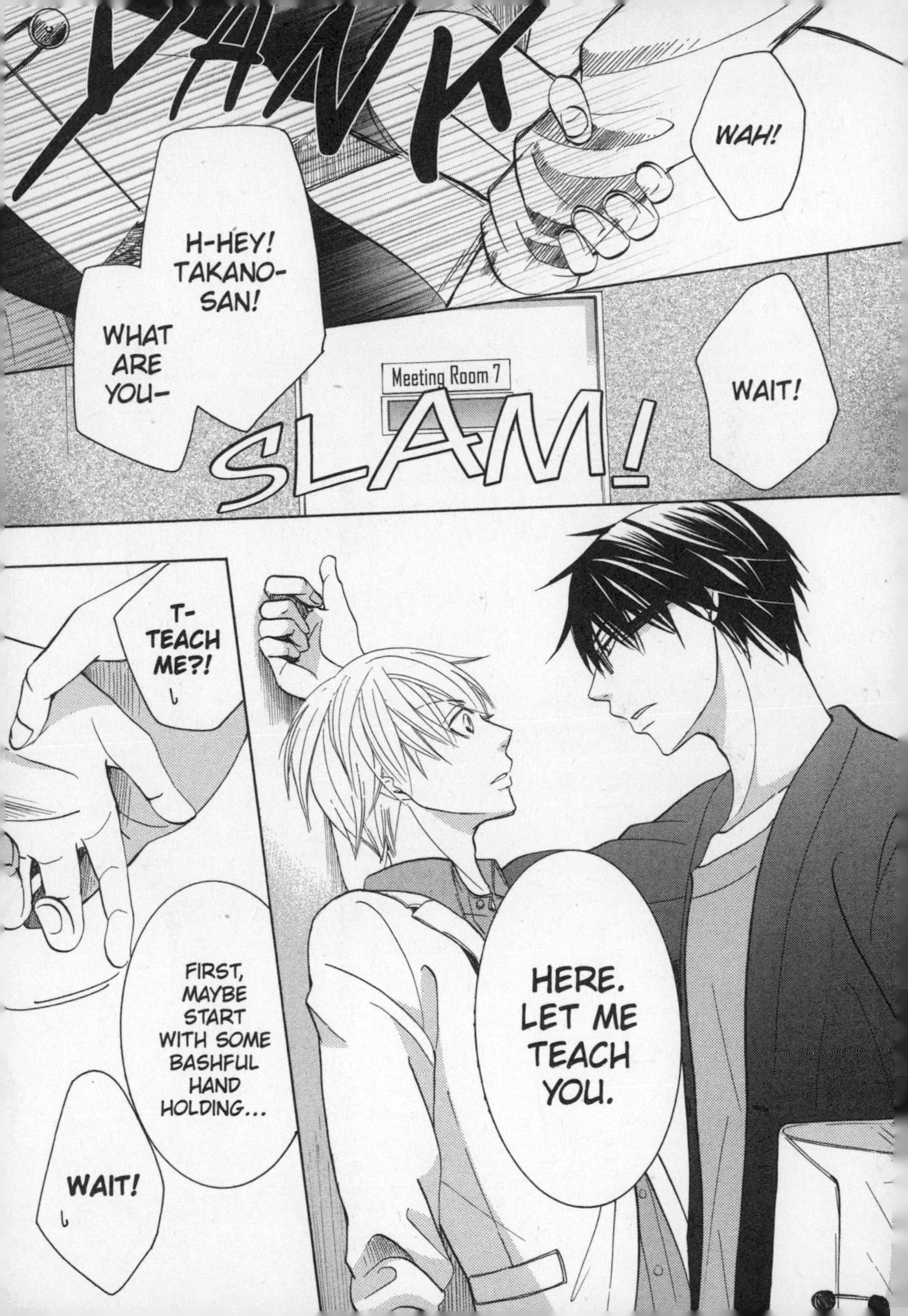
YANK
WAH!
WAIT!
H-HEY! TAKANO-SAN! WHAT ARE YOU-
Meeting Room 7
SLAM!
HERE. LET ME TEACH YOU.
T-TEACH ME?!
FIRST, MAYBE START WITH SOME BASHFUL HAND HOLDING...
WAIT!

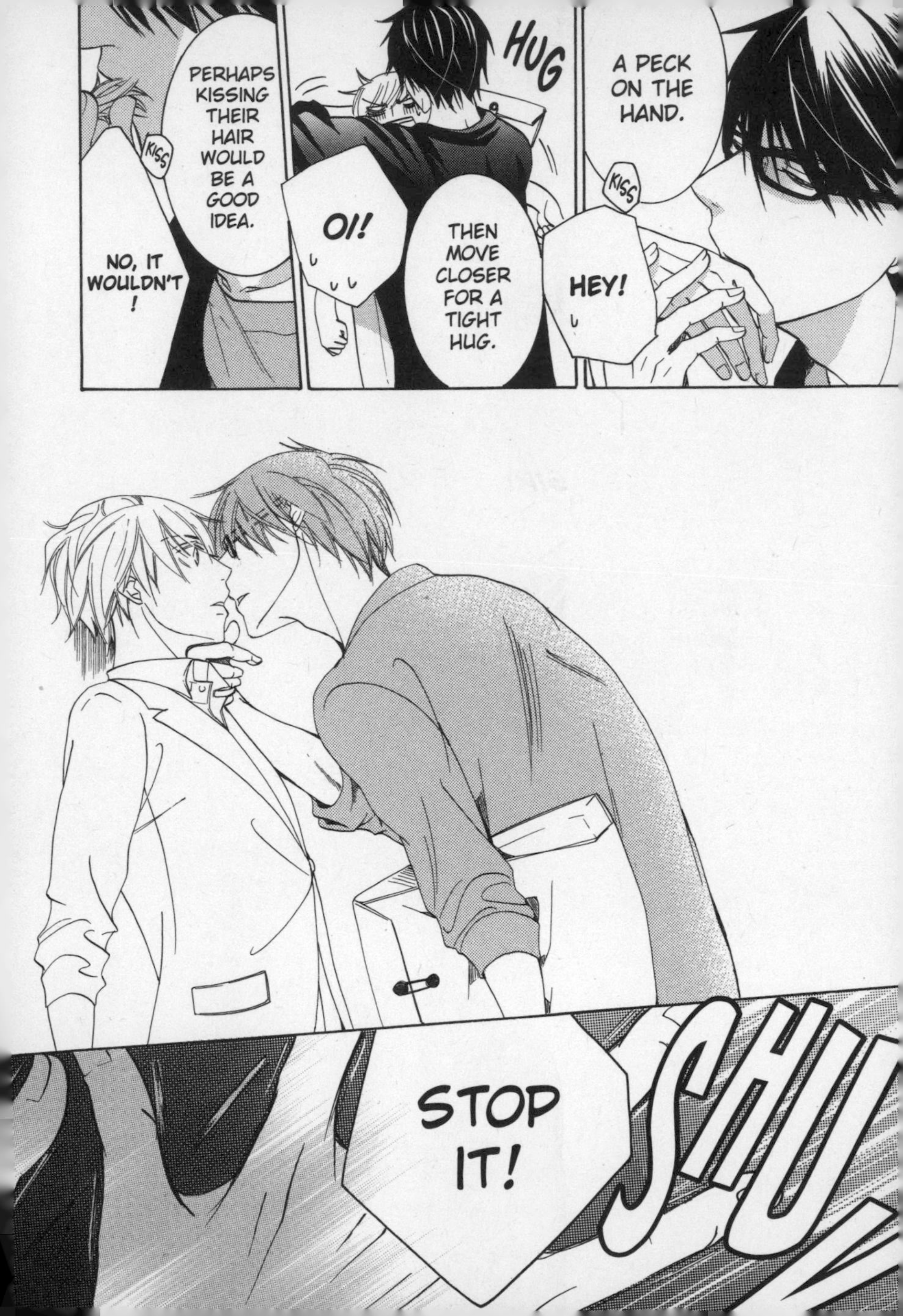
A PECK ON THE HAND.
KISS
HEY!
HUG
THEN MOVE CLOSER FOR A TIGHT HUG.
OI!
PERHAPS KISSING THEIR HAIR WOULD BE A GOOD IDEA.
KISS
NO, IT WOULDN'T!
SCHU
STOP IT!

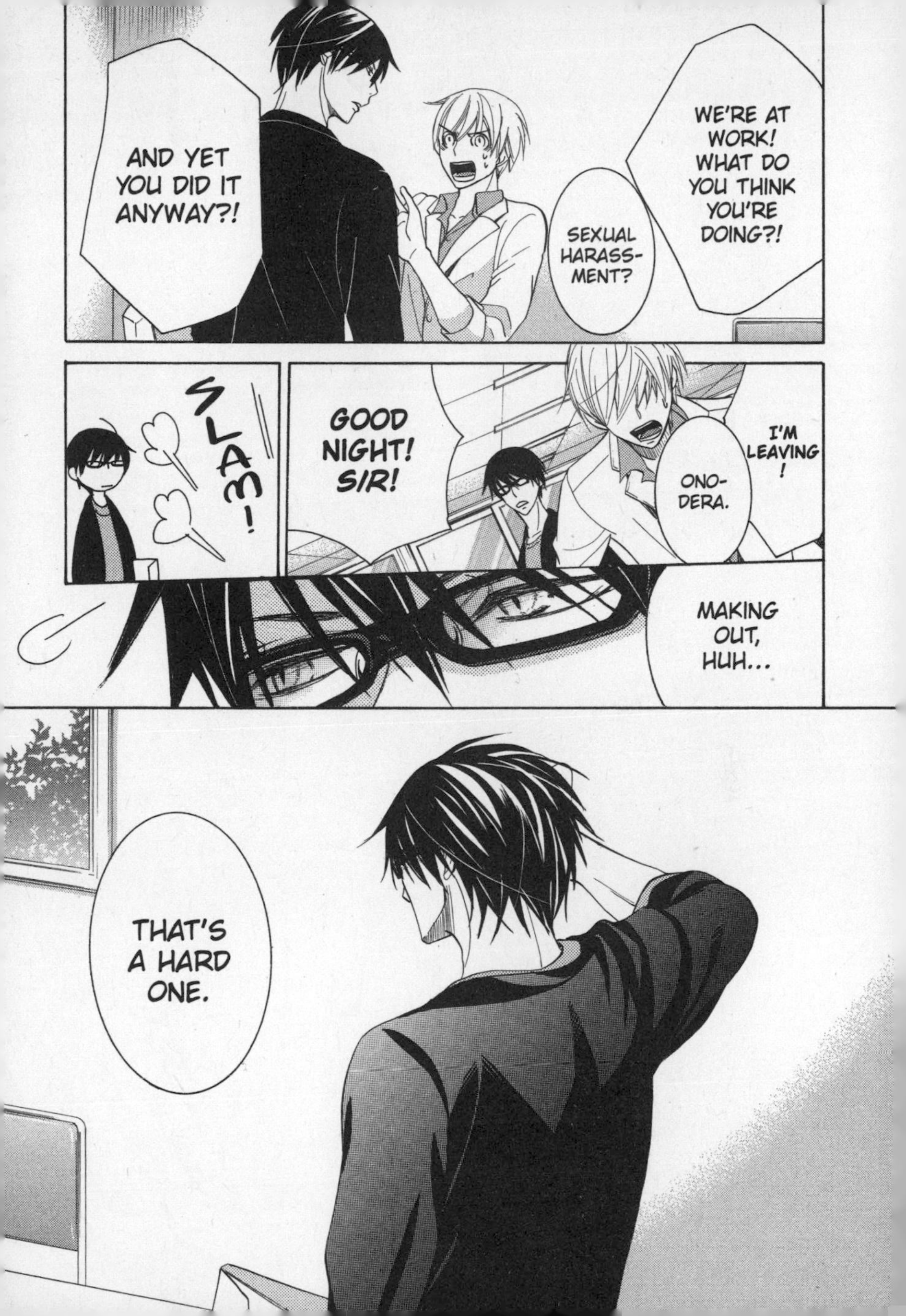
WE'RE AT WORK! WHAT DO YOU THINK YOU'RE DOING?!
SEXUAL HARASS-MENT?
AND YET YOU DID IT ANYWAY?!
I'M LEAVING!
ONO-DERA.
GOOD NIGHT! SIR!
SLAM!
MAKING OUT, HUH...
THAT'S A HARD ONE.

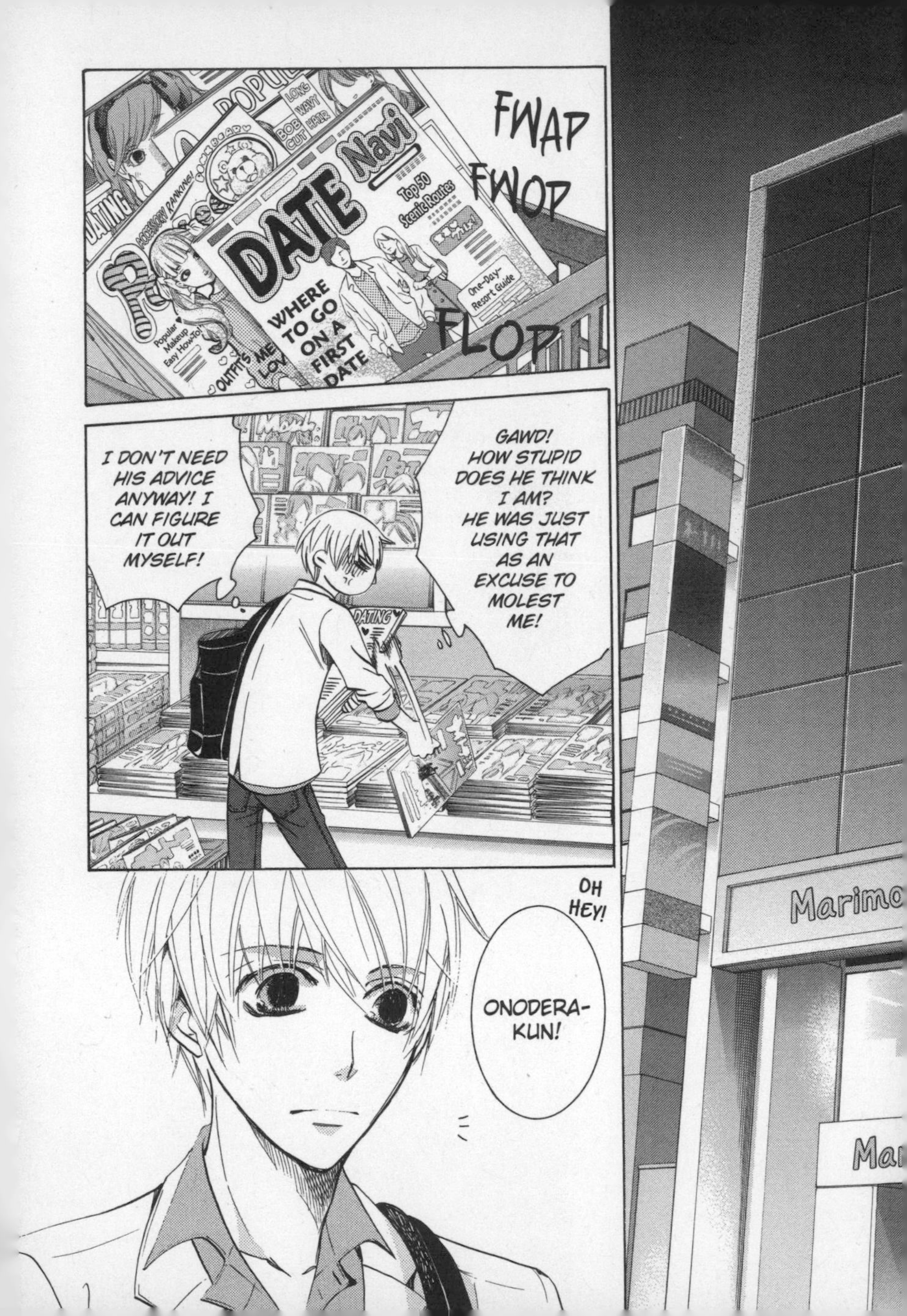
Marimo
FWAP
FWOP
FLOP
DATE Navi
Top 50 Scenic Routes
One-Day-Resort Guide
WHERE TO GO ON A FIRST DATE
LONG WAVY HAIR
BOB CUT
DATING
Popular Makeup Easy How-To!
GAWD! HOW STUPID DOES HE THINK I AM? HE WAS JUST USING THAT AS AN EXCUSE TO MOLEST ME!
I DON'T NEED HIS ADVICE ANYWAY! I CAN FIGURE IT OUT MYSELF!
DATING
OH HEY!
ONODERA-KUN!

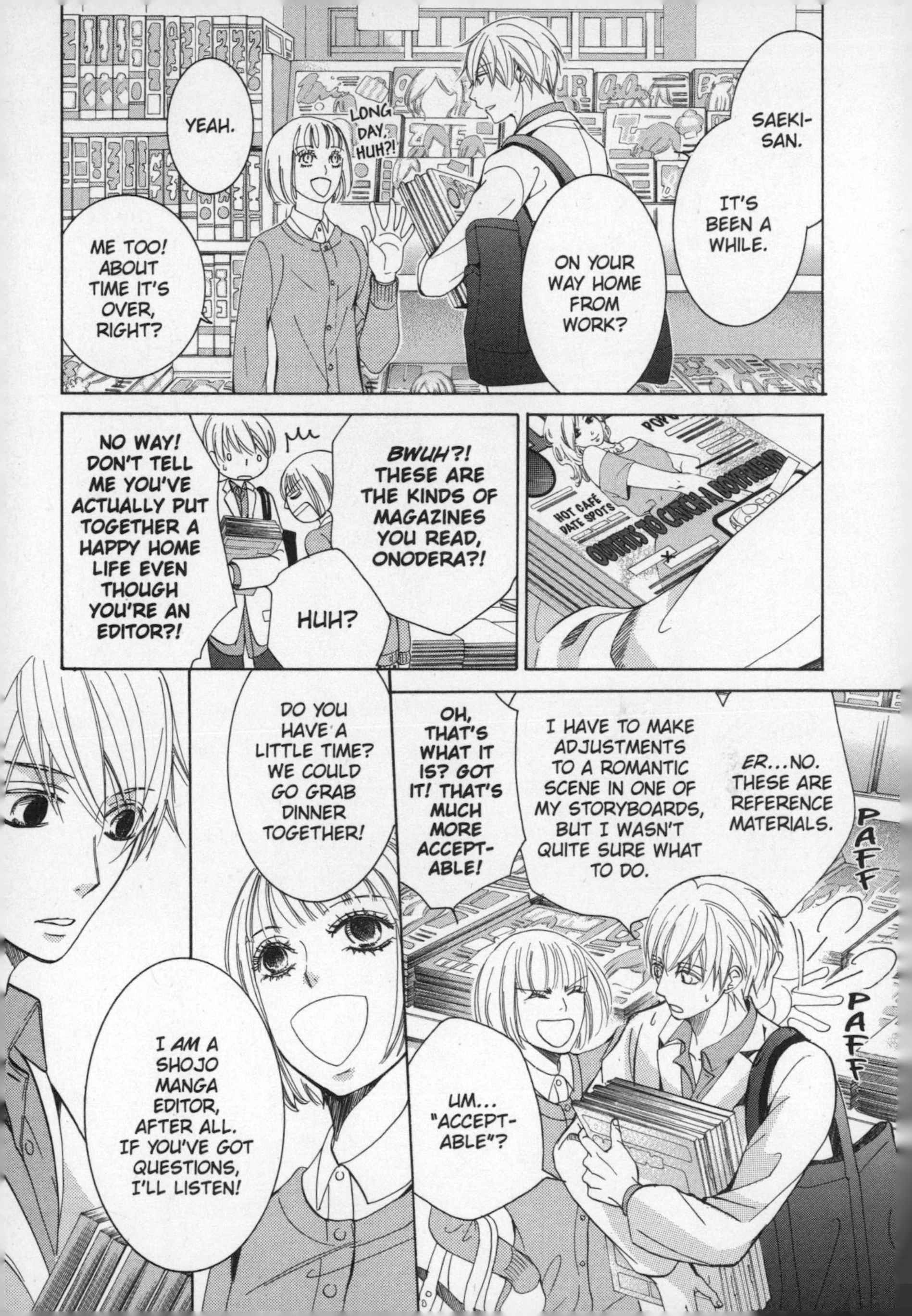
SAEKI-SAN.
IT'S BEEN A WHILE.
ON YOUR WAY HOME FROM WORK?
LONG DAY, HUH?!
YEAH.
ME TOO! ABOUT TIME IT'S OVER, RIGHT?
HOT CAFÉ DATE SPOTS
OUTFITS TO CATCH A BOYFRIEND
BWUH?! THESE ARE THE KINDS OF MAGAZINES YOU READ, ONODERA?!
HUH?
NO WAY! DON'T TELL ME YOU'VE ACTUALLY PUT TOGETHER A HAPPY HOME LIFE EVEN THOUGH YOU'RE AN EDITOR?!
ER...NO. THESE ARE REFERENCE MATERIALS.
PAFF
I HAVE TO MAKE ADJUSTMENTS TO A ROMANTIC SCENE IN ONE OF MY STORYBOARDS, BUT I WASN'T QUITE SURE WHAT TO DO.
OH, THAT'S WHAT IT IS? GOT IT! THAT'S MUCH MORE ACCEPTABLE!
PAFF
UM... "ACCEPTABLE"?
DO YOU HAVE A LITTLE TIME? WE COULD GO GRAB DINNER TOGETHER!
I AM A SHOJO MANGA EDITOR, AFTER ALL. IF YOU'VE GOT QUESTIONS, I'LL LISTEN!

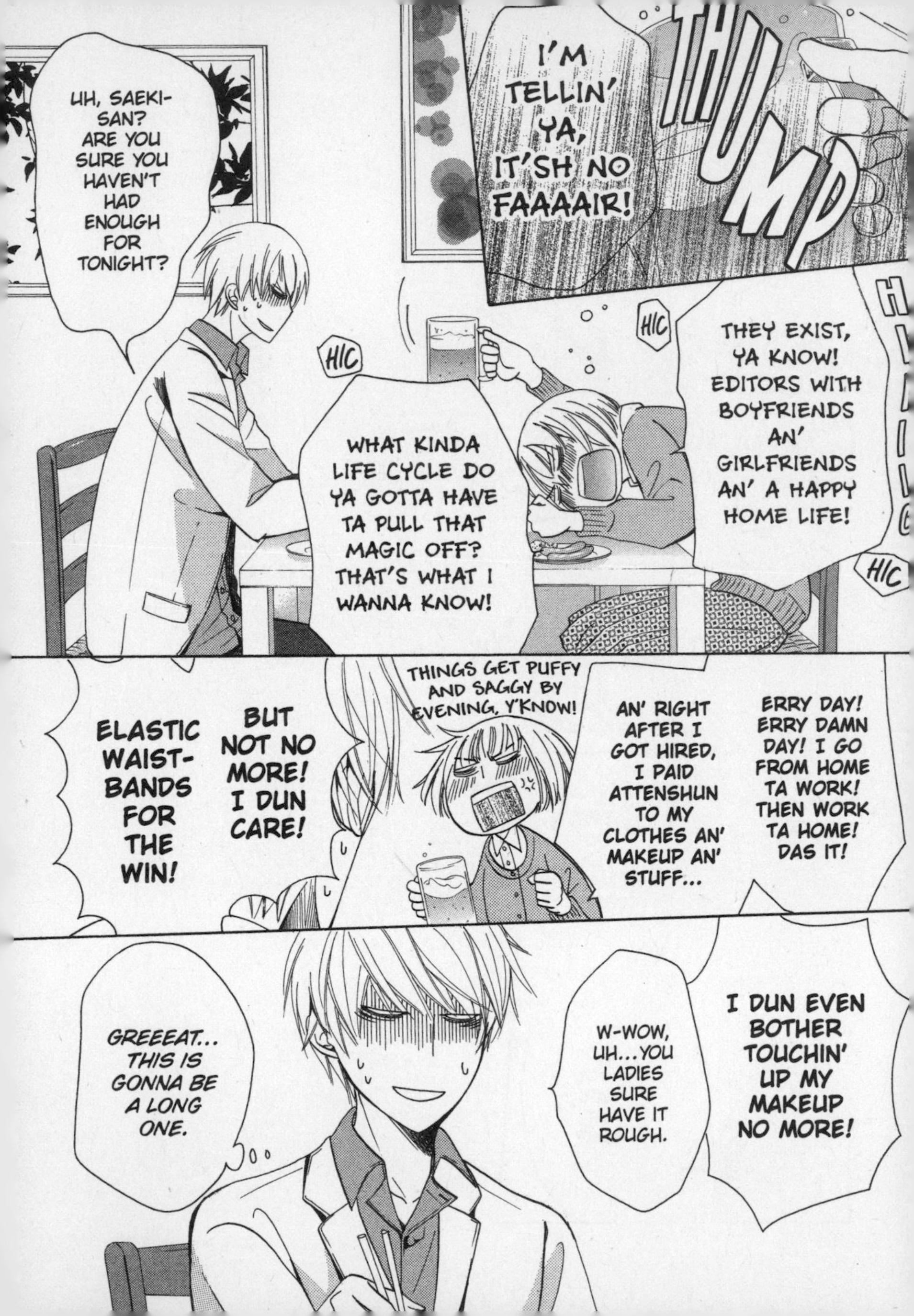
THUMP
I'M TELLIN' YA, IT'SH NO FAAAAIR!
HIC
THEY EXIST, YA KNOW! EDITORS WITH BOYFRIENDS AN' GIRLFRIENDS AN' A HAPPY HOME LIFE!
HIC
HIC
WHAT KINDA LIFE CYCLE DO YA GOTTA HAVE TA PULL THAT MAGIC OFF? THAT'S WHAT I WANNA KNOW!
UH, SAEKI-SAN? ARE YOU SURE YOU HAVEN'T HAD ENOUGH FOR TONIGHT?
ERRY DAY! ERRY DAMN DAY! I GO FROM HOME TA WORK! THEN WORK TA HOME! DAS IT!
AN' RIGHT AFTER I GOT HIRED, I PAID ATTENSHUN TO MY CLOTHES AN' MAKEUP AN' STUFF...
THINGS GET PUFFY AND SAGGY BY EVENING, Y'KNOW!
BUT NOT NO MORE! I DUN CARE!
ELASTIC WAIST-BANDS FOR THE WIN!
I DUN EVEN BOTHER TOUCHIN' UP MY MAKEUP NO MORE!
W-WOW, UH...YOU LADIES SURE HAVE IT ROUGH.
GREEEAT... THIS IS GONNA BE A LONG ONE.

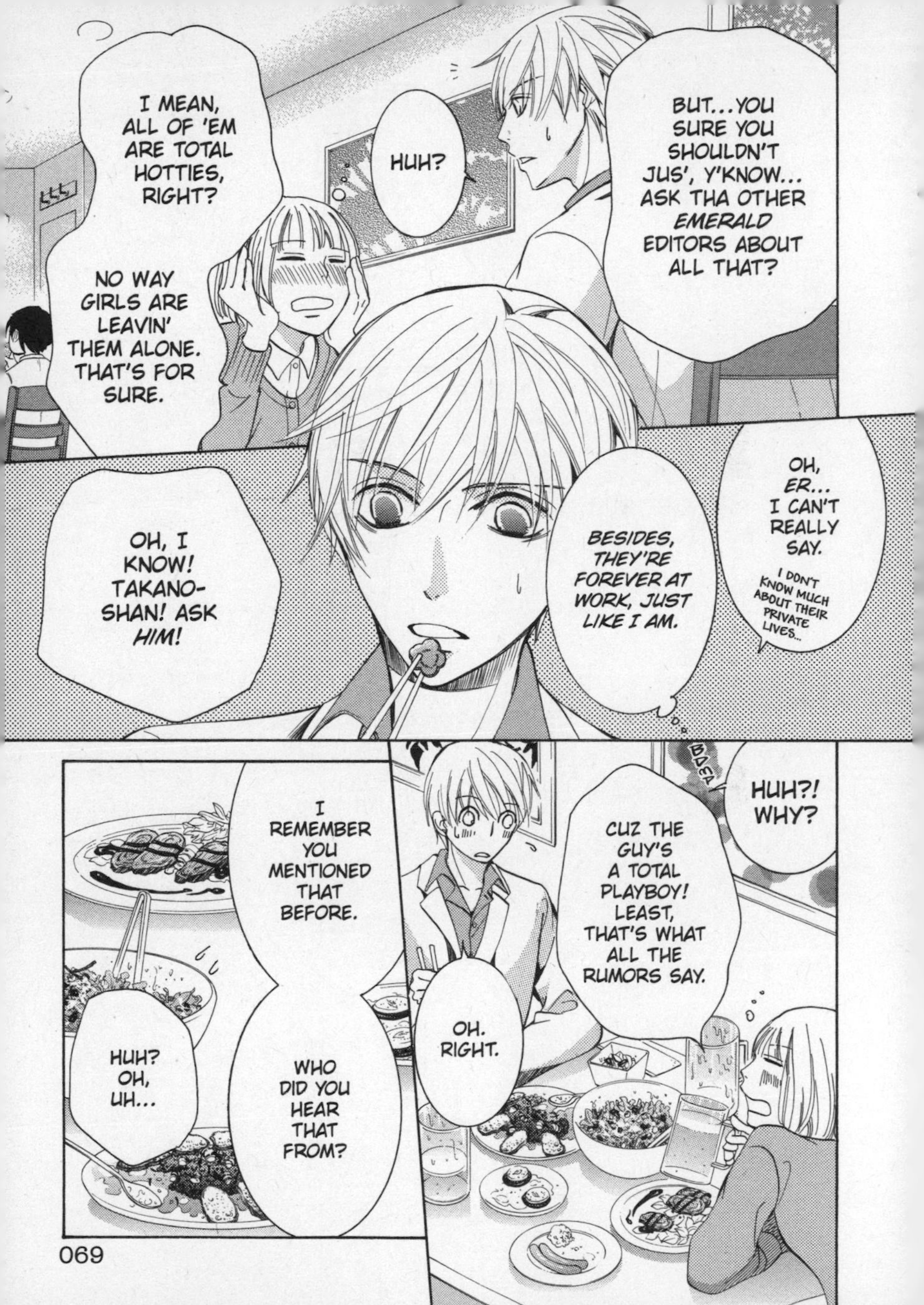
BUT...YOU SURE YOU SHOULDN'T JUS', Y'KNOW... ASK THA OTHER *EMERALD* EDITORS ABOUT ALL THAT?
HUH?
I MEAN, ALL OF 'EM ARE TOTAL HOTTIES, RIGHT?
NO WAY GIRLS ARE LEAVIN' THEM ALONE. THAT'S FOR SURE.
OH, ER... I CAN'T REALLY SAY.
I DON'T KNOW MUCH ABOUT THEIR PRIVATE LIVES...
BESIDES, THEY'RE FOREVER AT WORK, JUST LIKE I AM.
OH, I KNOW! TAKANO-SHAN! ASK *HIM*!
HUH?! WHY?
BDEA
CUZ THE GUY'S A TOTAL PLAYBOY! LEAST, THAT'S WHAT ALL THE RUMORS SAY.
OH. RIGHT.
I REMEMBER YOU MENTIONED THAT BEFORE.
WHO DID YOU HEAR THAT FROM?
HUH? OH, UH...

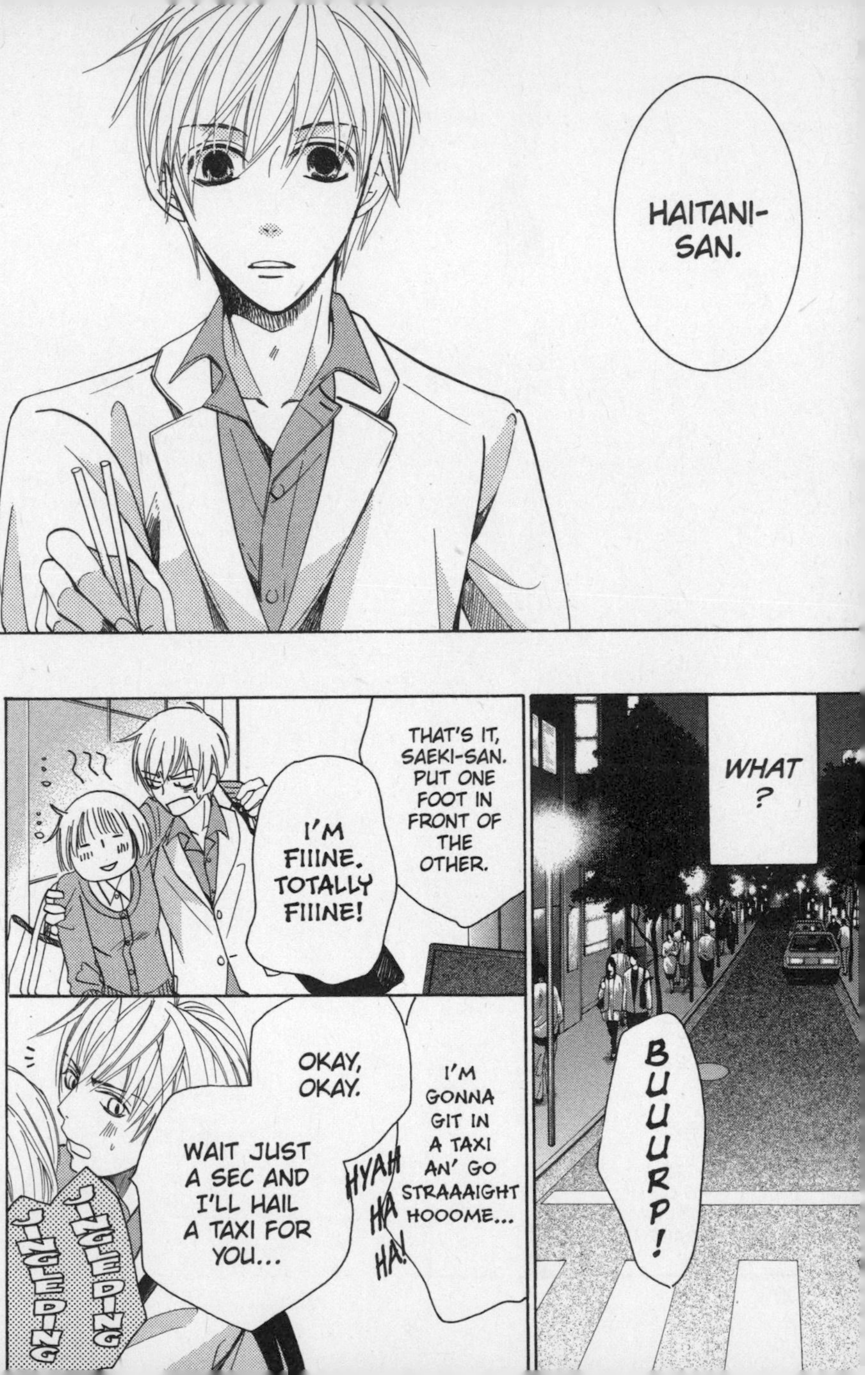
HAITANI-SAN.
WHAT?
BUUURP!
THAT'S IT, SAEKI-SAN. PUT ONE FOOT IN FRONT OF THE OTHER.
I'M FIIINE. TOTALLY FIIINE!
I'M GONNA GIT IN A TAXI AN' GO STRAAAIGHT HOOOME...
OKAY, OKAY.
HYAH HA HA!
WAIT JUST A SEC AND I'LL HAIL A TAXI FOR YOU...
JINGLEDING JINGLEDING

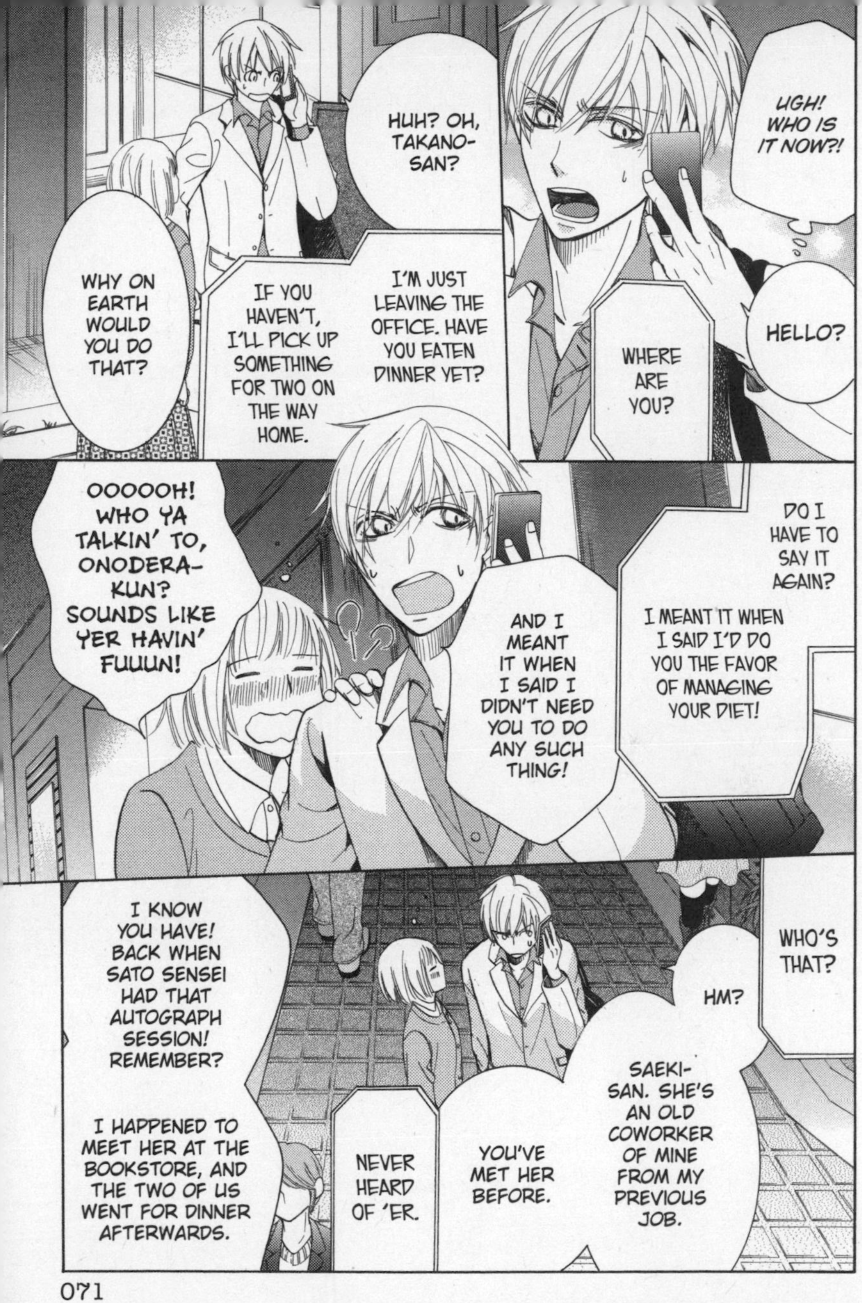
UGH! WHO IS IT NOW?!
HELLO?
WHERE ARE YOU?
HUH? OH, TAKANO-SAN?
I'M JUST LEAVING THE OFFICE. HAVE YOU EATEN DINNER YET?
IF YOU HAVEN'T, I'LL PICK UP SOMETHING FOR TWO ON THE WAY HOME.
WHY ON EARTH WOULD YOU DO THAT?
DO I HAVE TO SAY IT AGAIN?
I MEANT IT WHEN I SAID I'D DO YOU THE FAVOR OF MANAGING YOUR DIET!
AND I MEANT IT WHEN I SAID I DIDN'T NEED YOU TO DO ANY SUCH THING!
OOOOOH! WHO YA TALKIN' TO, ONODERA-KUN? SOUNDS LIKE YER HAVIN' FUUUN!
WHO'S THAT?
HM?
SAEKI-SAN. SHE'S AN OLD COWORKER OF MINE FROM MY PREVIOUS JOB.
YOU'VE MET HER BEFORE.
NEVER HEARD OF 'ER.
I KNOW YOU HAVE! BACK WHEN SATO SENSEI HAD THAT AUTOGRAPH SESSION! REMEMBER?
I HAPPENED TO MEET HER AT THE BOOKSTORE, AND THE TWO OF US WENT FOR DINNER AFTERWARDS.

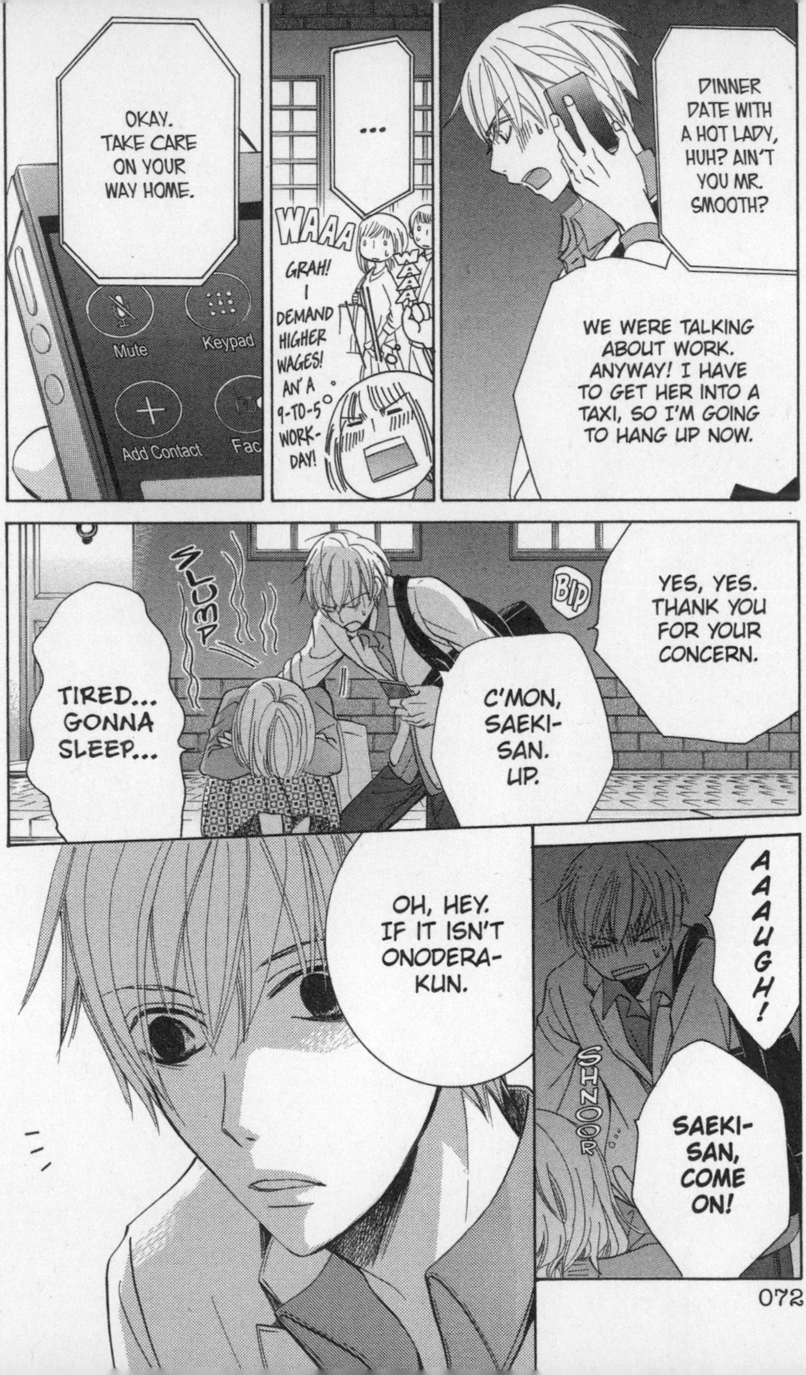
DINNER DATE WITH A HOT LADY, HUH? AIN'T YOU MR. SMOOTH?
WE WERE TALKING ABOUT WORK. ANYWAY! I HAVE TO GET HER INTO A TAXI, SO I'M GOING TO HANG UP NOW.
...
WAAA
WAAAA
GRAH! I DEMAND HIGHER WAGES! AN' A 9-TO-5 WORK-DAY!
OKAY. TAKE CARE ON YOUR WAY HOME.
Mute
Keypad
Add Contact
Fac
BIP
YES, YES. THANK YOU FOR YOUR CONCERN.
C'MON, SAEKI-SAN. UP.
SLUMP
TIRED... GONNA SLEEP...
AAAAUGH!
SHNOOR
SAEKI-SAN, COME ON!
OH, HEY. IF IT ISN'T ONODERA-KUN.

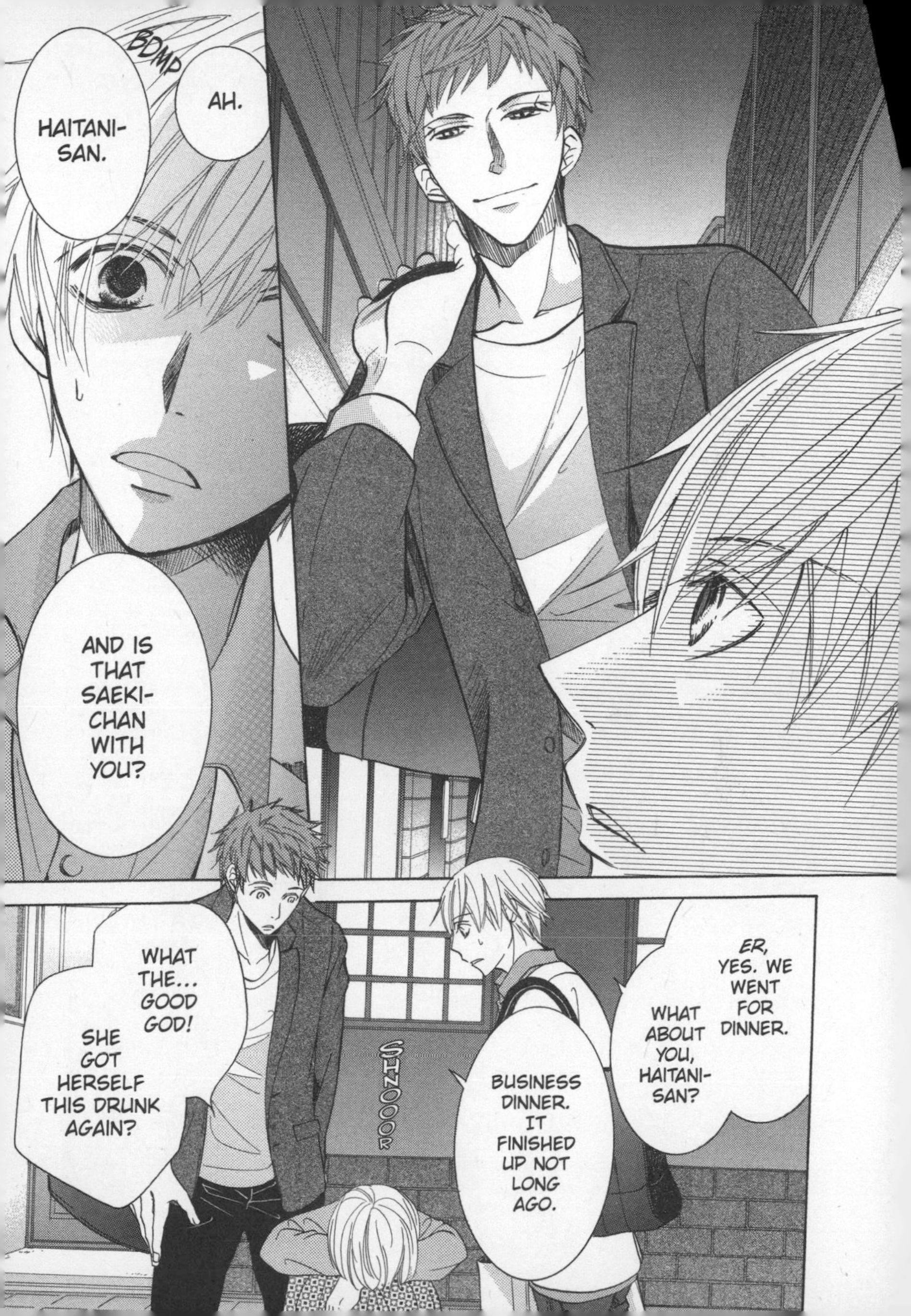
BDMP
AH.
HAITANI-SAN.
AND IS THAT SAEKI-CHAN WITH YOU?
ER, YES. WE WENT FOR DINNER.
WHAT ABOUT YOU, HAITANI-SAN?
BUSINESS DINNER. IT FINISHED UP NOT LONG AGO.
SHNOOOOR
WHAT THE... GOOD GOD!
SHE GOT HERSELF THIS DRUNK AGAIN?

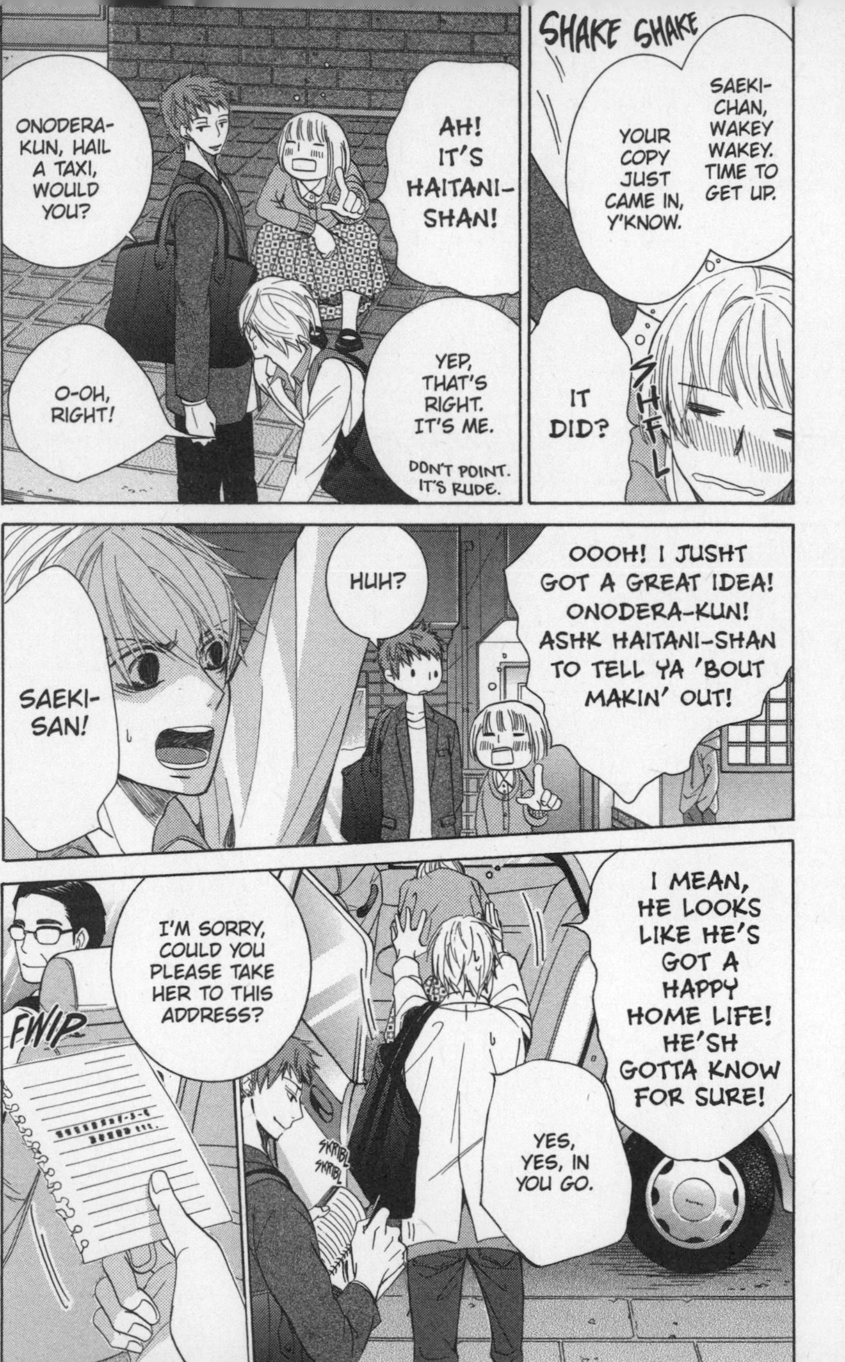
SHAKE SHAKE
SAEKI-CHAN, WAKEY WAKEY. TIME TO GET UP.
YOUR COPY JUST CAME IN, Y'KNOW.
IT DID?
SHFL
AH! IT'S HAITANI-SHAN!
ONODERA-KUN, HAIL A TAXI, WOULD YOU?
YEP, THAT'S RIGHT. IT'S ME.
DON'T POINT. IT'S RUDE.
O-OH, RIGHT!
OOOH! I JUSHT GOT A GREAT IDEA! ONODERA-KUN! ASHK HAITANI-SHAN TO TELL YA 'BOUT MAKIN' OUT!
HUH?
SAEKI-SAN!
I MEAN, HE LOOKS LIKE HE'S GOT A HAPPY HOME LIFE! HE'SH GOTTA KNOW FOR SURE!
I'M SORRY, COULD YOU PLEASE TAKE HER TO THIS ADDRESS?
FWIP
YES, YES, IN YOU GO.
SKRIBL SKRIBL

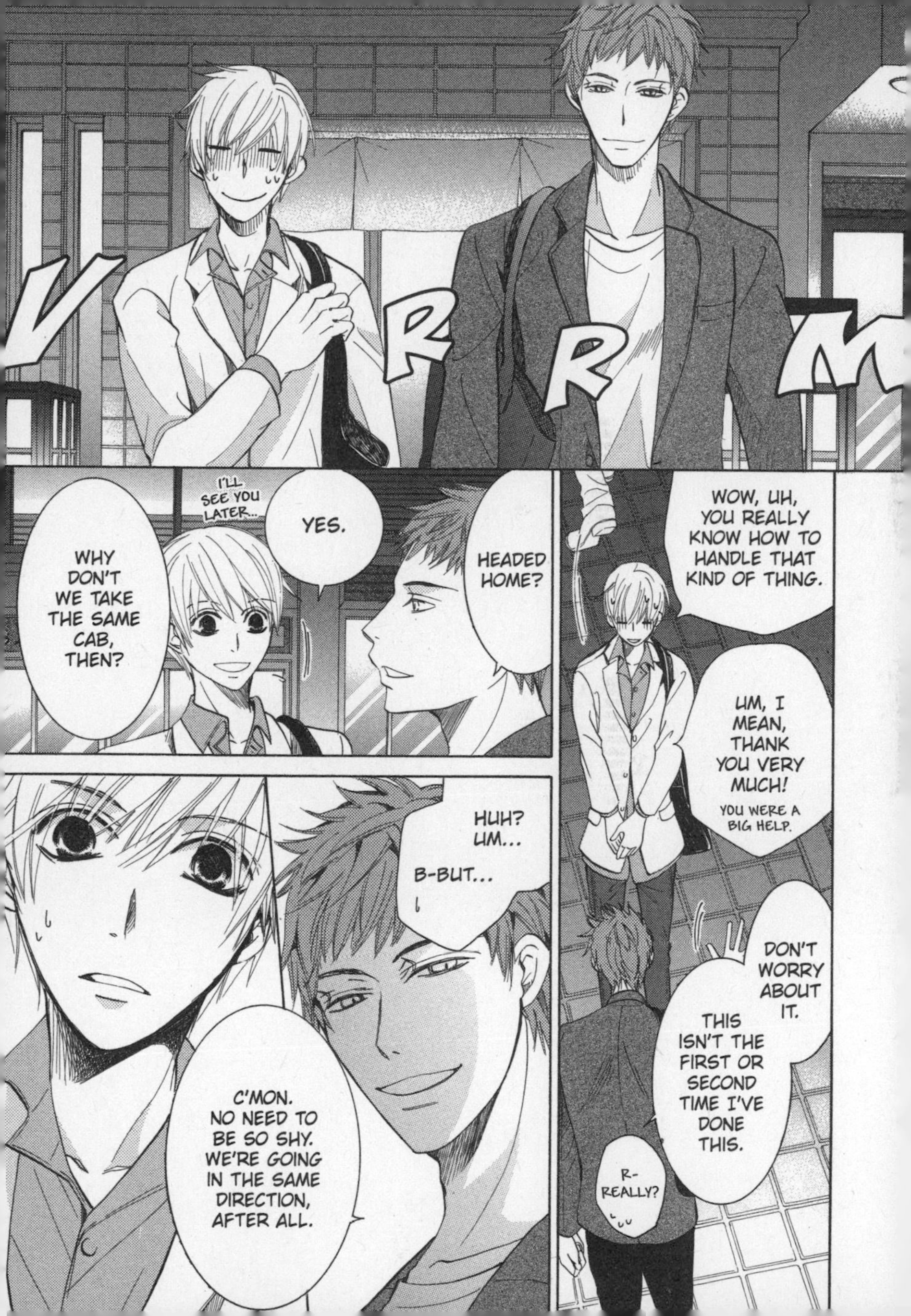
VRRM
WOW, UH, YOU REALLY KNOW HOW TO HANDLE THAT KIND OF THING.
UM, I MEAN, THANK YOU VERY MUCH!
YOU WERE A BIG HELP.
DON'T WORRY ABOUT IT.
THIS ISN'T THE FIRST OR SECOND TIME I'VE DONE THIS.
R-REALLY?
HEADED HOME?
YES.
I'LL SEE YOU LATER...
WHY DON'T WE TAKE THE SAME CAB, THEN?
HUH? UM...
B-BUT...
C'MON. NO NEED TO BE SO SHY. WE'RE GOING IN THE SAME DIRECTION, AFTER ALL.

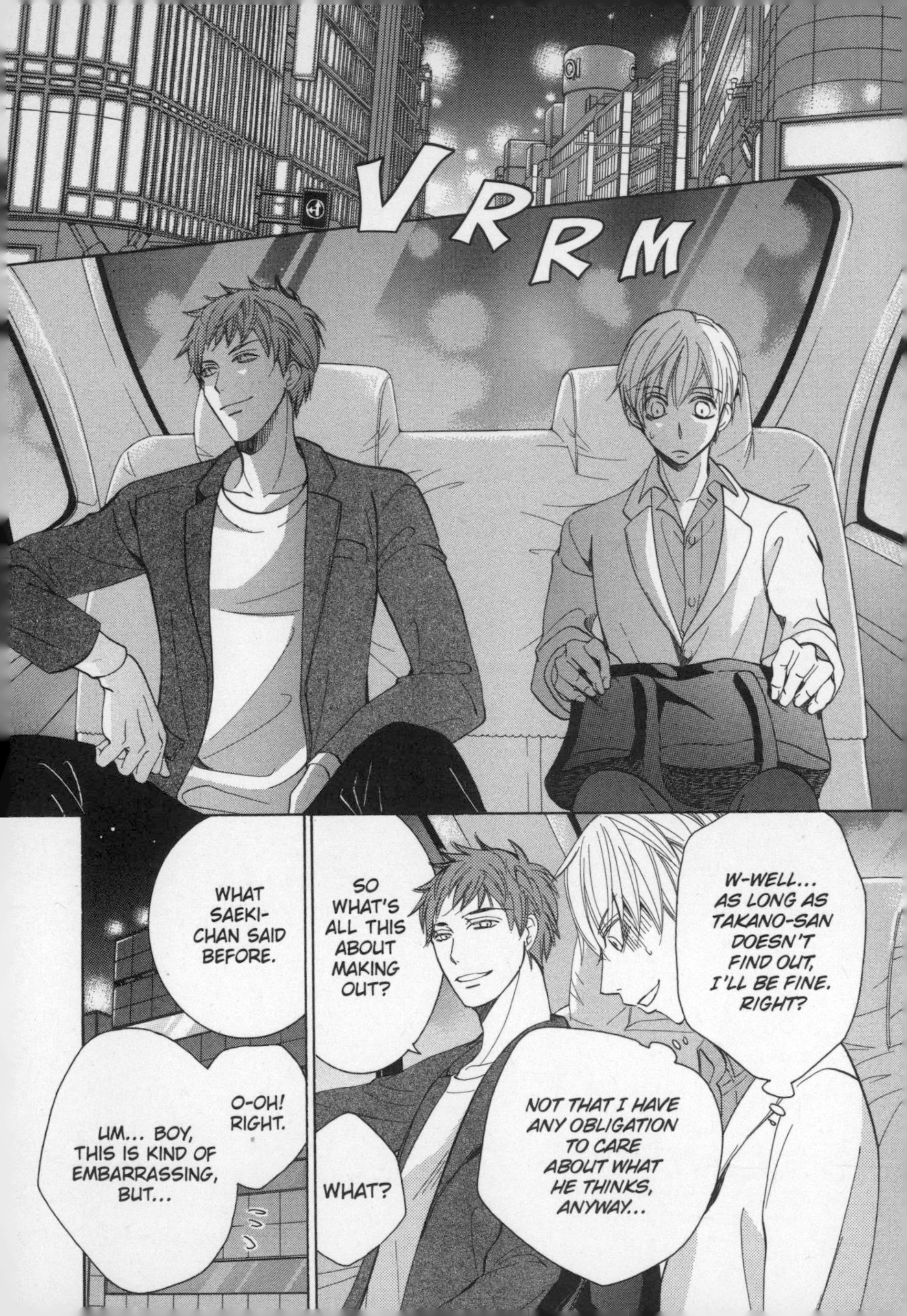
VRRM
W-WELL... AS LONG AS TAKANO-SAN DOESN'T FIND OUT, I'LL BE FINE. RIGHT?
SO WHAT'S ALL THIS ABOUT MAKING OUT?
NOT THAT I HAVE ANY OBLIGATION TO CARE ABOUT WHAT HE THINKS, ANYWAY...
WHAT?
WHAT SAEKI-CHAN SAID BEFORE.
O-OH! RIGHT.
UM... BOY, THIS IS KIND OF EMBARRASSING, BUT...

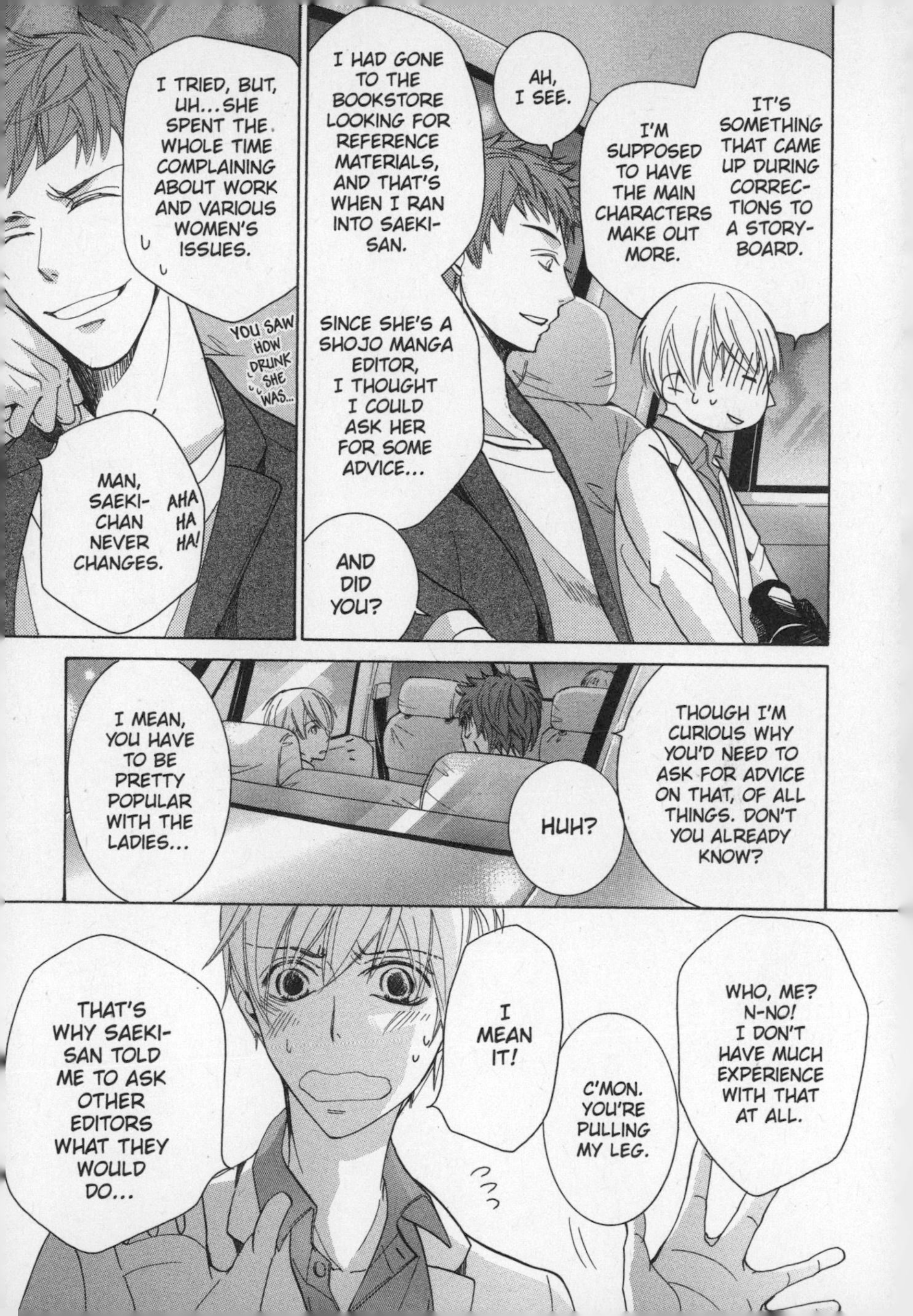

IT'S SOMETHING THAT CAME UP DURING CORRECTIONS TO A STORYBOARD.
I'M SUPPOSED TO HAVE THE MAIN CHARACTERS MAKE OUT MORE.
AH, I SEE.
I HAD GONE TO THE BOOKSTORE LOOKING FOR REFERENCE MATERIALS, AND THAT'S WHEN I RAN INTO SAEKI-SAN.
SINCE SHE'S A SHOJO MANGA EDITOR, I THOUGHT I COULD ASK HER FOR SOME ADVICE...
AND DID YOU?
I TRIED, BUT, UH...SHE SPENT THE WHOLE TIME COMPLAINING ABOUT WORK AND VARIOUS WOMEN'S ISSUES.
YOU SAW HOW DRUNK SHE WAS...
AHA HA HA!
MAN, SAEKI-CHAN NEVER CHANGES.
THOUGH I'M CURIOUS WHY YOU'D NEED TO ASK FOR ADVICE ON THAT, OF ALL THINGS. DON'T YOU ALREADY KNOW?
HUH?
I MEAN, YOU HAVE TO BE PRETTY POPULAR WITH THE LADIES...
WHO, ME? N-NO! I DON'T HAVE MUCH EXPERIENCE WITH THAT AT ALL.
C'MON. YOU'RE PULLING MY LEG.
I MEAN IT!
THAT'S WHY SAEKI-SAN TOLD ME TO ASK OTHER EDITORS WHAT THEY WOULD DO...

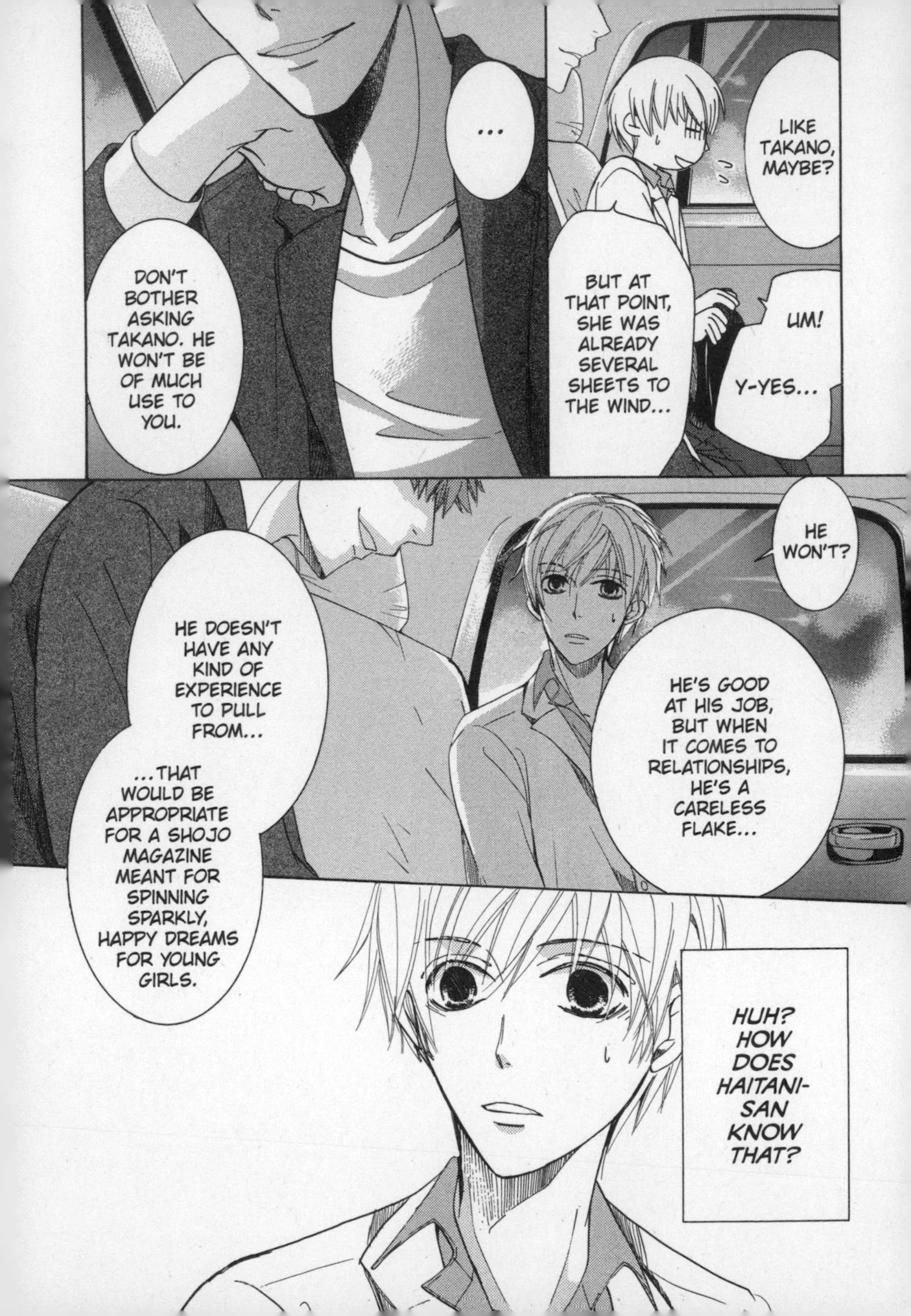
LIKE TAKANO, MAYBE?
UM!
Y-YES...
BUT AT THAT POINT, SHE WAS ALREADY SEVERAL SHEETS TO THE WIND...
...
DON'T BOTHER ASKING TAKANO. HE WON'T BE OF MUCH USE TO YOU.
HE WON'T?
HE'S GOOD AT HIS JOB, BUT WHEN IT COMES TO RELATIONSHIPS, HE'S A CARELESS FLAKE...
HE DOESN'T HAVE ANY KIND OF EXPERIENCE TO PULL FROM...
...THAT WOULD BE APPROPRIATE FOR A SHOJO MAGAZINE MEANT FOR SPINNING SPARKLY, HAPPY DREAMS FOR YOUNG GIRLS.
HUH? HOW DOES HAITANI-SAN KNOW THAT?

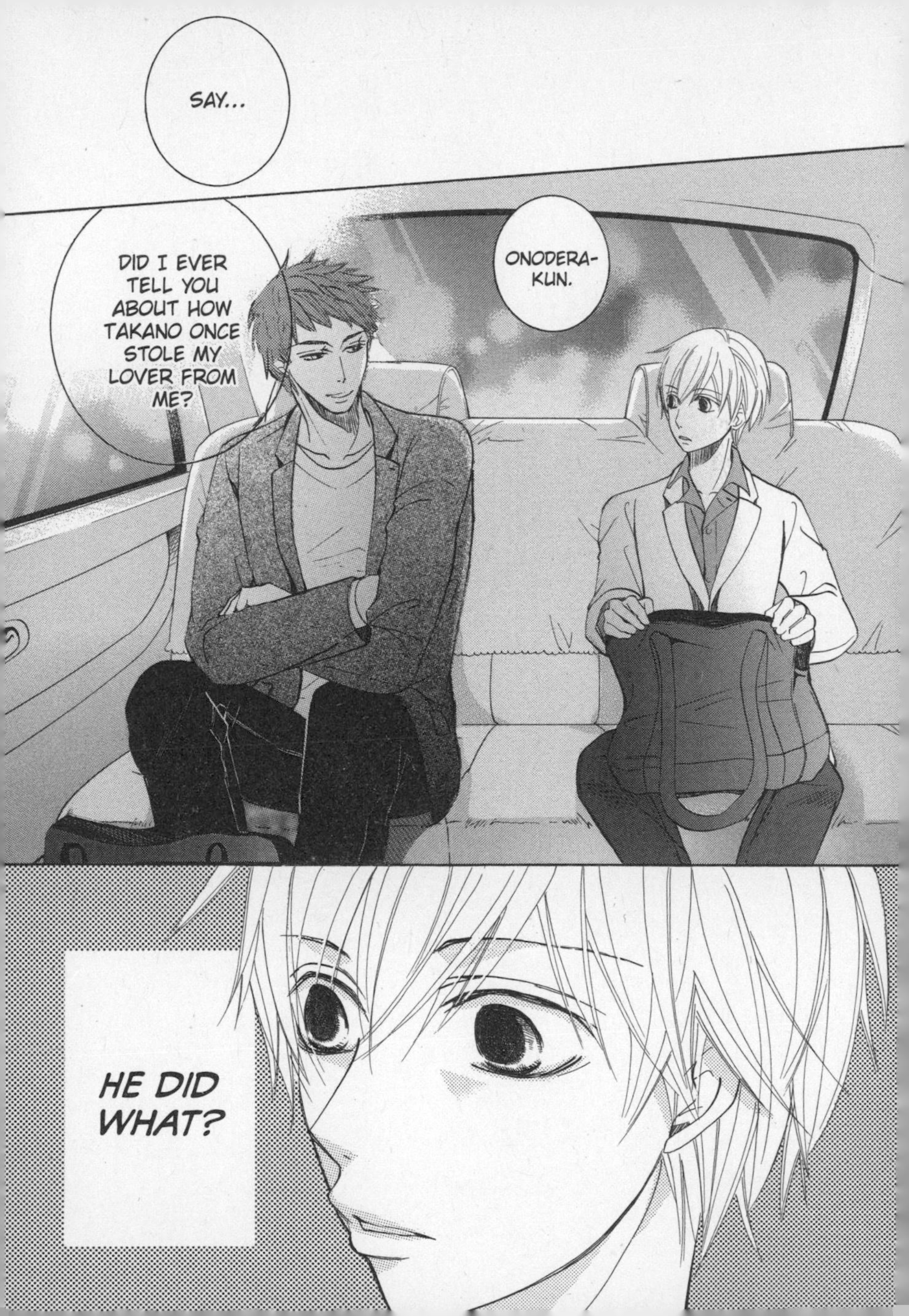
SAY...
ONODERA-KUN.
DID I EVER TELL YOU ABOUT HOW TAKANO ONCE STOLE MY LOVER FROM ME?
HE DID WHAT?

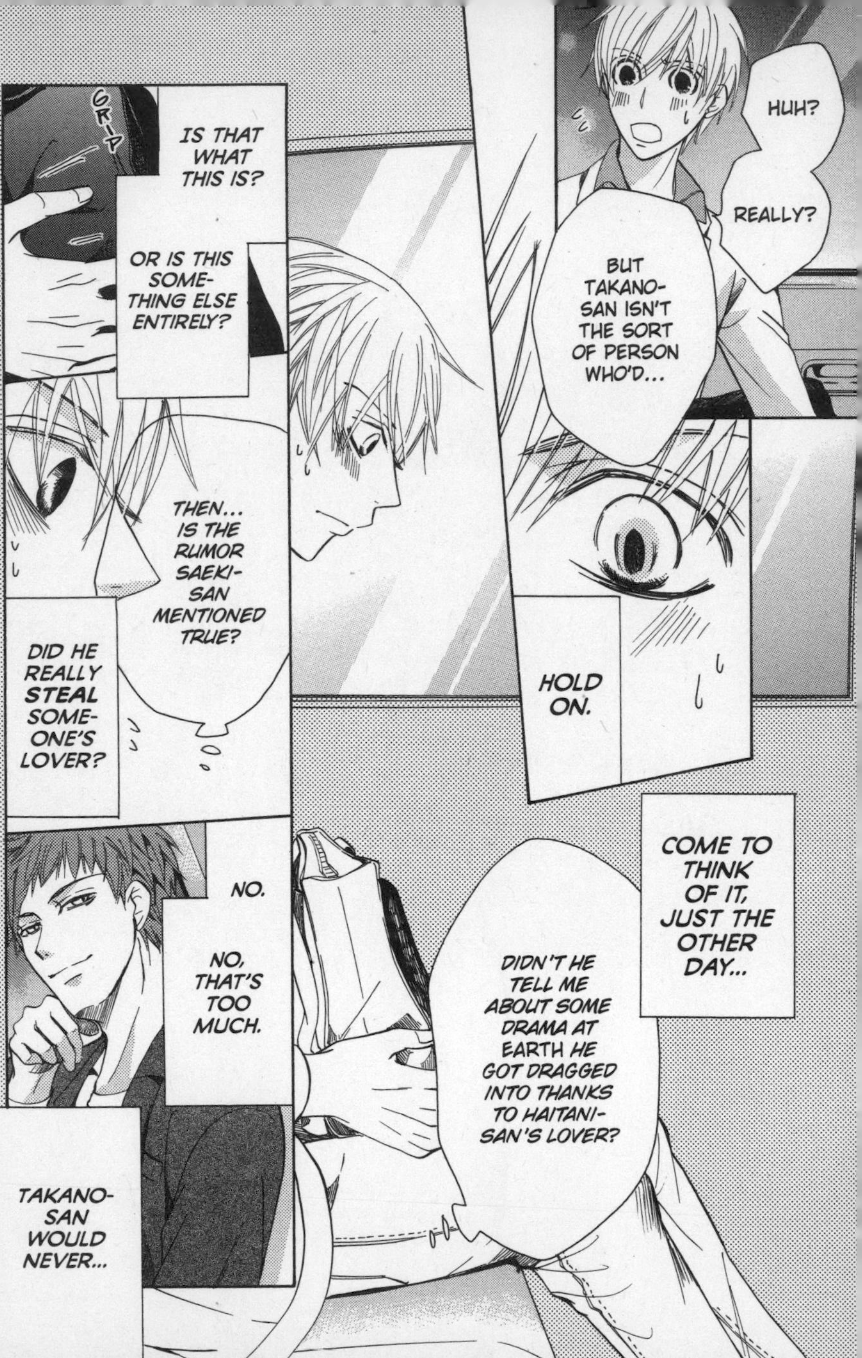
HUH?
REALLY?
BUT TAKANO-SAN ISN'T THE SORT OF PERSON WHO'D...
HOLD ON.
GRIP
IS THAT WHAT THIS IS?
OR IS THIS SOME-THING ELSE ENTIRELY?
THEN... IS THE RUMOR SAEKI-SAN MENTIONED TRUE?
DID HE REALLY STEAL SOME-ONE'S LOVER?
COME TO THINK OF IT, JUST THE OTHER DAY...
DIDN'T HE TELL ME ABOUT SOME DRAMA AT EARTH HE GOT DRAGGED INTO THANKS TO HAITANI-SAN'S LOVER?
NO.
NO, THAT'S TOO MUCH.
TAKANO-SAN WOULD NEVER...

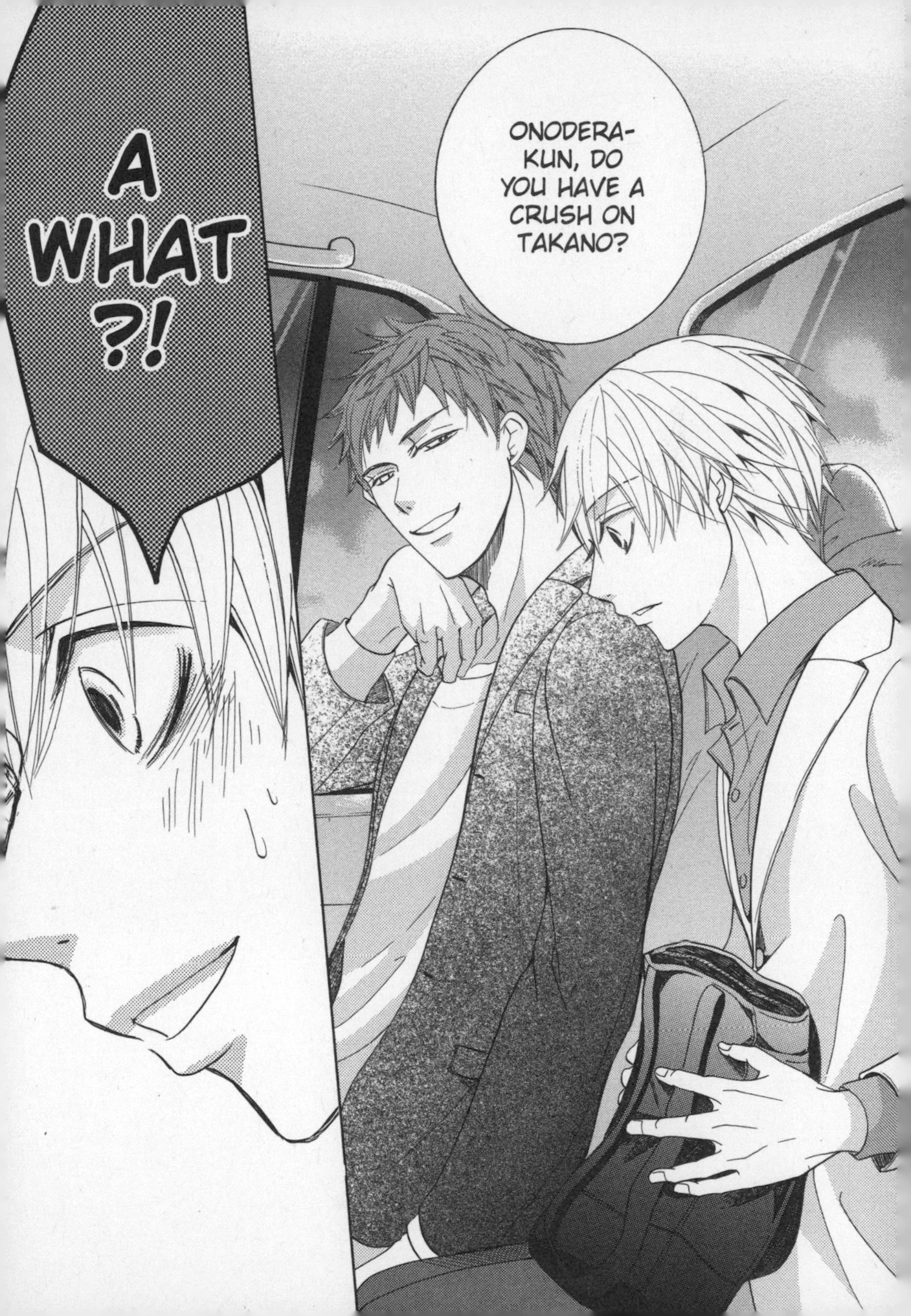
ONODERA-KUN, DO YOU HAVE A CRUSH ON TAKANO?
A WHAT?!

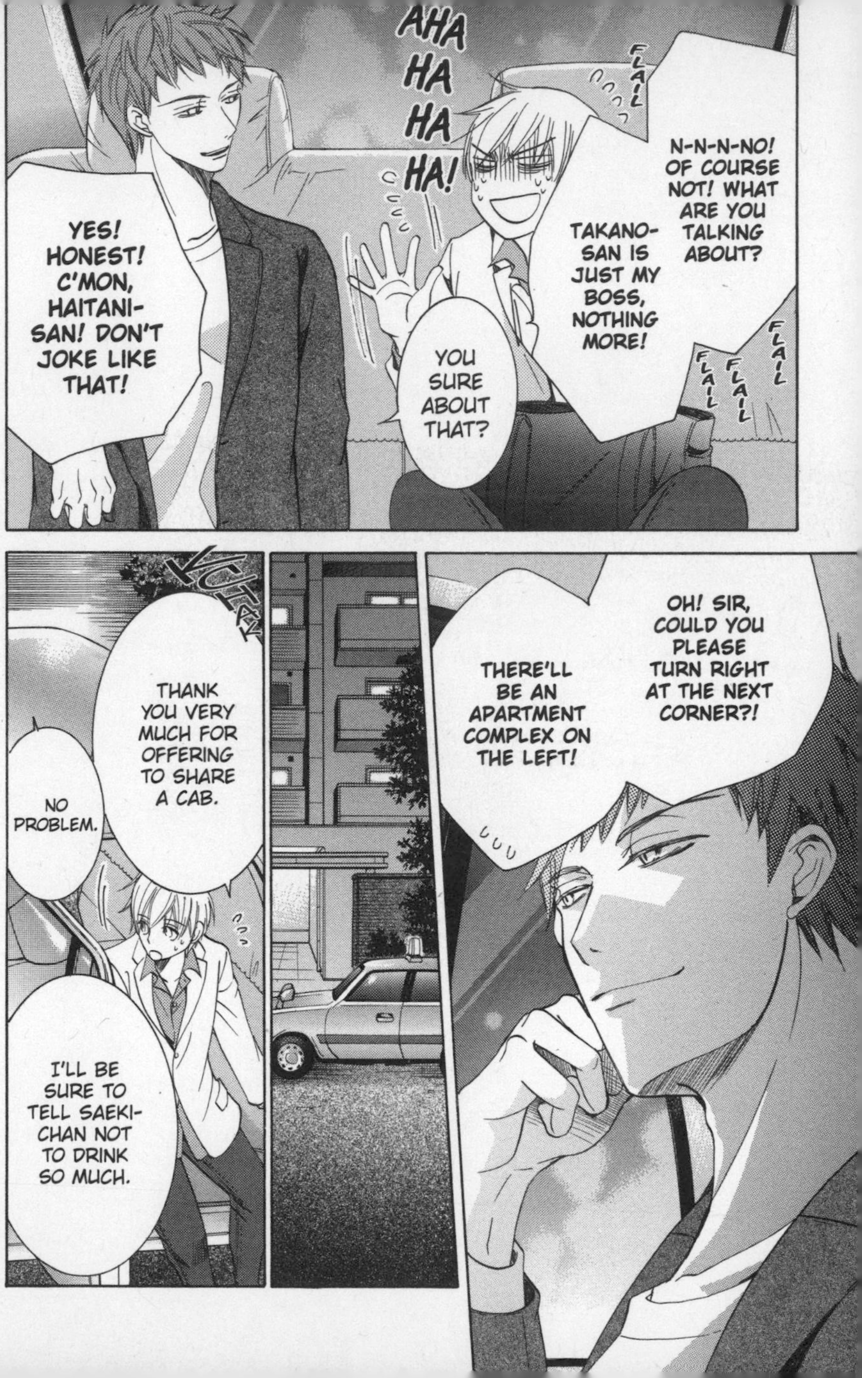

N-N-N-NO! OF COURSE NOT! WHAT ARE YOU TALKING ABOUT?
FLAIL
TAKANO-SAN IS JUST MY BOSS, NOTHING MORE!
FLAIL FLAIL FLAIL
AHA HA HA HA HA!
YOU SURE ABOUT THAT?
YES! HONEST! C'MON, HAITANI-SAN! DON'T JOKE LIKE THAT!
OH! SIR, COULD YOU PLEASE TURN RIGHT AT THE NEXT CORNER?!
THERE'LL BE AN APARTMENT COMPLEX ON THE LEFT!
KCHAK
THANK YOU VERY MUCH FOR OFFERING TO SHARE A CAB.
NO PROBLEM.
I'LL BE SURE TO TELL SAEKI-CHAN NOT TO DRINK SO MUCH.

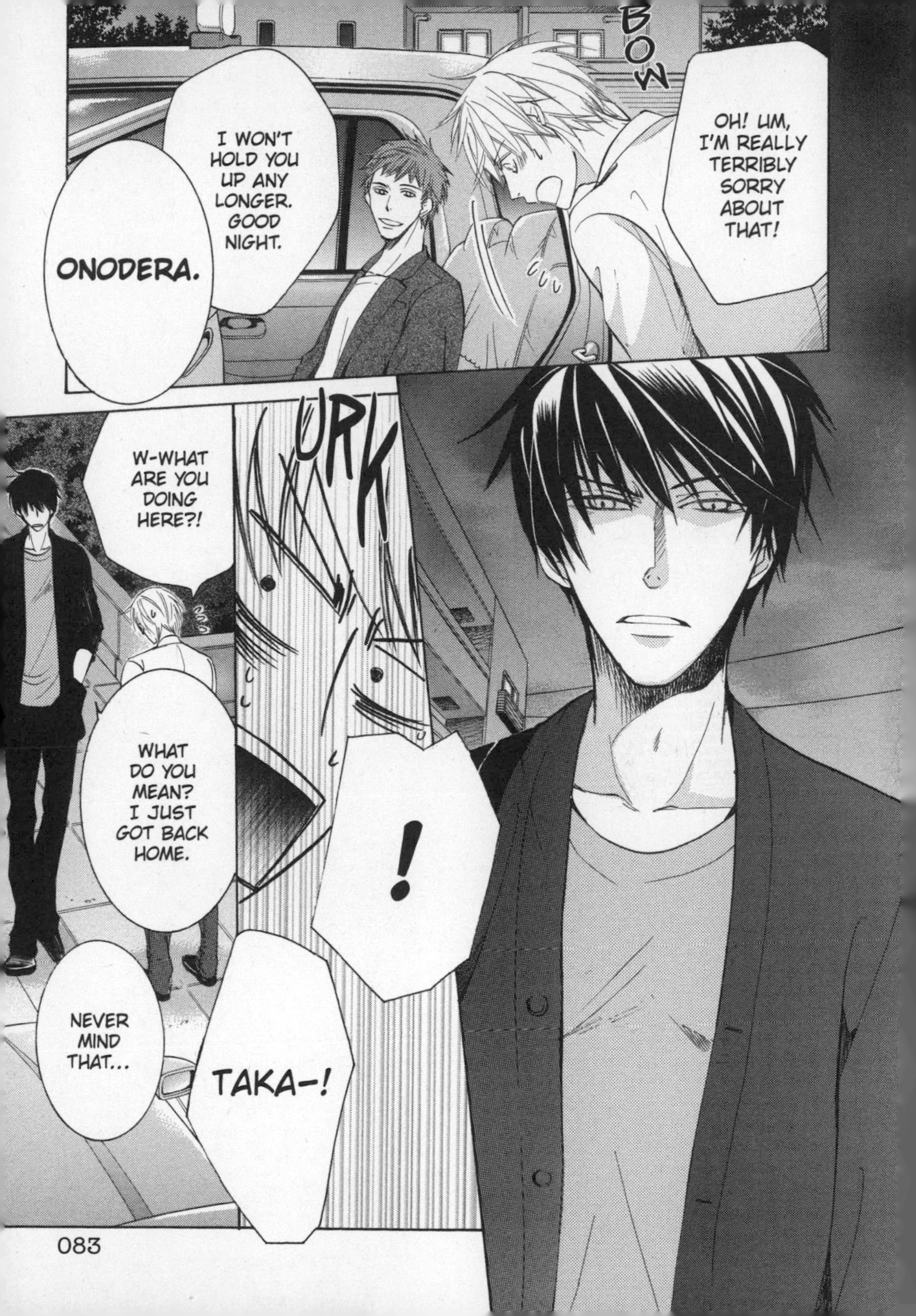
BOW
OH! UM, I'M REALLY TERRIBLY SORRY ABOUT THAT!
I WON'T HOLD YOU UP ANY LONGER. GOOD NIGHT.
ONODERA.
URK
!
TAKA-!
W-WHAT ARE YOU DOING HERE?!
WHAT DO YOU MEAN? I JUST GOT BACK HOME.
NEVER MIND THAT...

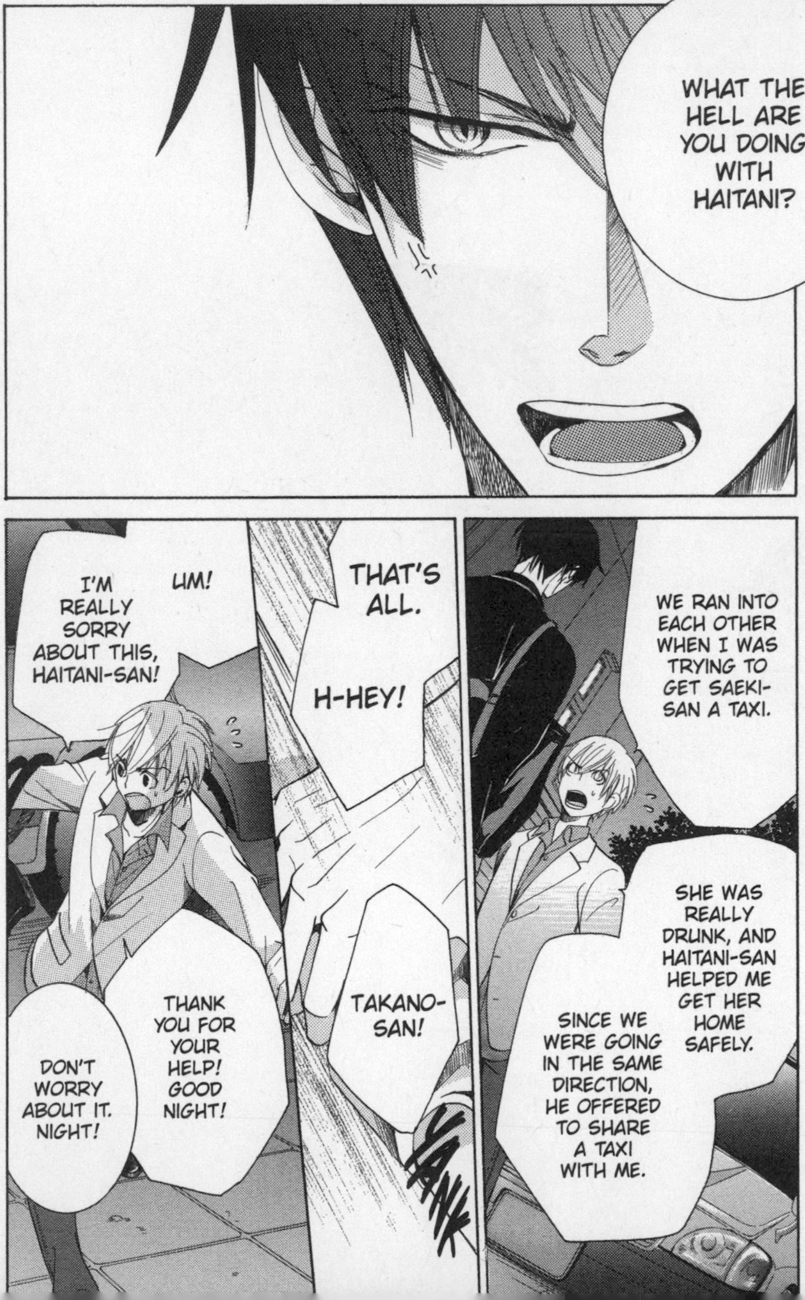
WHAT THE HELL ARE YOU DOING WITH HAITANI?
WE RAN INTO EACH OTHER WHEN I WAS TRYING TO GET SAEKI-SAN A TAXI.
SHE WAS REALLY DRUNK, AND HAITANI-SAN HELPED ME GET HER HOME SAFELY.
SINCE WE WERE GOING IN THE SAME DIRECTION, HE OFFERED TO SHARE A TAXI WITH ME.
THAT'S ALL.
H-HEY!
TAKANO-SAN!
YANK
UM!
I'M REALLY SORRY ABOUT THIS, HAITANI-SAN!
THANK YOU FOR YOUR HELP! GOOD NIGHT!
DON'T WORRY ABOUT IT. NIGHT!

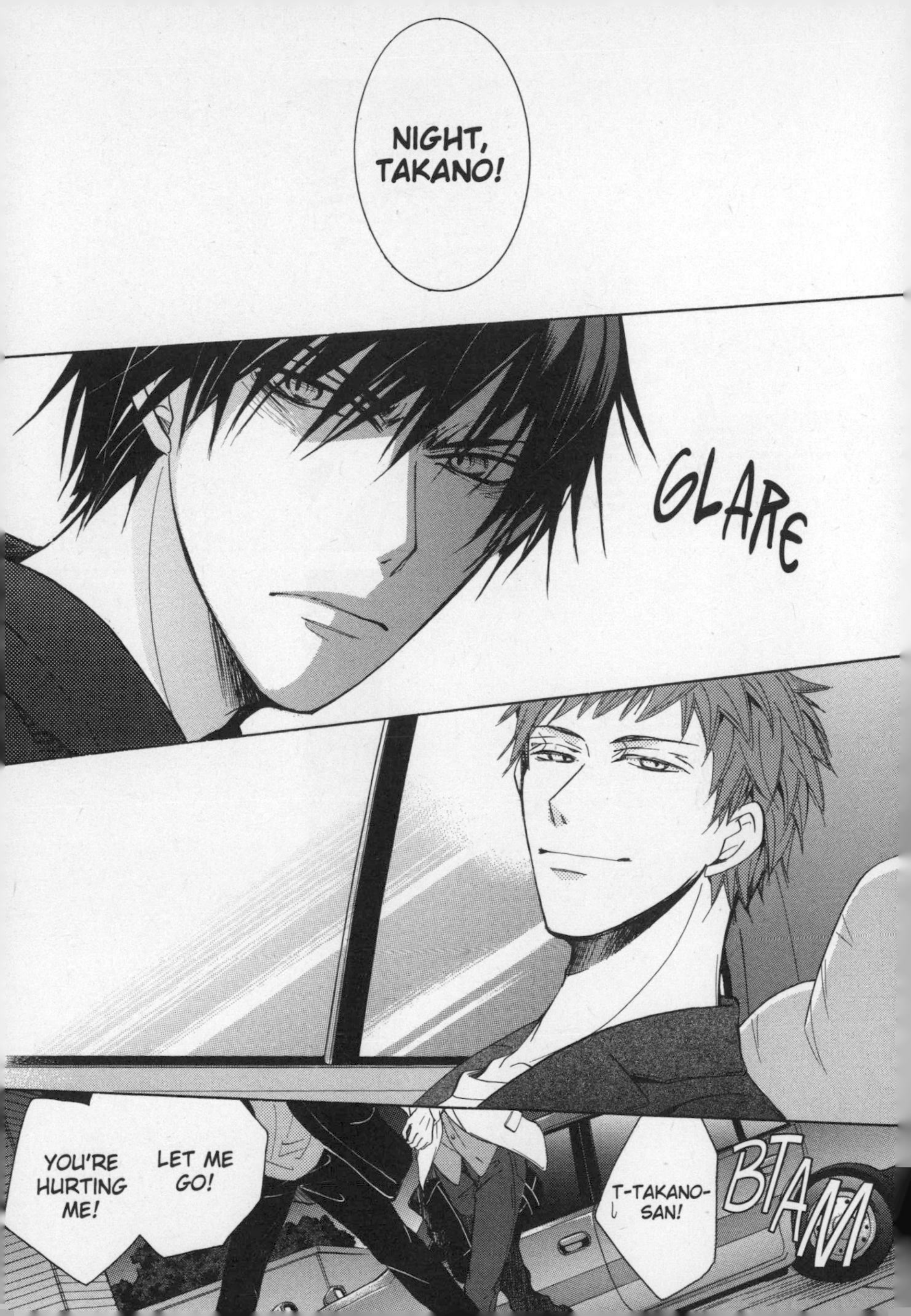
NIGHT, TAKANO!
GLARE
BTAM
T-TAKANO-SAN!
LET ME GO!
YOU'RE HURTING ME!

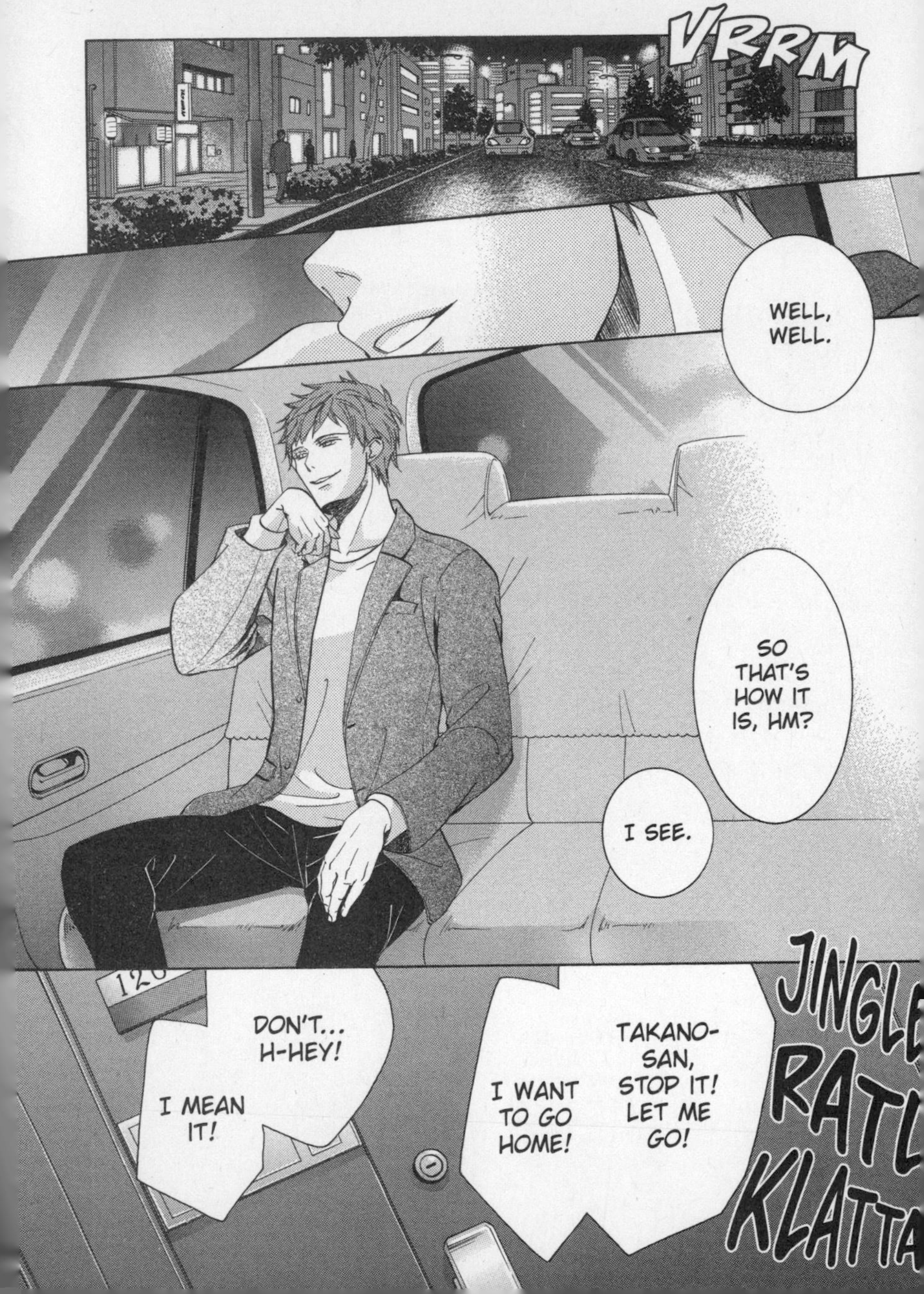
VRRM
WELL, WELL.
SO THAT'S HOW IT IS, HM?
I SEE.
JINGL
RATL
KLATTA
TAKANO-SAN, STOP IT! LET ME GO!
I WANT TO GO HOME!
DON'T... H-HEY!
I MEAN IT!

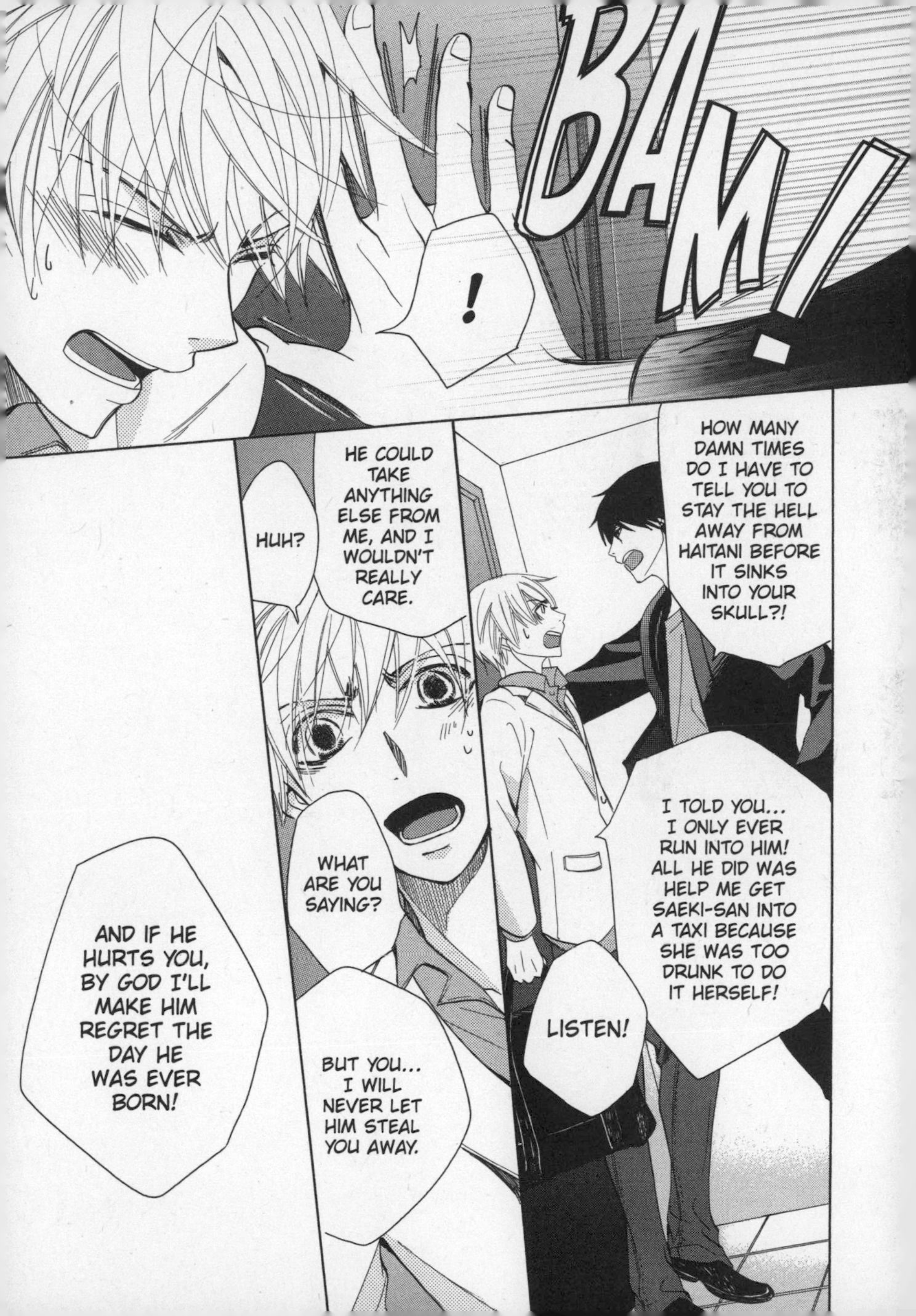
BAM!
!
HOW MANY DAMN TIMES DO I HAVE TO TELL YOU TO STAY THE HELL AWAY FROM HAITANI BEFORE IT SINKS INTO YOUR SKULL?!
I TOLD YOU... I ONLY EVER RUN INTO HIM! ALL HE DID WAS HELP ME GET SAEKI-SAN INTO A TAXI BECAUSE SHE WAS TOO DRUNK TO DO IT HERSELF!
LISTEN!
HE COULD TAKE ANYTHING ELSE FROM ME, AND I WOULDN'T REALLY CARE.
HUH?
WHAT ARE YOU SAYING?
BUT YOU... I WILL NEVER LET HIM STEAL YOU AWAY.
AND IF HE HURTS YOU, BY GOD I'LL MAKE HIM REGRET THE DAY HE WAS EVER BORN!

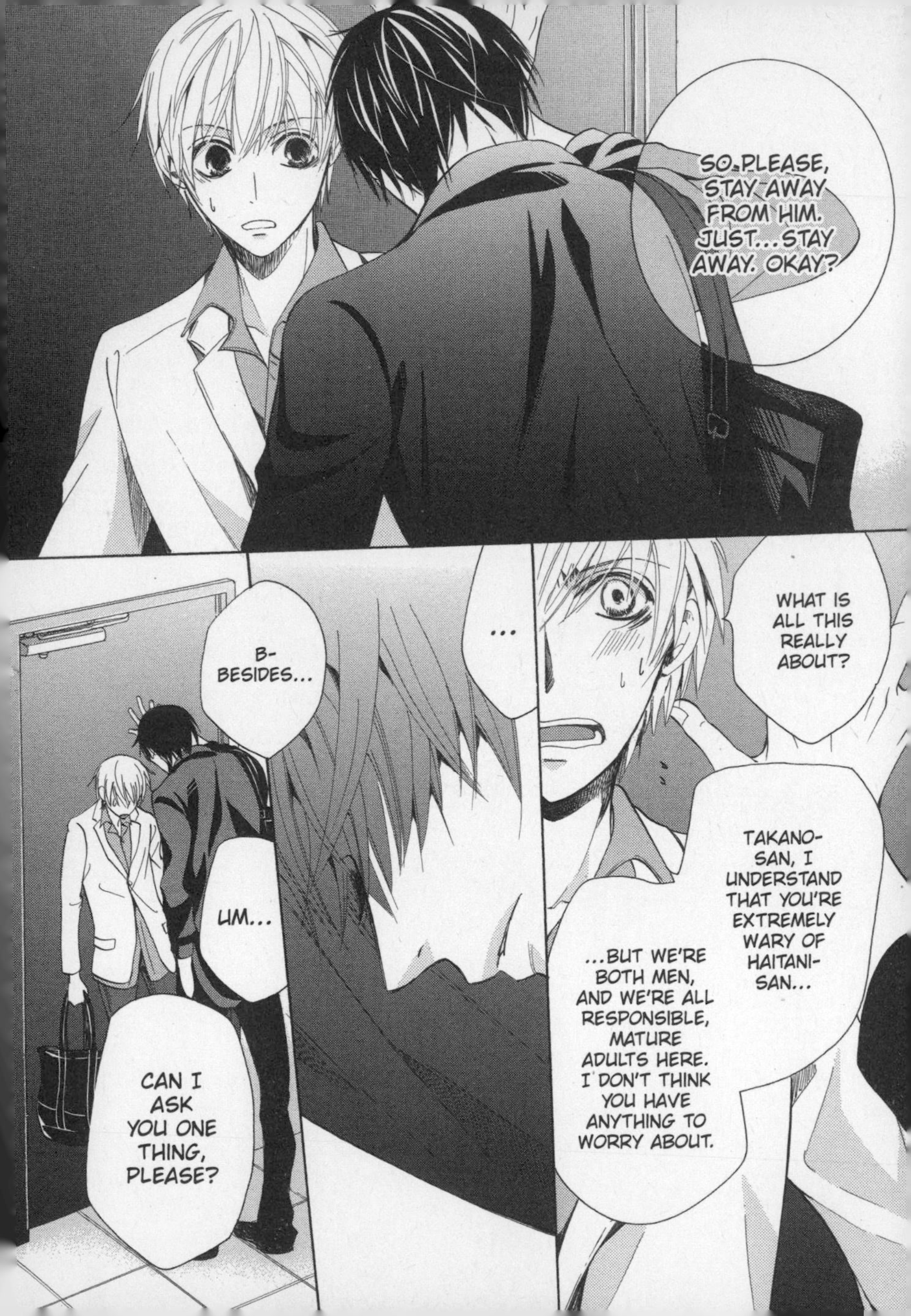
SO PLEASE, STAY AWAY FROM HIM. JUST... STAY AWAY. OKAY?
WHAT IS ALL THIS REALLY ABOUT?
TAKANO-SAN, I UNDERSTAND THAT YOU'RE EXTREMELY WARY OF HAITANI-SAN...
...BUT WE'RE BOTH MEN, AND WE'RE ALL RESPONSIBLE, MATURE ADULTS HERE. I DON'T THINK YOU HAVE ANYTHING TO WORRY ABOUT.
...
B-BESIDES...
UM...
CAN I ASK YOU ONE THING, PLEASE?

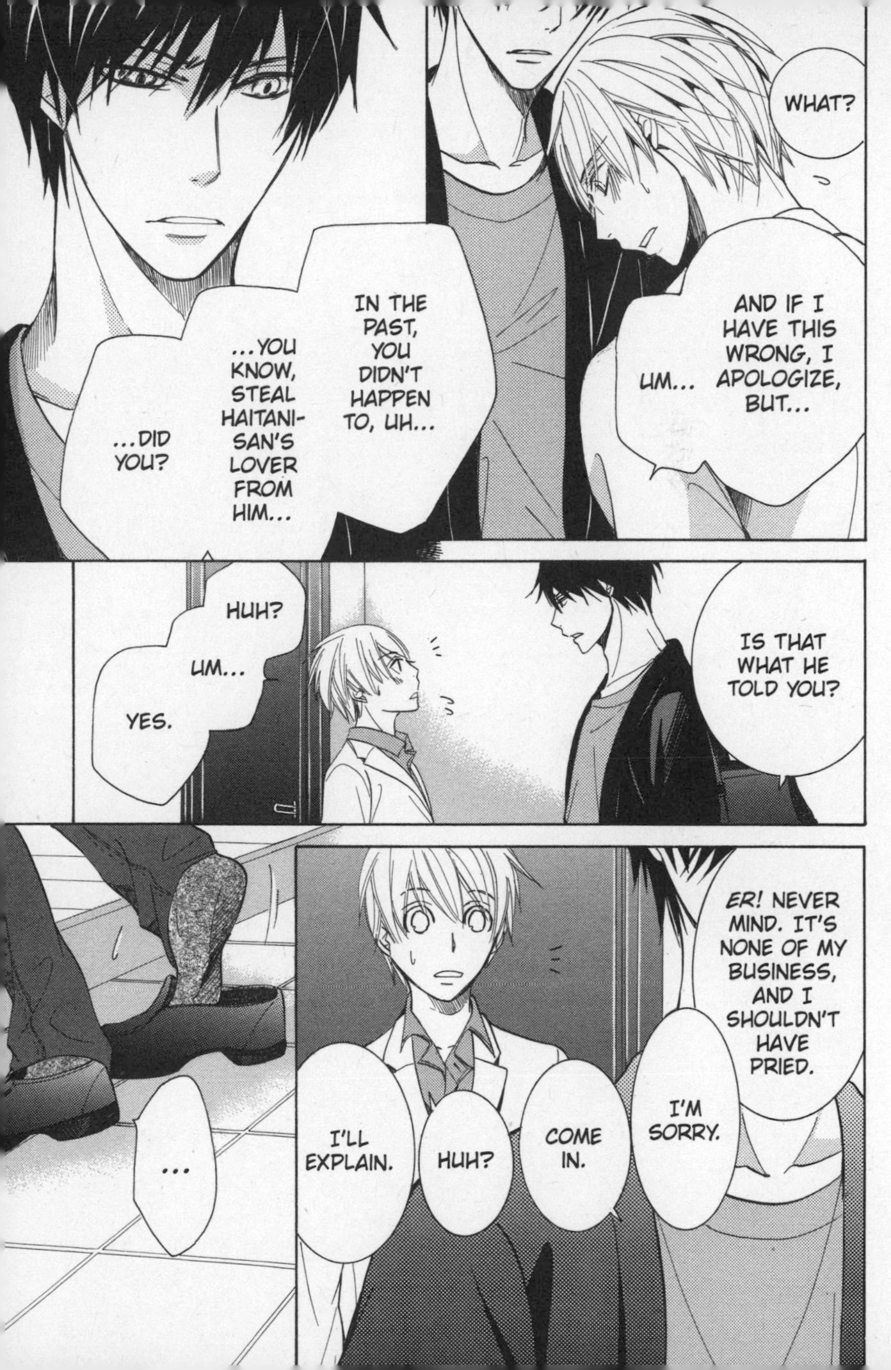
WHAT?
UM...
AND IF I HAVE THIS WRONG, I APOLOGIZE, BUT...
IN THE PAST, YOU DIDN'T HAPPEN TO, UH...
...YOU KNOW, STEAL HAITANI-SAN'S LOVER FROM HIM...
...DID YOU?
IS THAT WHAT HE TOLD YOU?
HUH?
UM...
YES.
ER! NEVER MIND. IT'S NONE OF MY BUSINESS, AND I SHOULDN'T HAVE PRIED.
I'M SORRY.
COME IN.
HUH?
I'LL EXPLAIN.
...

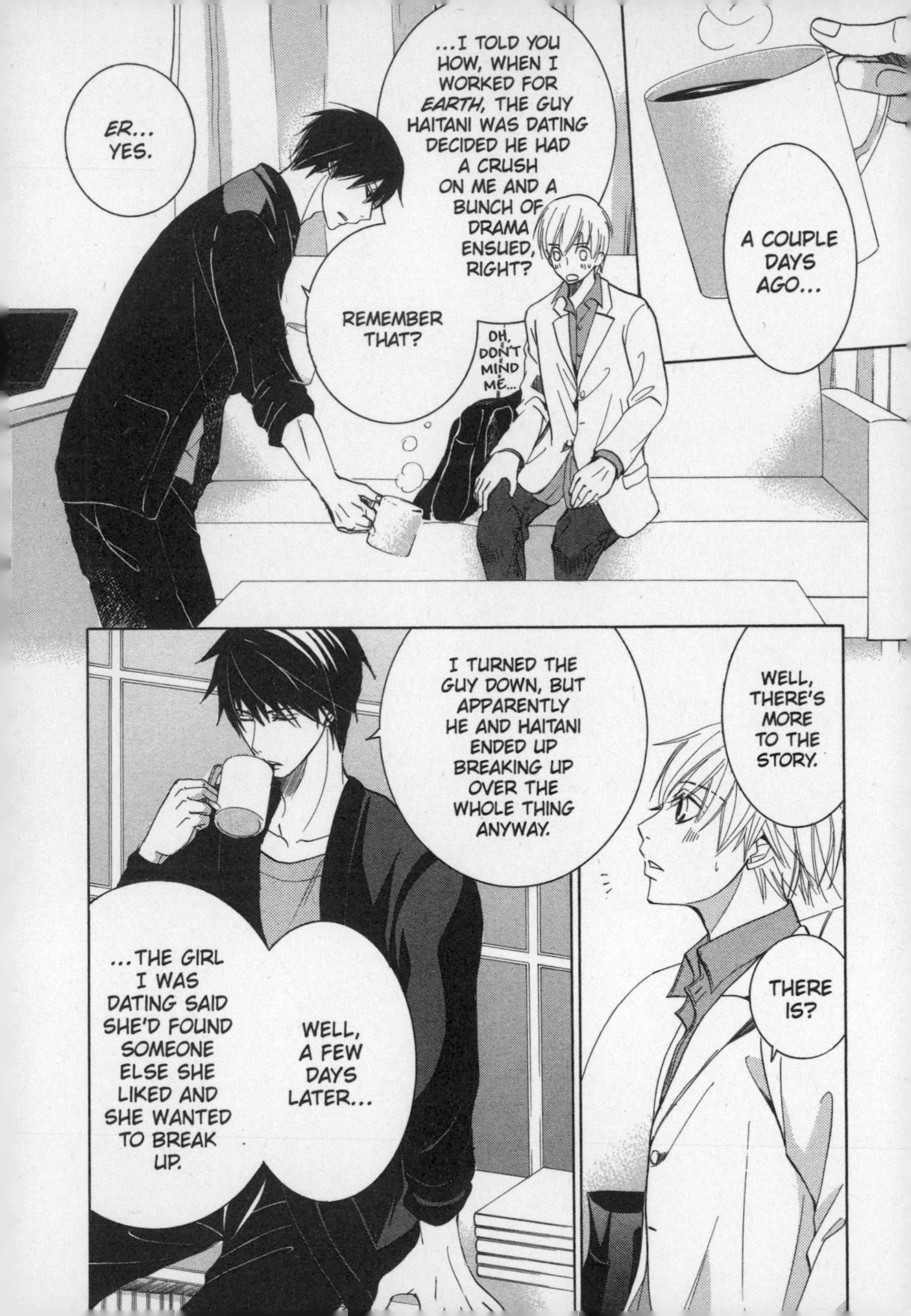
A COUPLE DAYS AGO...
...I TOLD YOU HOW, WHEN I WORKED FOR *EARTH*, THE GUY HAITANI WAS DATING DECIDED HE HAD A CRUSH ON ME AND A BUNCH OF DRAMA ENSUED, RIGHT?
REMEMBER THAT?
ER... YES.
OH, DON'T MIND ME...
I TURNED THE GUY DOWN, BUT APPARENTLY HE AND HAITANI ENDED UP BREAKING UP OVER THE WHOLE THING ANYWAY.
WELL, THERE'S MORE TO THE STORY.
THERE IS?
WELL, A FEW DAYS LATER...
...THE GIRL I WAS DATING SAID SHE'D FOUND SOMEONE ELSE SHE LIKED AND SHE WANTED TO BREAK UP.

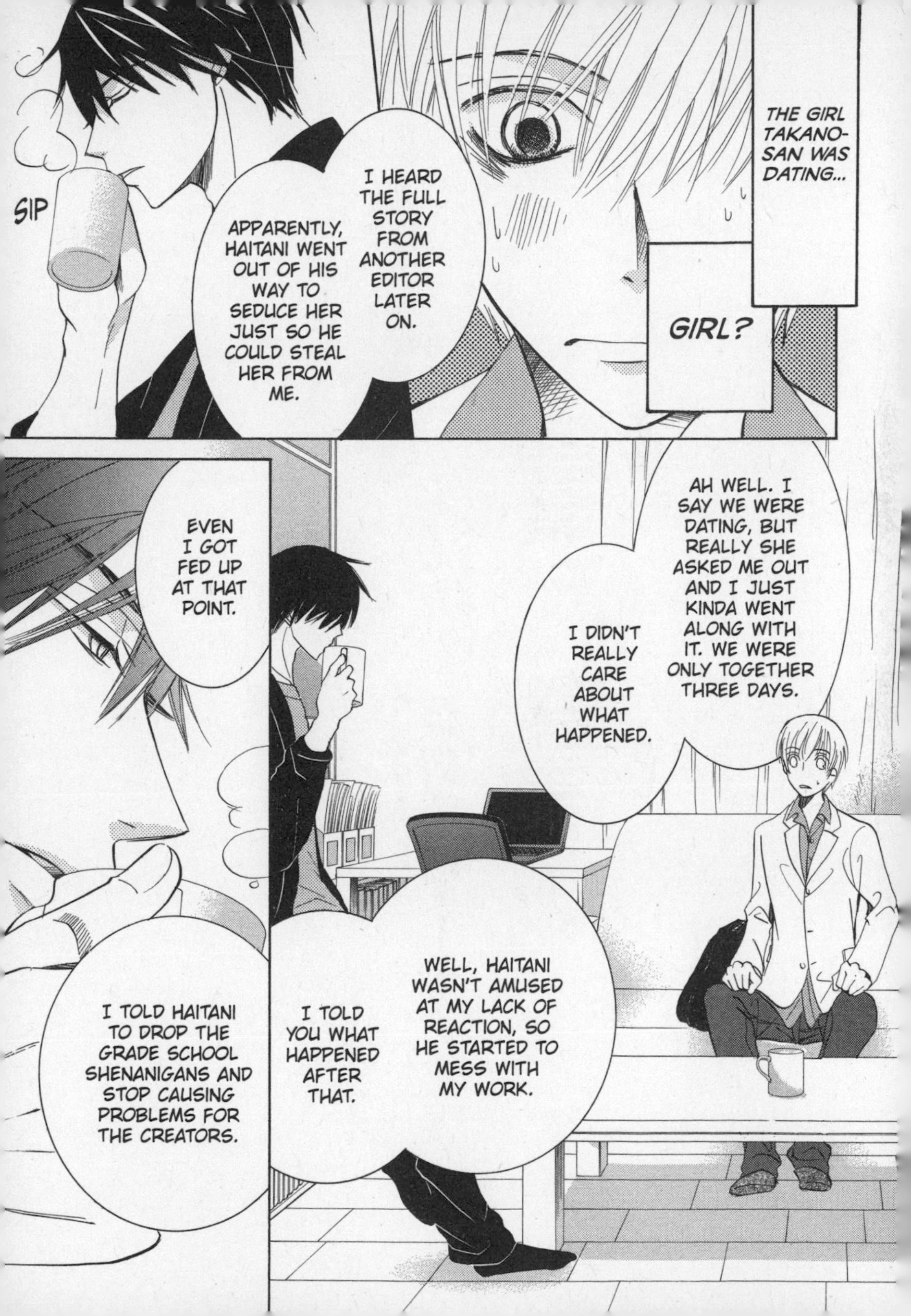
THE GIRL TAKANO-SAN WAS DATING...
GIRL?
I HEARD THE FULL STORY FROM ANOTHER EDITOR LATER ON.
APPARENTLY, HAITANI WENT OUT OF HIS WAY TO SEDUCE HER JUST SO HE COULD STEAL HER FROM ME.
SIP
AH WELL. I SAY WE WERE DATING, BUT REALLY SHE ASKED ME OUT AND I JUST KINDA WENT ALONG WITH IT. WE WERE ONLY TOGETHER THREE DAYS.
I DIDN'T REALLY CARE ABOUT WHAT HAPPENED.
WELL, HAITANI WASN'T AMUSED AT MY LACK OF REACTION, SO HE STARTED TO MESS WITH MY WORK.
I TOLD YOU WHAT HAPPENED AFTER THAT.
EVEN I GOT FED UP AT THAT POINT.
I TOLD HAITANI TO DROP THE GRADE SCHOOL SHENANIGANS AND STOP CAUSING PROBLEMS FOR THE CREATORS.

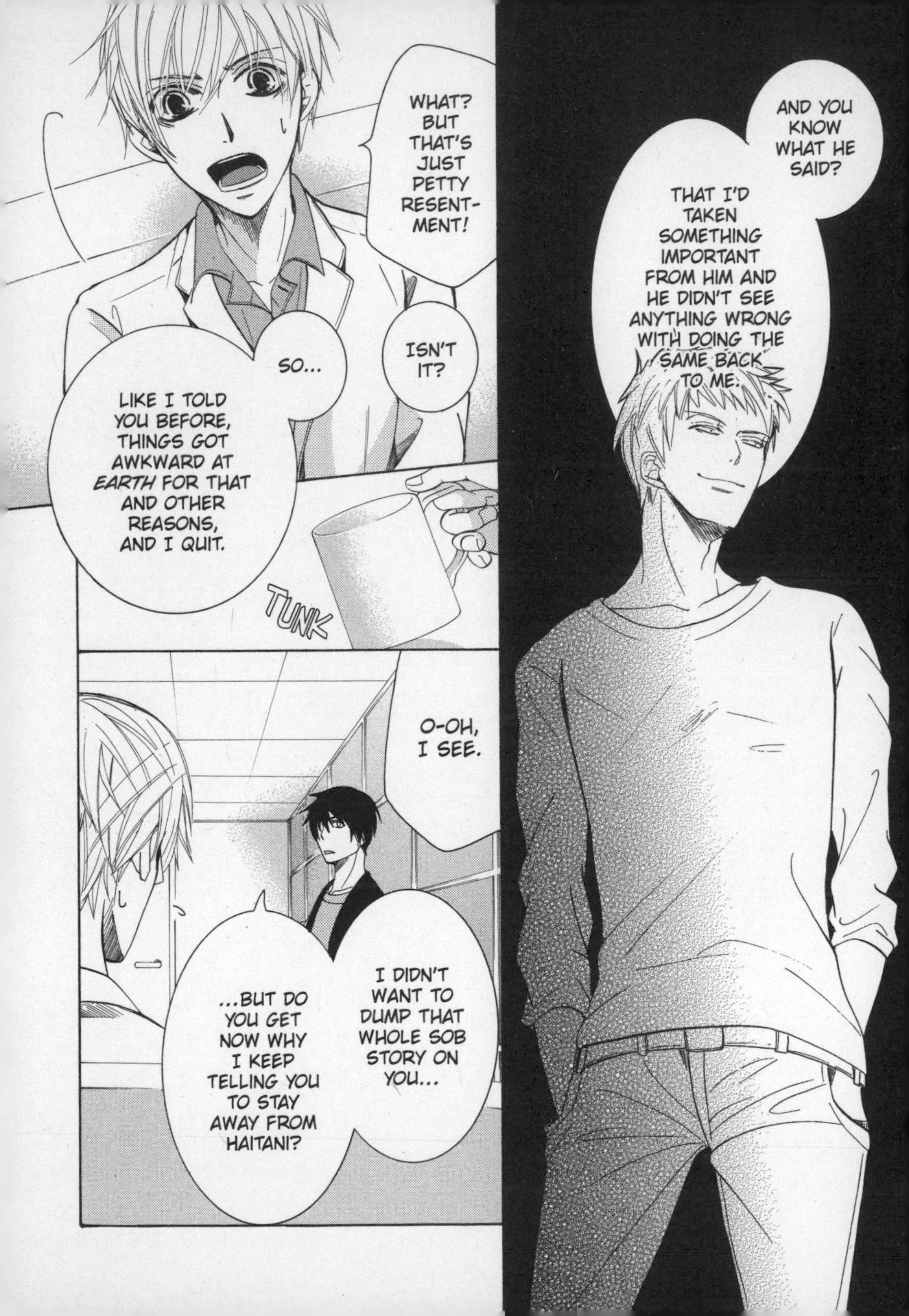
AND YOU KNOW WHAT HE SAID?
THAT I'D TAKEN SOMETHING IMPORTANT FROM HIM AND HE DIDN'T SEE ANYTHING WRONG WITH DOING THE SAME BACK TO ME.
WHAT? BUT THAT'S JUST PETTY RESENT-MENT!
ISN'T IT?
SO...
LIKE I TOLD YOU BEFORE, THINGS GOT AWKWARD AT *EARTH* FOR THAT AND OTHER REASONS, AND I QUIT.
TUNK
O-OH, I SEE.
I DIDN'T WANT TO DUMP THAT WHOLE SOB STORY ON YOU...
...BUT DO YOU GET NOW WHY I KEEP TELLING YOU TO STAY AWAY FROM HAITANI?

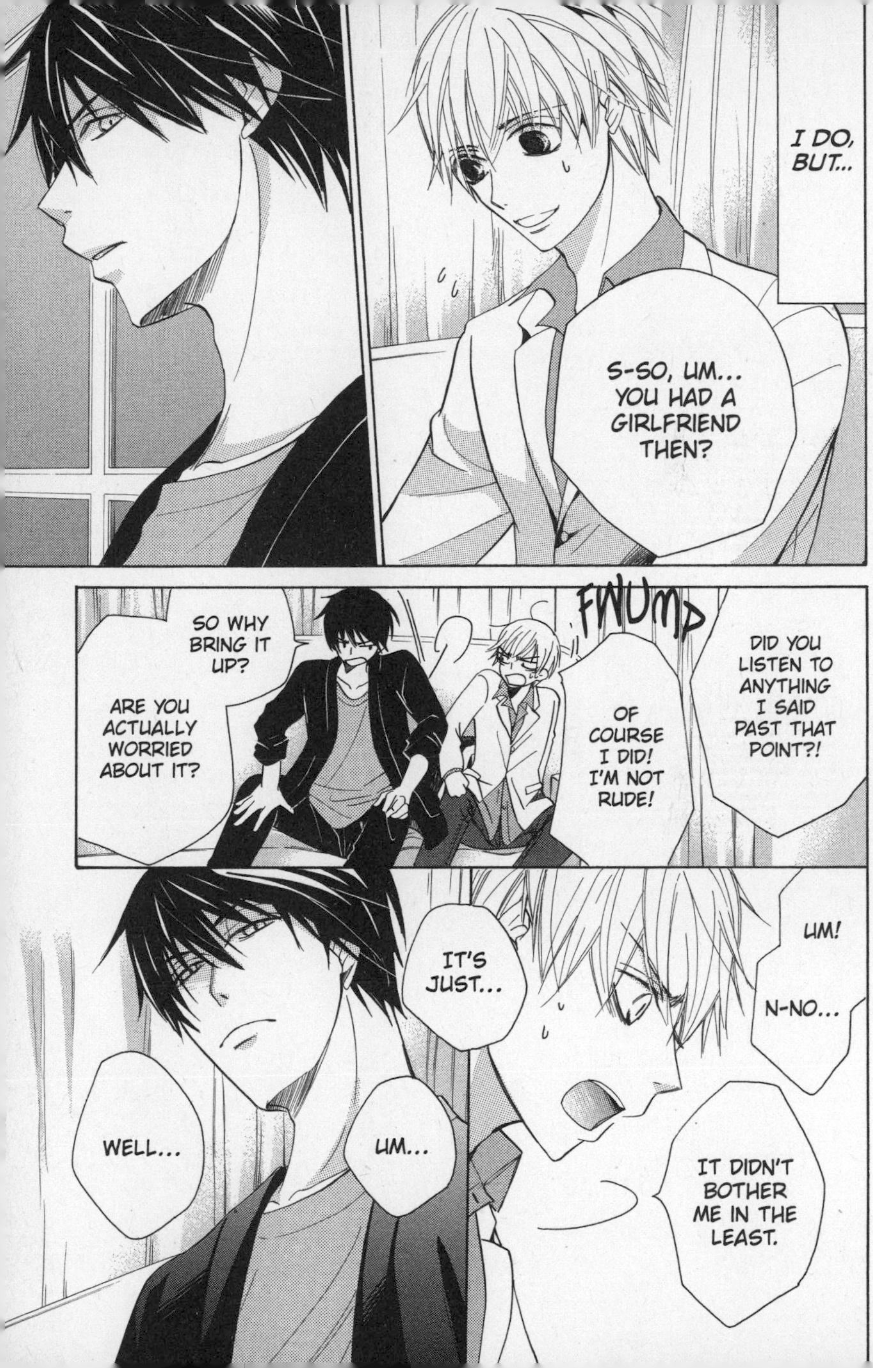
I DO, BUT...
S-SO, UM... YOU HAD A GIRLFRIEND THEN?
DID YOU LISTEN TO ANYTHING I SAID PAST THAT POINT?!
FWUMP
OF COURSE I DID! I'M NOT RUDE!
SO WHY BRING IT UP?
ARE YOU ACTUALLY WORRIED ABOUT IT?
UM!
N-NO...
IT'S JUST...
IT DIDN'T BOTHER ME IN THE LEAST.
UM...
WELL...

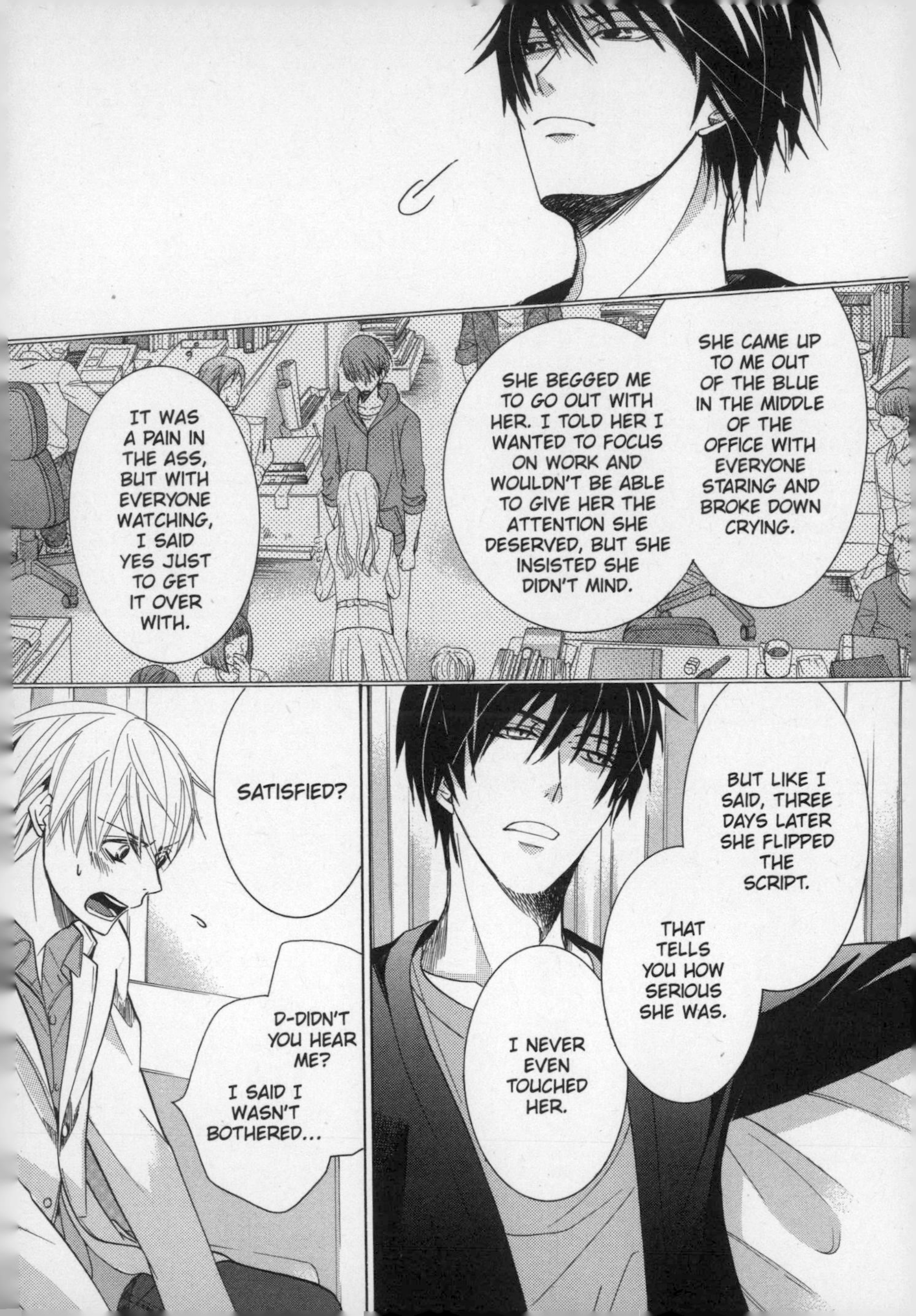
SHE CAME UP TO ME OUT OF THE BLUE IN THE MIDDLE OF THE OFFICE WITH EVERYONE STARING AND BROKE DOWN CRYING.
SHE BEGGED ME TO GO OUT WITH HER. I TOLD HER I WANTED TO FOCUS ON WORK AND WOULDN'T BE ABLE TO GIVE HER THE ATTENTION SHE DESERVED, BUT SHE INSISTED SHE DIDN'T MIND.
IT WAS A PAIN IN THE ASS, BUT WITH EVERYONE WATCHING, I SAID YES JUST TO GET IT OVER WITH.
BUT LIKE I SAID, THREE DAYS LATER SHE FLIPPED THE SCRIPT.
THAT TELLS YOU HOW SERIOUS SHE WAS.
I NEVER EVEN TOUCHED HER.
SATISFIED?
D-DIDN'T YOU HEAR ME?
I SAID I WASN'T BOTHERED...

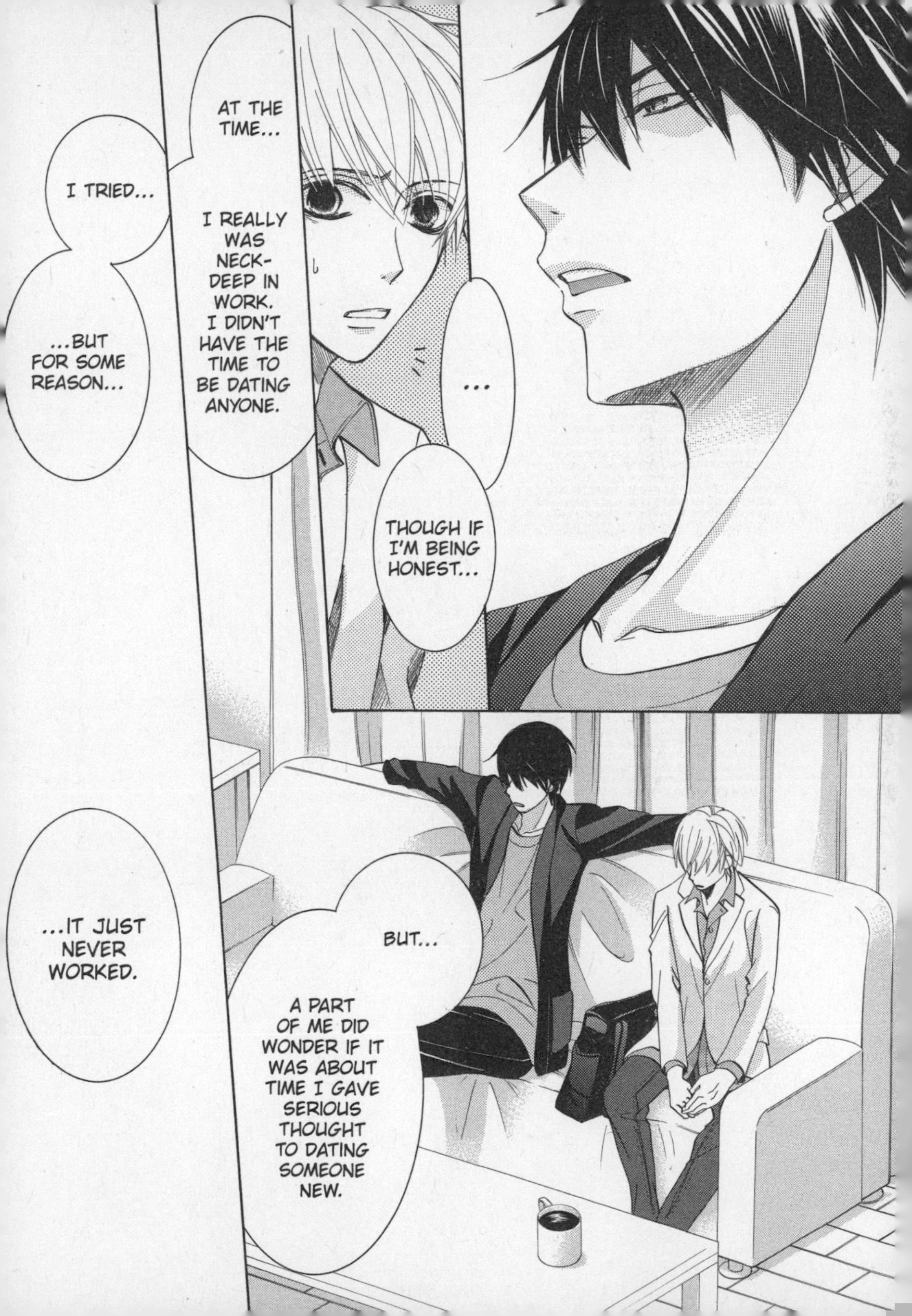
...
THOUGH IF I'M BEING HONEST...
AT THE TIME...
I REALLY WAS NECK-DEEP IN WORK. I DIDN'T HAVE THE TIME TO BE DATING ANYONE.
BUT...
A PART OF ME DID WONDER IF IT WAS ABOUT TIME I GAVE SERIOUS THOUGHT TO DATING SOMEONE NEW.
I TRIED...
...BUT FOR SOME REASON...
...IT JUST NEVER WORKED.

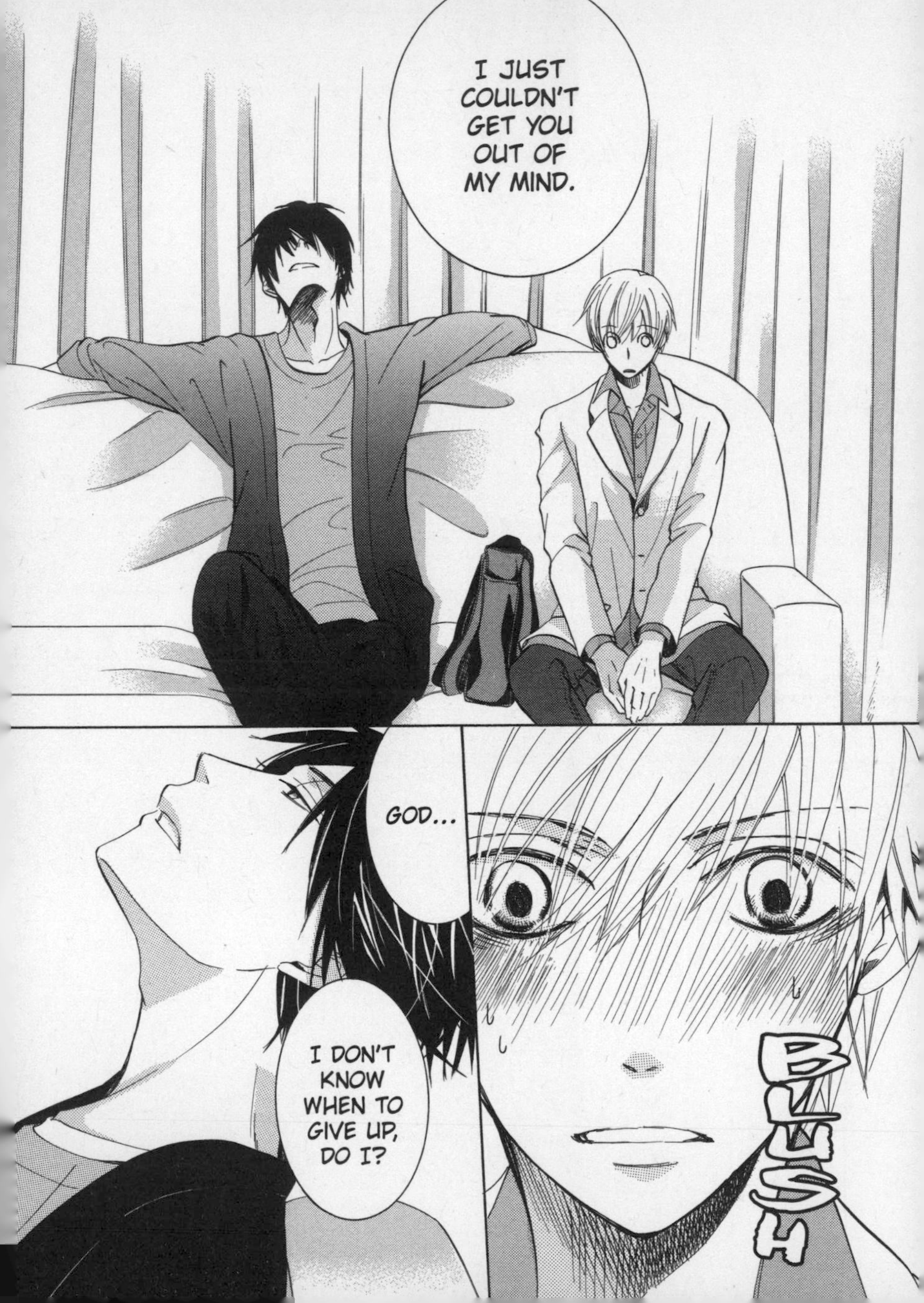
I JUST COULDN'T GET YOU OUT OF MY MIND.
GOD...
I DON'T KNOW WHEN TO GIVE UP, DO I?
BLUSH

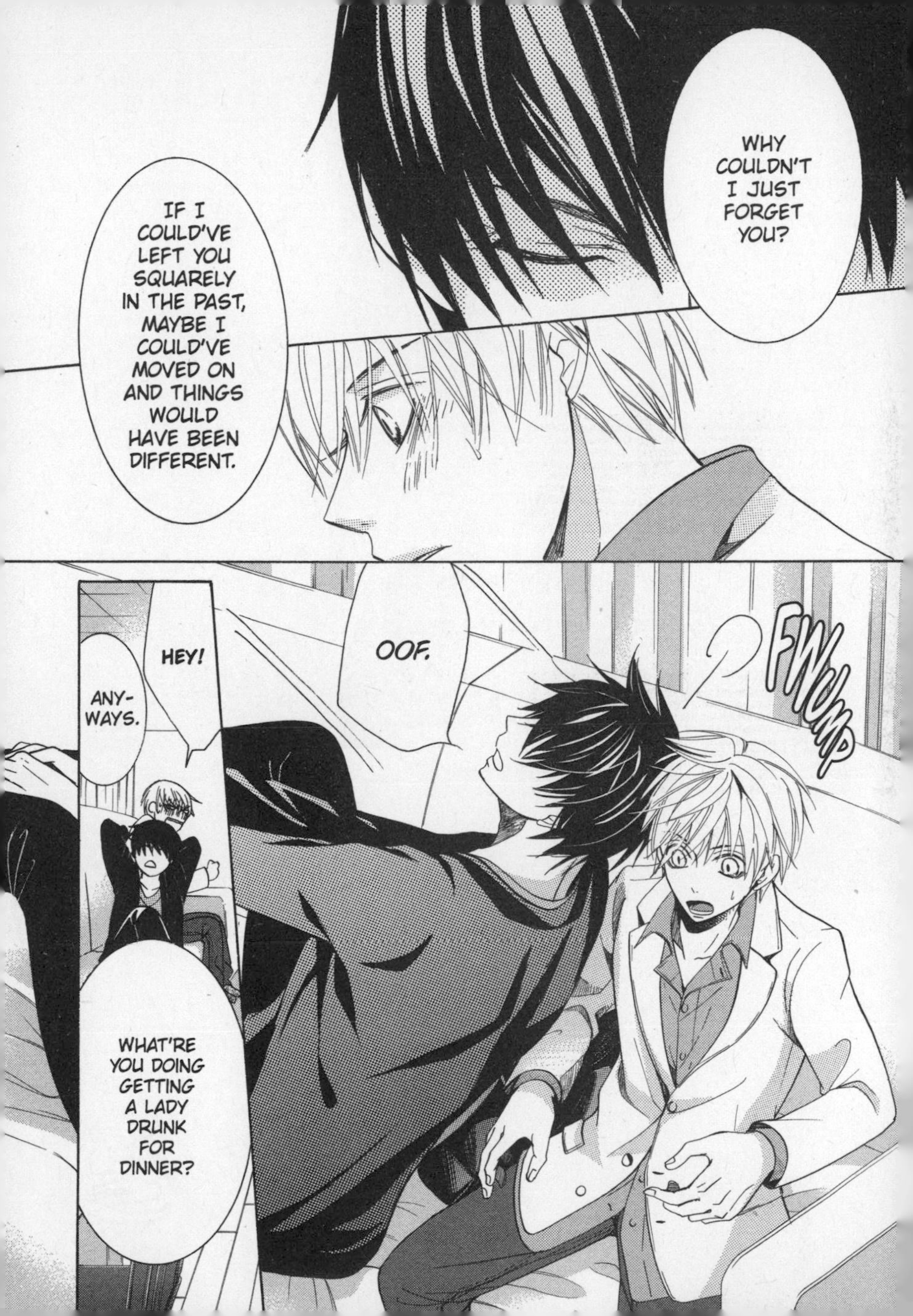
WHY COULDN'T I JUST FORGET YOU?
IF I COULD'VE LEFT YOU SQUARELY IN THE PAST, MAYBE I COULD'VE MOVED ON AND THINGS WOULD HAVE BEEN DIFFERENT.
FWUMP
OOF.
HEY!
ANY-WAYS.
WHAT'RE YOU DOING GETTING A LADY DRUNK FOR DINNER?

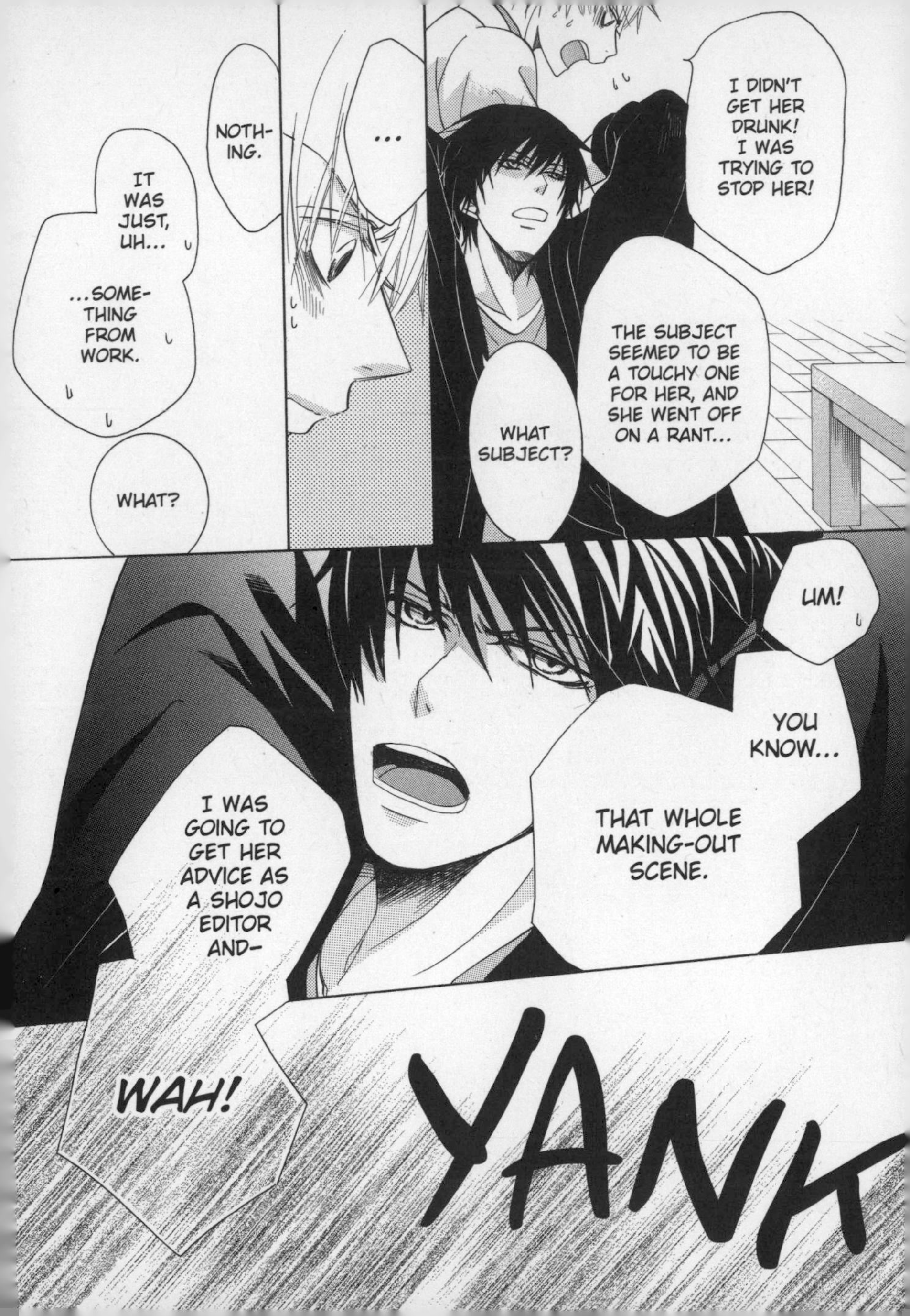
I DIDN'T GET HER DRUNK! I WAS TRYING TO STOP HER!
THE SUBJECT SEEMED TO BE A TOUCHY ONE FOR HER, AND SHE WENT OFF ON A RANT...
WHAT SUBJECT?
...
NOTH-ING.
IT WAS JUST, UH...
...SOME-THING FROM WORK.
WHAT?
UM!
YOU KNOW...
THAT WHOLE MAKING-OUT SCENE.
I WAS GOING TO GET HER ADVICE AS A SHOJO EDITOR AND-
YANK
WAH!

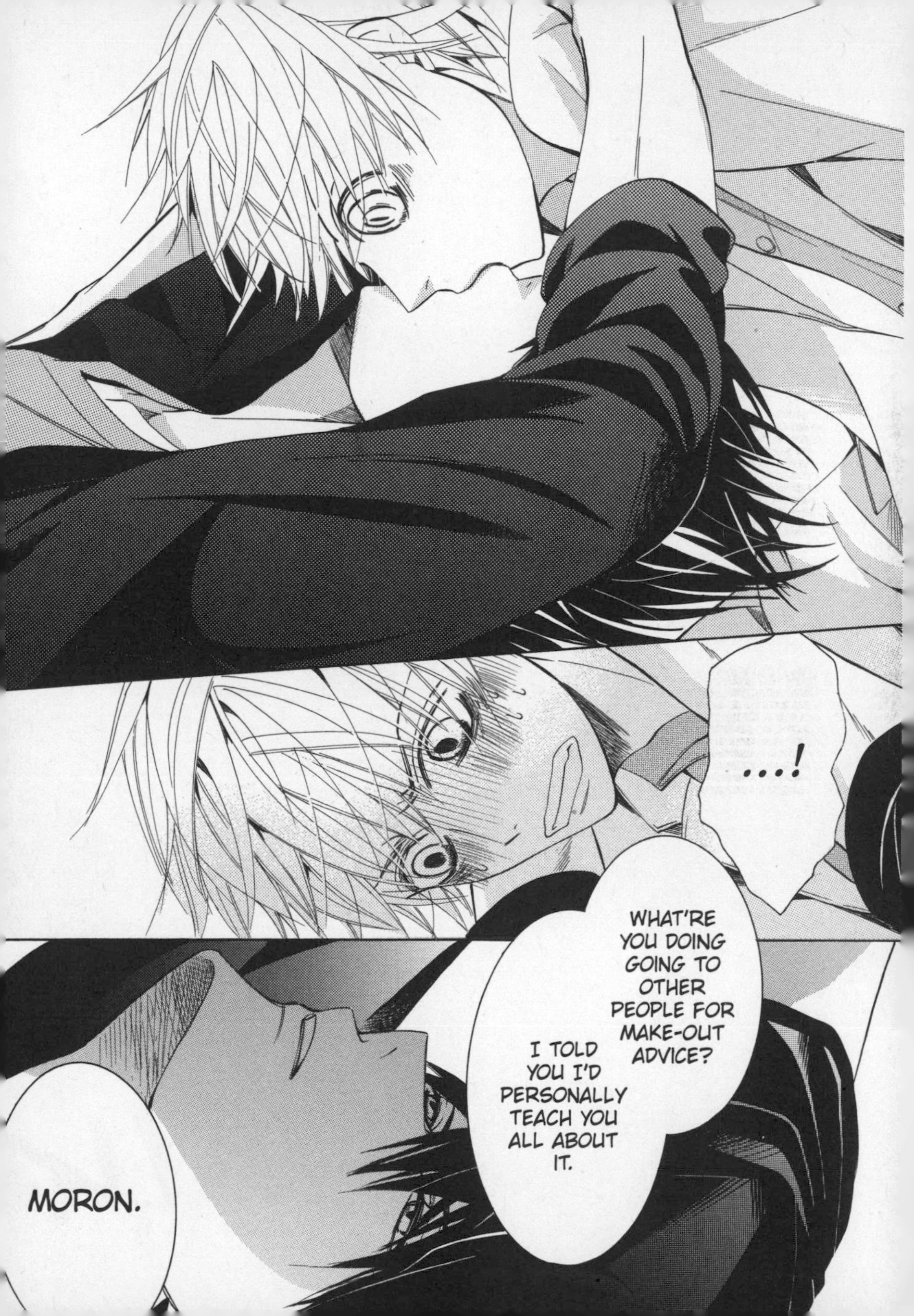
...!
WHAT'RE YOU DOING GOING TO OTHER PEOPLE FOR MAKE-OUT ADVICE?
I TOLD YOU I'D PERSONALLY TEACH YOU ALL ABOUT IT.
MORON.

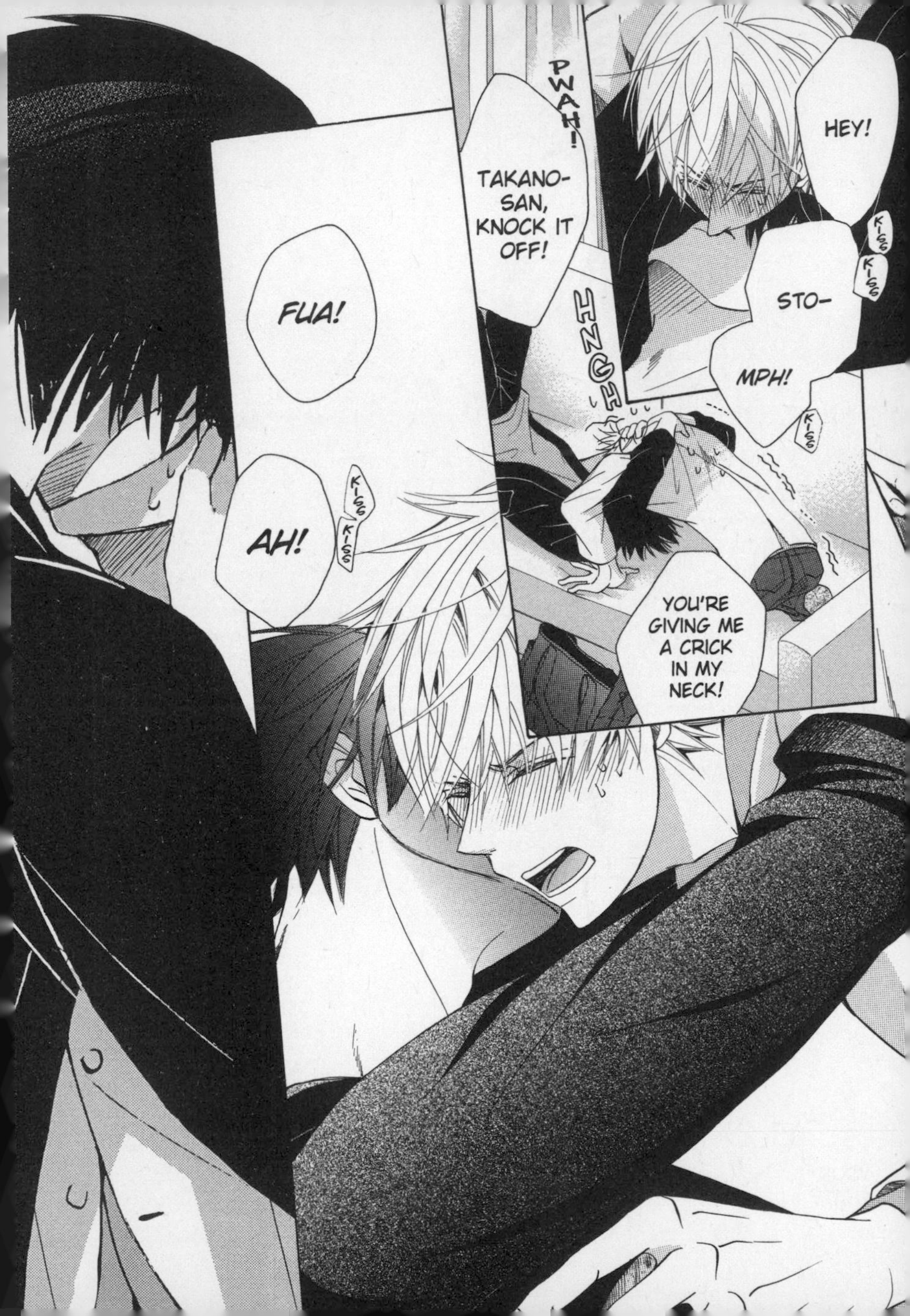
HEY!
KISS
KISS
STO-
MPH!
KISS
PWAH!
TAKANO-SAN, KNOCK IT OFF!
HNGH
YOU'RE GIVING ME A CRICK IN MY NECK!
FUA!
AH!
KISS
KISS

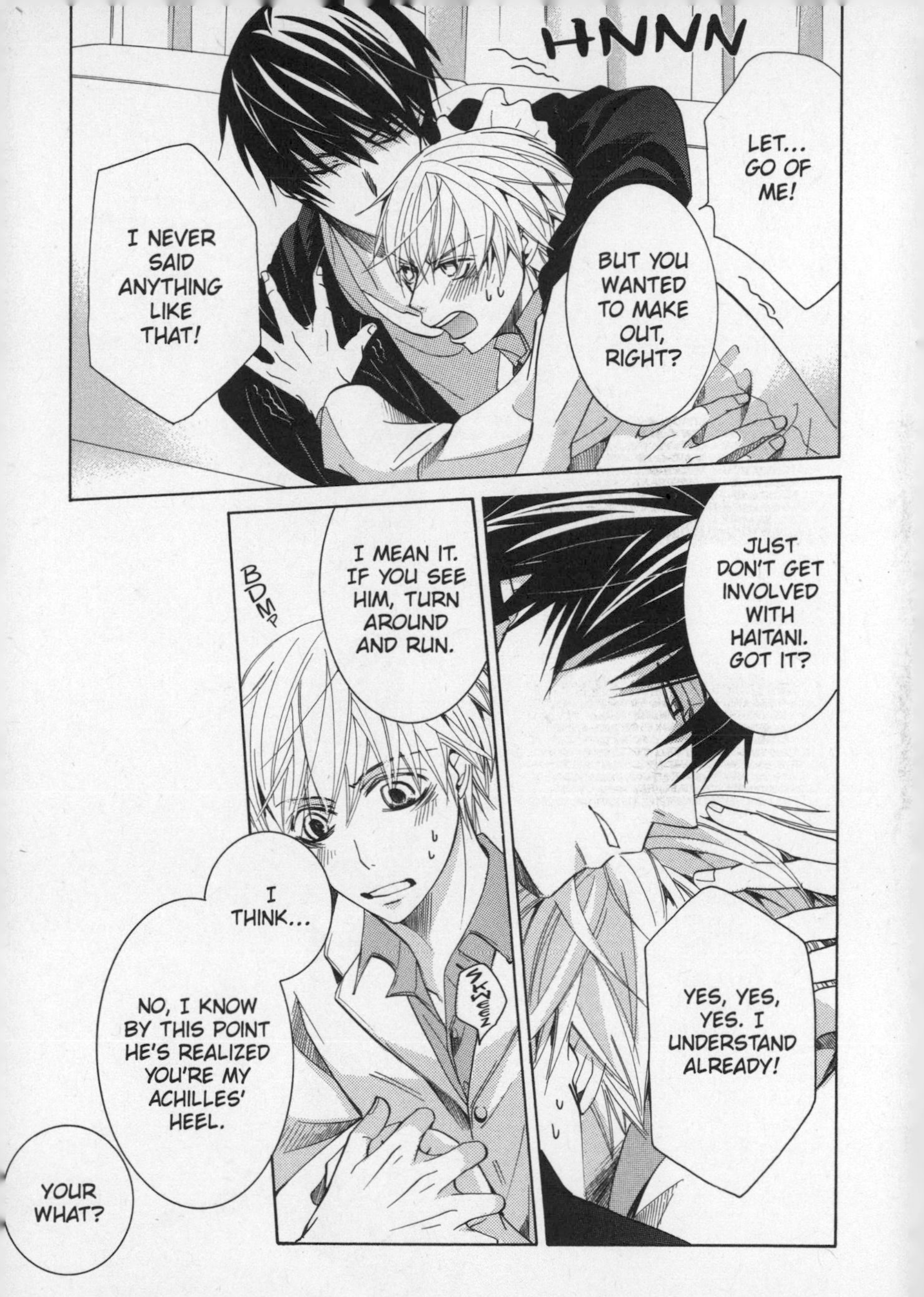
HNNN
LET... GO OF ME!
BUT YOU WANTED TO MAKE OUT, RIGHT?
I NEVER SAID ANYTHING LIKE THAT!
JUST DON'T GET INVOLVED WITH HAITANI. GOT IT?
YES, YES, YES. I UNDERSTAND ALREADY!
I MEAN IT. IF YOU SEE HIM, TURN AROUND AND RUN.
BDMP
I THINK...
NO, I KNOW BY THIS POINT HE'S REALIZED YOU'RE MY ACHILLES' HEEL.
SKWEEZ
YOUR WHAT?

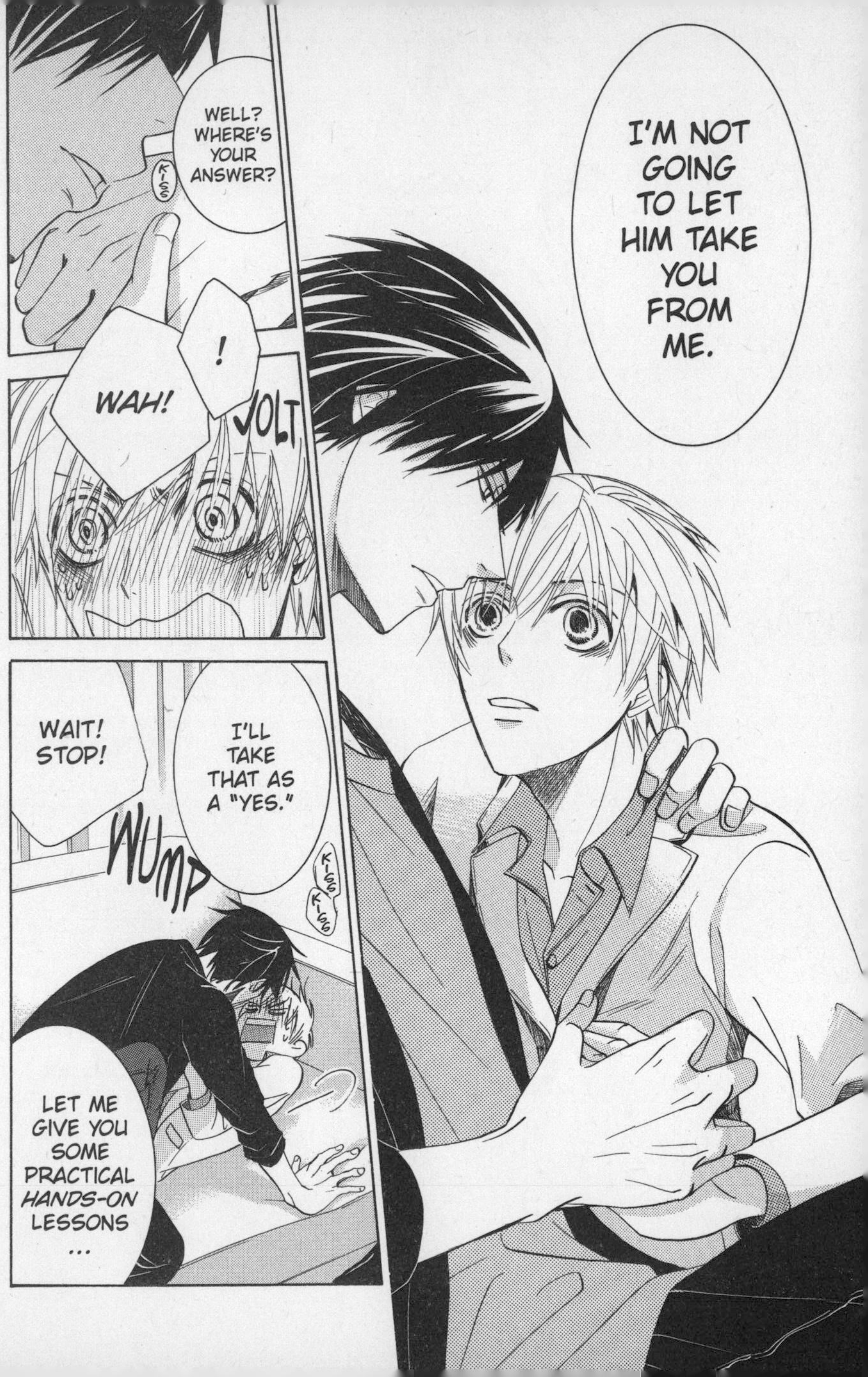
I'M NOT GOING TO LET HIM TAKE YOU FROM ME.
WELL? WHERE'S YOUR ANSWER?
KISS
!
JOLT
WAH!
I'LL TAKE THAT AS A "YES."
WAIT! STOP!
KISS
KISS
WUMP
LET ME GIVE YOU SOME PRACTICAL *HANDS-ON* LESSONS ...

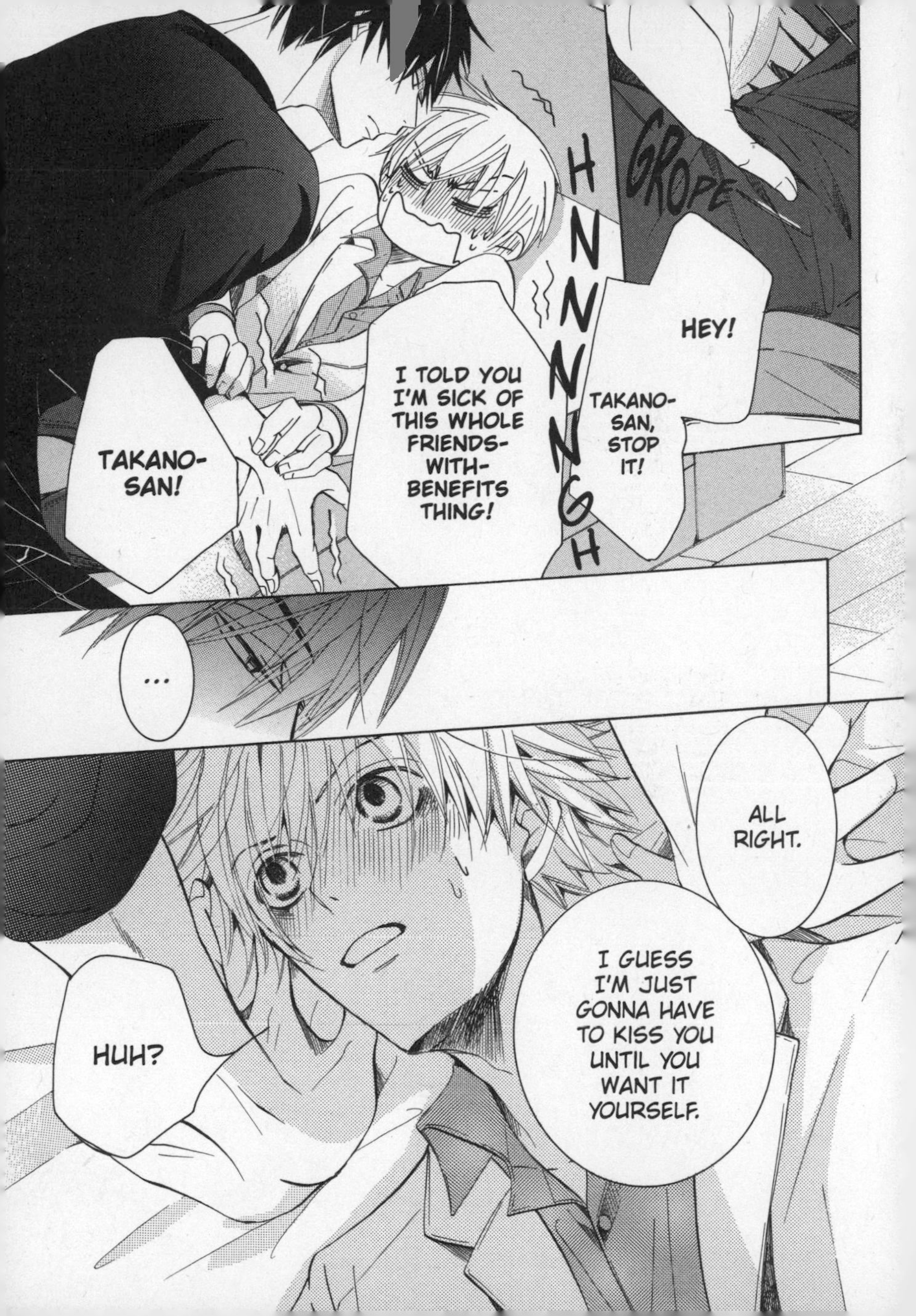
GROPE
HEY!
TAKANO-SAN, STOP IT!
HNNNNNGH
I TOLD YOU I'M SICK OF THIS WHOLE FRIENDS-WITH-BENEFITS THING!
TAKANO-SAN!
...
ALL RIGHT.
I GUESS I'M JUST GONNA HAVE TO KISS YOU UNTIL YOU WANT IT YOURSELF.
HUH?

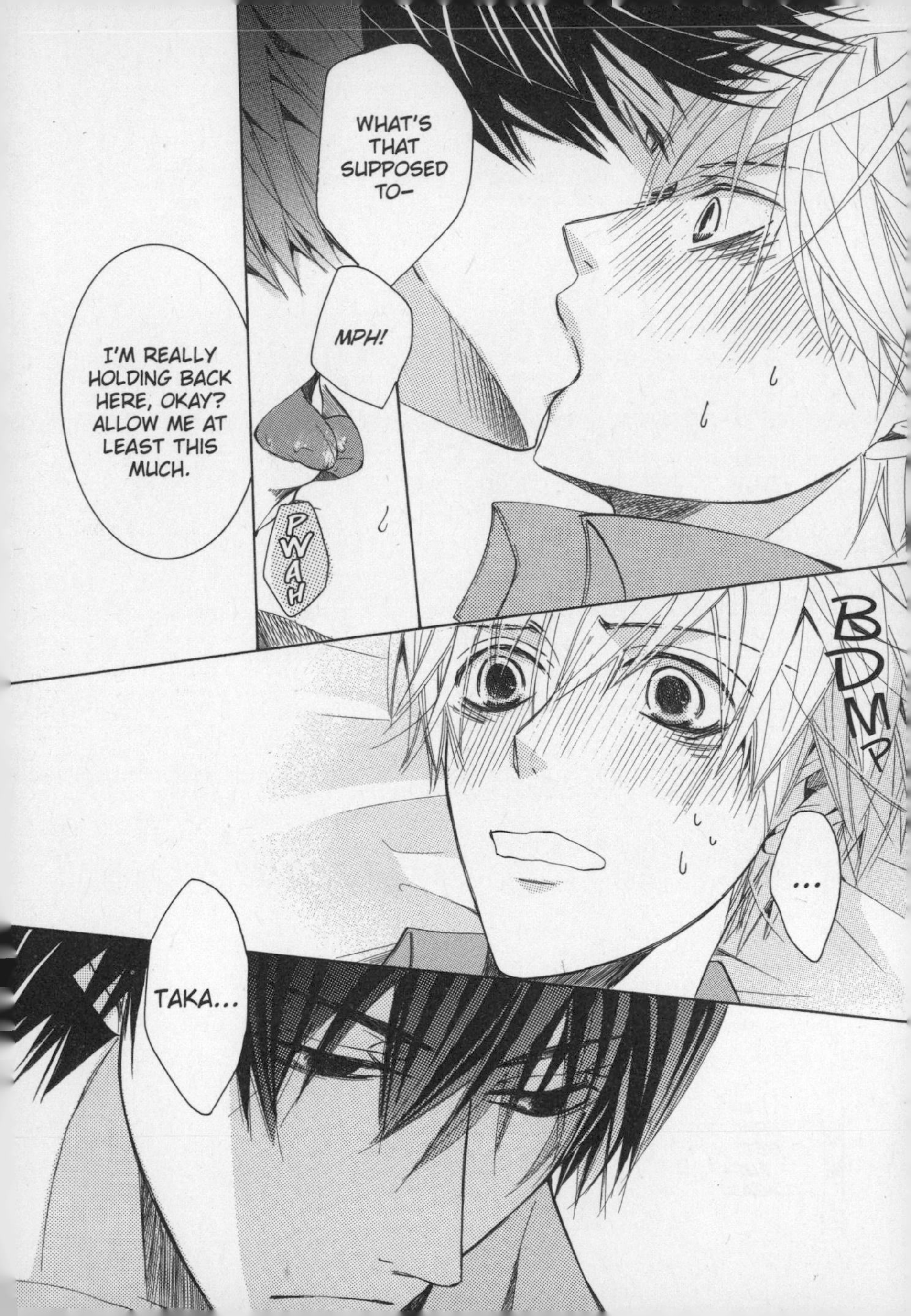
WHAT'S THAT SUPPOSED TO–
MPH!
PWAH
I'M REALLY HOLDING BACK HERE, OKAY? ALLOW ME AT LEAST THIS MUCH.
BDMP
...
TAKA...

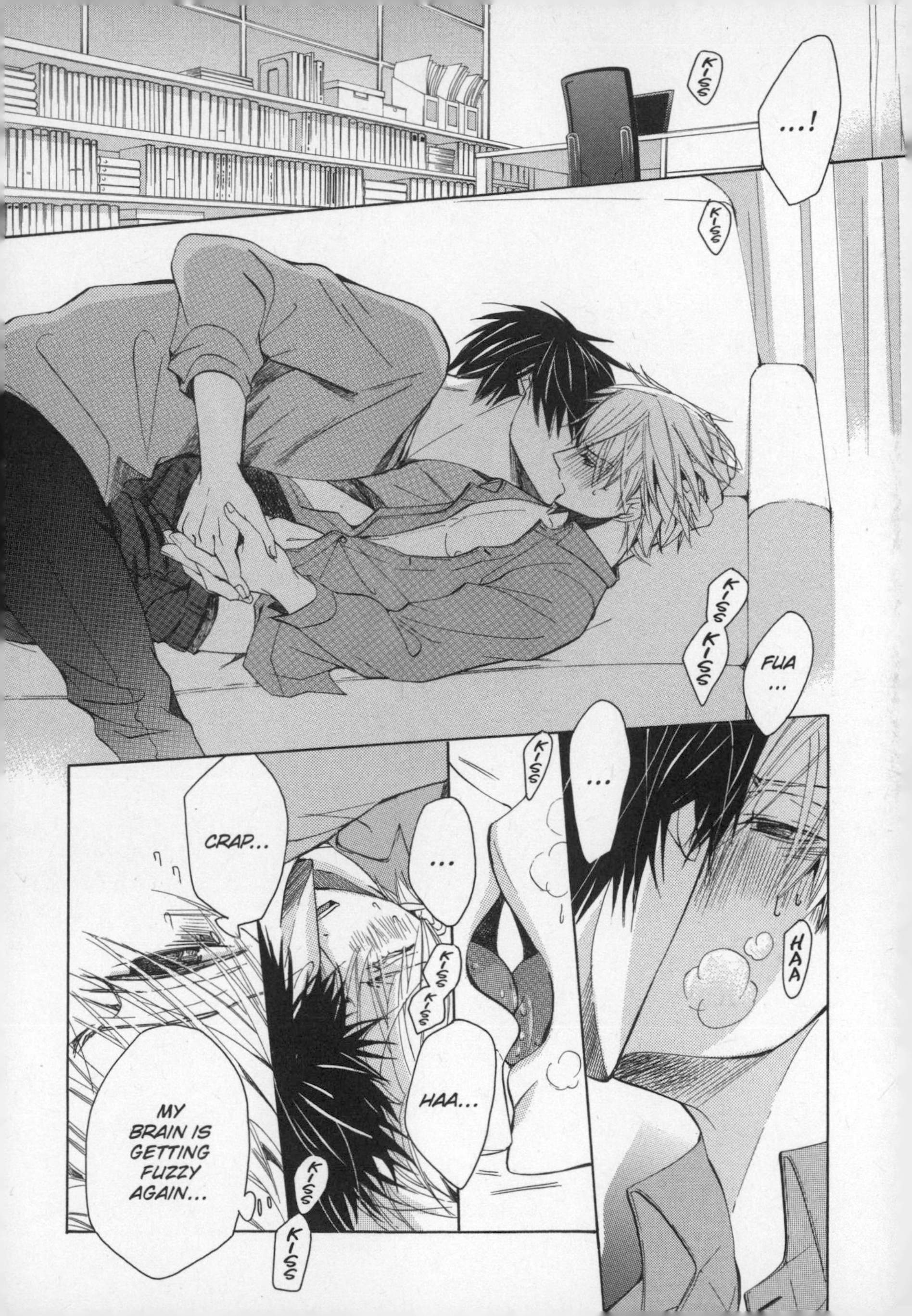

...!
KISS
KISS
KISS KISS
FUA ...
...
HAA
KISS
...
CRAP...
KISS KISS
HAA...
MY BRAIN IS GETTING FUZZY AGAIN...
KISS
KISS

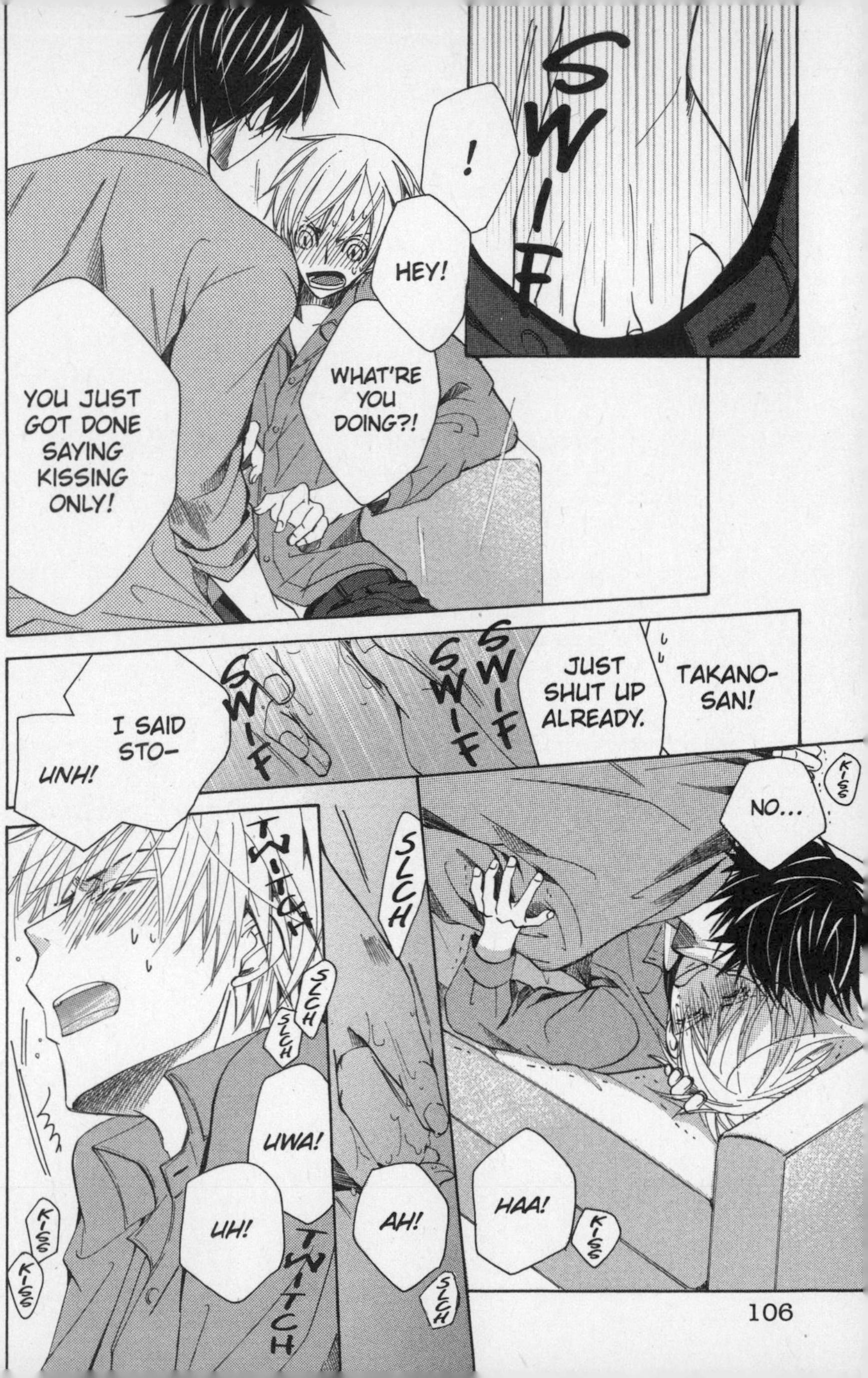
SWIF
!
HEY!
WHAT'RE YOU DOING?!
YOU JUST GOT DONE SAYING KISSING ONLY!
TAKANO-SAN!
JUST SHUT UP ALREADY.
SWIF
SWIF
SWIF
I SAID STO-
UNH!
KISS
NO...
HAA!
KISS
SLCH
TWITCH
SLCH
SLCH
UWA!
AH!
UH!
TWITCH
SLCH
KISS
KISS

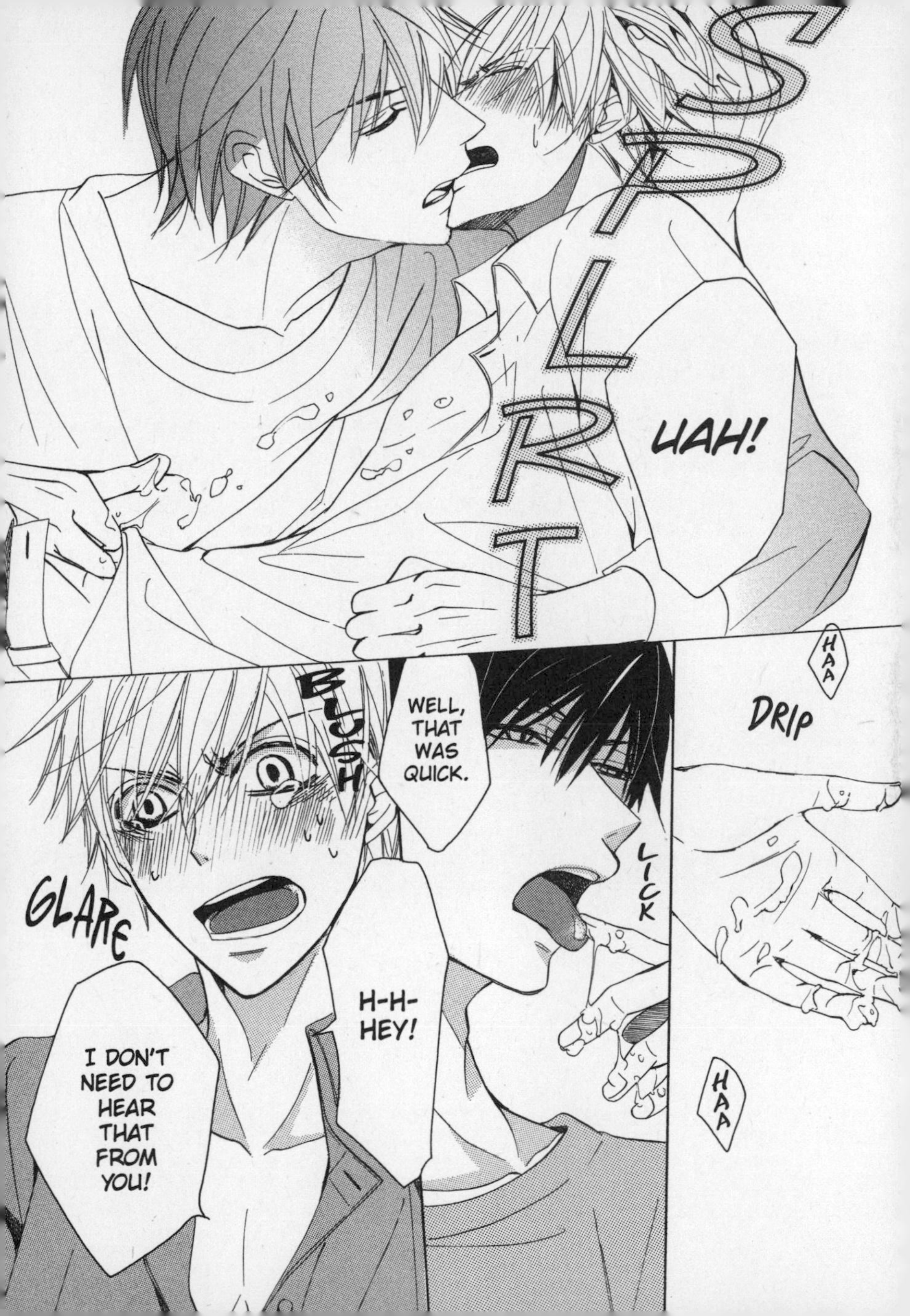
SPLRT
UAH!
HAA
DRIP
HAA
BLUSH
WELL, THAT WAS QUICK.
LICK
GLARE
H-H-HEY!
I DON'T NEED TO HEAR THAT FROM YOU!

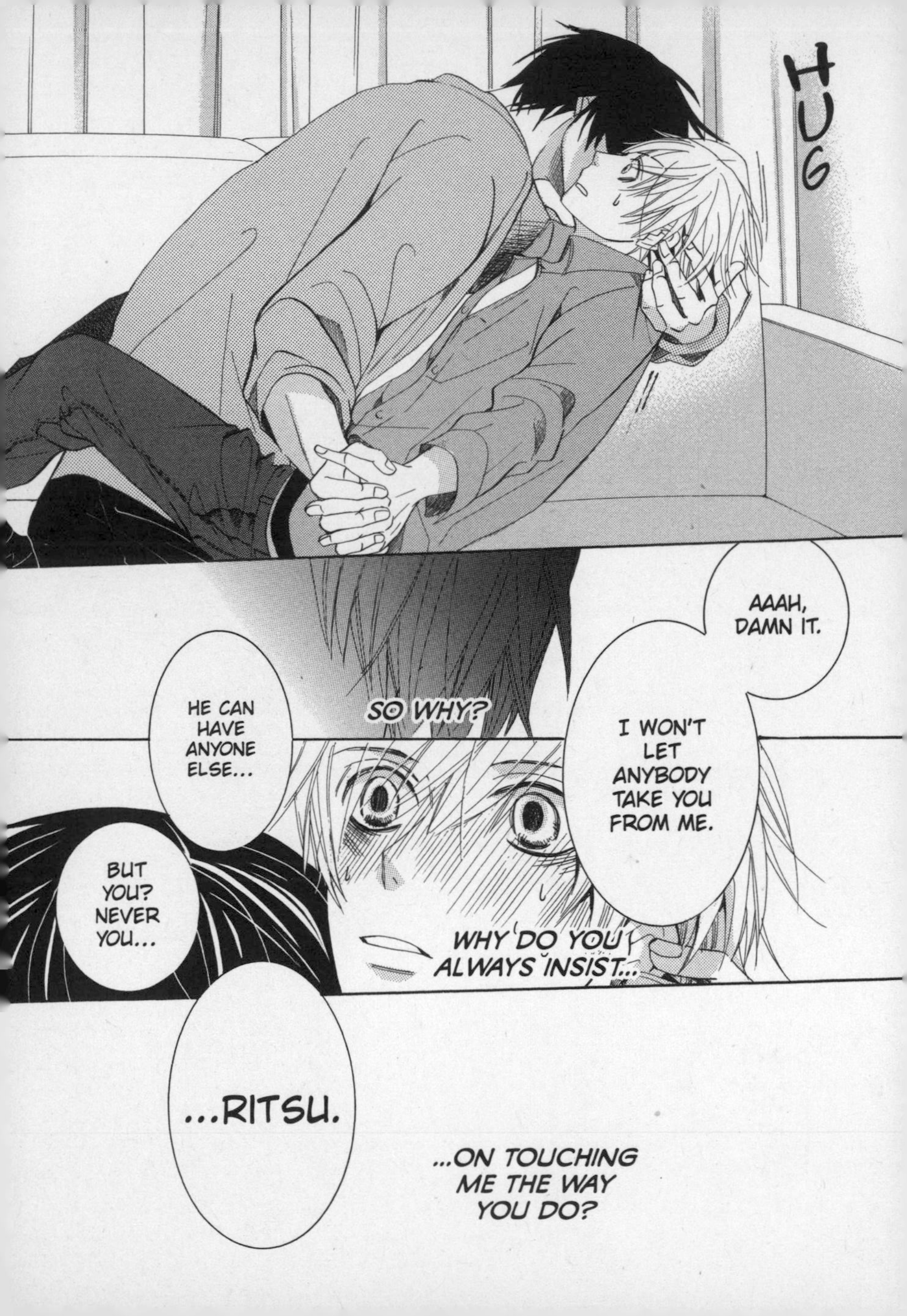
HUG
AAAH, DAMN IT.
SO WHY?
I WON'T LET ANYBODY TAKE YOU FROM ME.
HE CAN HAVE ANYONE ELSE...
BUT YOU? NEVER YOU...
WHY DO YOU ALWAYS INSIST...
...RITSU.
...ON TOUCHING ME THE WAY YOU DO?

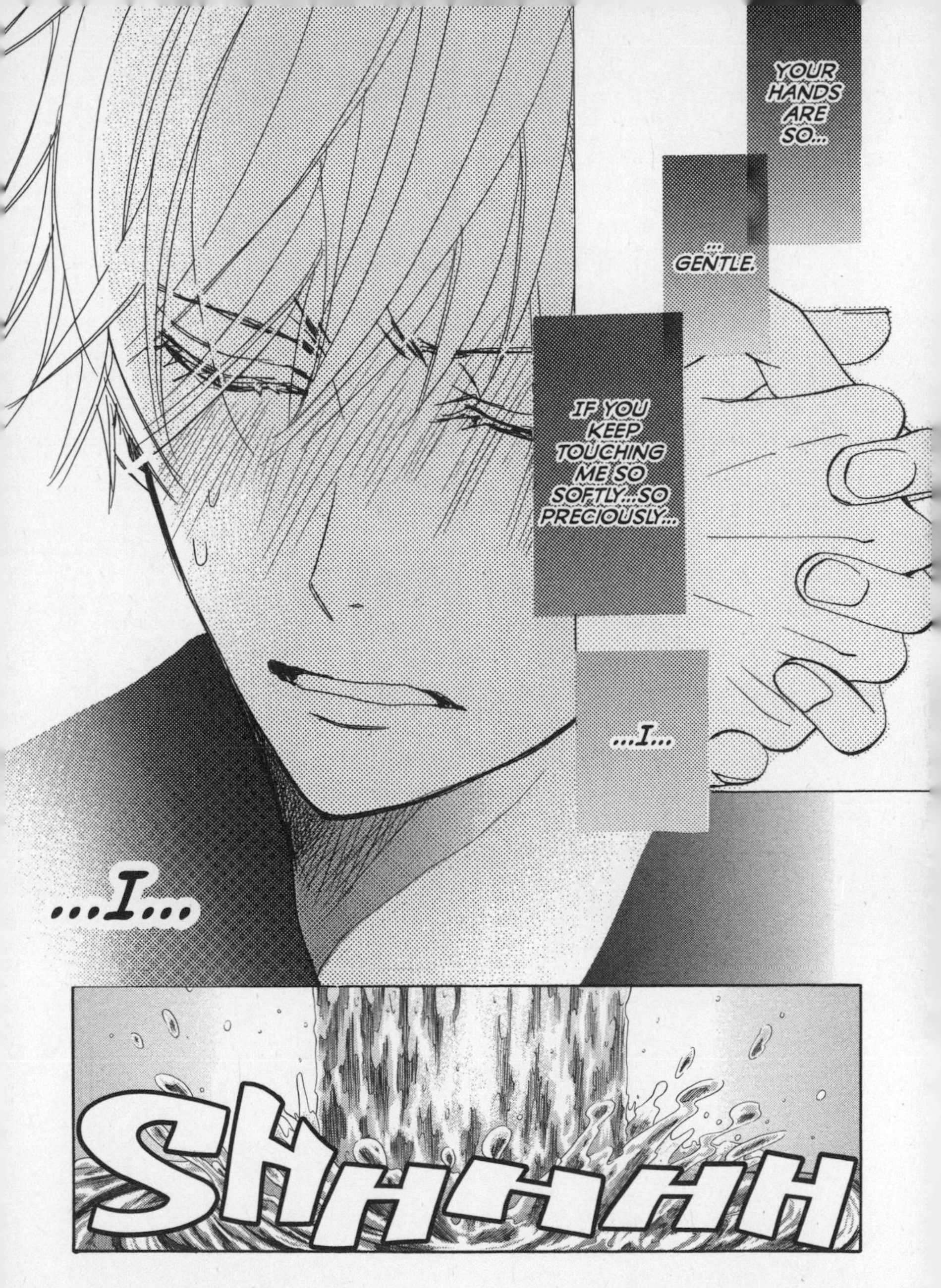
YOUR HANDS ARE SO...
...GENTLE.
IF YOU KEEP TOUCHING ME SO SOFTLY...SO PRECIOUSLY...
...I...
...I...
SHHHHH

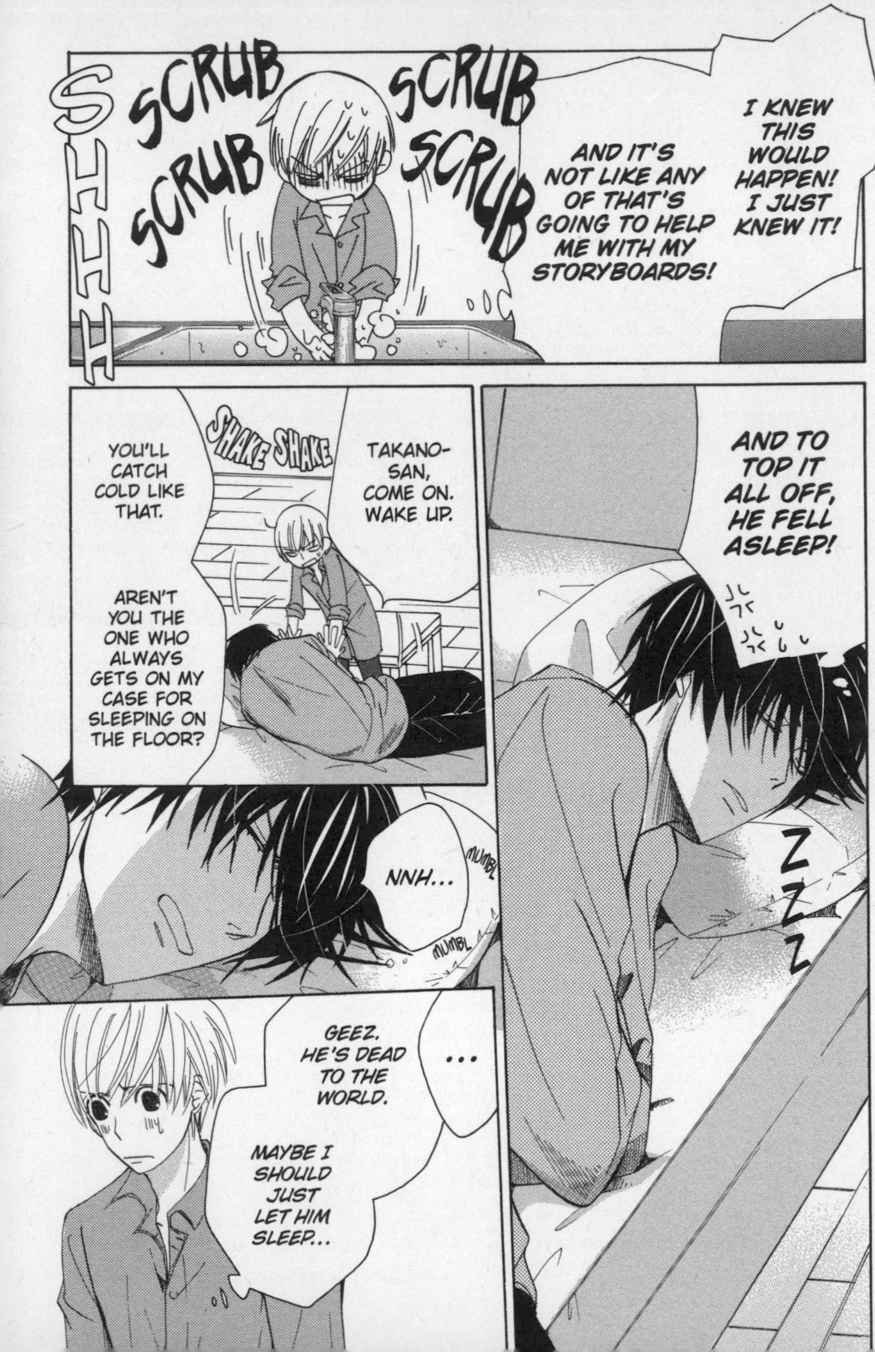
I KNEW THIS WOULD HAPPEN! I JUST KNEW IT!
AND IT'S NOT LIKE ANY OF THAT'S GOING TO HELP ME WITH MY STORYBOARDS!
SCRUB SCRUB
SCRUB SCRUB
SHHHH
AND TO TOP IT ALL OFF, HE FELL ASLEEP!
ZZZ
SHAKE SHAKE
TAKANO-SAN, COME ON. WAKE UP.
YOU'LL CATCH COLD LIKE THAT.
AREN'T YOU THE ONE WHO ALWAYS GETS ON MY CASE FOR SLEEPING ON THE FLOOR?
MUMBL
NNH...
MUMBL
...
GEEZ. HE'S DEAD TO THE WORLD.
MAYBE I SHOULD JUST LET HIM SLEEP...

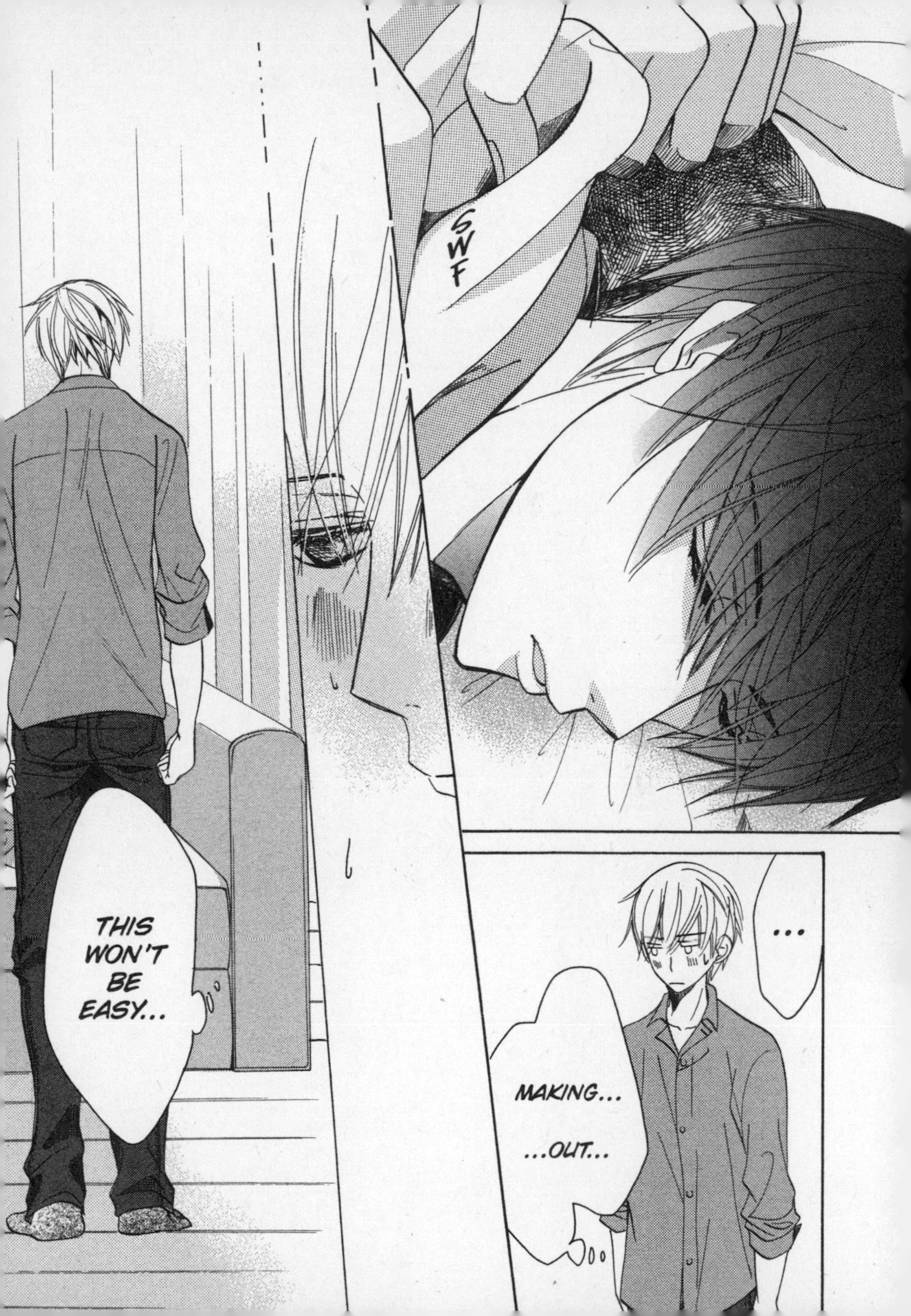
SWF
...
MAKING...
...OUT...
THIS WON'T BE EASY...

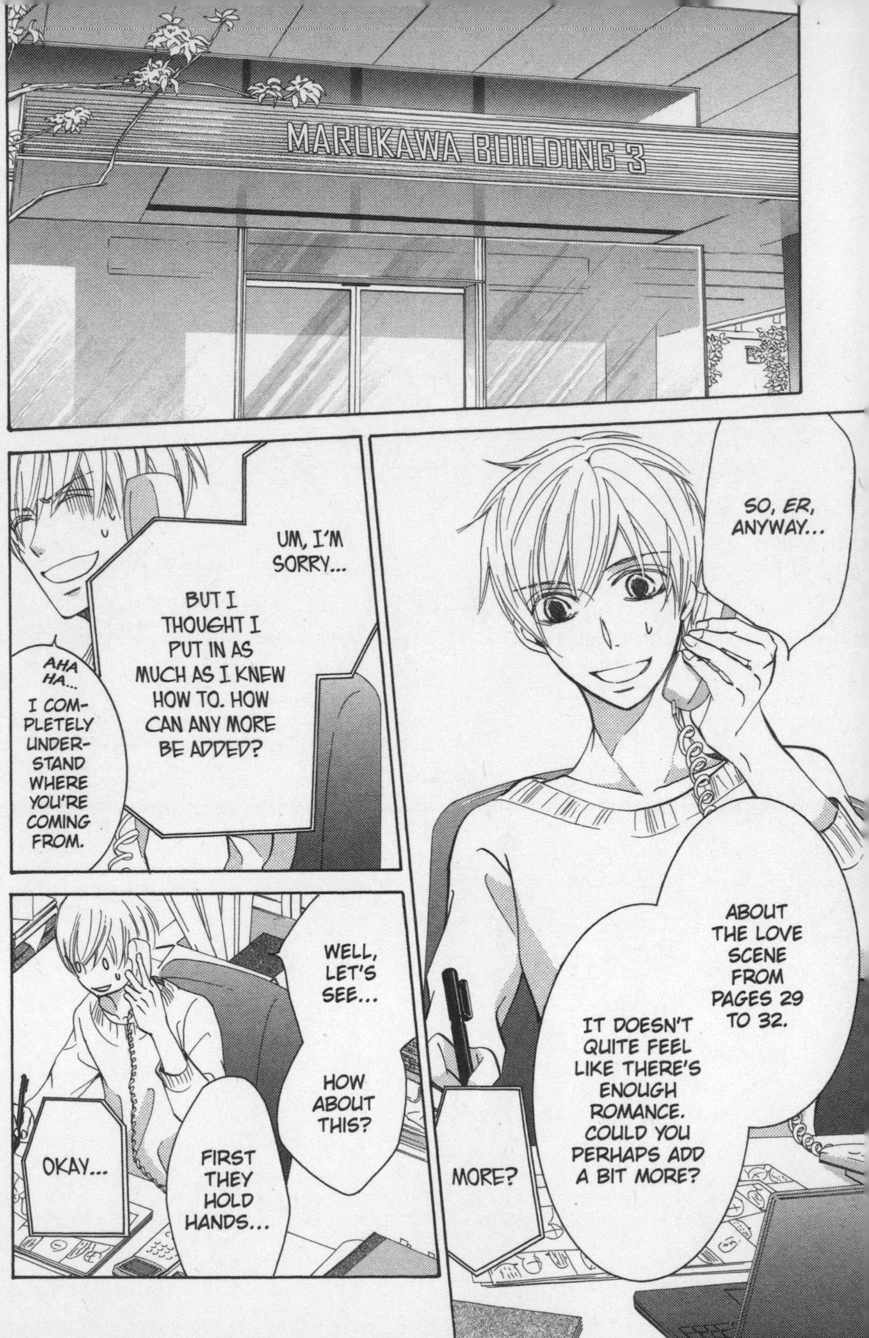
MARUKAWA BUILDING 3
SO, ER, ANYWAY...
ABOUT THE LOVE SCENE FROM PAGES 29 TO 32.
IT DOESN'T QUITE FEEL LIKE THERE'S ENOUGH ROMANCE. COULD YOU PERHAPS ADD A BIT MORE?
MORE?
UM, I'M SORRY...
BUT I THOUGHT I PUT IN AS MUCH AS I KNEW HOW TO. HOW CAN ANY MORE BE ADDED?
AHA HA... I COMPLETELY UNDERSTAND WHERE YOU'RE COMING FROM.
WELL, LET'S SEE...
HOW ABOUT THIS?
FIRST THEY HOLD HANDS...
OKAY...

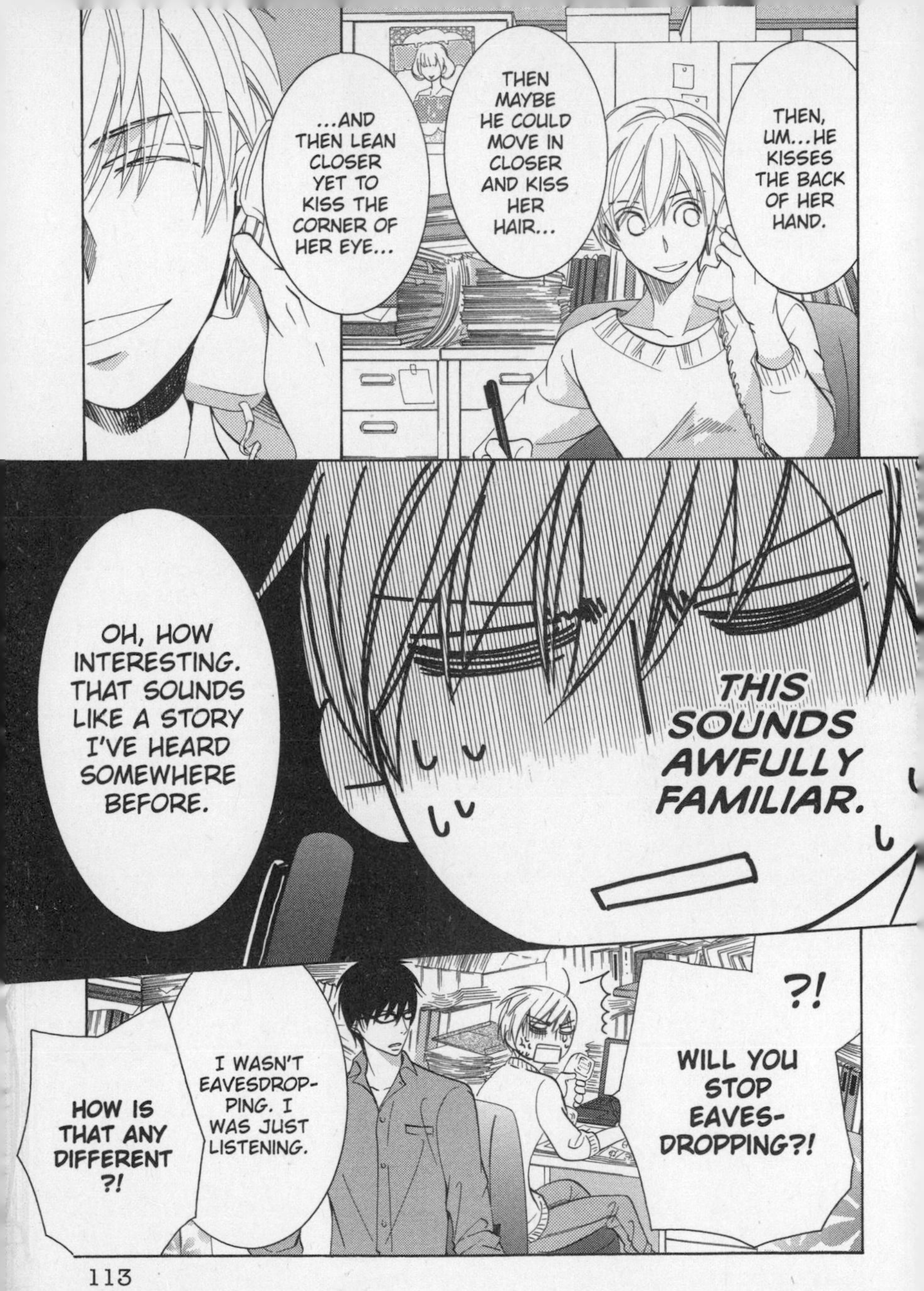
THEN, UM...HE KISSES THE BACK OF HER HAND.
THEN MAYBE HE COULD MOVE IN CLOSER AND KISS HER HAIR...
...AND THEN LEAN CLOSER YET TO KISS THE CORNER OF HER EYE...
THIS SOUNDS AWFULLY FAMILIAR.
OH, HOW INTERESTING. THAT SOUNDS LIKE A STORY I'VE HEARD SOMEWHERE BEFORE.
?!
WILL YOU STOP EAVES-DROPPING?!
I WASN'T EAVESDROP-PING. I WAS JUST LISTENING.
HOW IS THAT ANY DIFFERENT ?!

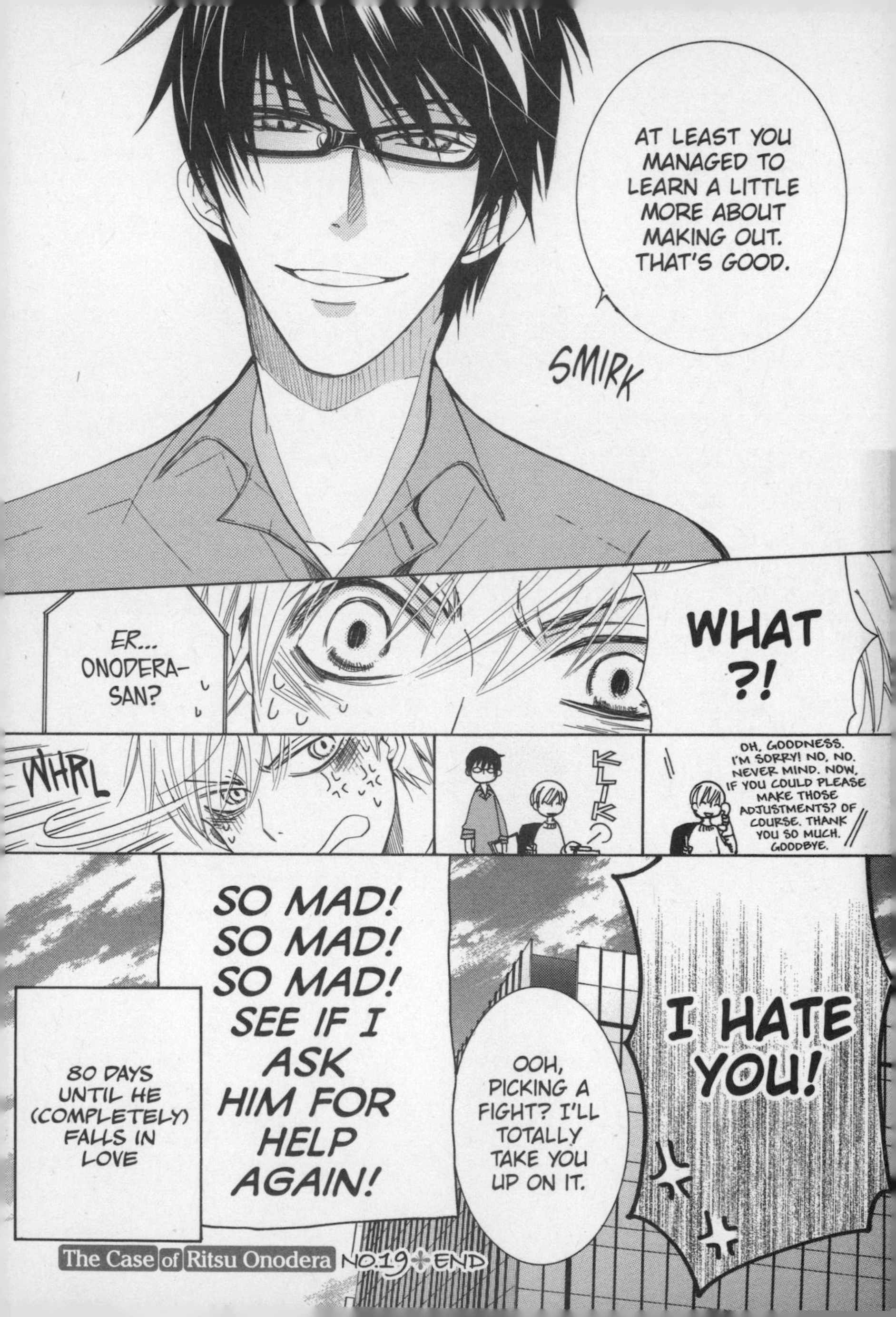
AT LEAST YOU MANAGED TO LEARN A LITTLE MORE ABOUT MAKING OUT. THAT'S GOOD.
SMIRK
WHAT ?!
ER... ONODERA-SAN?
OH, GOODNESS. I'M SORRY! NO, NO. NEVER MIND. NOW, IF YOU COULD PLEASE MAKE THOSE ADJUSTMENTS? OF COURSE. THANK YOU SO MUCH. GOODBYE.
KLIK
WHRL
I HATE YOU!
OOH, PICKING A FIGHT? I'LL TOTALLY TAKE YOU UP ON IT.
SO MAD! SO MAD! SO MAD! SEE IF I ASK HIM FOR HELP AGAIN!
80 DAYS UNTIL HE (COMPLETELY) FALLS IN LOVE
The Case of Ritsu Onodera NO.19 END

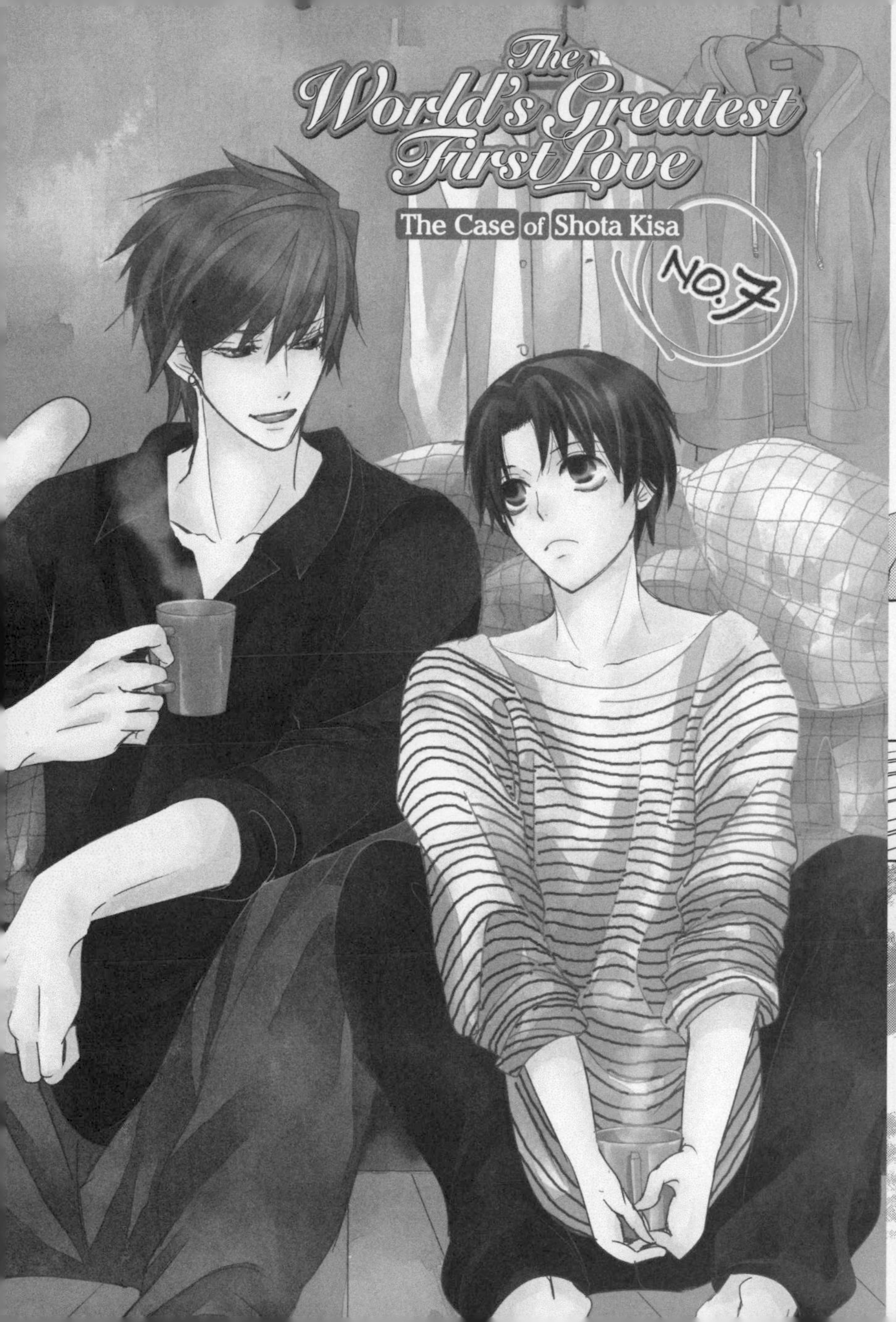
The World's Greatest First Love
The Case of Shota Kisa
NO.7

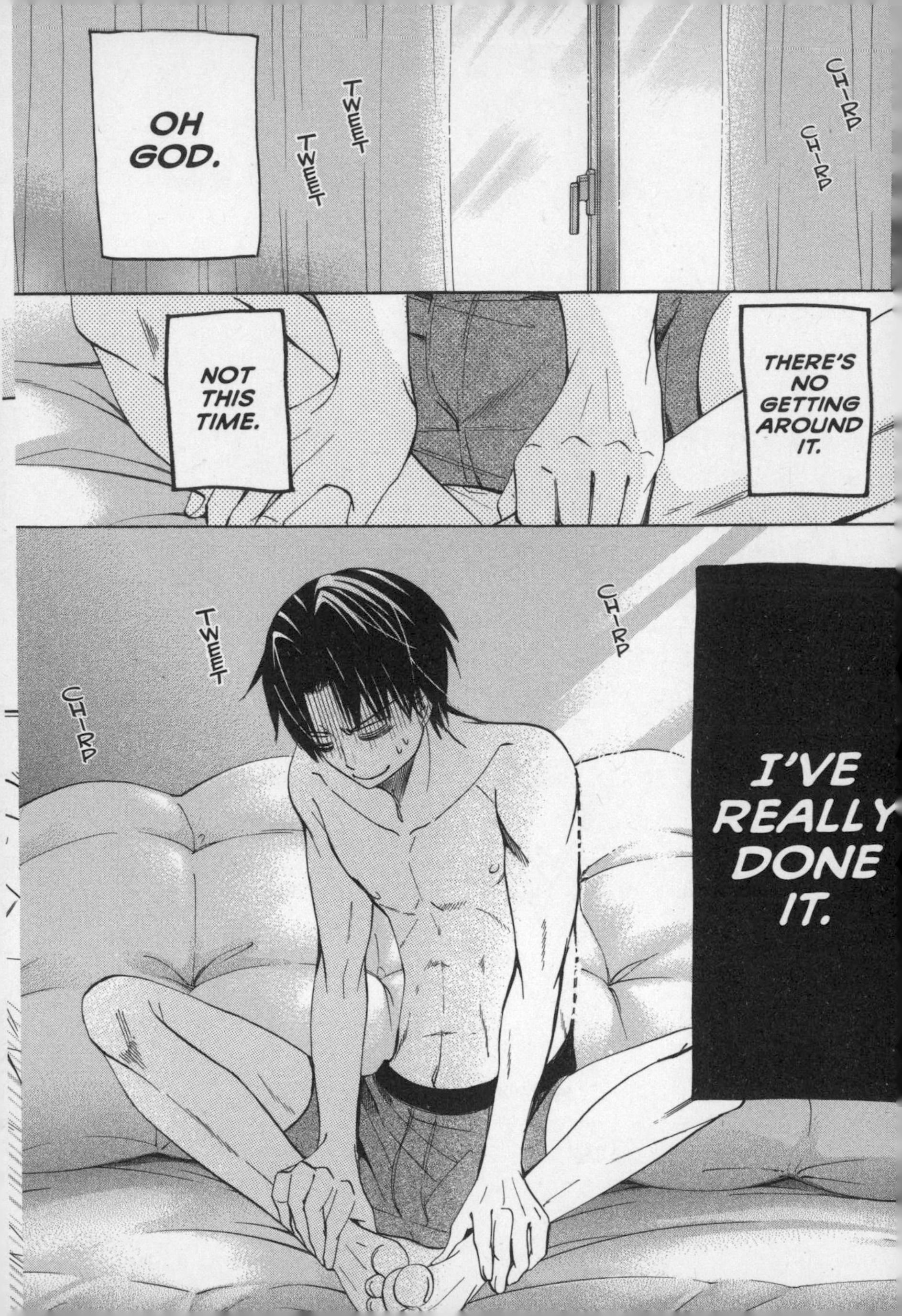
CHIRP CHIRP
TWEET TWEET
OH GOD.
THERE'S NO GETTING AROUND IT.
NOT THIS TIME.
I'VE REALLY DONE IT.
CHIRP
TWEET
CHIRP

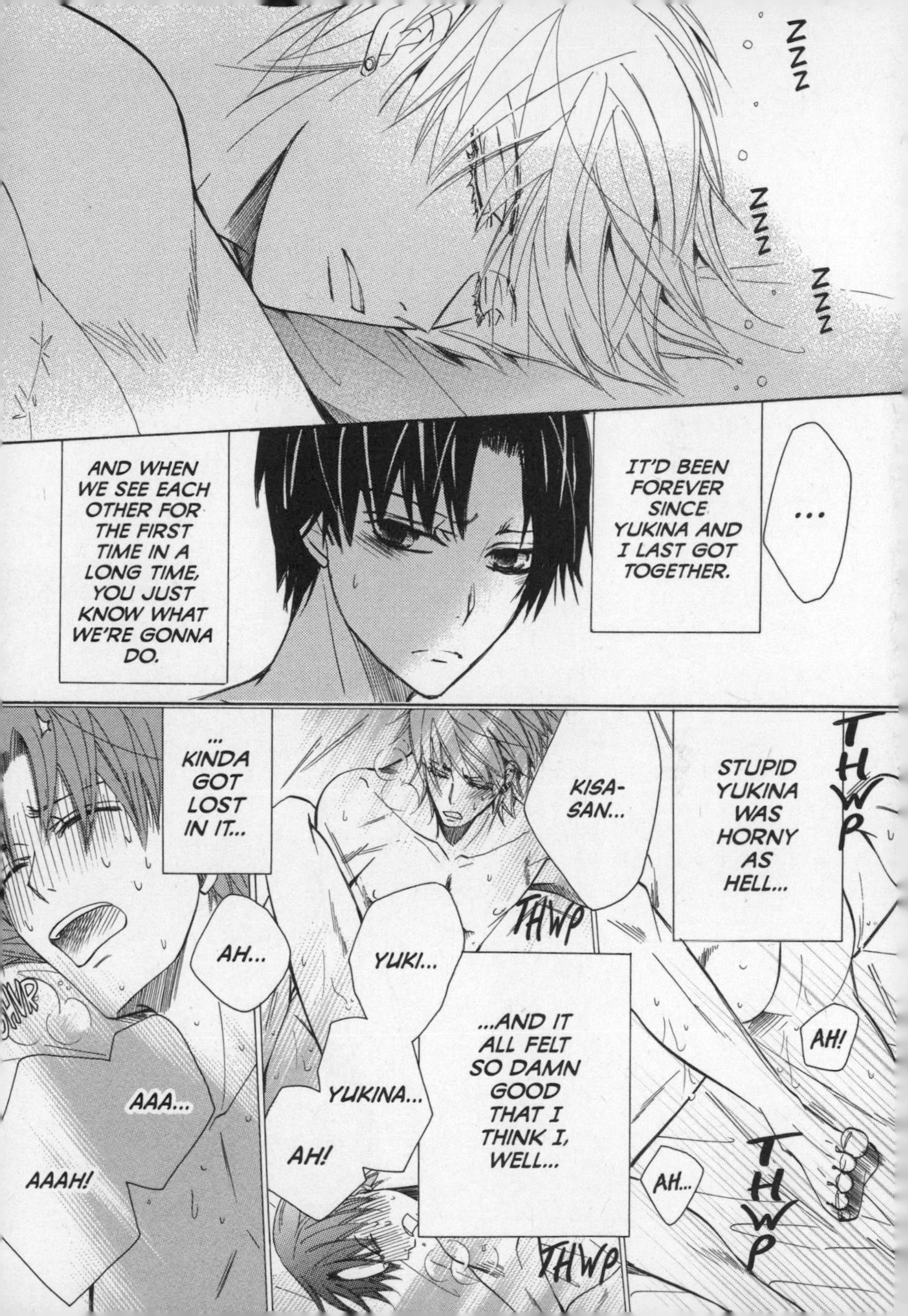
ZZZ
ZZZ
ZZZ
...
IT'D BEEN FOREVER SINCE YUKINA AND I LAST GOT TOGETHER.
AND WHEN WE SEE EACH OTHER FOR THE FIRST TIME IN A LONG TIME, YOU JUST KNOW WHAT WE'RE GONNA DO.
THWP
STUPID YUKINA WAS HORNY AS HELL...
KISA-SAN...
... KINDA GOT LOST IN IT...
THWP
AH!
YUKI...
AH...
...AND IT ALL FELT SO DAMN GOOD THAT I THINK I, WELL...
THWP
AH...
THWP
YUKINA...
AH!
AAA...
AAAH!

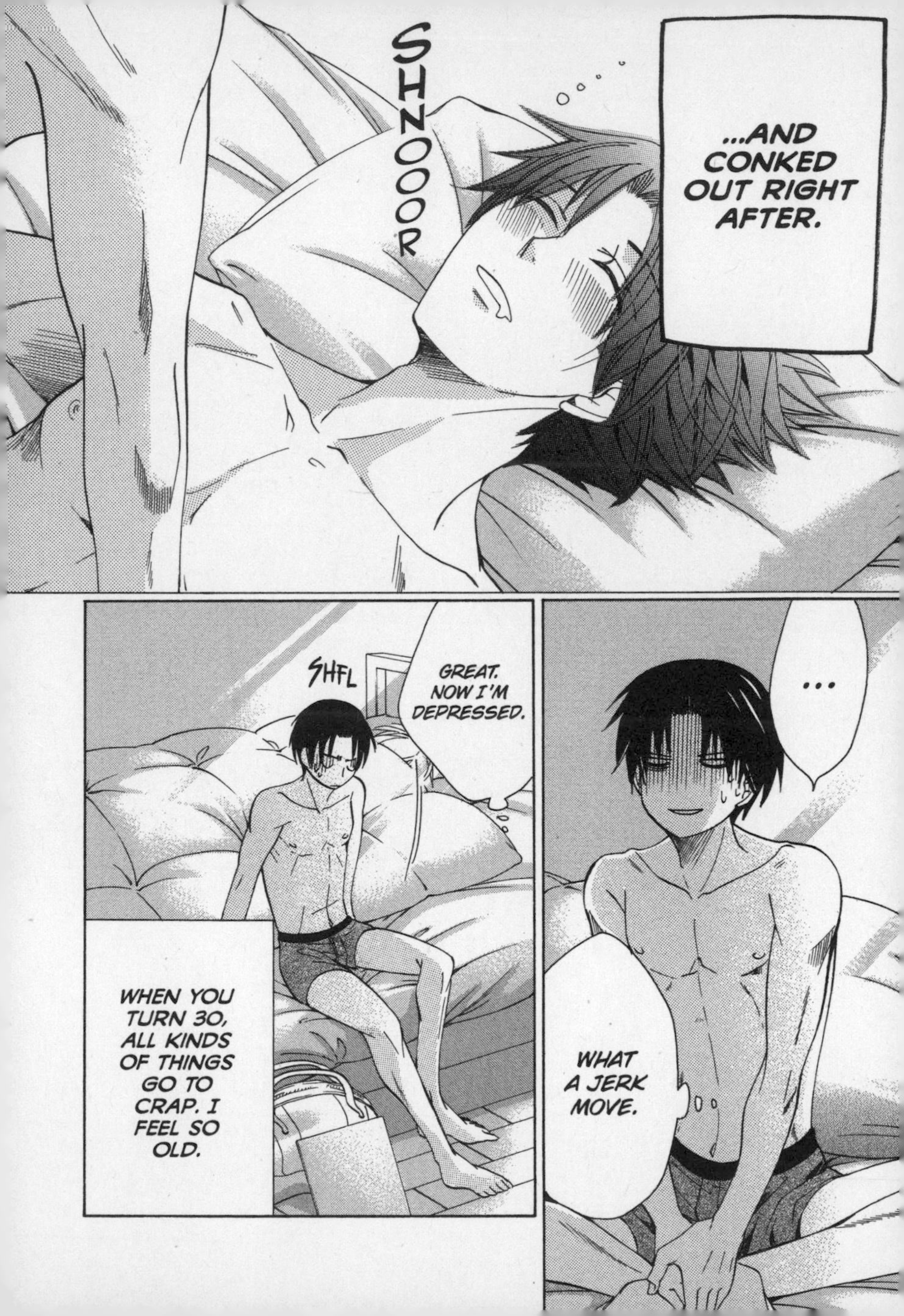
...AND CONKED OUT RIGHT AFTER.
SHNOOOR
...
WHAT A JERK MOVE.
GREAT. NOW I'M DEPRESSED.
SHFL
WHEN YOU TURN 30, ALL KINDS OF THINGS GO TO CRAP. I FEEL SO OLD.

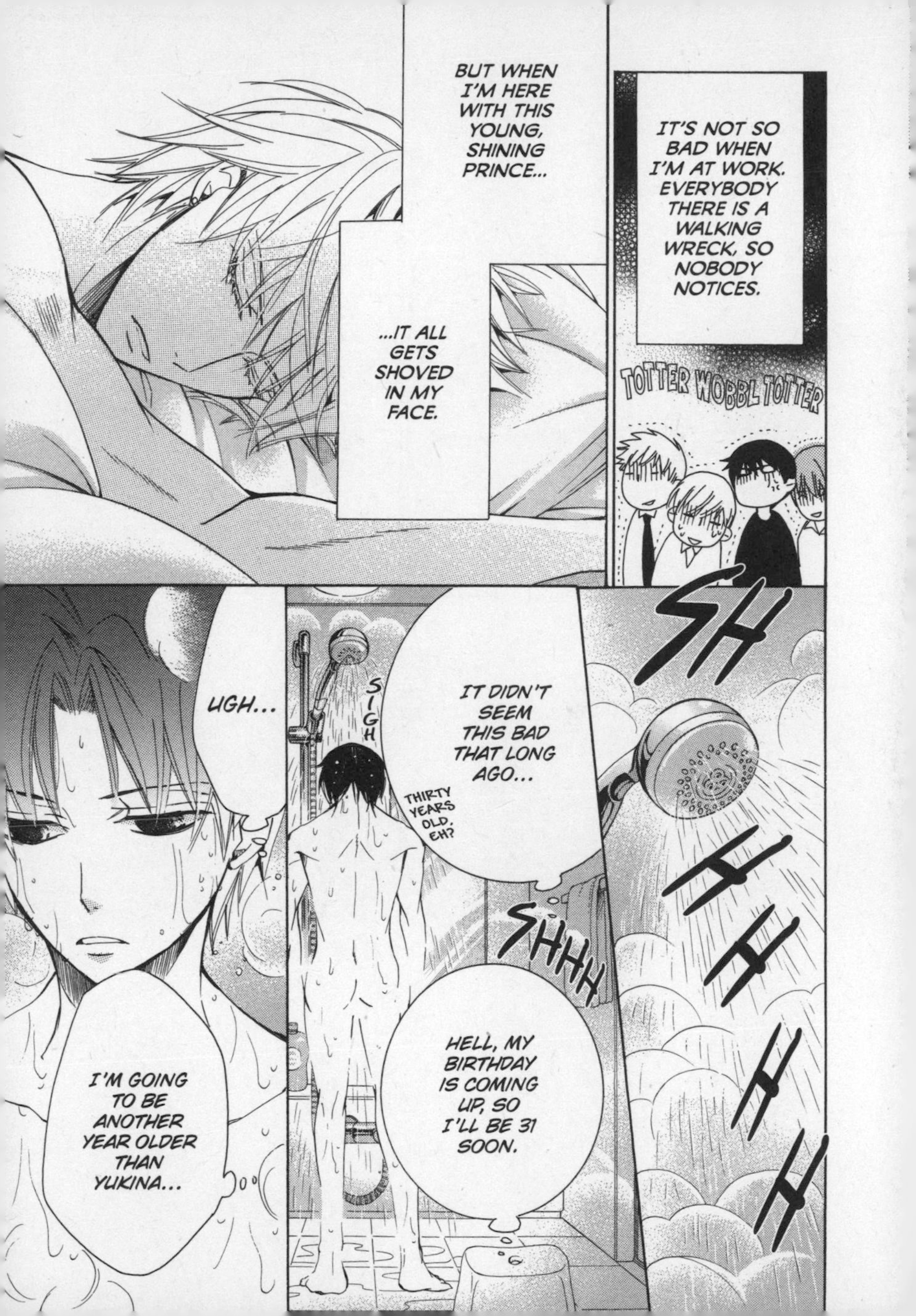
IT'S NOT SO BAD WHEN I'M AT WORK. EVERYBODY THERE IS A WALKING WRECK, SO NOBODY NOTICES.
TOTTER WOBBL TOTTER
BUT WHEN I'M HERE WITH THIS YOUNG, SHINING PRINCE...
...IT ALL GETS SHOVED IN MY FACE.
SHHHHHHH
IT DIDN'T SEEM THIS BAD THAT LONG AGO...
SIGH
THIRTY YEARS OLD, EH?
SHHH
HELL, MY BIRTHDAY IS COMING UP, SO I'LL BE 31 SOON.
UGH...
I'M GOING TO BE ANOTHER YEAR OLDER THAN YUKINA...

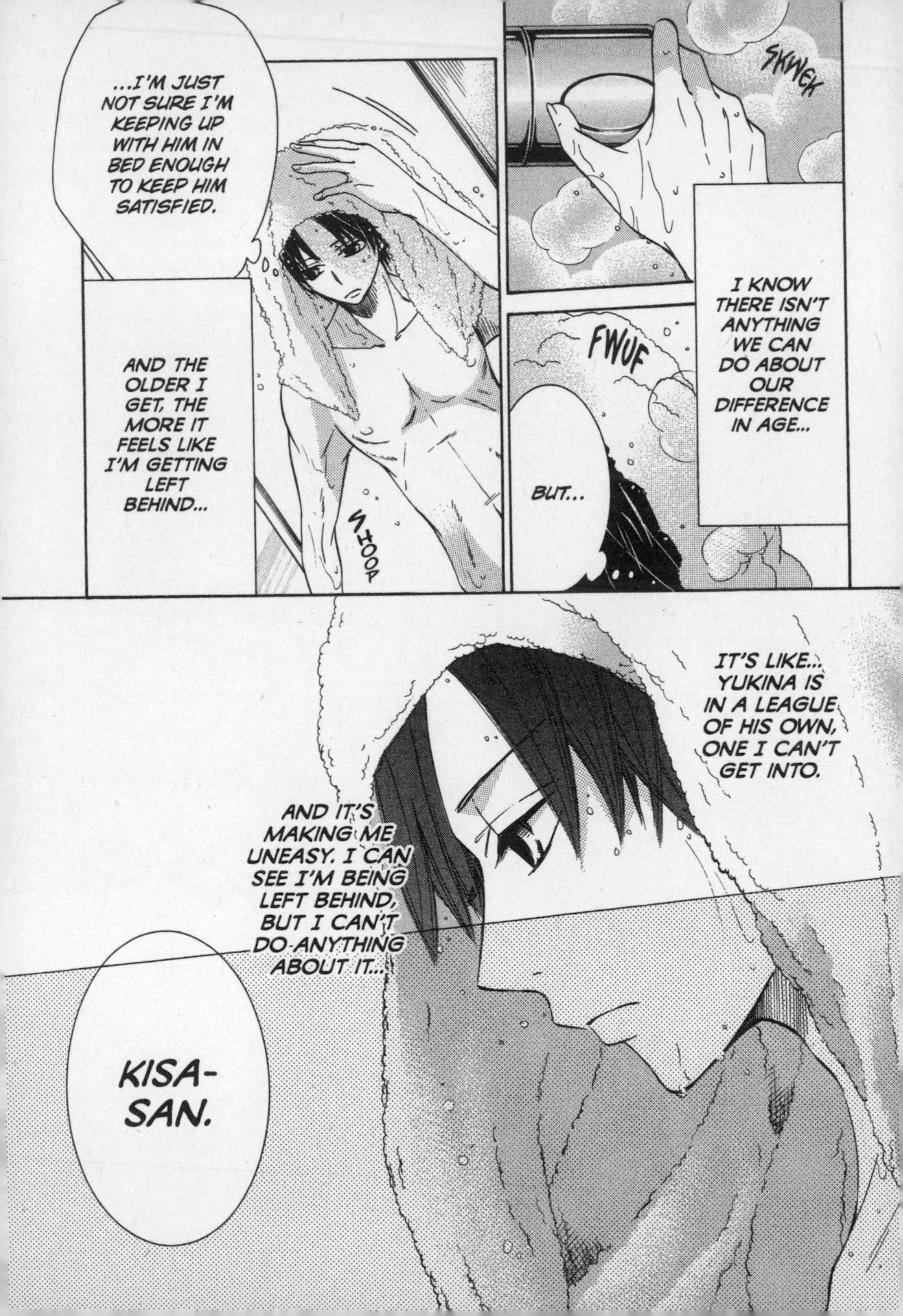
SKWEK
I KNOW THERE ISN'T ANYTHING WE CAN DO ABOUT OUR DIFFERENCE IN AGE...
FWUF
BUT...
...I'M JUST NOT SURE I'M KEEPING UP WITH HIM IN BED ENOUGH TO KEEP HIM SATISFIED.
AND THE OLDER I GET, THE MORE IT FEELS LIKE I'M GETTING LEFT BEHIND...
SHOOP
IT'S LIKE... YUKINA IS IN A LEAGUE OF HIS OWN, ONE I CAN'T GET INTO.
AND IT'S MAKING ME UNEASY. I CAN SEE I'M BEING LEFT BEHIND, BUT I CAN'T DO ANYTHING ABOUT IT...
KISA-SAN.

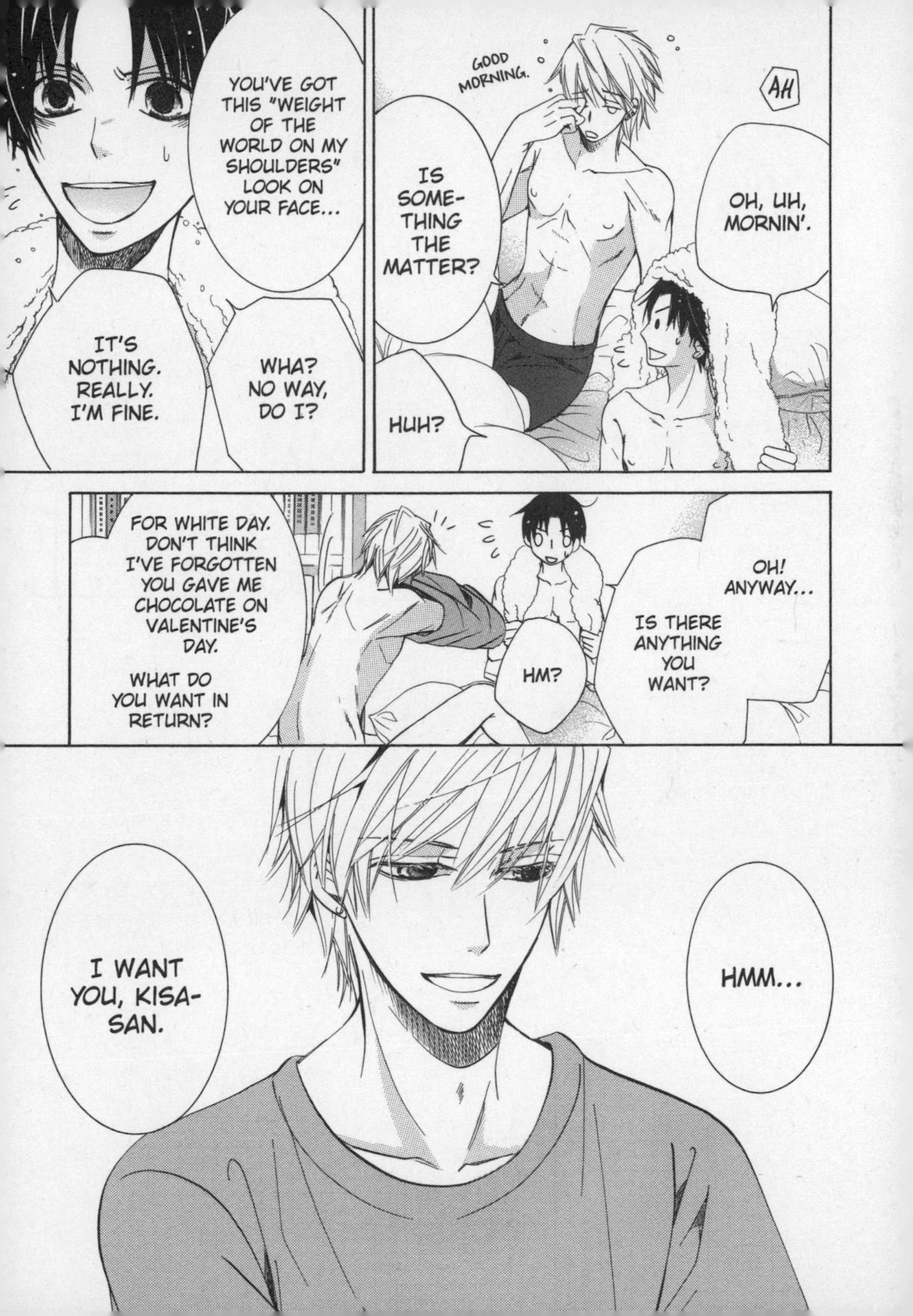
AH
GOOD MORNING.
OH, UH, MORNIN'.
IS SOMETHING THE MATTER?
HUH?
YOU'VE GOT THIS "WEIGHT OF THE WORLD ON MY SHOULDERS" LOOK ON YOUR FACE...
WHA? NO WAY, DO I?
IT'S NOTHING. REALLY. I'M FINE.
OH! ANYWAY...
IS THERE ANYTHING YOU WANT?
HM?
FOR WHITE DAY. DON'T THINK I'VE FORGOTTEN YOU GAVE ME CHOCOLATE ON VALENTINE'S DAY.
WHAT DO YOU WANT IN RETURN?
HMM...
I WANT YOU, KISA-SAN.

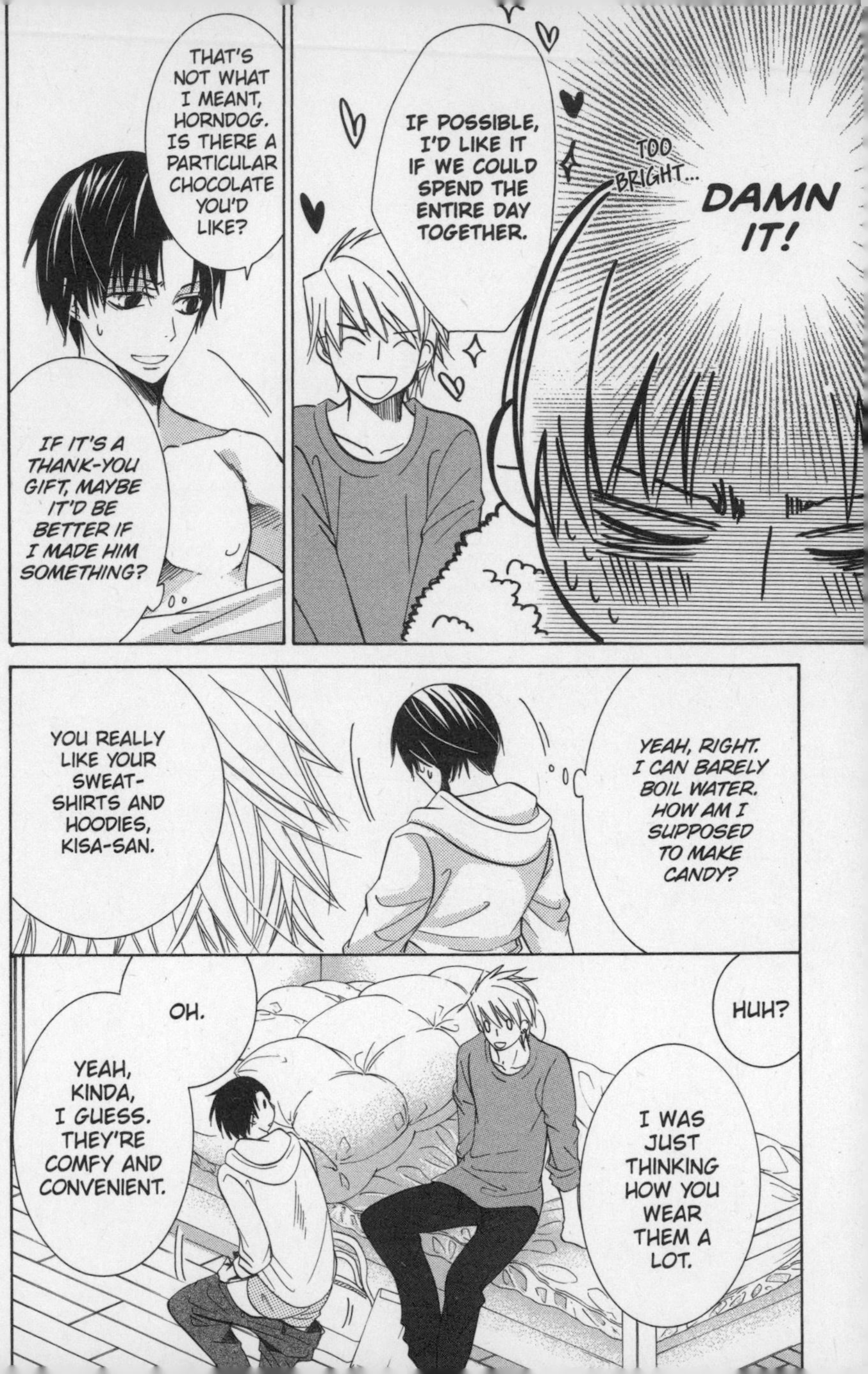
TOO BRIGHT...
DAMN IT!
IF POSSIBLE, I'D LIKE IT IF WE COULD SPEND THE ENTIRE DAY TOGETHER.
THAT'S NOT WHAT I MEANT, HORNDOG. IS THERE A PARTICULAR CHOCOLATE YOU'D LIKE?
IF IT'S A THANK-YOU GIFT, MAYBE IT'D BE BETTER IF I MADE HIM SOMETHING?
YEAH, RIGHT. I CAN BARELY BOIL WATER. HOW AM I SUPPOSED TO MAKE CANDY?
YOU REALLY LIKE YOUR SWEAT-SHIRTS AND HOODIES, KISA-SAN.
HUH?
I WAS JUST THINKING HOW YOU WEAR THEM A LOT.
OH.
YEAH, KINDA, I GUESS. THEY'RE COMFY AND CONVENIENT.

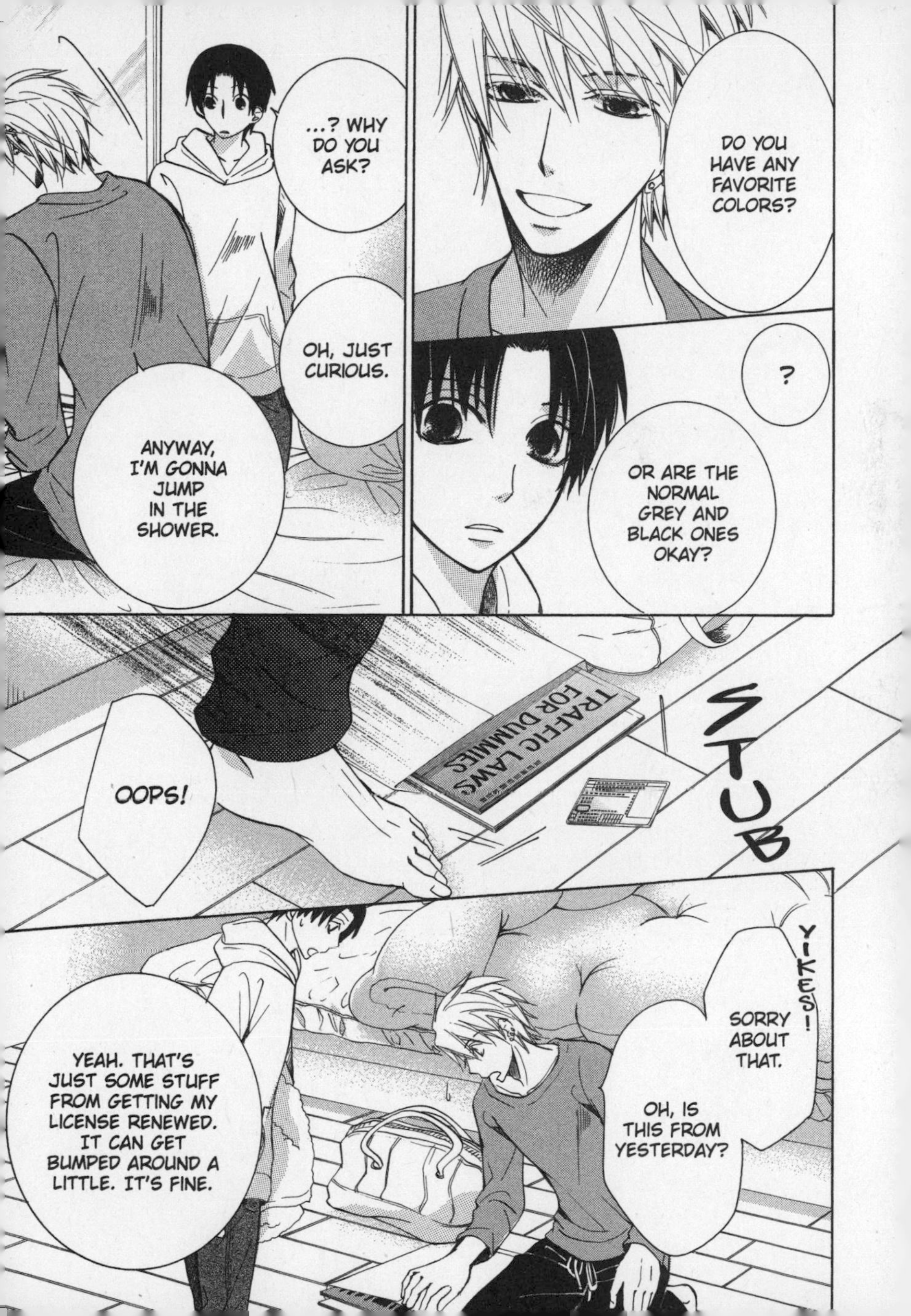
DO YOU HAVE ANY FAVORITE COLORS?
?
OR ARE THE NORMAL GREY AND BLACK ONES OKAY?
...? WHY DO YOU ASK?
OH, JUST CURIOUS.
ANYWAY, I'M GONNA JUMP IN THE SHOWER.
STUB
TRAFFIC LAWS FOR DUMMIES
OOPS!
YIKES!
SORRY ABOUT THAT.
OH, IS THIS FROM YESTERDAY?
YEAH. THAT'S JUST SOME STUFF FROM GETTING MY LICENSE RENEWED. IT CAN GET BUMPED AROUND A LITTLE. IT'S FINE.

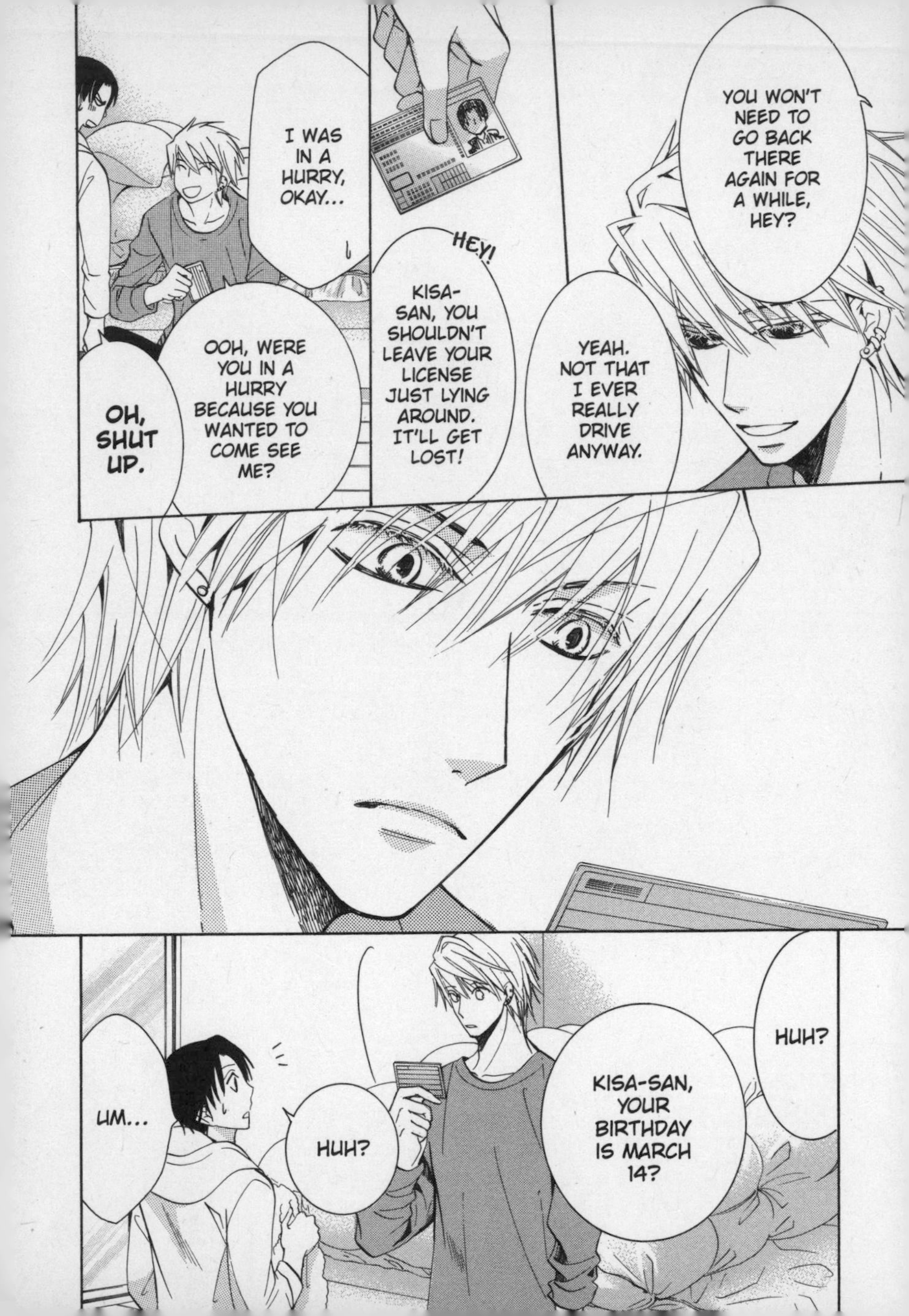
YOU WON'T NEED TO GO BACK THERE AGAIN FOR A WHILE, HEY?
YEAH. NOT THAT I EVER REALLY DRIVE ANYWAY.
HEY!
KISA-SAN, YOU SHOULDN'T LEAVE YOUR LICENSE JUST LYING AROUND. IT'LL GET LOST!
I WAS IN A HURRY, OKAY...
OOH, WERE YOU IN A HURRY BECAUSE YOU WANTED TO COME SEE ME?
OH, SHUT UP.
HUH?
KISA-SAN, YOUR BIRTHDAY IS MARCH 14?
HUH?
UM...

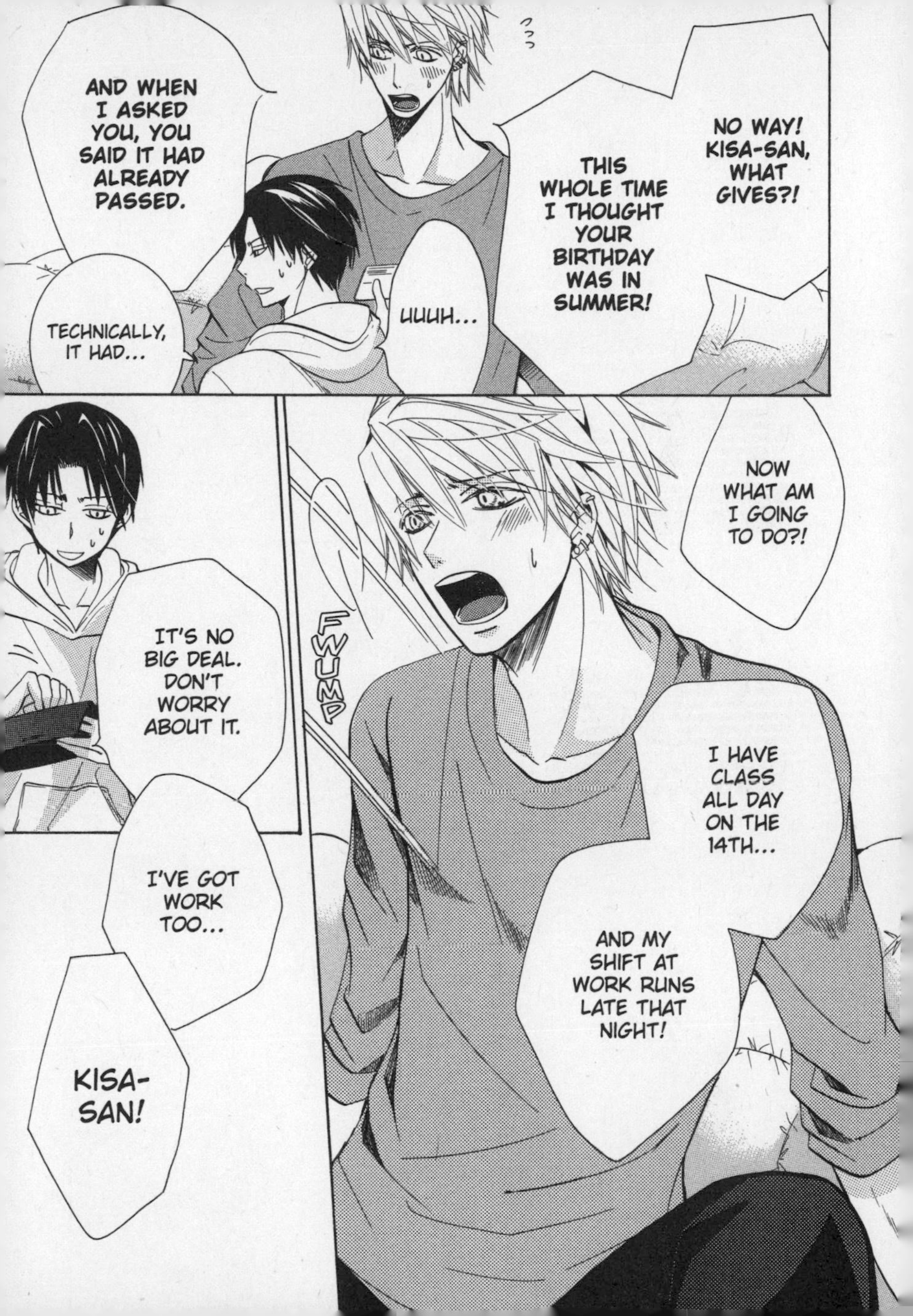
NO WAY! KISA-SAN, WHAT GIVES?!
THIS WHOLE TIME I THOUGHT YOUR BIRTHDAY WAS IN SUMMER!
AND WHEN I ASKED YOU, YOU SAID IT HAD ALREADY PASSED.
UUUH...
TECHNICALLY, IT HAD...
NOW WHAT AM I GOING TO DO?!
FWUMP
I HAVE CLASS ALL DAY ON THE 14TH...
AND MY SHIFT AT WORK RUNS LATE THAT NIGHT!
IT'S NO BIG DEAL. DON'T WORRY ABOUT IT.
I'VE GOT WORK TOO...
KISA-SAN!

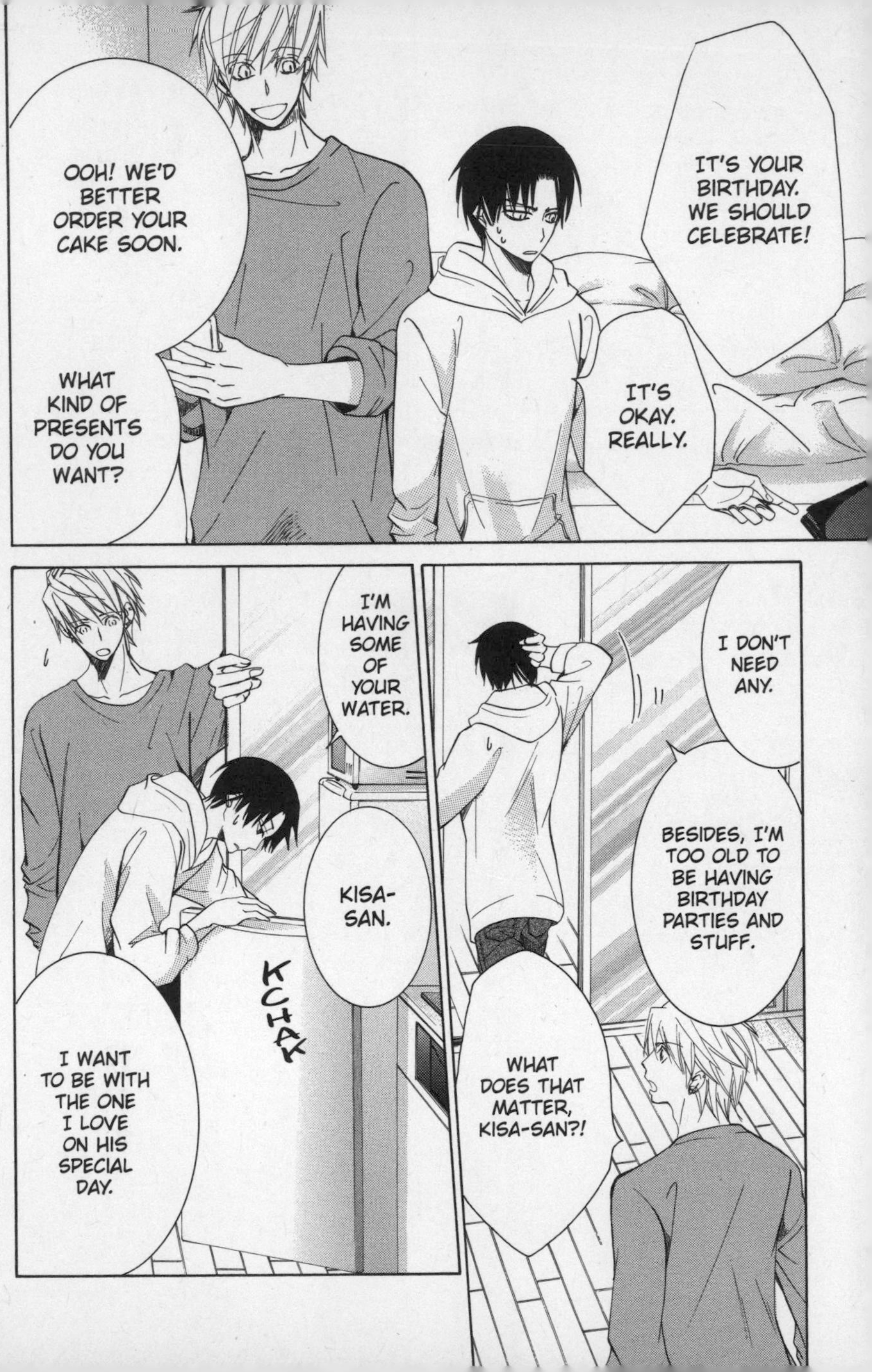
IT'S YOUR BIRTHDAY. WE SHOULD CELEBRATE!
OOH! WE'D BETTER ORDER YOUR CAKE SOON.
IT'S OKAY. REALLY.
WHAT KIND OF PRESENTS DO YOU WANT?
I DON'T NEED ANY.
BESIDES, I'M TOO OLD TO BE HAVING BIRTHDAY PARTIES AND STUFF.
WHAT DOES THAT MATTER, KISA-SAN?!
I'M HAVING SOME OF YOUR WATER.
KISA-SAN.
KCHAK
I WANT TO BE WITH THE ONE I LOVE ON HIS SPECIAL DAY.

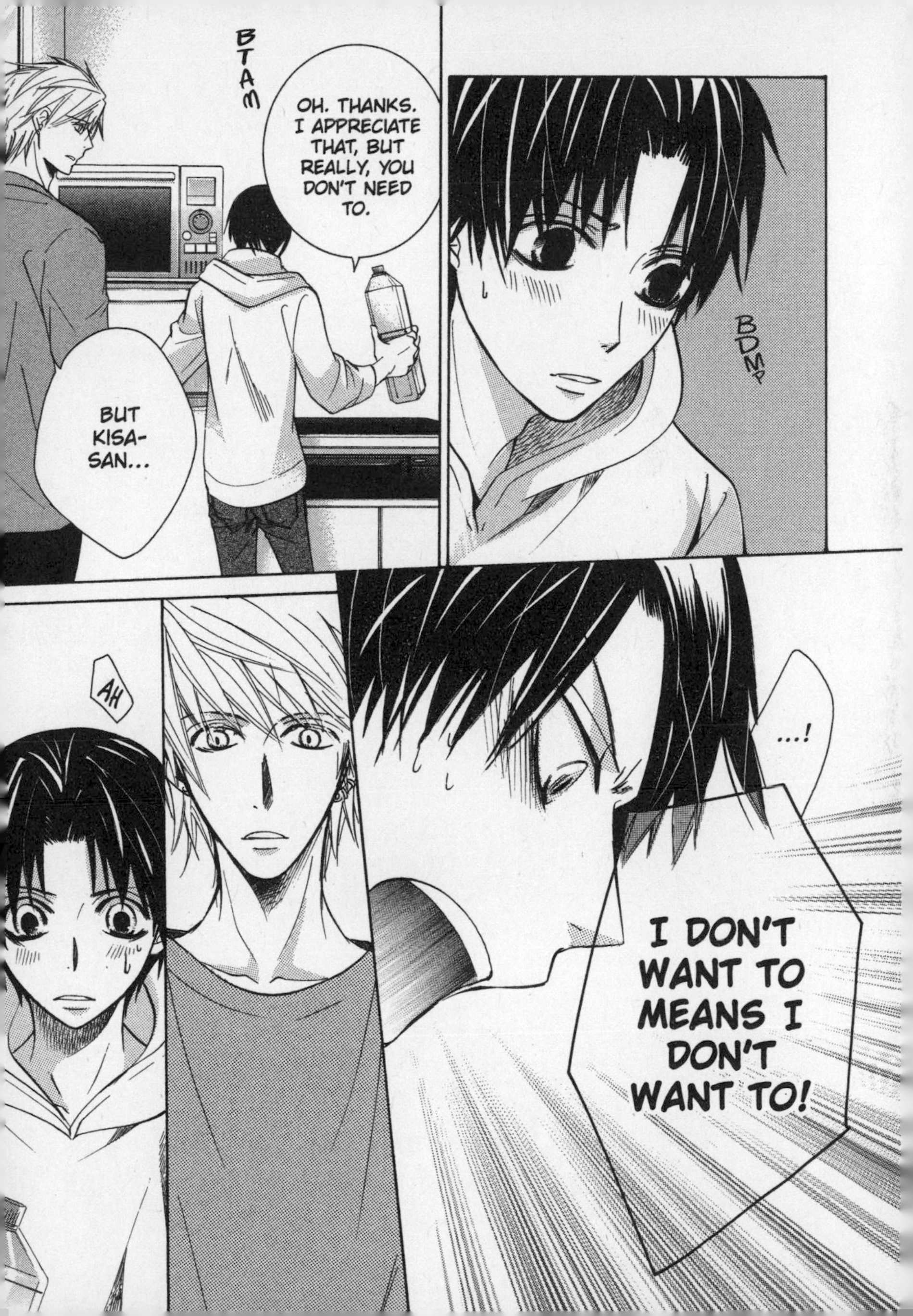
BDMP
OH. THANKS. I APPRECIATE THAT, BUT REALLY, YOU DON'T NEED TO.
BTAM
BUT KISA-SAN...
...!
I DON'T WANT TO MEANS I DON'T WANT TO!
AH

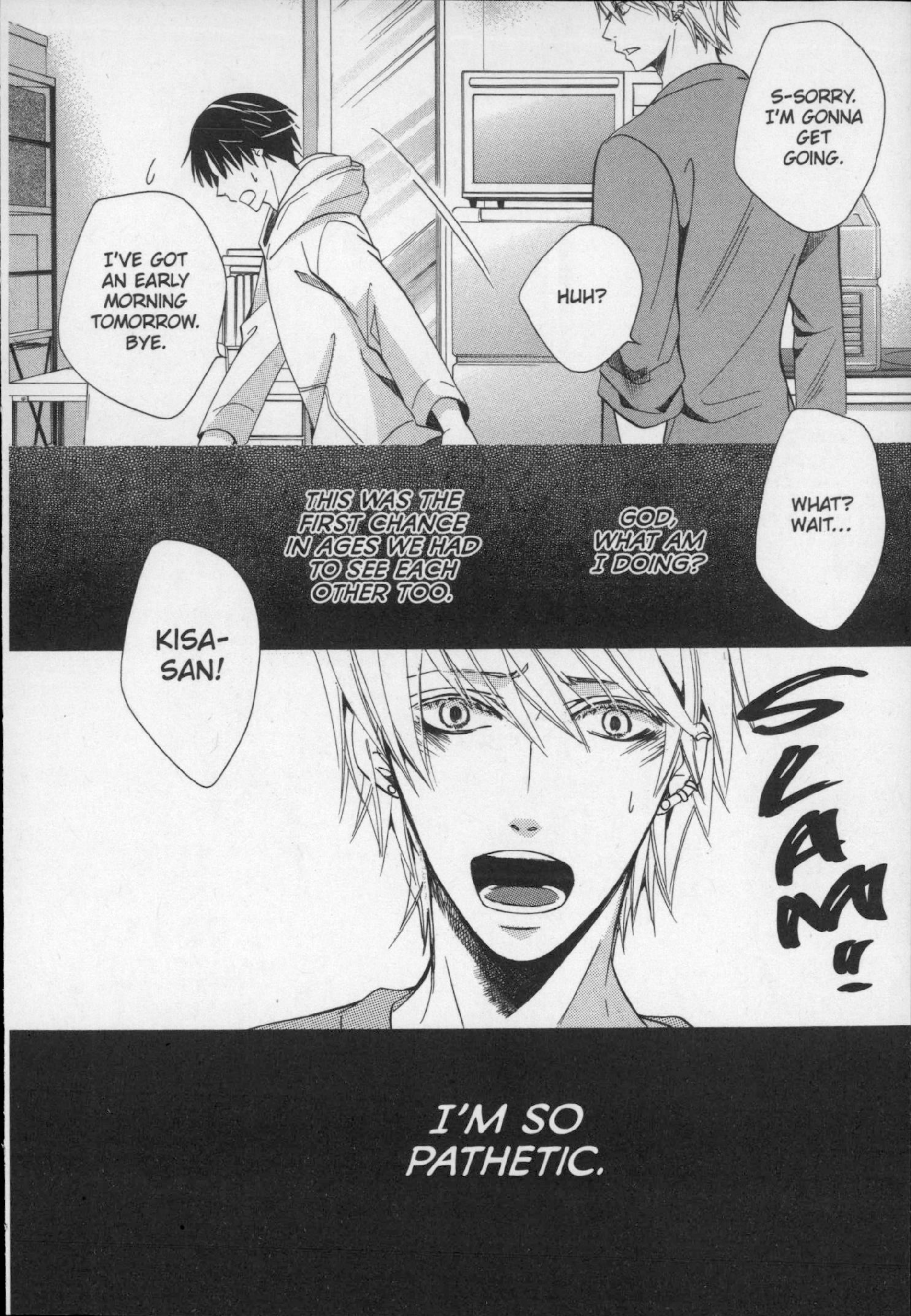
S-SORRY. I'M GONNA GET GOING.
HUH?
I'VE GOT AN EARLY MORNING TOMORROW. BYE.
WHAT? WAIT...
GOD, WHAT AM I DOING?
THIS WAS THE FIRST CHANCE IN AGES WE HAD TO SEE EACH OTHER TOO.
KISA-SAN!
SLAM!
I'M SO PATHETIC.

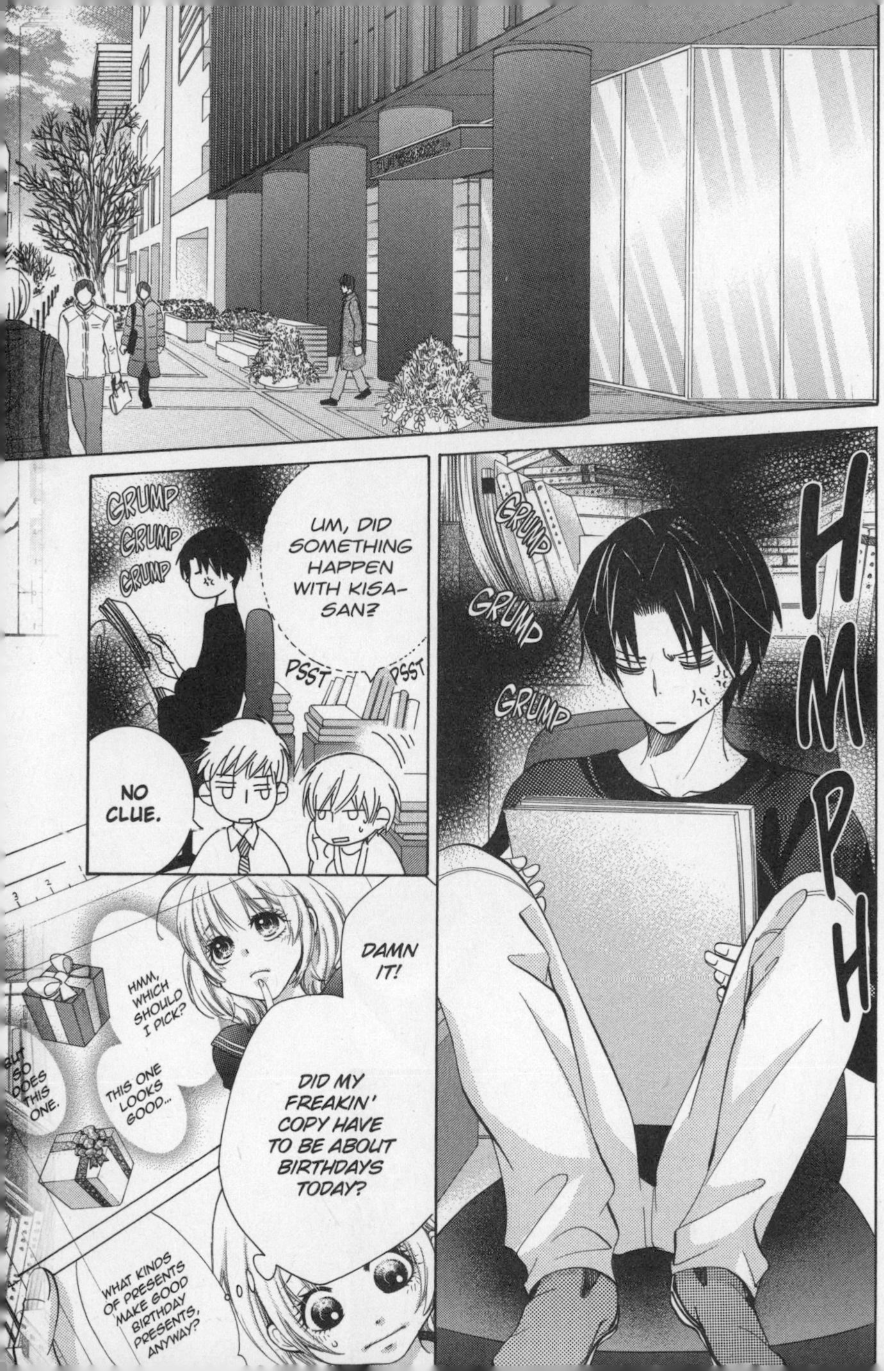
HMMPH
GRUMP
GRUMP
GRUMP
UM, DID SOMETHING HAPPEN WITH KISA-SAN?
GRUMP
GRUMP
GRUMP
PSST
PSST
NO CLUE.
DAMN IT!
HMM, WHICH SHOULD I PICK?
THIS ONE LOOKS GOOD...
SO DOES THIS ONE.
DID MY FREAKIN' COPY HAVE TO BE ABOUT BIRTHDAYS TODAY?
WHAT KINDS OF PRESENTS MAKE GOOD BIRTHDAY PRESENTS, ANYWAY?

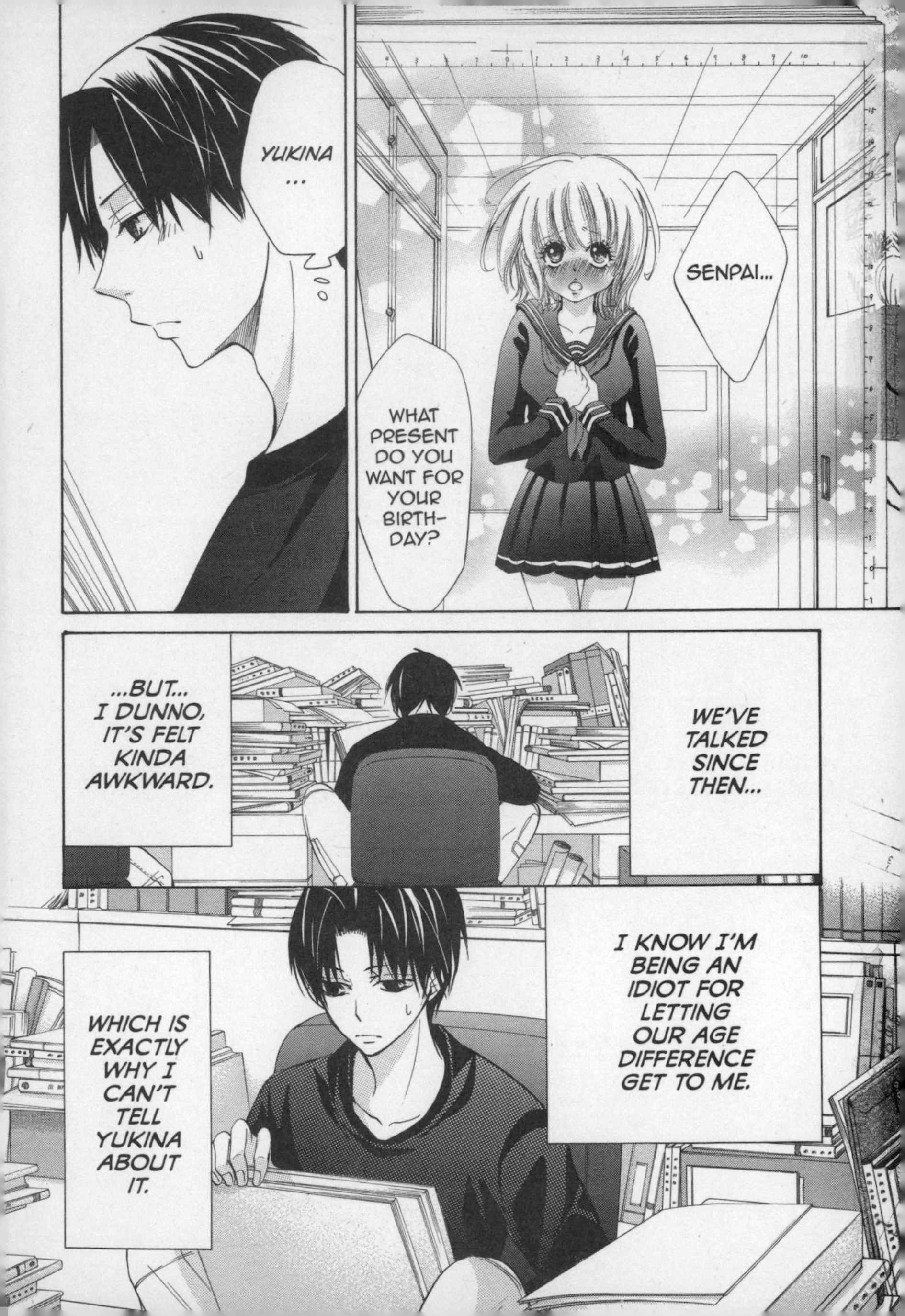
SENPAI...
WHAT PRESENT DO YOU WANT FOR YOUR BIRTH-DAY?
YUKINA ...
WE'VE TALKED SINCE THEN...
...BUT... I DUNNO, IT'S FELT KINDA AWKWARD.
I KNOW I'M BEING AN IDIOT FOR LETTING OUR AGE DIFFERENCE GET TO ME.
WHICH IS EXACTLY WHY I CAN'T TELL YUKINA ABOUT IT.

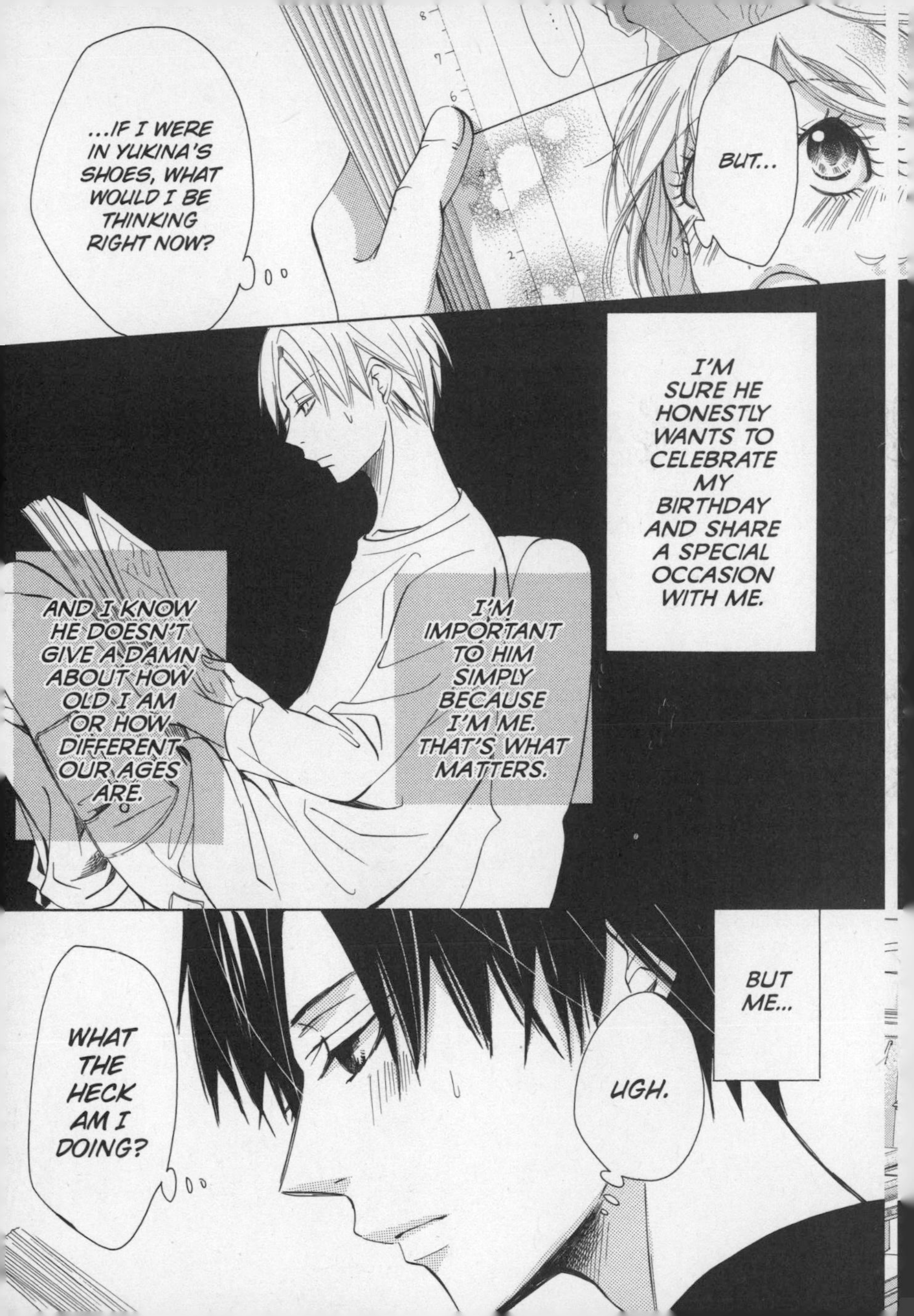
BUT...
...IF I WERE IN YUKINA'S SHOES, WHAT WOULD I BE THINKING RIGHT NOW?
I'M SURE HE HONESTLY WANTS TO CELEBRATE MY BIRTHDAY AND SHARE A SPECIAL OCCASION WITH ME.
I'M IMPORTANT TO HIM SIMPLY BECAUSE I'M ME. THAT'S WHAT MATTERS.
AND I KNOW HE DOESN'T GIVE A DAMN ABOUT HOW OLD I AM OR HOW DIFFERENT OUR AGES ARE.
BUT ME...
UGH.
WHAT THE HECK AM I DOING?

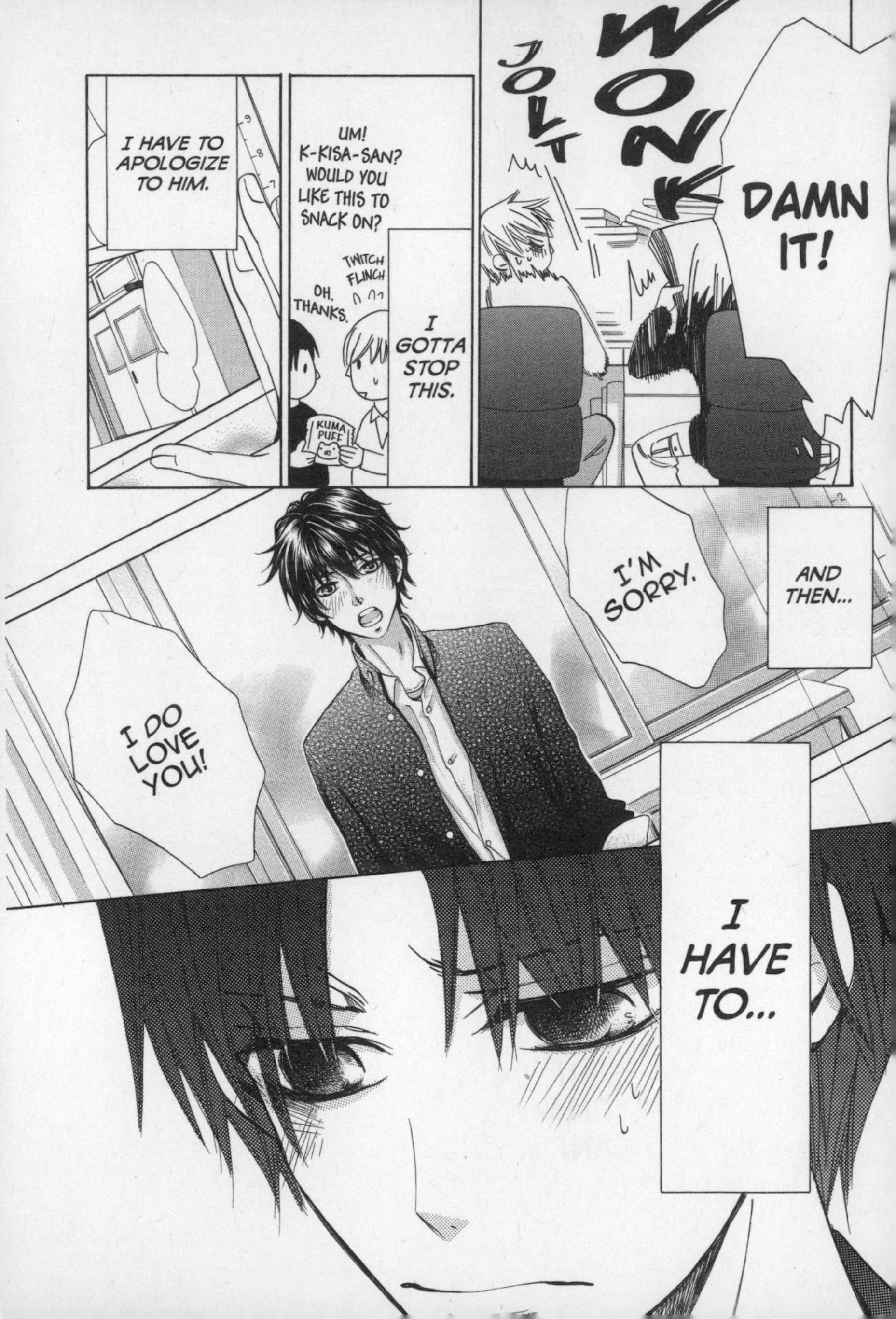
WONK
JOLT
DAMN IT!
UM! K-KISA-SAN? WOULD YOU LIKE THIS TO SNACK ON?
I GOTTA STOP THIS.
TWITCH FLINCH
OH. THANKS.
KUMA PUFF
I HAVE TO APOLOGIZE TO HIM.
AND THEN...
I'M SORRY.
I DO LOVE YOU!
I HAVE TO...

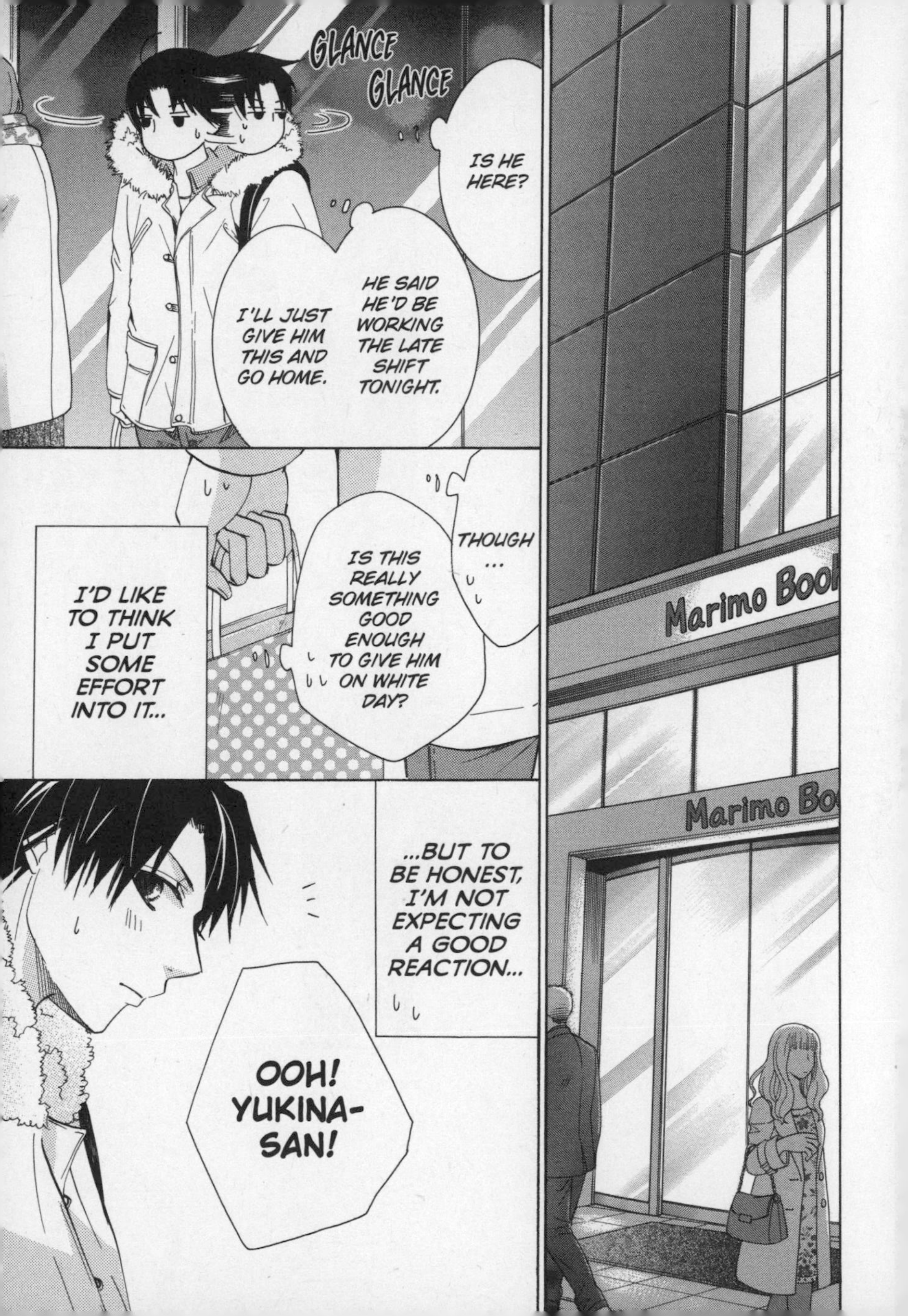
Marimo Boo
Marimo Bo
GLANCE GLANCE
IS HE HERE?
HE SAID HE'D BE WORKING THE LATE SHIFT TONIGHT.
I'LL JUST GIVE HIM THIS AND GO HOME.
THOUGH...
IS THIS REALLY SOMETHING GOOD ENOUGH TO GIVE HIM ON WHITE DAY?
I'D LIKE TO THINK I PUT SOME EFFORT INTO IT...
...BUT TO BE HONEST, I'M NOT EXPECTING A GOOD REACTION...
OOH! YUKINA-SAN!

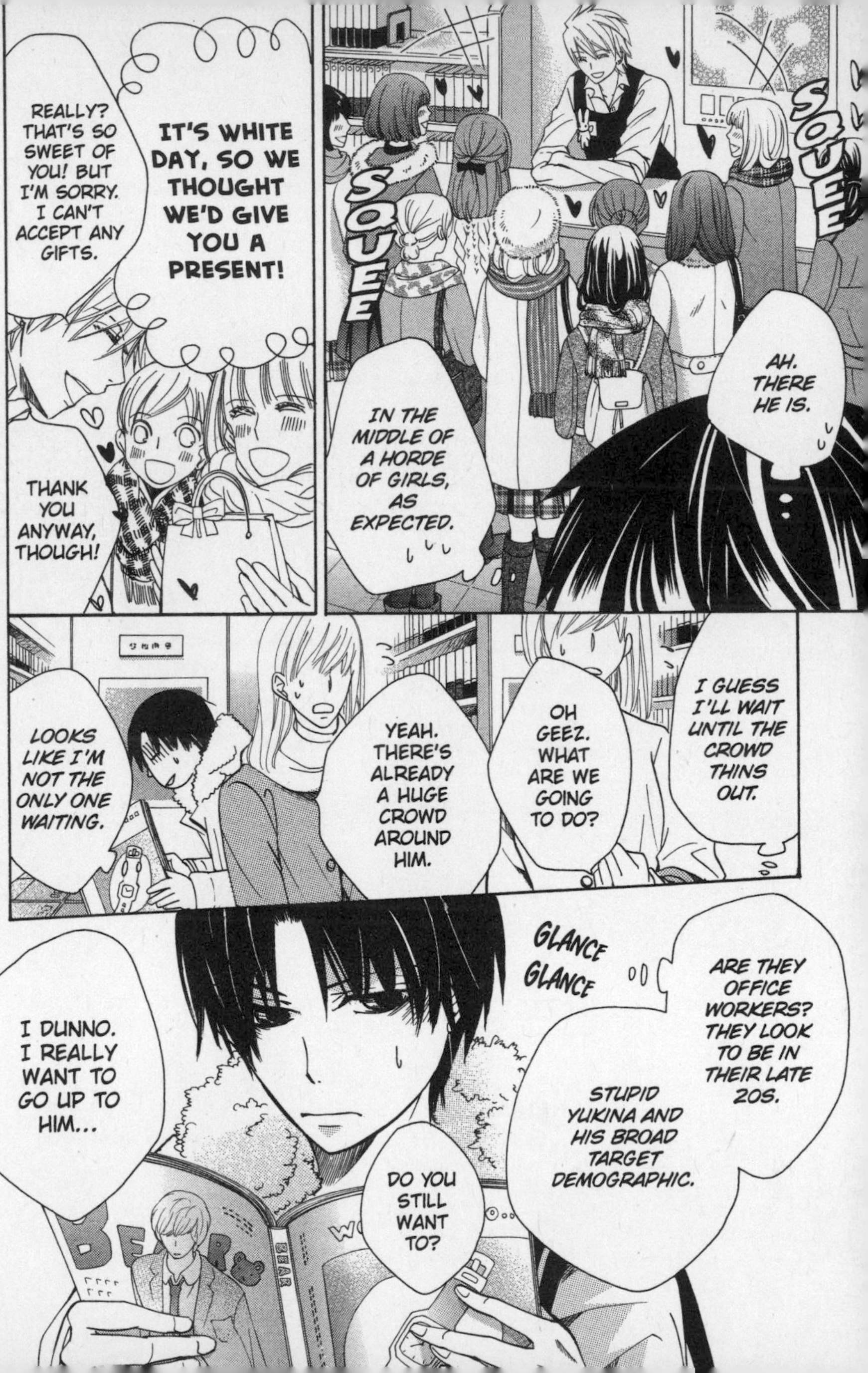
SQUEE
SQUEE
AH. THERE HE IS.
IN THE MIDDLE OF A HORDE OF GIRLS, AS EXPECTED.
IT'S WHITE DAY, SO WE THOUGHT WE'D GIVE YOU A PRESENT!
REALLY? THAT'S SO SWEET OF YOU! BUT I'M SORRY. I CAN'T ACCEPT ANY GIFTS.
THANK YOU ANYWAY, THOUGH!
I GUESS I'LL WAIT UNTIL THE CROWD THINS OUT.
OH GEEZ. WHAT ARE WE GOING TO DO?
YEAH. THERE'S ALREADY A HUGE CROWD AROUND HIM.
LOOKS LIKE I'M NOT THE ONLY ONE WAITING.
ARE THEY OFFICE WORKERS? THEY LOOK TO BE IN THEIR LATE 20S.
GLANCE GLANCE
STUPID YUKINA AND HIS BROAD TARGET DEMOGRAPHIC.
I DUNNO. I REALLY WANT TO GO UP TO HIM...
DO YOU STILL WANT TO?

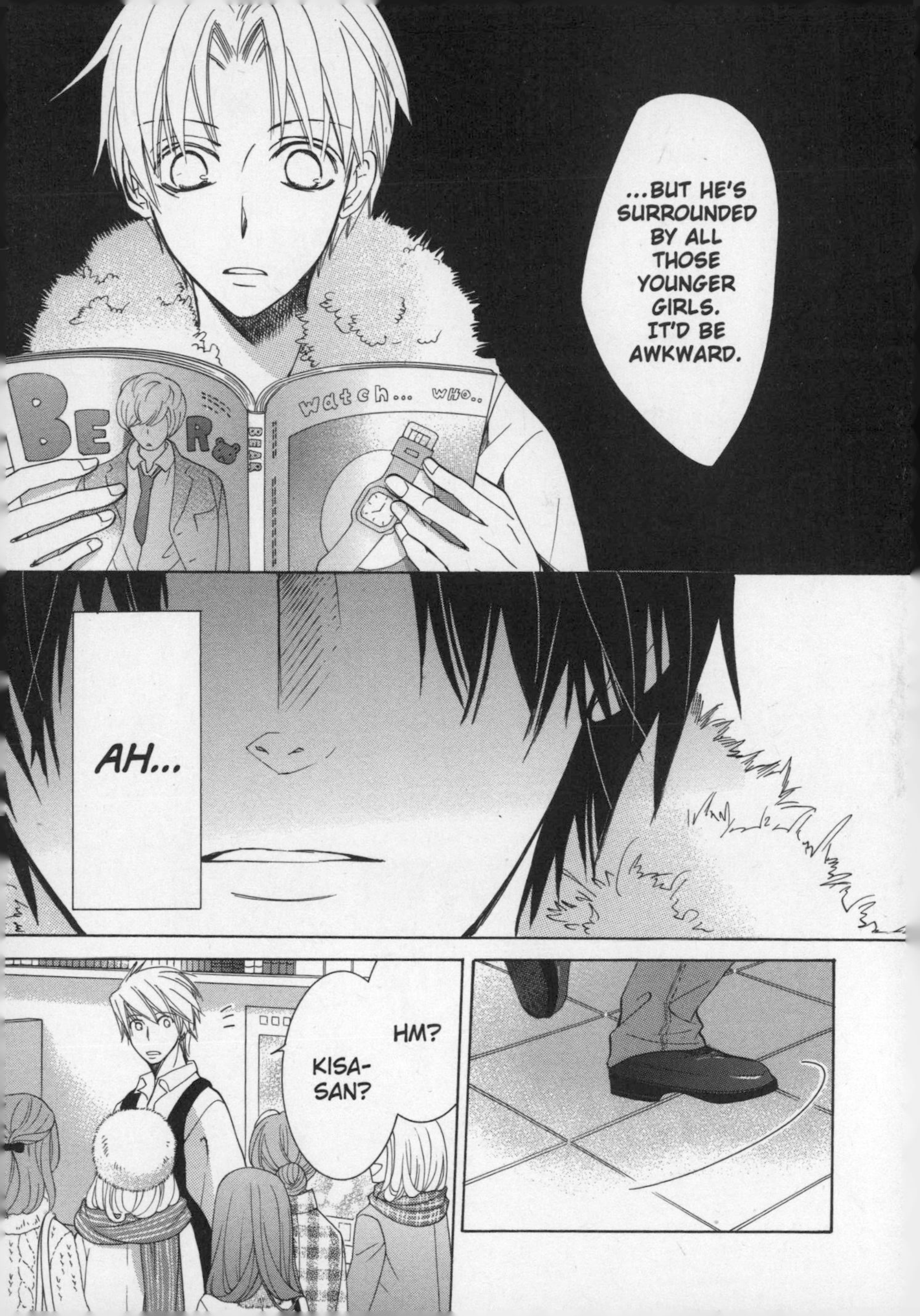
...BUT HE'S SURROUNDED BY ALL THOSE YOUNGER GIRLS. IT'D BE AWKWARD.
watch... WHO..
AH...
HM?
KISA-SAN?

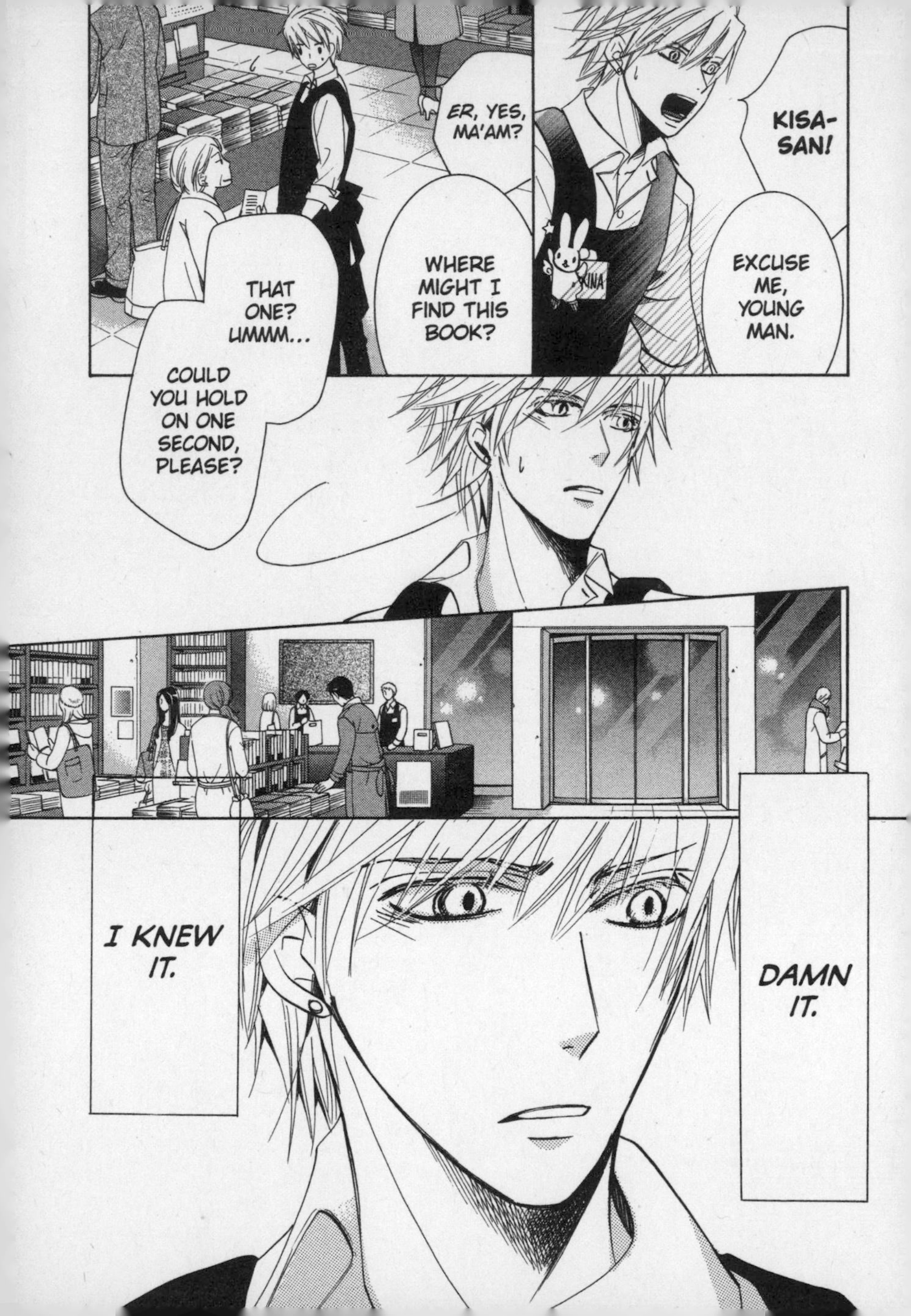
KISA-SAN!
EXCUSE ME, YOUNG MAN.
ER, YES, MA'AM?
WHERE MIGHT I FIND THIS BOOK?
THAT ONE? UMMM...
COULD YOU HOLD ON ONE SECOND, PLEASE?
DAMN IT.
I KNEW IT.

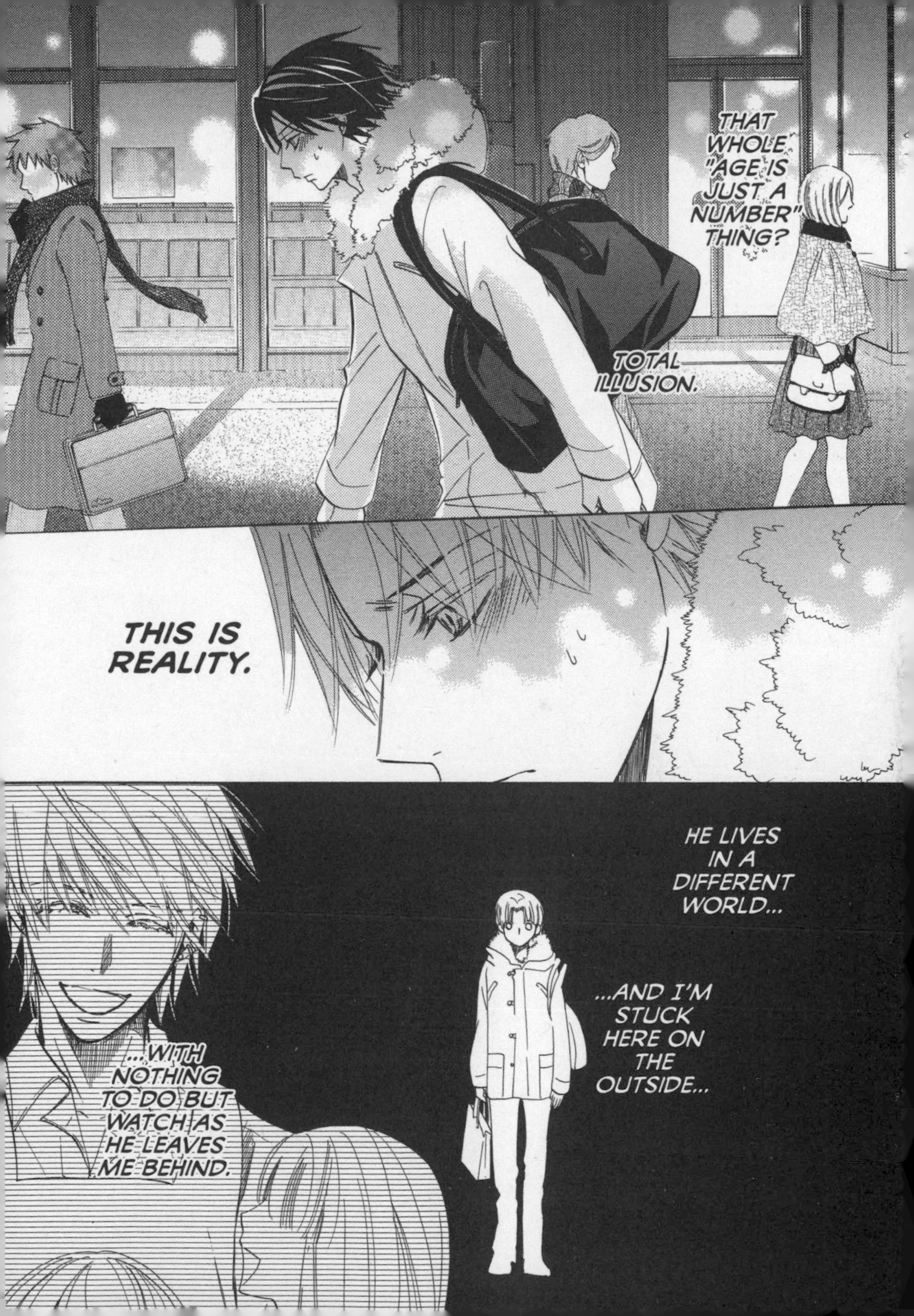
THAT WHOLE "AGE IS JUST A NUMBER" THING?
TOTAL ILLUSION.
THIS IS REALITY.
HE LIVES IN A DIFFERENT WORLD...
...AND I'M STUCK HERE ON THE OUTSIDE...
...WITH NOTHING TO DO BUT WATCH AS HE LEAVES ME BEHIND.

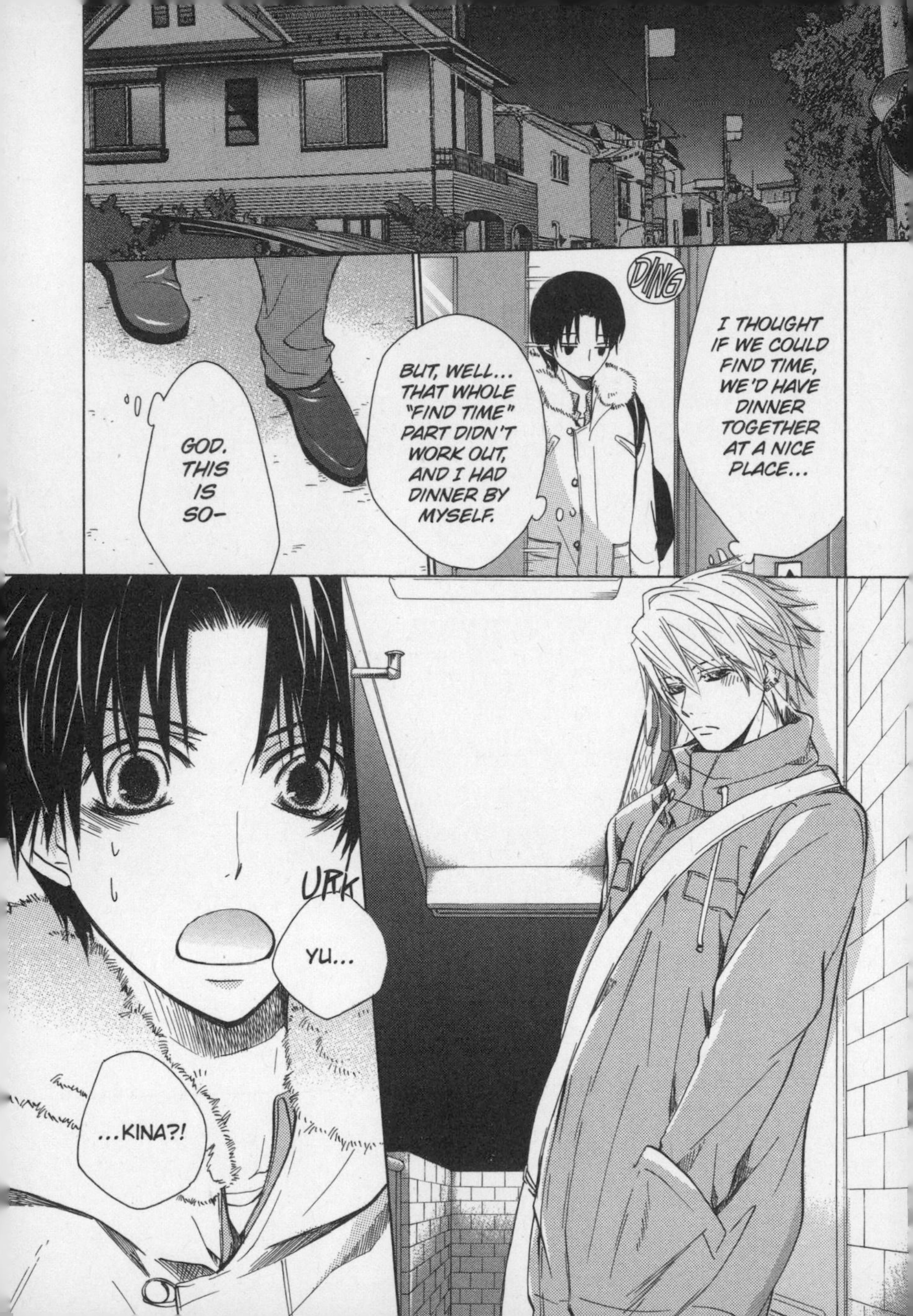
I THOUGHT IF WE COULD FIND TIME, WE'D HAVE DINNER TOGETHER AT A NICE PLACE...
DING
BUT, WELL... THAT WHOLE "FIND TIME" PART DIDN'T WORK OUT, AND I HAD DINNER BY MYSELF.
GOD. THIS IS SO-
URK
YU...
...KINA?!

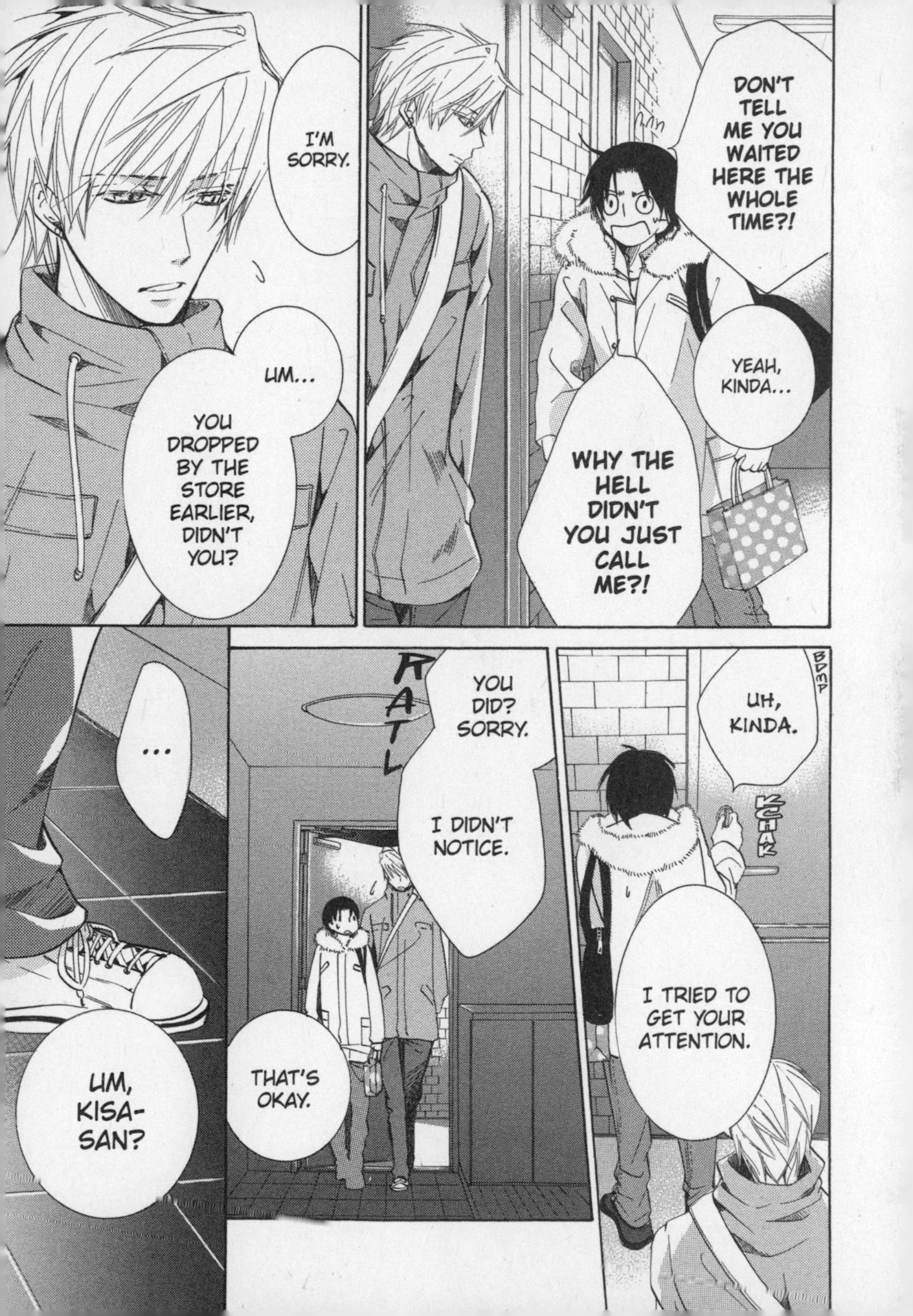
DON'T TELL ME YOU WAITED HERE THE WHOLE TIME?!
YEAH, KINDA...
WHY THE HELL DIDN'T YOU JUST CALL ME?!
I'M SORRY.
UM...
YOU DROPPED BY THE STORE EARLIER, DIDN'T YOU?
BDMP
UH, KINDA.
KCHAK
I TRIED TO GET YOUR ATTENTION.
RATTL
YOU DID? SORRY.
I DIDN'T NOTICE.
THAT'S OKAY.
...
UM, KISA-SAN?

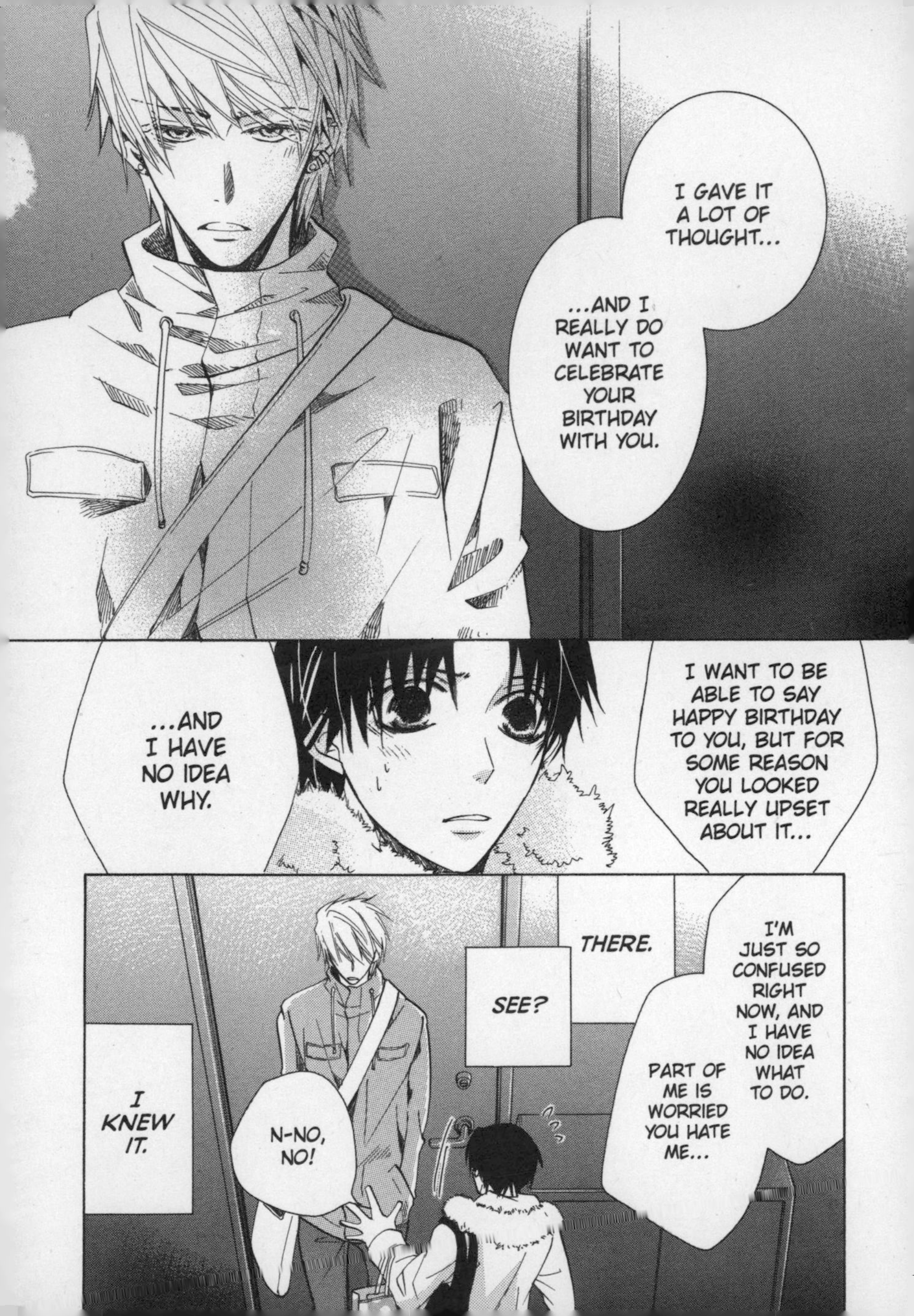
I GAVE IT A LOT OF THOUGHT...
...AND I REALLY DO WANT TO CELEBRATE YOUR BIRTHDAY WITH YOU.
I WANT TO BE ABLE TO SAY HAPPY BIRTHDAY TO YOU, BUT FOR SOME REASON YOU LOOKED REALLY UPSET ABOUT IT...
...AND I HAVE NO IDEA WHY.
I'M JUST SO CONFUSED RIGHT NOW, AND I HAVE NO IDEA WHAT TO DO.
PART OF ME IS WORRIED YOU HATE ME...
THERE.
SEE?
N-NO, NO!
I KNEW IT.

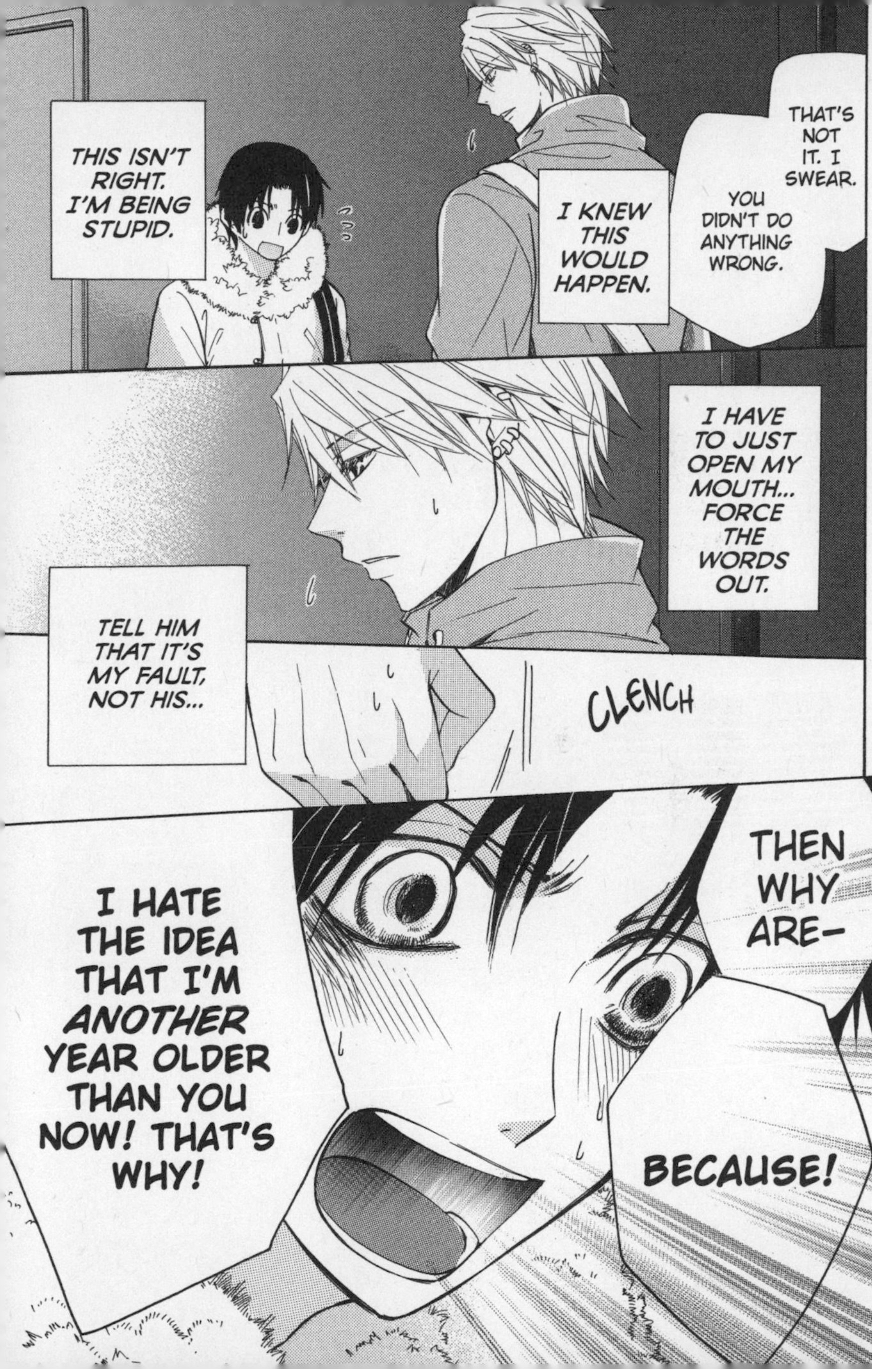
THAT'S NOT IT. I SWEAR.
YOU DIDN'T DO ANYTHING WRONG.
I KNEW THIS WOULD HAPPEN.
THIS ISN'T RIGHT. I'M BEING STUPID.
I HAVE TO JUST OPEN MY MOUTH... FORCE THE WORDS OUT.
TELL HIM THAT IT'S MY FAULT, NOT HIS...
CLENCH
THEN WHY ARE-
BECAUSE!
I HATE THE IDEA THAT I'M *ANOTHER* YEAR OLDER THAN YOU NOW! THAT'S WHY!

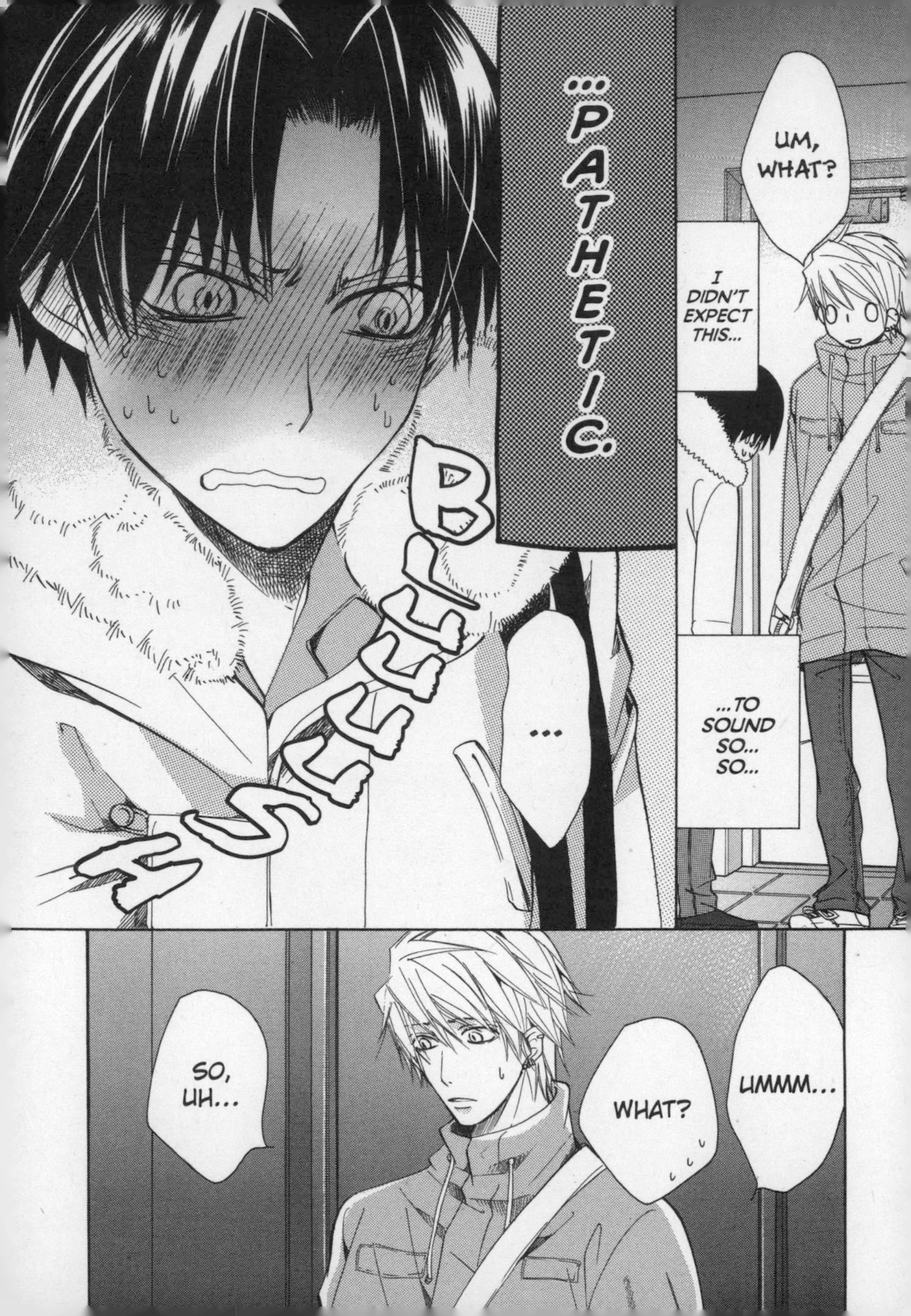
UM, WHAT?
I DIDN'T EXPECT THIS...
...TO SOUND SO... SO...
...PATHETIC.
...
BLUUUUSH
UMMM...
WHAT?
SO, UH...

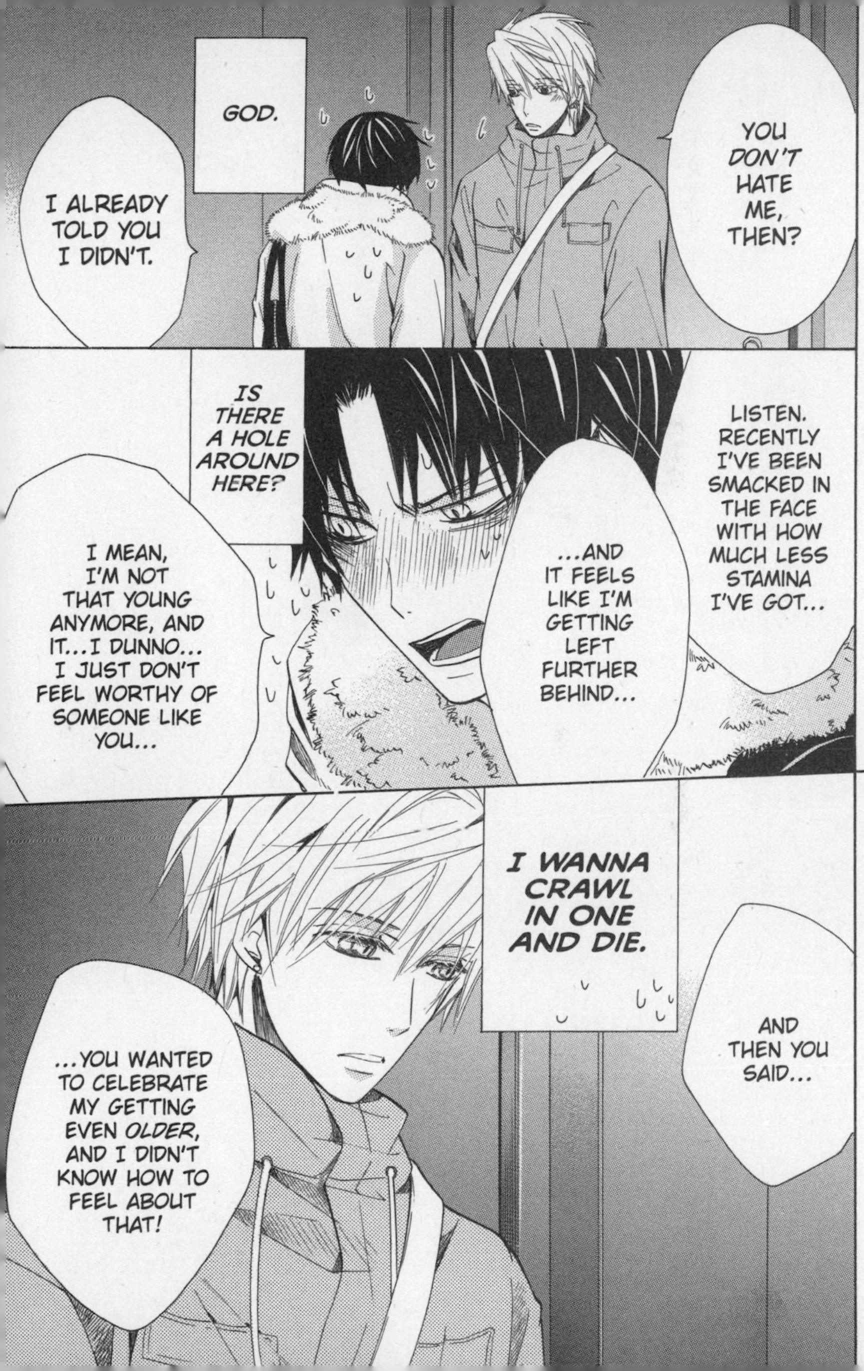
YOU DON'T HATE ME, THEN?
GOD.
I ALREADY TOLD YOU I DIDN'T.
LISTEN. RECENTLY I'VE BEEN SMACKED IN THE FACE WITH HOW MUCH LESS STAMINA I'VE GOT...
...AND IT FEELS LIKE I'M GETTING LEFT FURTHER BEHIND...
IS THERE A HOLE AROUND HERE?
I MEAN, I'M NOT THAT YOUNG ANYMORE, AND IT...I DUNNO... I JUST DON'T FEEL WORTHY OF SOMEONE LIKE YOU...
AND THEN YOU SAID...
I WANNA CRAWL IN ONE AND DIE.
...YOU WANTED TO CELEBRATE MY GETTING EVEN OLDER, AND I DIDN'T KNOW HOW TO FEEL ABOUT THAT!

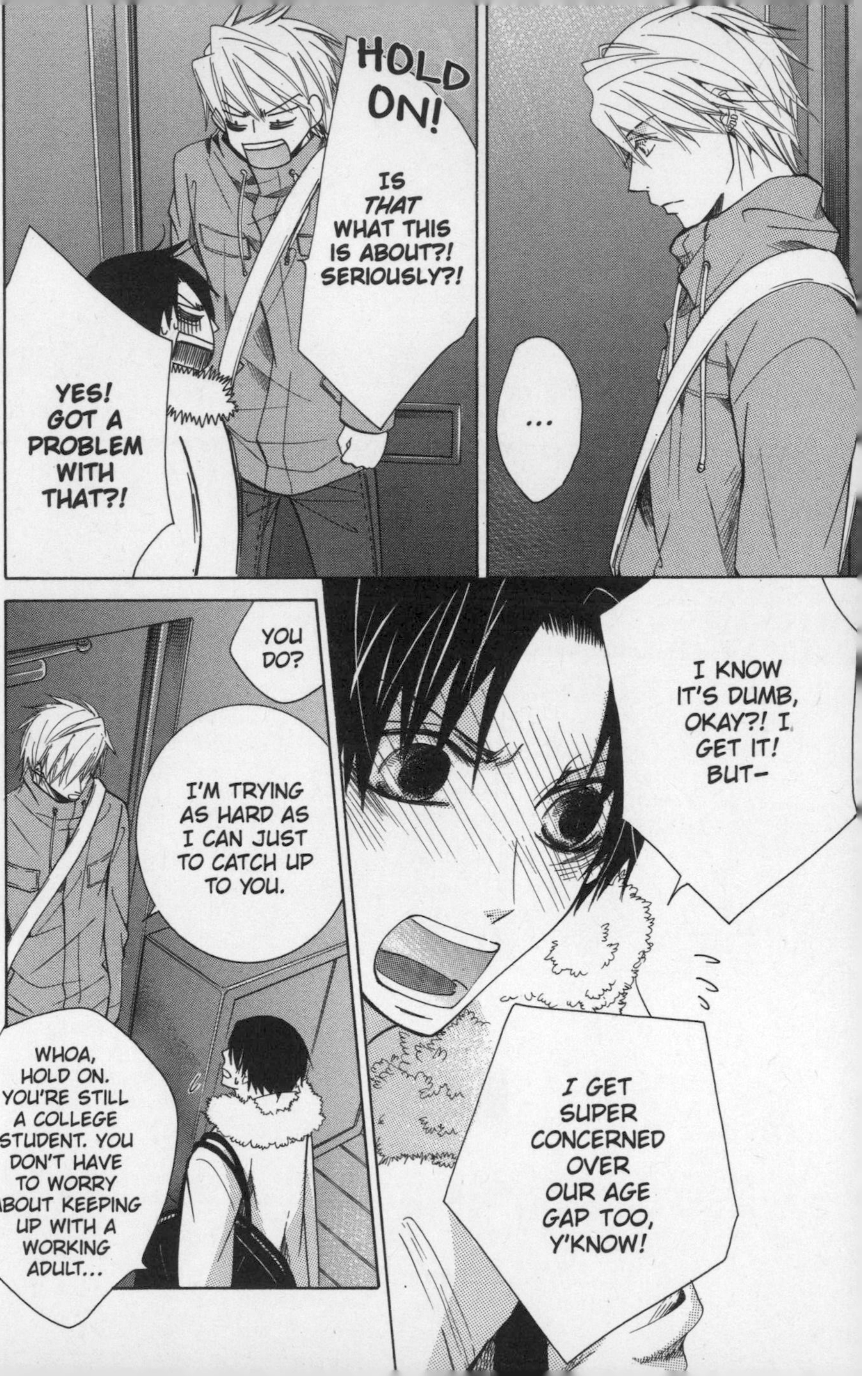
...
HOLD ON!
IS *THAT* WHAT THIS IS ABOUT?! SERIOUSLY?!
YES! GOT A PROBLEM WITH THAT?!
I KNOW IT'S DUMB, OKAY?! I GET IT! BUT-
I GET SUPER CONCERNED OVER OUR AGE GAP TOO, Y'KNOW!
YOU DO?
I'M TRYING AS HARD AS I CAN JUST TO CATCH UP TO YOU.
WHOA, HOLD ON. YOU'RE STILL A COLLEGE STUDENT. YOU DON'T HAVE TO WORRY ABOUT KEEPING UP WITH A WORKING ADULT...

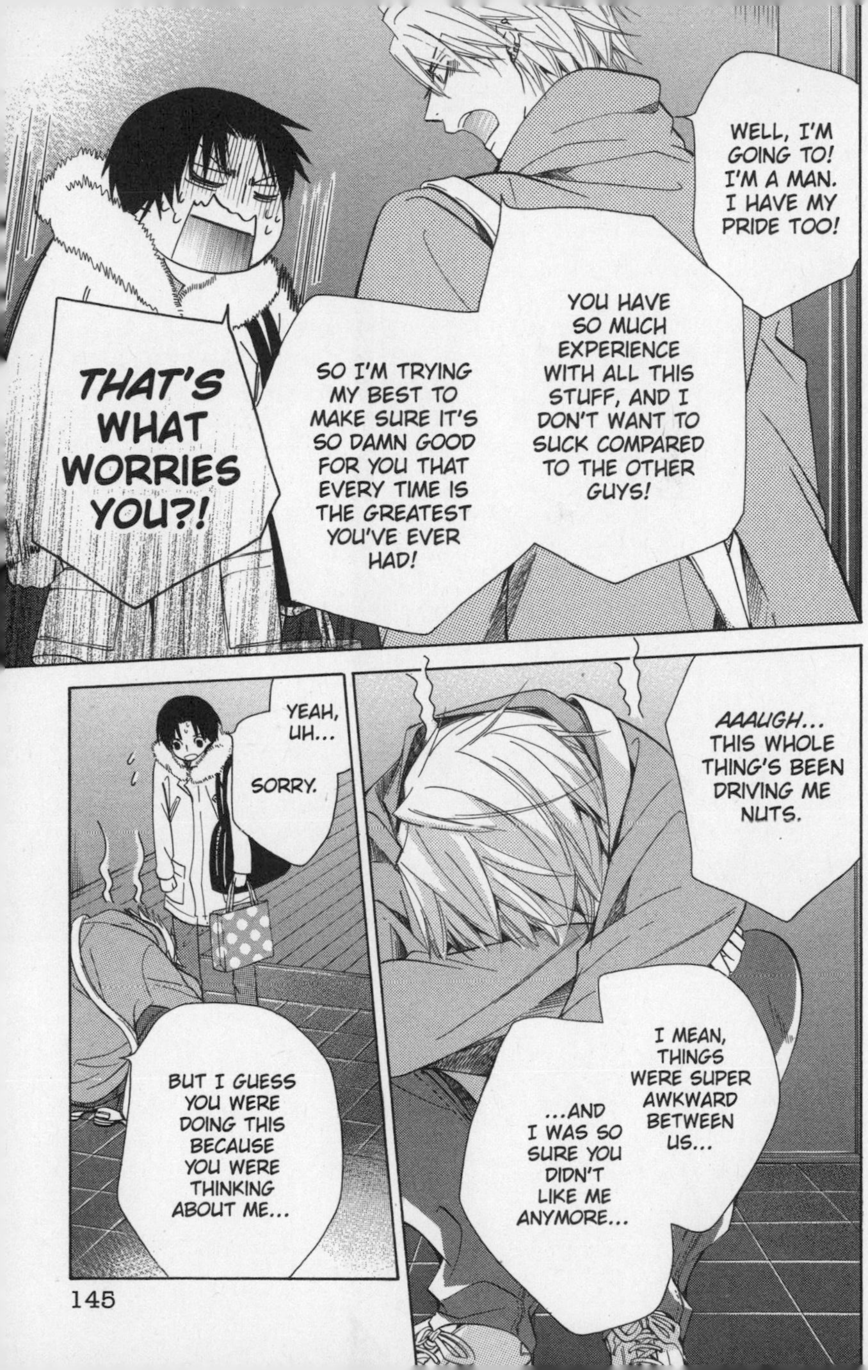
WELL, I'M GOING TO! I'M A MAN. I HAVE MY PRIDE TOO!
YOU HAVE SO MUCH EXPERIENCE WITH ALL THIS STUFF, AND I DON'T WANT TO SUCK COMPARED TO THE OTHER GUYS!
SO I'M TRYING MY BEST TO MAKE SURE IT'S SO DAMN GOOD FOR YOU THAT EVERY TIME IS THE GREATEST YOU'VE EVER HAD!
THAT'S WHAT WORRIES YOU?!
AAAUGH... THIS WHOLE THING'S BEEN DRIVING ME NUTS.
I MEAN, THINGS WERE SUPER AWKWARD BETWEEN US...
...AND I WAS SO SURE YOU DIDN'T LIKE ME ANYMORE...
YEAH, UH...
SORRY.
BUT I GUESS YOU WERE DOING THIS BECAUSE YOU WERE THINKING ABOUT ME...

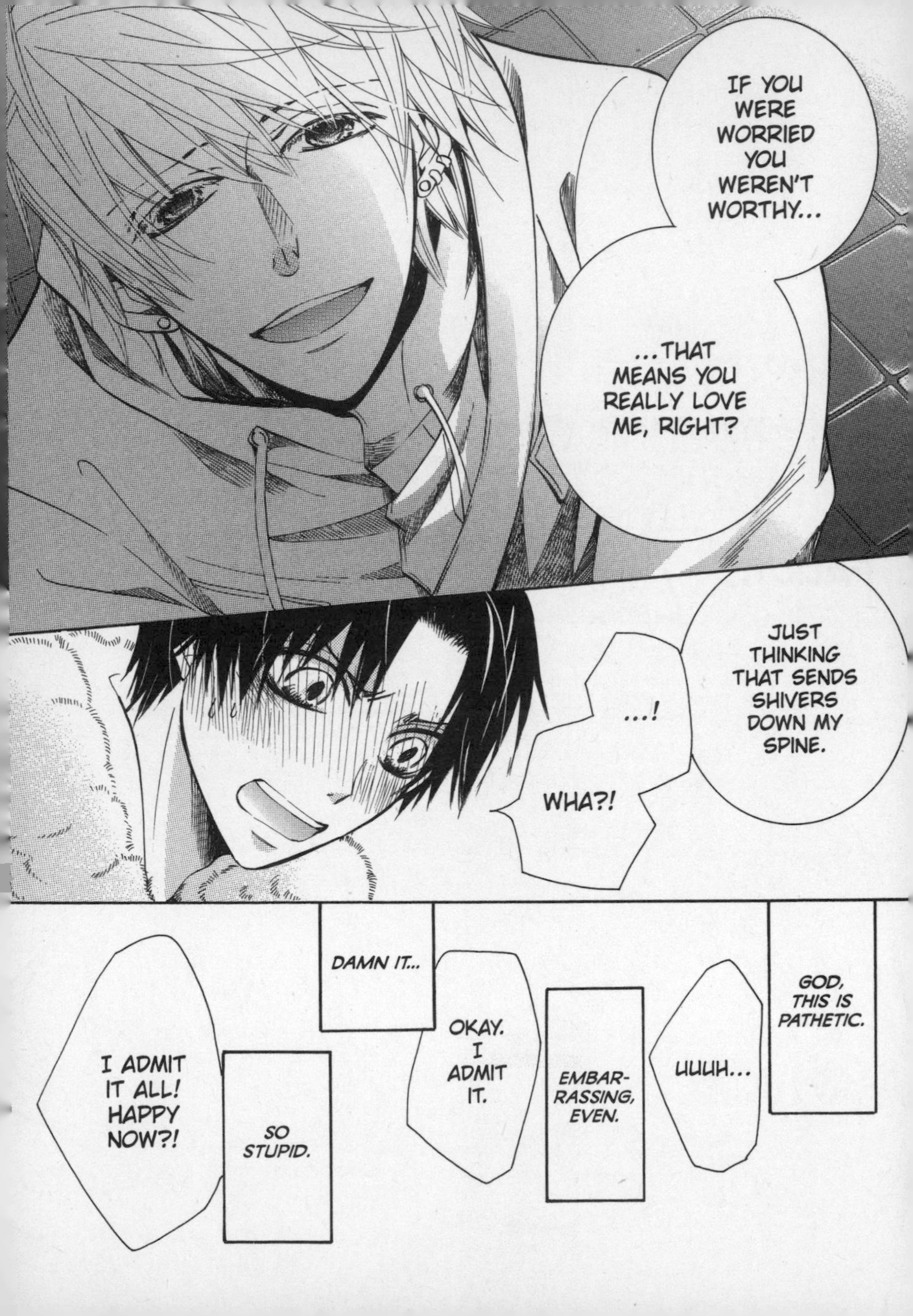
IF YOU WERE WORRIED YOU WEREN'T WORTHY...
...THAT MEANS YOU REALLY LOVE ME, RIGHT?
JUST THINKING THAT SENDS SHIVERS DOWN MY SPINE.
...! WHA?!
GOD, THIS IS PATHETIC.
UUUH...
EMBAR-RASSING, EVEN.
DAMN IT...
OKAY. I ADMIT IT.
SO STUPID.
I ADMIT IT ALL! HAPPY NOW?!

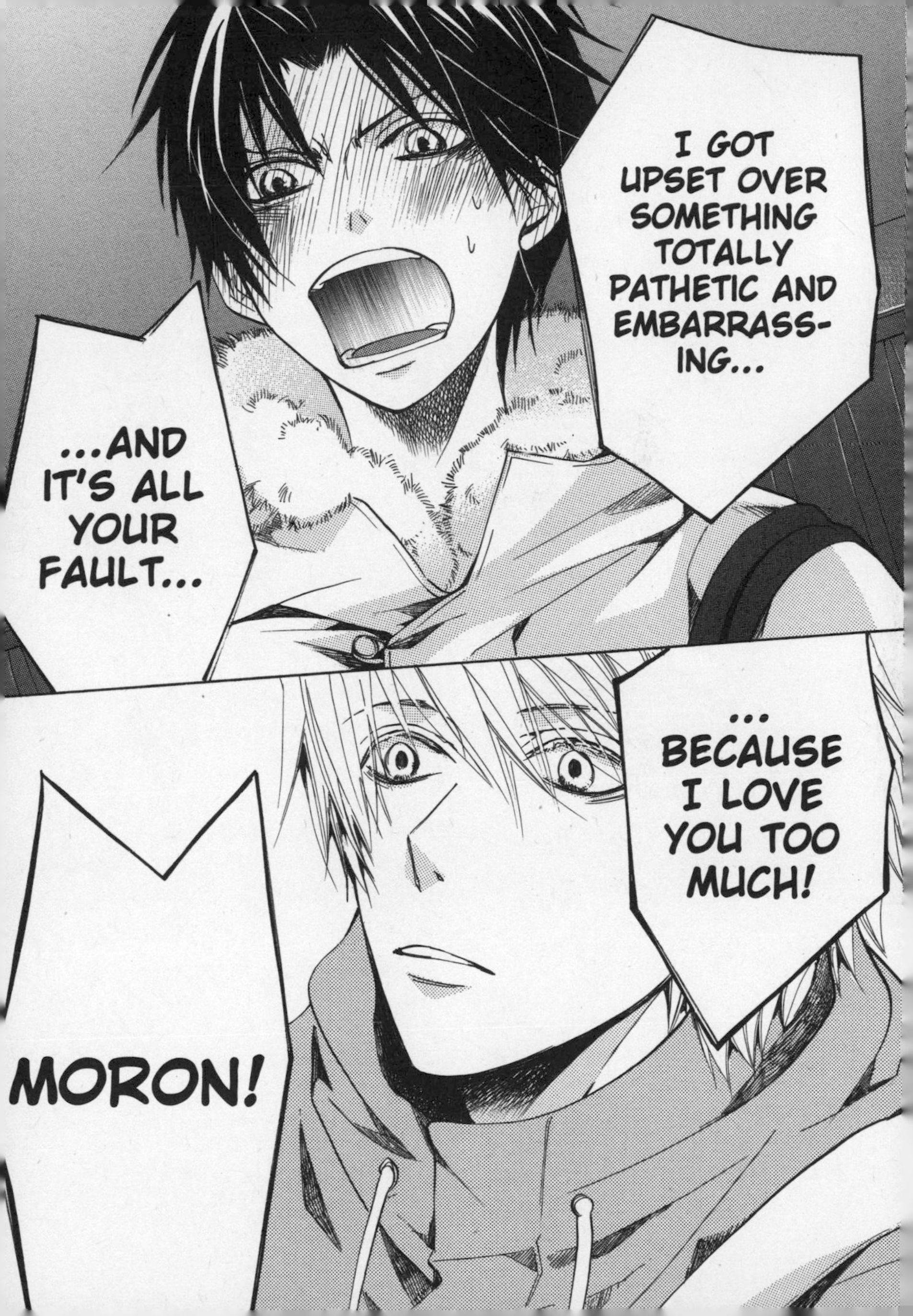
I GOT UPSET OVER SOMETHING TOTALLY PATHETIC AND EMBARRASS-ING...
...AND IT'S ALL YOUR FAULT...
...BECAUSE I LOVE YOU TOO MUCH!
MORON!

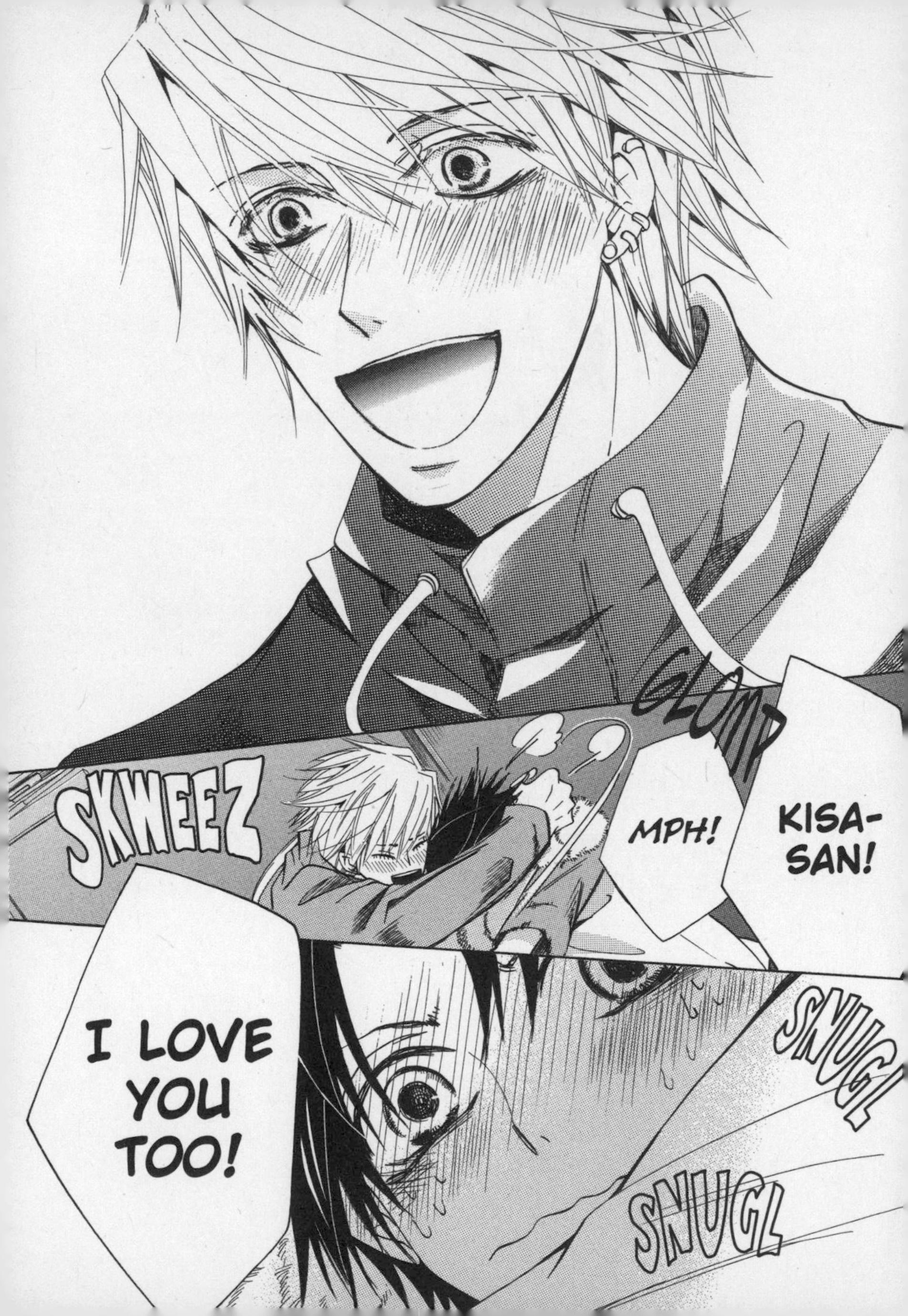
GLOMP
KISA-SAN!
MPH!
SKWEEZ
SNUGL
SNUGL
I LOVE YOU TOO!

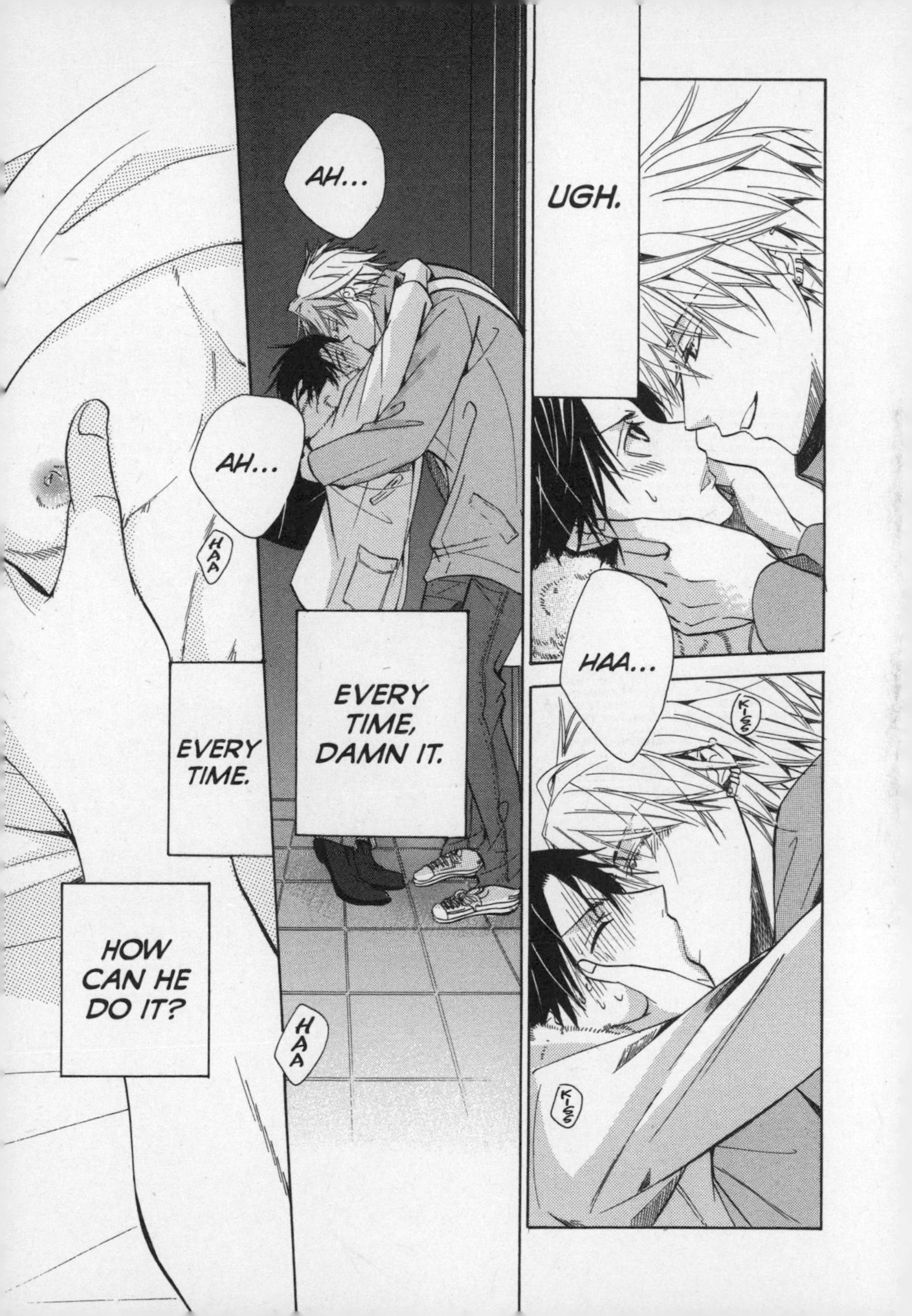
UGH.
HAA...
KISS
KISS
AH...
AH...
HAA
EVERY TIME, DAMN IT.
EVERY TIME.
HOW CAN HE DO IT?
HAA

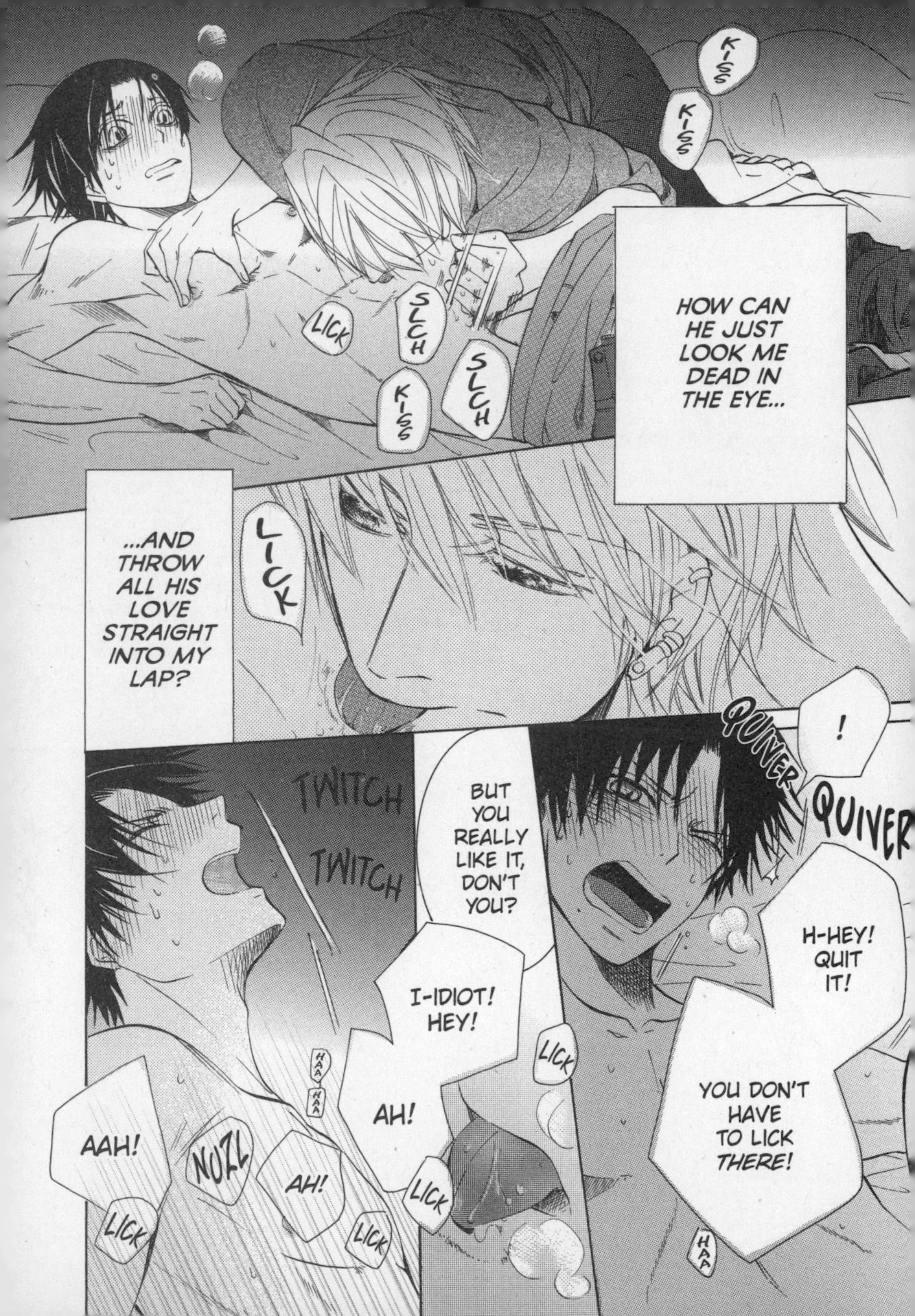

KISS
KISS
HOW CAN HE JUST LOOK ME DEAD IN THE EYE...
SLCH
SLCH
LICK
KISS
LICK
...AND THROW ALL HIS LOVE STRAIGHT INTO MY LAP?
!
QUIVER
QUIVER
H-HEY! QUIT IT!
YOU DON'T HAVE TO LICK THERE!
LICK
LICK
HAA
BUT YOU REALLY LIKE IT, DON'T YOU?
TWITCH
TWITCH
I-IDIOT! HEY!
HAA
HAA
AH!
AAH!
NUZZ
AH!
LICK
LICK

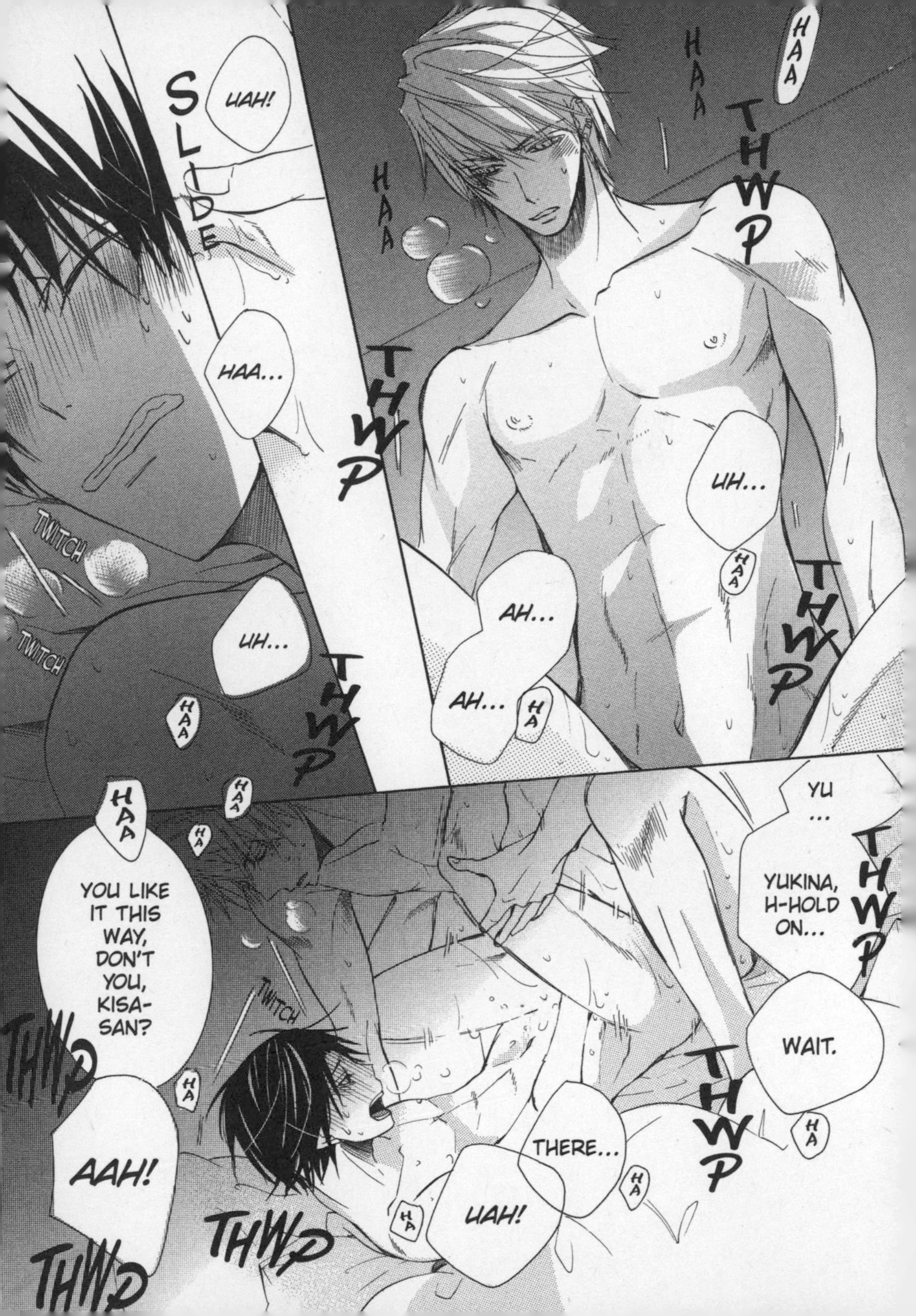
HAA HAA
HAA HAA
THWP
HAA HAA
UH...
HAA
THWP
AH...
AH...
HA
UAH!
SLIDE
HAA...
THWP
TWITCH
TWITCH
UH...
HAA
THWP
YU...
YUKINA, H-HOLD ON...
THWP
WAIT.
THWP
HA
THERE...
HA
UAH!
HA
HAA
HAA
HA
YOU LIKE IT THIS WAY, DON'T YOU, KISA-SAN?
TWITCH
THWP
HA
AAH!
THWP
THWP

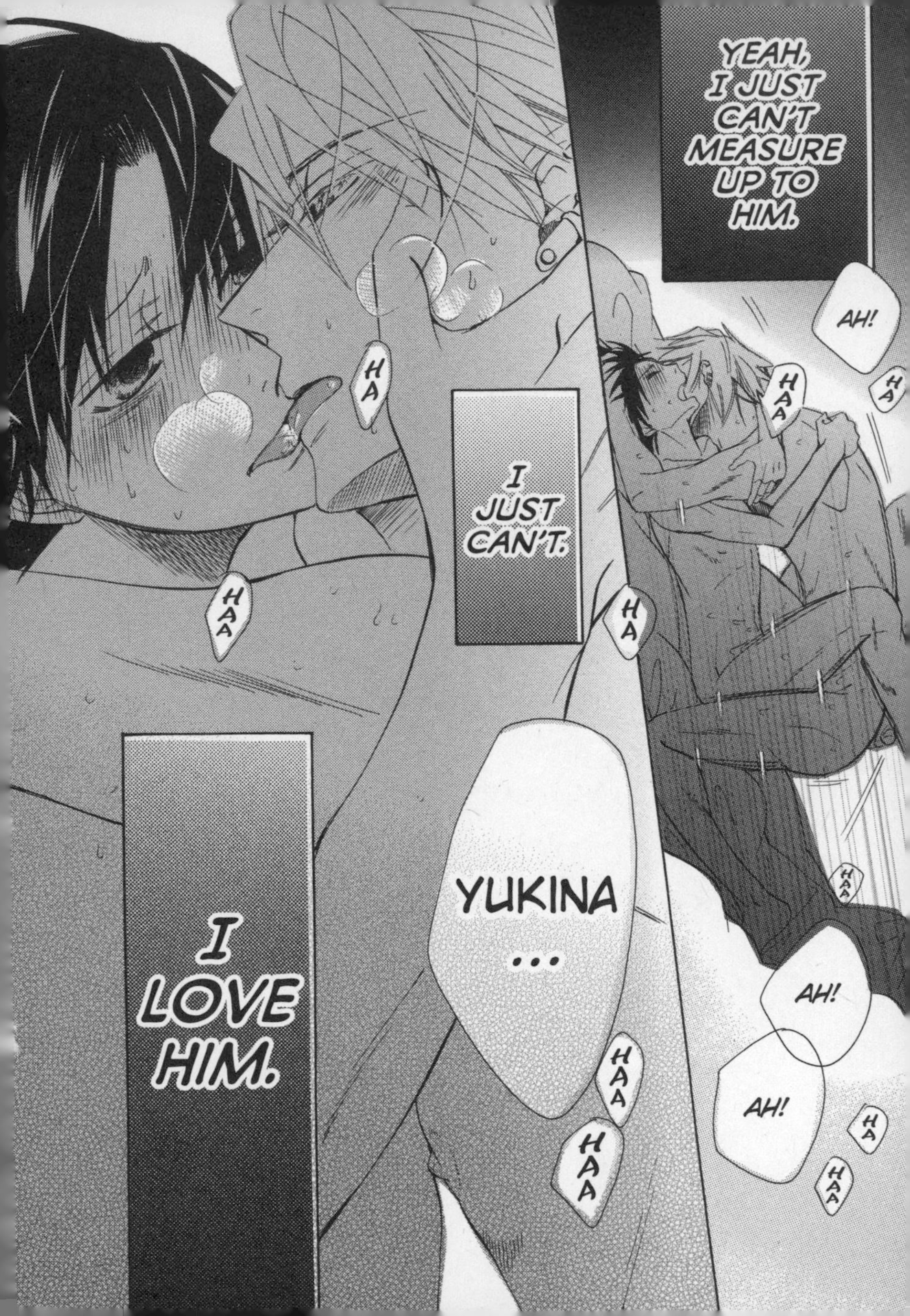
YEAH, I JUST CAN'T MEASURE UP TO HIM.
AH!
HA
HAA
HA
HAA
AH!
AH!
HA
HAA
HA
I JUST CAN'T.
HAA
YUKINA ...
I LOVE HIM.
HAA
HAA

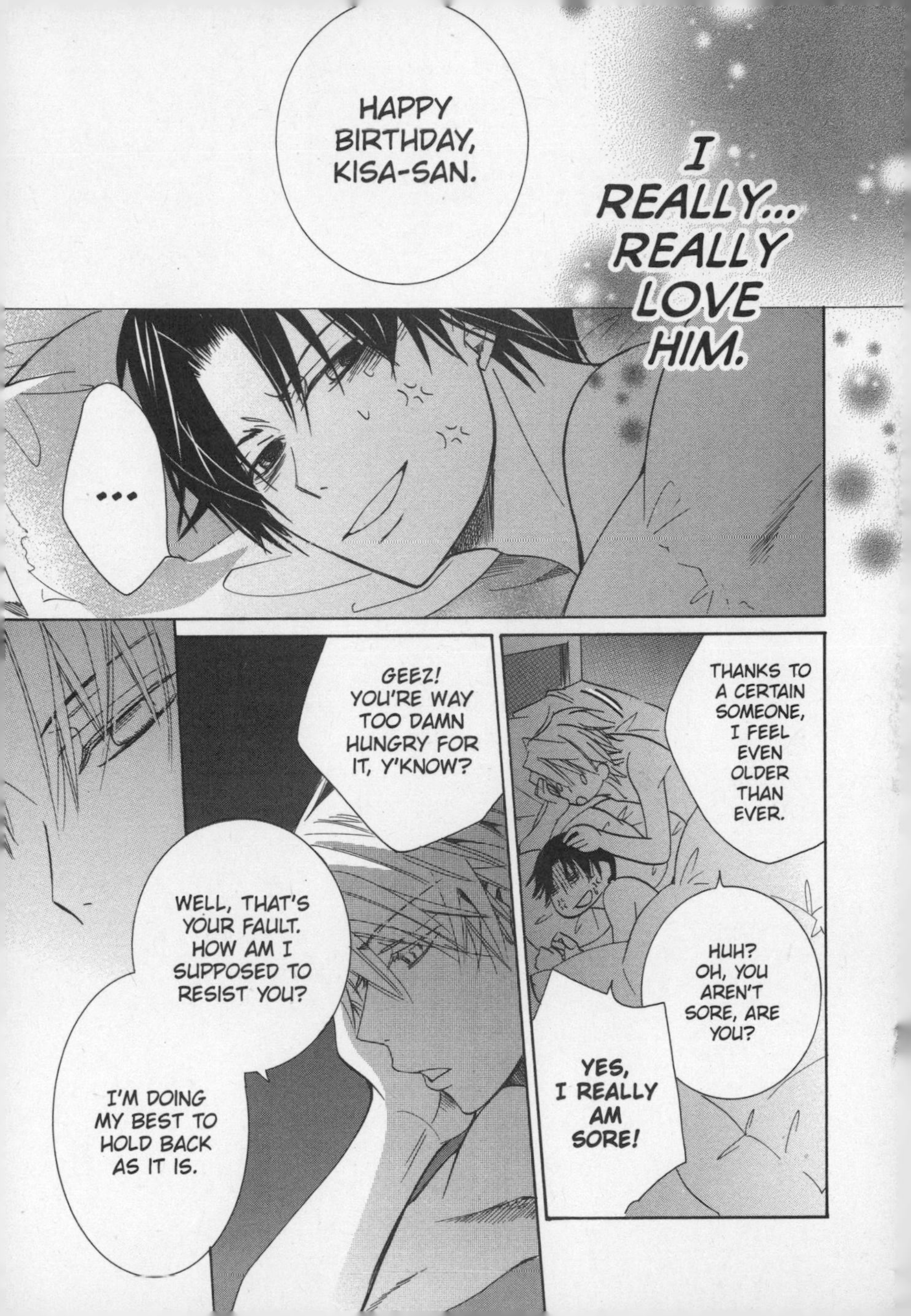
HAPPY BIRTHDAY, KISA-SAN.
I REALLY... REALLY LOVE HIM.
...
THANKS TO A CERTAIN SOMEONE, I FEEL EVEN OLDER THAN EVER.
HUH? OH, YOU AREN'T SORE, ARE YOU?
YES, I REALLY AM SORE!
GEEZ! YOU'RE WAY TOO DAMN HUNGRY FOR IT, Y'KNOW?
WELL, THAT'S YOUR FAULT. HOW AM I SUPPOSED TO RESIST YOU?
I'M DOING MY BEST TO HOLD BACK AS IT IS.

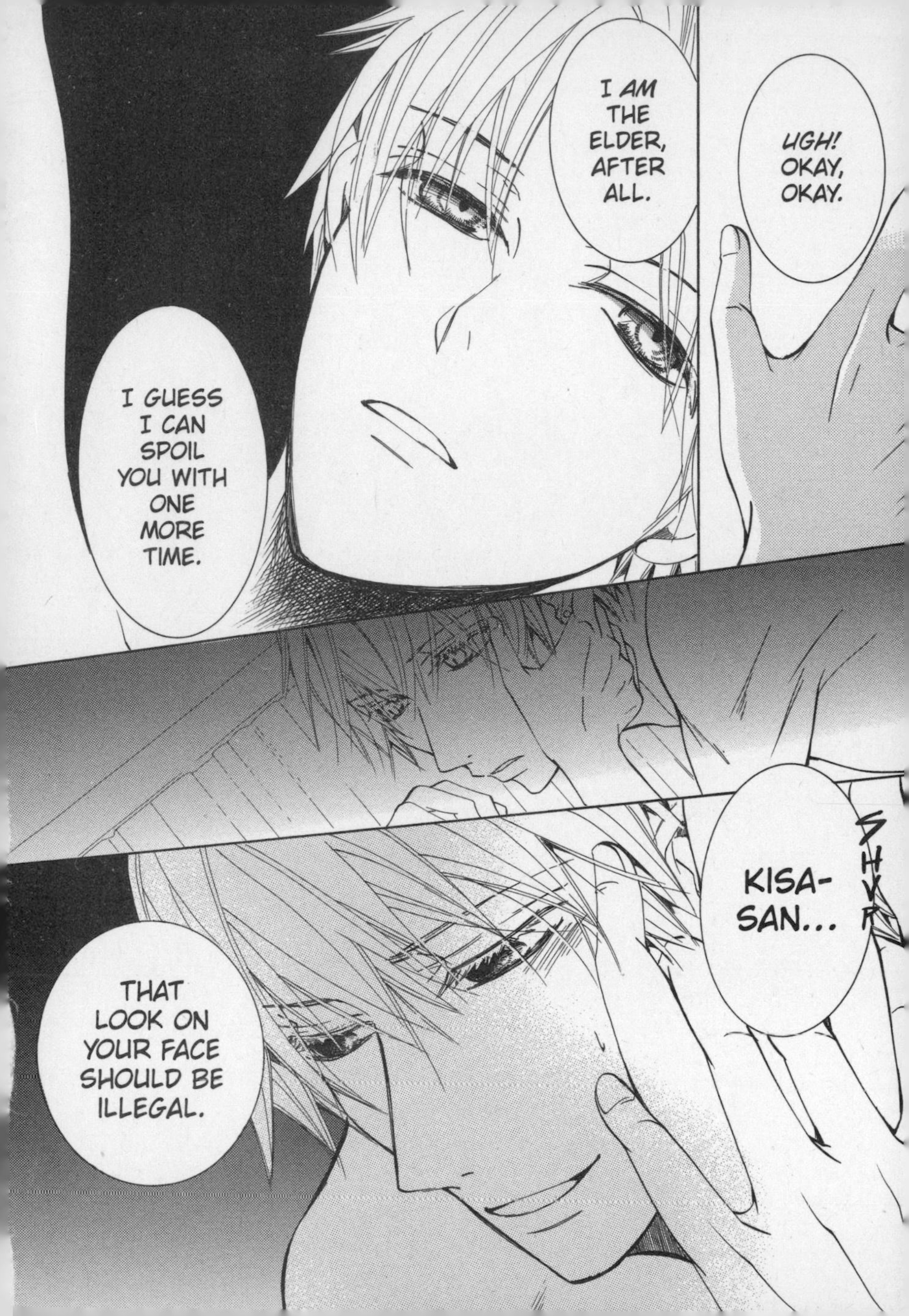
UGH! OKAY, OKAY.
I AM THE ELDER, AFTER ALL.
I GUESS I CAN SPOIL YOU WITH ONE MORE TIME.
SHVR
KISA-SAN...
THAT LOOK ON YOUR FACE SHOULD BE ILLEGAL.

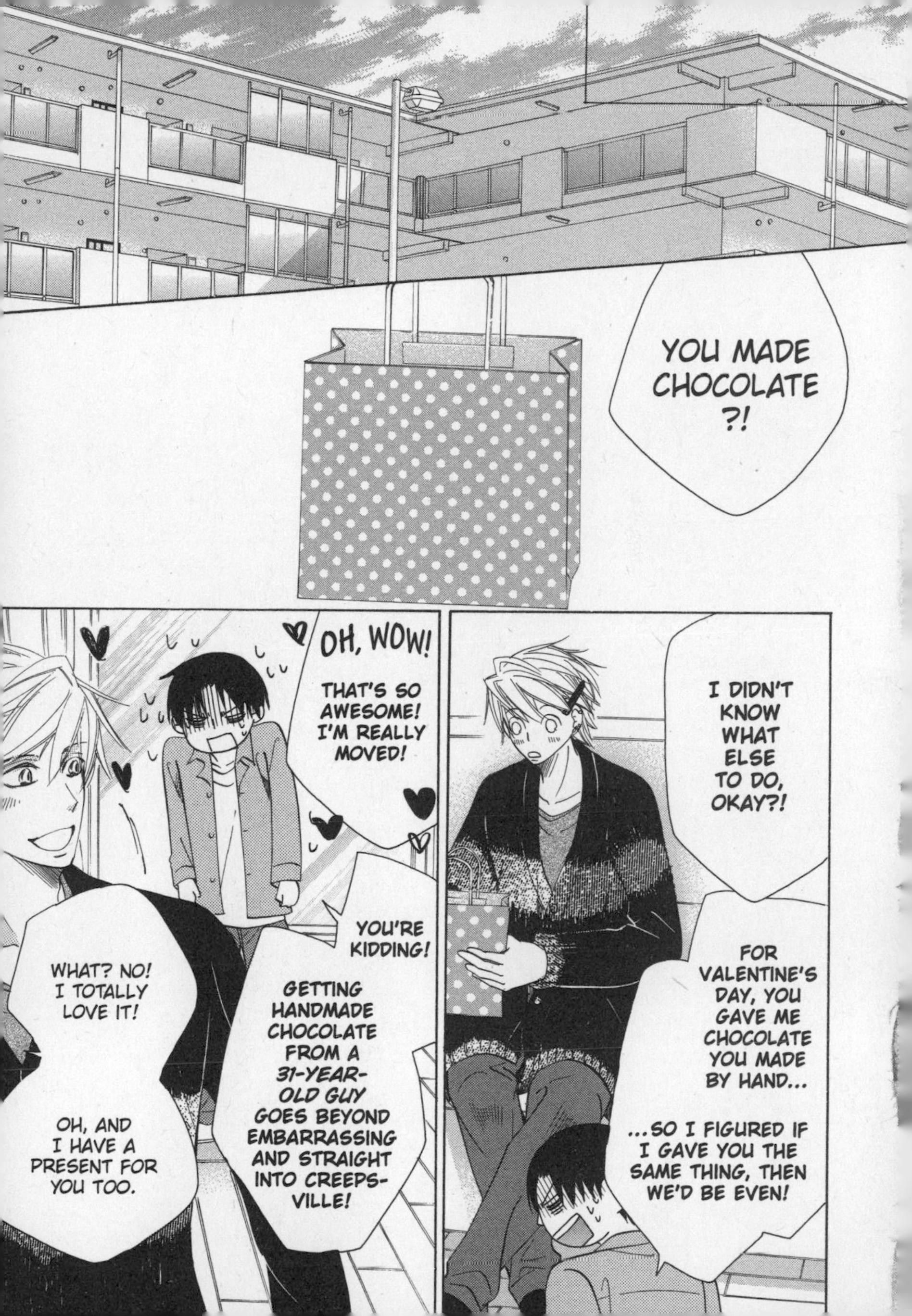
YOU MADE CHOCOLATE ?!
I DIDN'T KNOW WHAT ELSE TO DO, OKAY?!
FOR VALENTINE'S DAY, YOU GAVE ME CHOCOLATE YOU MADE BY HAND...
...SO I FIGURED IF I GAVE YOU THE SAME THING, THEN WE'D BE EVEN!
OH, WOW!
THAT'S SO AWESOME! I'M REALLY MOVED!
YOU'RE KIDDING!
GETTING HANDMADE CHOCOLATE FROM A 31-YEAR-OLD GUY GOES BEYOND EMBARRASSING AND STRAIGHT INTO CREEPS-VILLE!
WHAT? NO! I TOTALLY LOVE IT!
OH, AND I HAVE A PRESENT FOR YOU TOO.

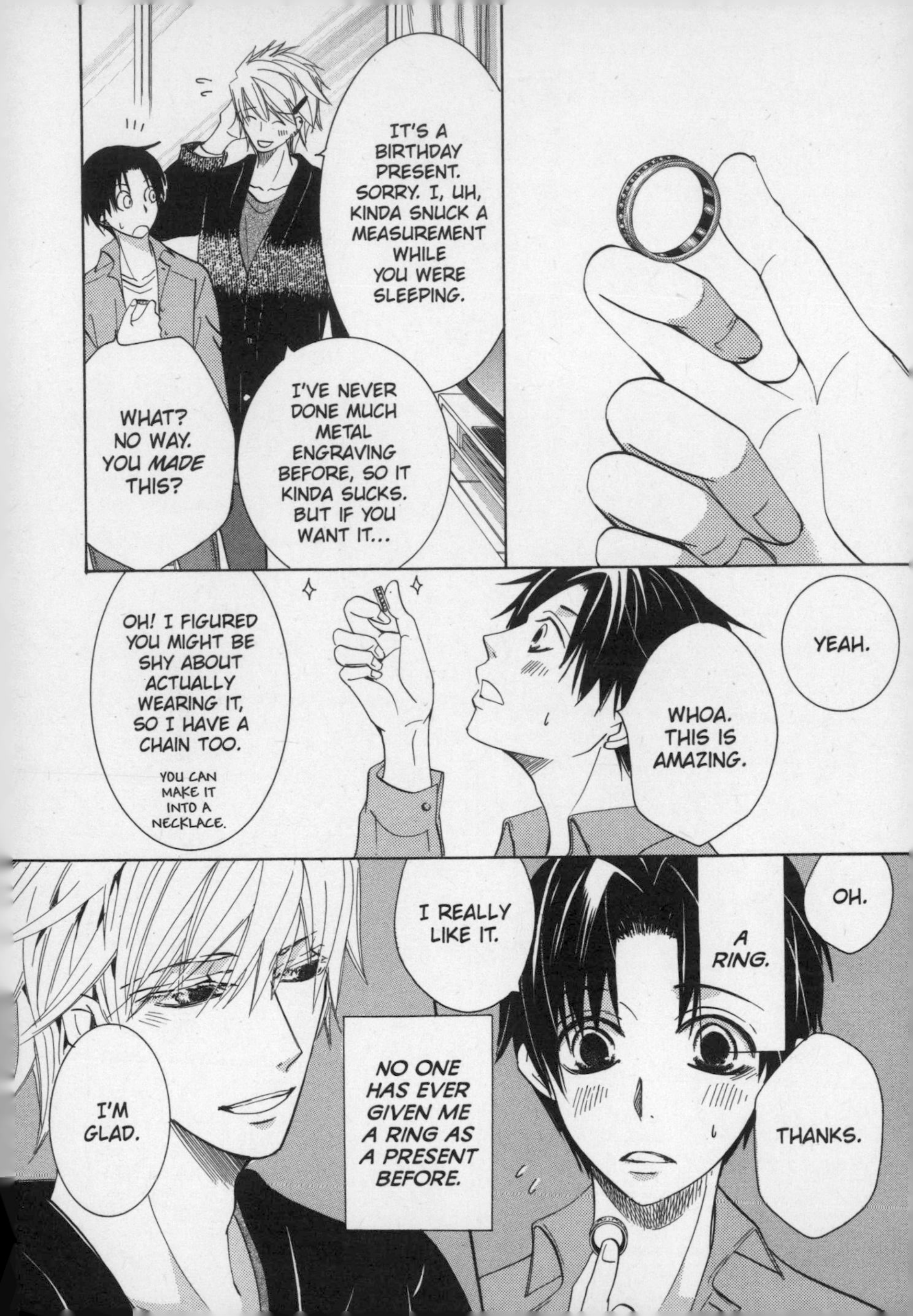
IT'S A BIRTHDAY PRESENT. SORRY. I, UH, KINDA SNUCK A MEASUREMENT WHILE YOU WERE SLEEPING.
WHAT? NO WAY. YOU *MADE* THIS?
I'VE NEVER DONE MUCH METAL ENGRAVING BEFORE, SO IT KINDA SUCKS. BUT IF YOU WANT IT...
YEAH.
WHOA. THIS IS AMAZING.
OH! I FIGURED YOU MIGHT BE SHY ABOUT ACTUALLY WEARING IT, SO I HAVE A CHAIN TOO.
YOU CAN MAKE IT INTO A NECKLACE.
OH.
A RING.
THANKS.
I REALLY LIKE IT.
NO ONE HAS EVER GIVEN ME A RING AS A PRESENT BEFORE.
I'M GLAD.

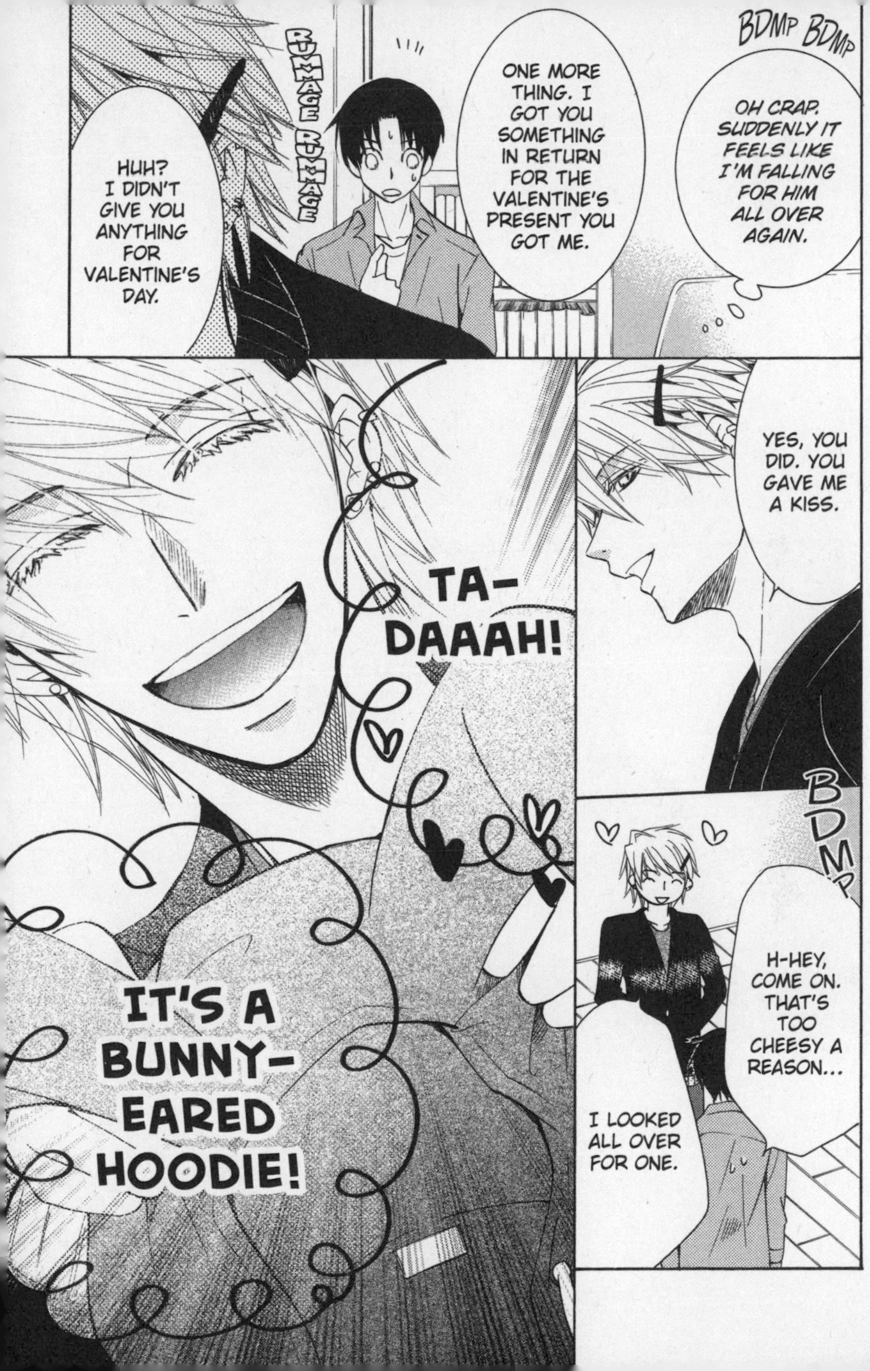
BDMP BDMP
OH CRAP. SUDDENLY IT FEELS LIKE I'M FALLING FOR HIM ALL OVER AGAIN.
ONE MORE THING. I GOT YOU SOMETHING IN RETURN FOR THE VALENTINE'S PRESENT YOU GOT ME.
RUMMAGE RUMMAGE
HUH? I DIDN'T GIVE YOU ANYTHING FOR VALENTINE'S DAY.
YES, YOU DID. YOU GAVE ME A KISS.
BDMP
H-HEY, COME ON. THAT'S TOO CHEESY A REASON...
I LOOKED ALL OVER FOR ONE.
TA-DAAAH!
IT'S A BUNNY-EARED HOODIE!

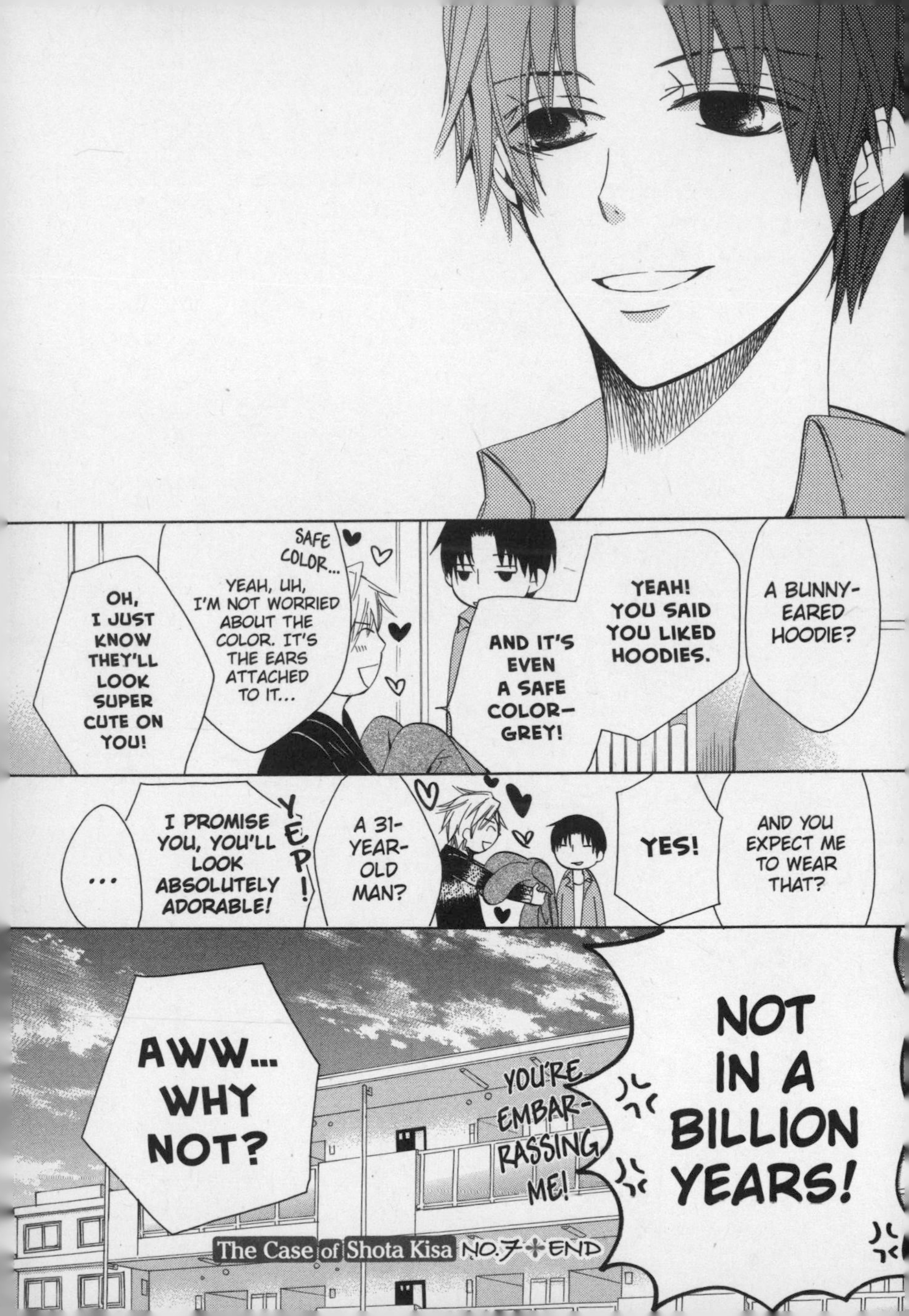
A BUNNY-EARED HOODIE?
YEAH! YOU SAID YOU LIKED HOODIES.
AND IT'S EVEN A SAFE COLOR—GREY!
SAFE COLOR...
YEAH, UH, I'M NOT WORRIED ABOUT THE COLOR. IT'S THE EARS ATTACHED TO IT...
OH, I JUST KNOW THEY'LL LOOK SUPER CUTE ON YOU!
AND YOU EXPECT ME TO WEAR THAT?
YES!
A 31-YEAR-OLD MAN?
YEP!
I PROMISE YOU, YOU'LL LOOK ABSOLUTELY ADORABLE!
...
NOT IN A BILLION YEARS!
YOU'RE EMBARRASSING ME!
AWW... WHY NOT?
The Case of Shota Kisa NO.7 ✦ END

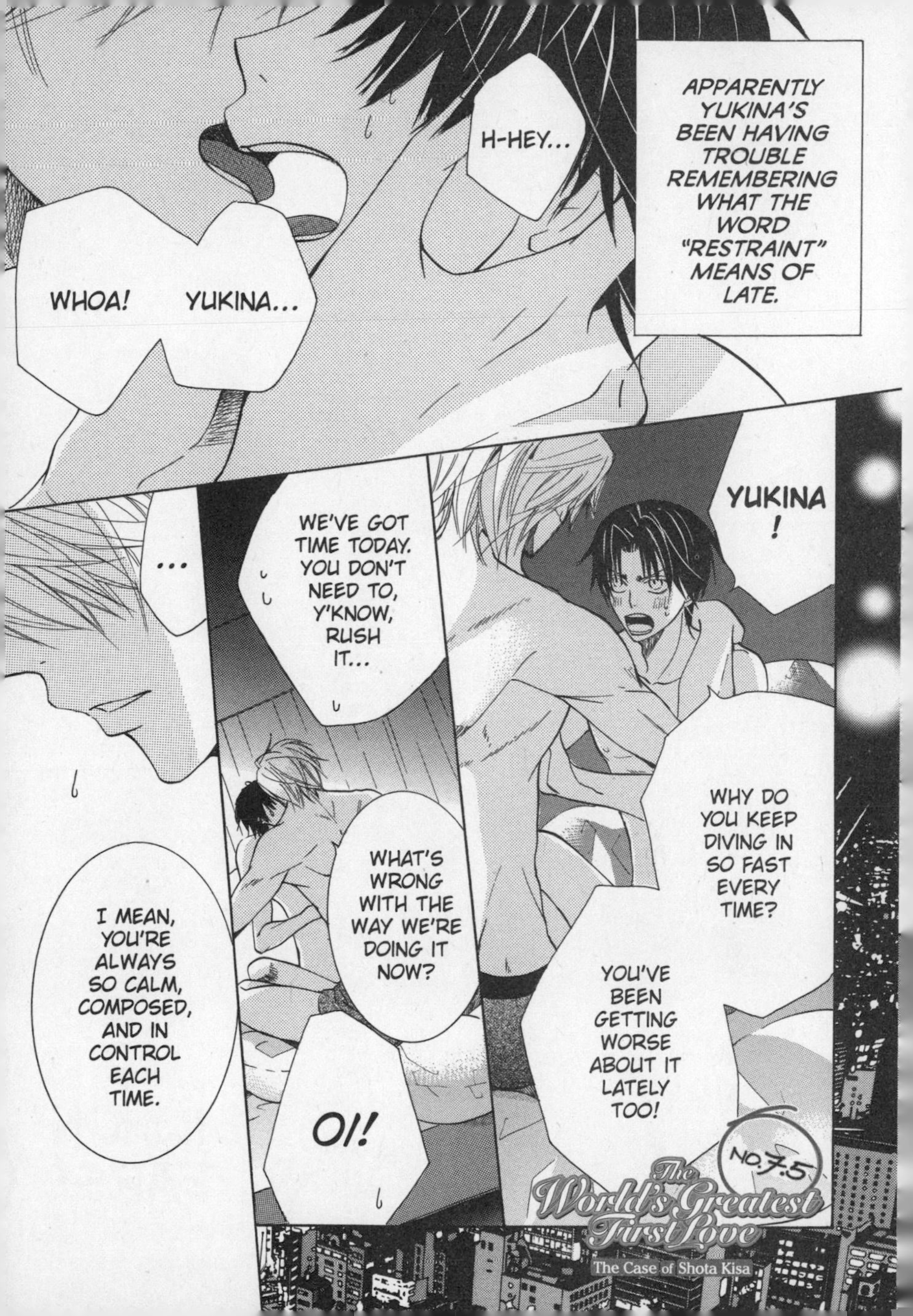
APPARENTLY YUKINA'S BEEN HAVING TROUBLE REMEMBERING WHAT THE WORD "RESTRAINT" MEANS OF LATE.
H-HEY...
WHOA! YUKINA...
YUKINA!
WHY DO YOU KEEP DIVING IN SO FAST EVERY TIME?
YOU'VE BEEN GETTING WORSE ABOUT IT LATELY TOO!
NO. 7.5
The World's Greatest First Love
The Case of Shota Kisa
WE'VE GOT TIME TODAY. YOU DON'T NEED TO, Y'KNOW, RUSH IT...
WHAT'S WRONG WITH THE WAY WE'RE DOING IT NOW?
OI!
...
I MEAN, YOU'RE ALWAYS SO CALM, COMPOSED, AND IN CONTROL EACH TIME.

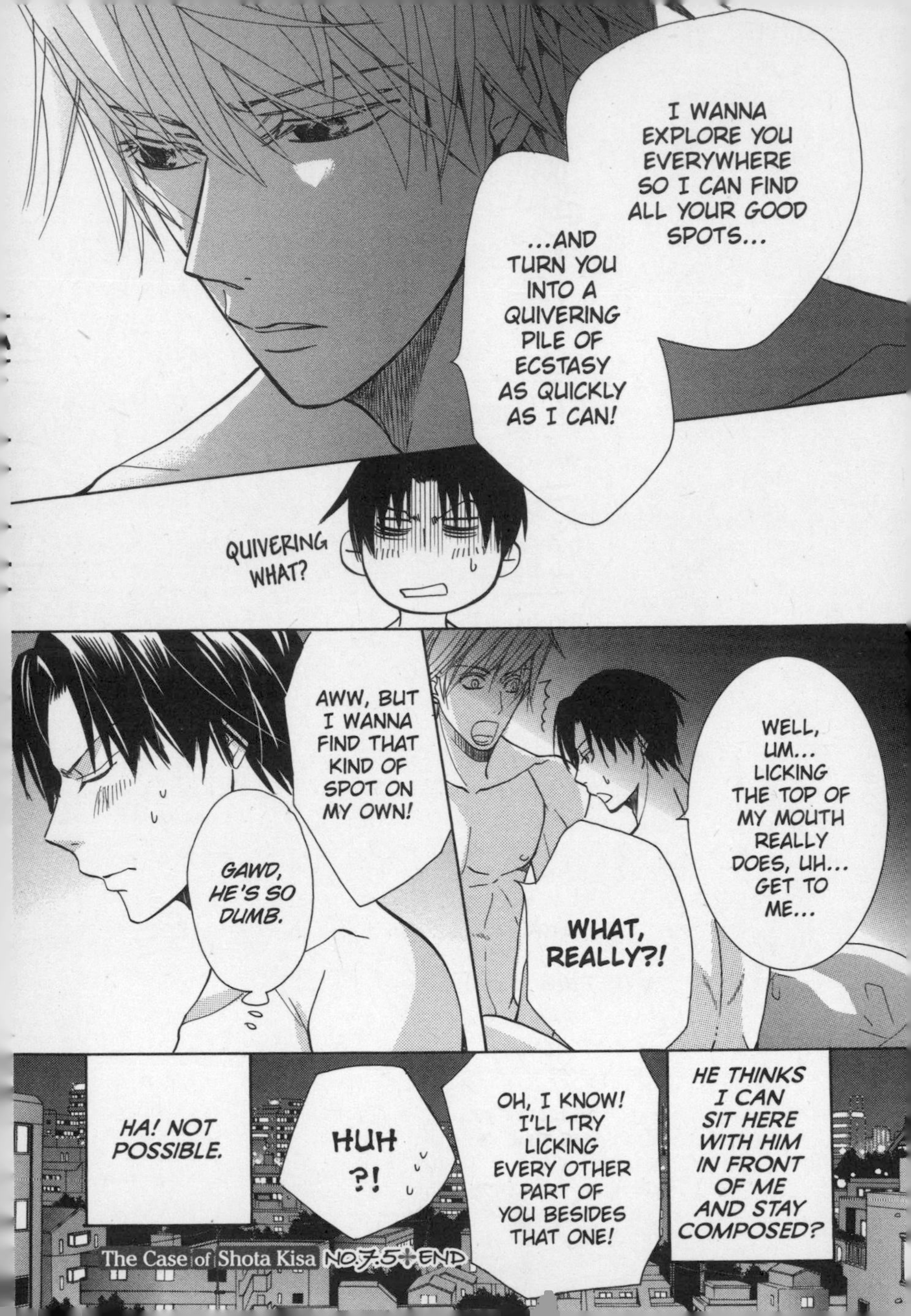
I WANNA EXPLORE YOU EVERYWHERE SO I CAN FIND ALL YOUR GOOD SPOTS...
...AND TURN YOU INTO A QUIVERING PILE OF ECSTASY AS QUICKLY AS I CAN!
QUIVERING WHAT?
WELL, UM... LICKING THE TOP OF MY MOUTH REALLY DOES, UH... GET TO ME...
WHAT, REALLY?!
AWW, BUT I WANNA FIND THAT KIND OF SPOT ON MY OWN!
GAWD, HE'S SO DUMB.
HE THINKS I CAN SIT HERE WITH HIM IN FRONT OF ME AND STAY COMPOSED?
OH, I KNOW! I'LL TRY LICKING EVERY OTHER PART OF YOU BESIDES THAT ONE!
HUH ?!
HA! NOT POSSIBLE.
The Case of Shota Kisa NO.7.5 END

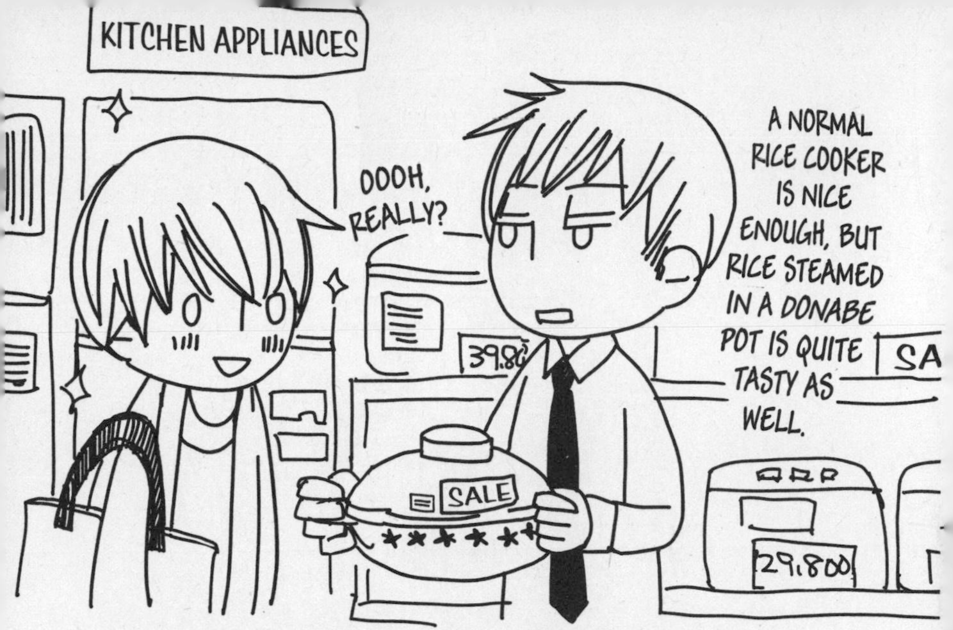
KITCHEN APPLIANCES
A NORMAL RICE COOKER IS NICE ENOUGH, BUT RICE STEAMED IN A DONABE POT IS QUITE TASTY AS WELL.
OOOH, REALLY?
SALE
29,800

○ HELLO. THIS IS SHUNGIKU NAKAMURA. THANK YOU FOR BUYING VOLUME 10 OF *THE WORLD'S GREATEST FIRST LOVE ~THE CASE OF RITSU ONODERA~*! THANKS TO ALL YOUR HELP, WE'VE REACHED DOUBLE DIGITS! YAY! WOO!

SHAMELESS PLUG

● *THE WORLD'S GREATEST FIRST LOVE* AND *JUNJO ROMANTICA* ARE CURRENTLY BEING SERIALIZED IN *EMERALD MAGAZINE*!

● IN MAY OF 2015, *J.W.P.B.*, A PERIOD FANTASY SERIES I DID FOR A DIFFERENT COMPANY YEARS AGO, WAS GIVEN A RERELEASE BY KADOKAWA. IT'S A LITTLE STORY ABOUT HEROINE SUZURI AND LEGEND MOMOTARO ADVENTURING TOGETHER. IF YOU'D LIKE, PLEASE CHECK IT OUT! BY THE WAY, IF PERIOD FANTASY IS YOUR THING, I SUGGEST YOU CHECK OUT THESE TITLES TOO:

- *TOZANDO TENTSUI IBUN* (2 VOLUMES)
- *TSUKI WA YAMIYO NI KAKURU GA GOTOKU*
- *MANGETSU MONOGATARI*
- *HYBRID CHILD*

NOW THEN, THE STORY WILL CONTINUE TO RAMBLE ALONG AT A LEISURELY PACE FOR SOME TIME YET, SO I HOPE YOU'LL STICK AROUND. THANK YOU VERY MUCH!

-SHUNGIKU NAKAMURA

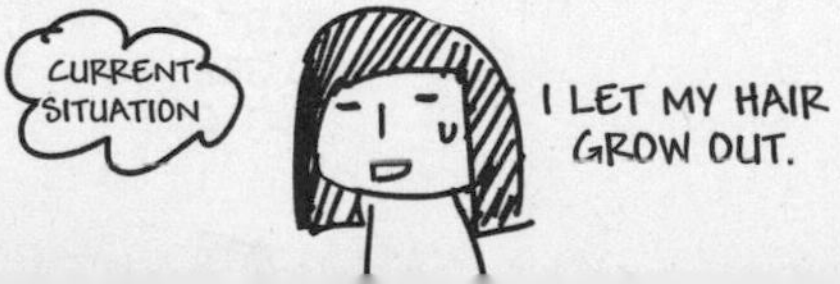
CURRENT SITUATION
I LET MY HAIR GROW OUT.

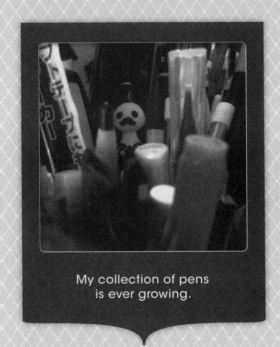

My collection of pens
is ever growing.

About the Author

Shungiku Nakamura
DOB December 13
Sagittarius
Blood Type O

The World's Greatest First Love: The Case of Ritsu Onodera

Volume 10
SuBLime Manga Edition

Story and Art by **Shungiku Nakamura**

Translation—**Adrienne Beck**
Touch-Up Art and Lettering—**Eric Erbes**
Cover and Graphic Design—**Izumi Evers**
Editor—**Jennifer LeBlanc**

SEKAIICHI HATSUKOI ~ONODERA RITSU NO BAAI~ Volume 10
© Shungiku NAKAMURA 2015
Edited by KADOKAWA SHOTEN
First published in Japan in 2015 by KADOKAWA CORPORATION, Tokyo.
English translation rights arranged with KADOKAWA CORPORATION,
Tokyo.

ASUKA
COMICS
CL^D_X

Printed in the U.S.A.

Published by SuBLime Manga
P.O. Box 77010
San Francisco, CA 94107

10 9 8 7 6 5 4 3 2 1
First printing, July 2018

 PARENTAL ADVISORY
THE WORLD'S GREATEST FIRST LOVE is rated M for Mature and is
recommended for mature readers. This volume contains graphic
MATURE imagery and mature themes.

www.SuBLimeManga.com

For more information

on all our products, along with the most up-to-date news on releases, series announcements, and contests, please visit us at:

 SuBLimeManga.com

 twitter.com/**SuBLimeManga**

 facebook.com/**SuBLimeManga**

 instagram.com/**SuBLimeManga**

 SuBLimeManga.tumblr.com

SUBLIME
MANGA

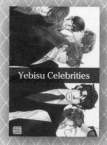

Downloading is as easy as:

1

2

3

The Scent of Apple Blossoms
SUBLIME
BLOG
How's Your Ex?
The Night Before the Wedding
Punch Up!
Bond of Dreams, Bond of Love
Honey Darling
Do You Like Me?
Three Wolves Mountain

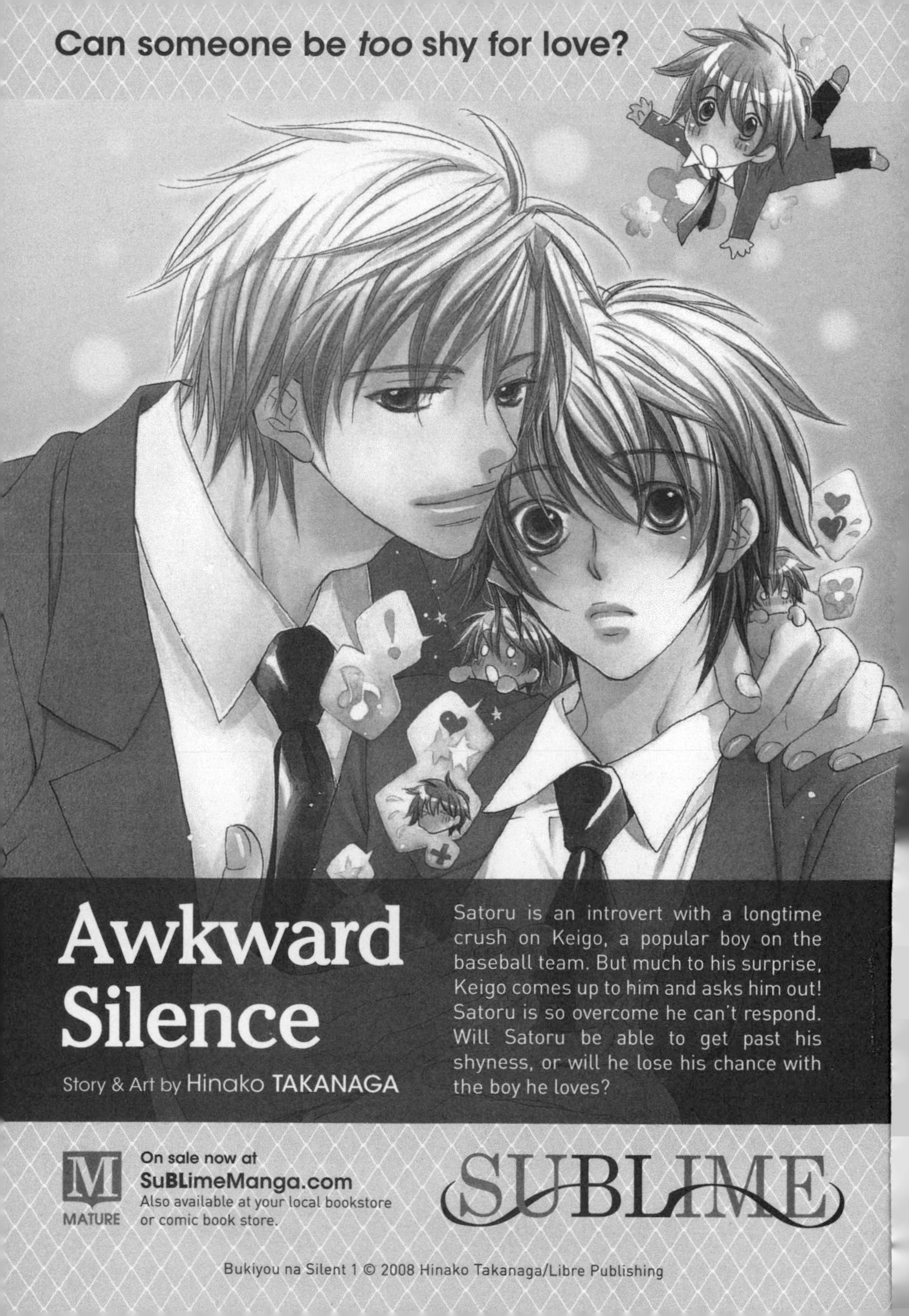
Can someone be *too* shy for love?
Awkward Silence
Story & Art by Hinako TAKANAGA
Satoru is an introvert with a longtime crush on Keigo, a popular boy on the baseball team. But much to his surprise, Keigo comes up to him and asks him out! Satoru is so overcome he can't respond. Will Satoru be able to get past his shyness, or will he lose his chance with the boy he loves?
M
MATURE
On sale now at
SuBLimeManga.com
Also available at your local bookstore or comic book store.
SUBLIME
Bukiyou na Silent 1 © 2008 Hinako Takanaga/Libre Publishing